JOHN ARMSTRONG, JR.,
1758–1843

A NEW YORK STATE STUDY

John Armstrong, Jr., by John Vanderlyn, ca. 1809.
Courtesy of Mrs. W. Vincent Astor

JOHN ARMSTRONG, JR., 1758–1843

A BIOGRAPHY

C. Edward Skeen

SYRACUSE UNIVERSITY PRESS
1981

This book is published with the assistance
of a grant from the John Ben Snow Foundation.

Library of Congress Cataloging in Publication Data
Skeen, Carl Edward.
   John Armstrong, Jr., 1758–1843.
   (A New York State study)
   Bibliography: p.
   Includes index.
   1. Armstrong, John, 1758–1843. 2. United States
—Politics and government—1783–1809. 3. United
States—History—War of 1812. 4. Statesmen—
United States—Biography. I. Title. II. Series.
E302.6.A7S55   973.5'092'4 [B]   81-9381
ISBN 0-8156-2242-2   AACR2

To my parents

C. Edward Skeen received M.A. and Ph.D. degrees from Ohio State University. He is Associate Professor of History, Memphis State University, and has written articles for *The William and Mary Quarterly, New-York Historical Society Quarterly, New York History,* and *Journal of the Early Republic.*

CONTENTS

ILLUSTRATIONS

MAPS

PREFACE

I T IS AN UNDERSTANDABLE but regrettable fact that major figures of any
historical period are subject to repeated and continuous analysis,
while minor figures are frequently neglected and forgotten. Many of the
major figures of the early American Republic, for example, have had their
characters, contributions, even their sex lives subjected to painstaking
scrutiny by several generations of scholars. The preoccupation with
"great men" is a distortion of history, for we lose the perspective of the
past as well as an appreciation of the contributions of those who labored
in the shadow of these giants. John Armstrong is one such figure whose
career has been overlooked and forgotten. Yet he was by no means an insignificant individual in his era.

To put his story in capsule form, his public career spanned the
period from the Revolutionary War through the War of 1812. He was a
Revolutionary officer and a participant in many important battles. He
was the anonymous author of the Newburgh Addresses which seemed to
threaten the mutiny of the Revolutionary army at the end of the war. He
was a key figure in the so-called Pennamite War, a struggle between Pennsylvanians and Connecticut settlers. He was secretary of the Supreme Executive Council of Pennsylvania and later a representative of that state to
the Congress under the Articles of Confederation. A fortuitous marriage
into the powerful Livingston family of New York led to his removal to
that state and his subsequent election as a senator from New York. This
exposure to national politics and national political leaders led to his selection by President Jefferson as the United States minister to France. Armstrong served six stormy years in France (1804–1810) contesting the pirati-
cal and rapacious policies of Emperor Napoleon Bonaparte toward

United States commerce. Strangely, this valuable service to his country
has been largely overlooked. Armstrong's best-known service was as secretary of war during the War of 1812. This war, the first fought under the
Constitution, has been amply studied both from the standpoint of causa-
tion as well as from the military aspects. Nevertheless, the role of the secretary of war and his relationship to the conduct of the war has been all
but neglected. In many military histories of that conflict, Armstrong has
been frequently relegated to passing references.

When Armstrong has not been overlooked, he has been misunderstood. Most references are critical of him; some of the criticisms are deserved, but many others are misrepresentations. For example, in a recent
important historical work, Marshall Smelser (*The Democratic Republic,
1801–1815*, p. 140) blithely refers to Armstrong as "an intellectual light-
weight." Smelser's source was Napoleon Bonaparte himself, but Napoleon had suffered too long under Armstrong's slashing indictments of his
policies to be considered an impartial observer of Armstrong's intellectual
capacity. Even Armstrong's bitterest enemies would have admitted that
he was one of the best-educated men and perhaps the best writer of his
generation. Misrepresentation such as this is not surprising, however, for
if there is any one word that would describe Armstrong's services or public career, it would be "controversial." There was probably no public figure of the early American Republic who was engaged so frequently or so
incessantly in disputes of one sort or the other. Armstrong was possessed
of an extremely abrasive personality, and he accumulated a large number
of enemies, many of whom were in powerful positions. Their enmity partially explains Armstrong's failure to achieve a more distinguished career.
Their view of him has been perpetuated by their biographers, and Armstrong has come down to us in an unenviable light — as seen by his enemies.

Although Armstrong was not born into an aristocratic family, he
nevertheless affected a haughty, aristocratic demeanor. A man of un-
doubted abilities, but perhaps not as great as he imagined them to be, he
could not abide mediocrity in others. He seems to have lacked a spirit of
compassion and a rational tolerance for the faults of others. He often un-
derestimated the sensitivity of others to his judgments of them. Their enmity, frequently taking the form of pamphlet attacks after the fashion of
that day, received spirited replies from Armstrong. In fact, Armstrong
was easily one of the most accomplished polemicists of his era. Adding to
these negative characteristics was a general indolence and indifference to
his public labors that many of his contemporaries found incomprehensible.

Despite the fact that Armstrong was singularly lacking in many of
the characteristics necessary for success in public life, he nevertheless

achieved many eminent positions and made many important contributions to his country. It is quite possible that had he exercised greater tact
and better judgment in certain instances, he might have enjoyed an illustrious career indeed. Although it would be interesting to speculate along
these lines, I have sought to limit the narrative to what Armstrong did
rather than what he should have done.

The focus throughout is upon Armstrong. Historical events are included only when they impinge upon his life. His point of view is stressed
— which is to say that he, rather than his enemies, has been given the benefit of the doubt. It is, after all, his biography, and it is difficult for any biographer to spend several years studying an individual without incurring
some sympathy for his subject. I have endeavored, however, to be honest
in my assessments and true to the historical record. My primary aim has
been to place John Armstrong in his era and evaluate his contributions to
his country. It has also been my goal to show that these contributions
were far from insignificant and that he deserves to be better remembered.
Finally, it has been my purpose to add to the historical record the personal
life of an interesting but little-known figure of the early American
Republic.

In the course of research and writing I have received the assistance
of many, and I am happy to acknowledge the contribution that others
have made to this project. First of all, Dr. Harry L. Coles suggested the
need for a study of John Armstrong and directed my dissertation on one
aspect of his career. Since that time he has encouraged me to continue my
work. At the inception of my work a travel grant for research from Ohio
State University was very useful, and a grant from Memphis State University also assisted me in my research.

I am especially grateful to Mrs. Richard Aldrich and her two sons,
Richard and John Winthrop (Winty). They not only opened their estate
along the Hudson to me (Armstrong's Rokeby), as well as their trove of
documents, they were also very encouraging and kind to me. Winty in
particular went out of his way to assist me in tracking down documents
and helping me to verify family traditions. Armstrong himself could have
asked no more from a descendant.

Among the many libraries I visited, the staffs of the Historical Society of Pennsylvania and the New-York Historical Society were particularly helpful. I also wish to thank Ms. Paula Christian, who typed an
earlier draft of this manuscript.

Finally, the encouragement of my family has been a most sustaining
and rewarding experience. My daughters Marianne and Laura have encouraged me throughout my research and writing. I cannot express ade-

quately my obligation to my wife, Linda. Not only has she willingly accepted many lonely evenings and weekends, she has been my staunchest supporter even when I have become discouraged. She knows that she's "okay in my book."

C. Edward Skeen

JOHN ARMSTRONG, JR.,

1758–1843

1

REVOLUTIONARY SOLDIER

No doubt John Armstrong, Jr., heard many times of the actions of his father on the day he was born, November 25, 1758. That very day, Colonel John Armstrong marched his Pennsylvania militia into the smoking, deserted ruins of Fort Duquesne. His force was part of the main army commanded by General John Forbes, and as the first to enter the fort, Colonel Armstrong was given the honor of raising the British flag over that post, rechristened Fort Pitt. The capture of Fort Duquesne was a decisive event in the French and Indian War, and it helped to seal the fate of the French in North America.

John Armstrong, Sr., who had a formative influence over his son, was a remarkable representative of a hardy band of Scotch-Irish frontiersmen who migrated to western Pennsylvania in the mid-eighteenth century. His parents were Scottish, but he was born in Ireland, probably on October 13, 1717. His parents were apparently prosperous, for their son was well-educated and he became a surveyor. In 1739, Armstrong married Rebecca Lyon, and around 1746, with his family and some of his wife's family, he came to America. They settled on the west side of the Susquehanna River, which was then the frontier. Soon Armstrong was employed by the Penn family to survey the tracts of land in this area which had been formed into Cumberland County. He surveyed and laid out the town of Carlisle, and here he built his own home. His obvious abilities and his hard work soon established him as a leader of the new community. In 1749 he was elected to the provincial legislature, and that same year his first son, James, was born.[1]

When the French and Indian War began, Armstrong became a colonel of the militia. The frontier was a dangerous place, and Carlisle sat on the edge of the frontier. In the sporadic warfare that ensued, Indians and whites alike committed many barbarities, and hatreds ran high. Late in July 1756 one of Armstrong's brothers was killed in an Indian raid. Furious, Armstrong led about 300 men early in September on a daring raid deep into the Indian country and destroyed the principal Delaware Indian village of Kittanning, about forty miles above Fort Duquesne on the east side of the Allegheny River. Captain Jacobs, the Delaware chieftain, was killed and scalped, and approximately forty members of his tribe were killed. Although Armstrong was wounded and seventeen of his men were killed, he had dealt a great blow to the Indians. Armstrong was hailed throughout the colonies, medals were struck in his honor, and eventually in 1775 the Penn family rewarded the "Hero of Kittanning" with a valuable land grant in western Pennsylvania which included Kittanning itself.[2]

Armstrong was very proud of his two sons, and he was very concerned with providing them with the best education possible. His elder son, James, expressed an early interest in medicine and was enrolled at the Academy of Philadelphia. In 1769 he became one of the first graduates of the school of medicine of the College of Philadelphia (later the University of Pennsylvania). His younger son, John, was placed in a school in Carlisle directed by an Irish clergyman named McKinley. He remembered this experience fondly in later years. "McKinley was kind without indulgence, and strict, without severity," Armstrong recalled. "He had a rare and happy faculty of stimulating the ambition of his pupils, and to him I owe that love of books which I have found the source of the purest and highest pleasure." During these happy years of childhood, his constant companion was his cousin, James Armstrong. Their vacations were spent at Carlisle or at John's cousin's home at Chambersburg. John's father kept a pack of hounds, and the favorite sport of the two young boys was following the chase. Both became expert riders.[3]

At the age of thirteen John was transferred to a more advanced school, and at the age of sixteen he entered as a sophomore the College of New Jersey (Princeton), then rising to prominence under the presidency of John Witherspoon. Sixty years later, in a letter to the historian Jared Sparks, Armstrong was still crediting Witherspoon with exerting a major influence on his writing style. The interesting preliminaries of the revolution, however, intruded into the scholarly atmosphere of the campus at Princeton, and Armstrong never finished his college training. His father, on the recommendation of General George Washington, with whom he had formed a friendship on the march with Forbes, had accepted an appointment as a brigadier general and was assigned a command in the South. His brother James soon entered the service as a doctor, and young John soon followed.[4]

In August 1776 Armstrong and a companion followed a militia company to New Brunswick. When the company was ordered back to Princeton, Armstrong and his friend went on to New York City. He eventually joined Potter's Pennsylvania regiment as a volunteer. For many weeks he lingered in camp unnoticed and no doubt questioning the wisdom of his decision. Then General Hugh Mercer, who had served with Armstrong's father in the Kittanning expedition, invited him to join his staff as a brigade major and aide. Armstrong gratefully remembered this appointment. "He found me friendless in the camp . . . a boy in years, and exposed to the influence of licentious example. He received me in his family, and elevated me at once to a station, perhaps higher than I deserved, but the duties of which my gratitude no less than my ambition, prompted me to discharge in such a manner, as to justify the appointment."[5]

There is a hint in this statement, written fifty years after the event, that gives an important clue to Armstrong's character. He was apparently sensitive about attaining such a high rank in his youth. Placed in a situation of giving orders to much older men, desperately wanting to prove his worth, he adopted an attitude of superiority or haughtiness that was to mark his behavior for the remainder of his life. To those he considered his equals he could be warm and genial. No doubt he had already developed many of these character traits, but his new position undoubtedly did much to fix the tendencies and give them play.

Armstrong was not to hold his position long. He participated in the battles of Trenton and Princeton under General Mercer. In the latter battle Mercer was mortally wounded, however, and Armstrong barely escaped the same fate. His horse was shot, and Armstrong was pinned briefly before he was rescued. Mercer died from his injuries, and Armstrong accompanied the remnants of Mercer's command with the main army to the neighborhood of Morristown. There Mercer's forces merged with those of General Arthur St. Clair. Armstrong had lost his position, and when none was offered by St. Clair, he left Washington's army intending to make his way to the northern army, where he hoped the prospects of finding a suitable position for the coming campaign would be better. His departure preceded by a few days the arrival of his father in Washington's camp. The elder Armstrong provided a letter of introduction to Major General Horatio Gates. Gates met young Armstrong at Esopus (present-day Kingston), then the seat of the state government of New York. Impressed by the young man, Gates offered him a position as a major and aide-de-camp. Armstrong promptly accepted. This was the beginning of a friendship that persisted, despite the difference in their ages, long after the Revolutionary War.[6]

Horatio Gates's was a complex personality. He has been described as "balanced, often able, usually good-hearted, and apt to be liked by his men. But a mean, if not treacherous, streak of intrigue ran through him; not meanness to his cause, in which he never wavered, but toward those about him, up to and including his commander-in-chief."[7] He was English born, the son of an upper servant, and he had risen to the rank of major in the British army. Seeing no opportunity for advancement, he sold his commission and emigrated to America in 1772, settling in the Shenandoah Valley on a plantation called Traveller's Rest. He renewed his acquaintance with George Washington, with whom he had served on the Forbes expedition. When the revolution began, Gates was appointed a brigadier general in June 1775 on Washington's recommendation. Gates was an able man, but not perhaps as able as he believed himself to be.

When Armstrong joined him, Gates had just successfully wrested a separate command in the North, carved out of the command of his erstwhile superior, General Philip Schuyler of New York. Schuyler, however, not without political friends, rushed to Congress and soon returned vindicated and restored to complete control of the northern department. This was a short-lived victory, however, for a British army under the command of Lieutenant General John Burgoyne, proceeding from Canada down Lake Champlain, captured Fort Ticonderoga and was apparently moving irresistibly toward Albany. Dismay and alarm swept through the colonies. Schuyler, although making great exertions, could do nothing but retreat and render pessimistic reports to Congress, spreading gloom among his troops. On August 4 he was removed from command and replaced by Gates.

Gates assumed command on August 19, but the military situation, far from being desperate, had actually improved. A detachment of Burgoyne's force was virtually annihilated near Bennington, Vermont, by Brigadier General John Stark and his New Hampshire and Vermont militia on August 16. Further, the threat of an attack in the rear was removed when a British force under Lieutenant Colonel Barry St. Leger, advancing down the Mohawk Valley to join with Burgoyne, was checked by Brigadier General Nicholas Herkimer and then was forced to turn back by the approach of Major General Benedict Arnold. Gates was able to gather about 4500 men and was soon reinforced by Colonel Daniel Morgan with a valuable addition of about 350 riflemen from Washington's command. Arnold's return from the Mohawk Valley added another 1200 men.

With his force growing steadily, Gates moved his troops northward, and with the aid of the Polish engineer, Thaddeus Kosciuszko, he selected a strong position to await the arrival of Burgoyne. Gates has been criticized for his timidity in assuming a defensive posture, but his troops were not nearly so professional as the British force, and he realized that time was on his side because Burgoyne's supplies were dwindling.

Critics of Gates have even withheld from him credit for the ultimate defeat of Burgoyne and given it to the impetuous Benedict Arnold. Armstrong was a personal witness to the heroism of Arnold in the crucial battle of Bemis Heights on October 7. Arnold had quarreled with Gates over who should be second in command, and he was sulking in his tent when the battle began. Suddenly, he bolted out of his tent and recklessly led the charge against the British positions. Gates directed his young aide to order Arnold back into camp. Armstrong caught up with him, but only after Arnold had successfully breached the British line and forced their retreat. In the charge Arnold sustained a bullet wound that fractured his thigh bone. Gates, perhaps from the account of his aide, commended the "Gallant Major General Arnold" in his report of the battle. Armstrong's first claim to fame was thus at the battle of Saratoga — when he did not catch up with Benedict Arnold.[8]

Burgoyne surrendered his entire army to Gates on October 17. Gates, who truly deserved the credit, was hailed as the conquerer of Burgoyne. By any measure the battle of Saratoga was a tremendous victory for the Americans and a stunning setback for the British. But for Gates the triumph was soon dimmed by the pettiness of politics and his involvement in an obscure imbroglio known as the Conway Cabal. This incident began as a result of the indiscretion, intentional or otherwise, of Colonel James Wilkinson, Gates's deputy adjutant general, who revealed to a friend of Washington the contents of a letter written by Thomas Conway, an Irishman recently in the service of France and at that time a brigadier general in the Continental army. Conway's letter to Gates, Washington learned, suggested that Gates should replace Washington as commander-in-chief. Washington, who had already chided Gates for failing to inform him of the results of the battle of Saratoga, and perhaps because he was aware that many members of Congress shared Conway's view, chose to bring the matter out into the open. When he confronted Gates with his knowledge of the letter, Gates was forced to deny that he had any such pretensions. Gates and Wilkinson fought a harmless duel over the matter, and Conway himself was severely wounded in another related duel. Although there was never any plot, there is little doubt that Gates's reputation suffered then, as it has ever since as a consequence of the Conway affair.[9]

Congress rewarded Gates with an appointment to the newly created Board of War, but his experience on the board did not enhance his reputation. A planned invasion of Canada fell through due to politics and the lack of troops and supplies. Gates was eventually sent back north to take charge of the army and the forts along the Hudson. Armstrong, who had been ill for a prolonged period after the battle of Saratoga, journeyed to Boston in the spring of 1778 to join Gates, who had established his headquarters there. On his way there, Armstrong visited Kosciuszko who was superintending the construction of a fortress at West Point on the Hudson. Armstrong had met this young soldier of fortune the year before at Albany. Three years older than Armstrong, the grave, reserved Kosciuszko and the cocky, outgoing, rather indolent aide-de-camp became fast friends. Kosciuszko served the American cause well, but he won even greater fame as a Polish patriot. Armstrong later celebrated his friendship with Kosciuszko by naming a son in his honor.

In the year that followed, Armstrong was involved in routine activity. The tedium of camp life held no horrors as long as it was relieved by occasional rounds of social activity. One correspondent, Kosciuszko, noted that he was informed Armstrong lived "very jolly." He chided Armstrong for not writing more often, but he added in his tortured English, "knowing that you have a good Reason to give that the handsome Girls ingross the whole of your time and attention and realy If I was in your place I should of Choise do the same."[10]

A year of relative inactivity added no luster or distinction to Armstrong's military career. In fact, his father, concerned about his son's health, urged him to leave the army. But Armstrong still hoped for glory, and with Gates's permission he joined an expedition in the fall of 1779 organized by Massachusetts against the British at Castine, Maine. But the expedition was quickly routed, and Armstrong dejectedly made his way to Providence, Rhode Island, where Gates was now headquartered.[11]

This was not the only disappointment for Armstrong that fall of 1779. He was appointed acting adjutant general, only to be replaced by a Connecticut man when Gates bowed to public pressure. Armstrong's letters reveal his state of depression. He wrote a friend that he was in "the most unfriendly ill-natured humor I ever felt." Referring to being replaced as adjutant he said, "I feel myself injured to the last degree and turn in disgust from a life in which is so much dependency on my part and caprice on the other." Yet despite his disgust, he would not quit. He admitted candidly, "ambition still holds me by the hand and urges prospects of promotion to me."[12]

General Gates was well aware of the disappointment of his young aide. When the British evacuated Newport, Rhode Island, on October 25, he sent Armstrong to carry the message to Congress, along with a letter to Samuel Huntington, the president of Congress, recommending "some

Honorable Mark" for Armstrong's services. No promotion, however, was forthcoming.[13]

No suitable position was found in 1780 for Gates, who retired to his plantation to await assignment. Armstrong returned to Carlisle. At last, on July 13, 1780, Congress found a station befitting the victor of Saratoga. Gates was appointed commander of the Southern Department where the war had heated up considerably, and where the American situation had become critical. Armstrong was appointed deputy adjutant general, but the best that General Gates could secure for him was a brevet rank of lieutenant colonel.

Abandoning the caution that marked his activity at Saratoga, Gates took command on July 25 and shortly thereafter ordered his approximately 2000 troops on an ill-advised forced march from Hillsborough, North Carolina, toward Camden, South Carolina. Despite the sickly condition of his troops, Gates resolved to attack. On the night of August 15–16, the Americans were advancing under the cover of darkness to attack the British when they were startled to find the British under Lord Cornwallis advancing in the opposite direction to surprise the Americans! The American militia was no match for the British regulars. Gates lost about 1000 men killed and captured. The battle of Camden was a disastrous defeat for the Americans, and it was, of course, a stunning blow to Gates's reputation.

Armstrong missed all the action. He had hardly arrived in North Carolina when he came down with a fever (probably malaria). His condition was very grave for a time, but he recovered sufficiently to be moved to Richmond, Virginia, where he improved very slowly. His exertions there to defend his commander's reputation did not assist his recovery.[14]

Gates was relieved of his command on October 5, and he was replaced by Major General Nathanael Greene. This blow to Gates was followed a week later by the death of his very promising only son, Robert, who was twenty-two years old. Robert had been a friend and personal favorite of Armstrong. These events, although melancholy, strengthened the bonds of friendship between the old general and the young aide. Armstrong expressed this growing attachment in January 1781 in a letter to Gates written at his home in Carlisle, where he had gone to recuperate. "If I know my own heart," he wrote, "I can well assure you that parting from you in Carolina was among the most painful incidents of my life."[15]

In April Armstrong accompanied Gates to Philadelphia to ask Congress for an inquiry into Gates's conduct during the last campaign. Congress seemed reluctant to press the matter, which disgusted Armstrong. He wrote his father that members of Congress "confess themselves bankrupt in credit, sense, honesty and spirit." Eventually, in August 1782, Congress as a result of the inquiry brought no charges of misconduct. When Gates followed Washington into winter quarters at Newburgh, New York, in 1782, the prospects for peace were nearly certain. The victory over Cornwallis at Yorktown on October 19, 1781, made the remainder of the war anticlimactic. The biggest problem facing Congress and the military commanders was phasing out the troops, which proved to be as vexing as it had been to keep an army in the field to fight the war.

Congress announced in August 1782 a plan for voluntary retirement of officers according to a pre-arranged plan, to begin on January 1, 1783; but nothing was said about the promise made during the dark days of 1780 of half-pay for life for the eligible officers at the end of the war. It was known generally in the army that Congress had since reconsidered its promise and now opposed any such generous measure. Nor was it known when or how the soldiers would be compensated for back pay of salaries due them.

Lack of pay burdened soldiers and officers with mounting debts and loss of credit, causing distress to their families. On the other hand, civil officers regularly received their pay. Other grievances included the stopping of promotions, and the withholding of commissions and the proposed half-pay. Most members of Congress agreed that the soldiers should have their back pay, but many bitterly opposed the half-pay promise. Most of the army officers recognized this, and probably a majority of them were willing to accept a "commutation pay," that is, a gross amount in lieu of half-pay.

There was doubt whether Congress, lacking a permanent source of revenue, could fulfill its promise even if it were so inclined. That was the fundamental issue. Congress was badly divided between those who advocated strengthening the central government to provide it with the power to raise a revenue and meet its obligations and those who feared such centralizing tendencies. The latter group, however, was sensitive to the clamor raised by the army and the cries of the public creditors. It was widely believed that if pressures could be applied to the reluctant congressmen the government might be provided with a revenue.[16]

In December 1782 the officers sent a "memorial" to Congress offering to accept a commutation pay, but they noted in a menacing tone that "any further experiments on their patience may have fatal effects." A small group of nationalists in Philadelphia, including Robert Morris, the superintendent of finances, Gouverneur Morris, his assistant, and Alexander Hamilton sought to use the threat of the army to pressure Congress into adopting some dependable source of revenue for the government.

They convinced the army representatives who carried the memorial to Philadelphia that their only hope was to link their cause to that of the public creditors. Shortly thereafter assorted innuendoes about the growing discontent in the army were put into circulation to alarm the reluctant congressmen. Heavy pressure was also applied by the civilian creditors. Robert Morris even threatened to resign if by the end of May there was no "permanent provision for the public debts." His resignation could be expected to further weaken the faith of the army and the public creditors in the fiscal integrity of the government. Congress was alarmed, but many congressmen were bound by instructions from their states. Twice Congress failed to pass bills for commutation pay.[17]

The nationalists probably believed that this news would touch off an explosion of indignation in the camp at Newburgh. Leaving nothing to chance, they sought to enlist the highly respected Major General Henry Knox, who had drafted the first memorial, to draw up another statement that the army would not disband until Congress met its obligations to the army. Hamilton also wrote Washington "coaching" him on what to do. He should "not discountenance" the army's efforts to seek redress and, without appearing to do so, should *take the direction of them* through another individual, presumably Knox. Playing subtly on the general's vanity, Hamilton intimated that an idea was being propagated in the army "that delicacy carried to an extreme prevents your espousing its interests." He concluded that the establishment of general funds for the government and the restoration of credit was "the object of all men of sense; in this the influence of the army, properly directed, may cooperate."[18]

Knox, however, rebuffed the nationalists, and there was a certain ambivalence in Washington's reply to Hamilton. If Hamilton was recommending the use of the army for political ends, then Washington expressly rejected the advice. The intervention of the army, he asserted, would have a "fatal tendency" and would "end in blood." If, on the other hand, it was intended as a warning against insidious influences in the army, then the source "may be easily traced, as the old leaven *it is said,* for I have no proof of it, is beginning to work under the mask of the most perfect dissimulation and apparent cordiality." This reference was obviously to General Gates. Washington added that the "sensible and discerning part of the army cannot be unacquainted, (altho' I never took pains to inform them), with the services I have rendered it on more occasions than one." He had no great apprehension that the army would exceed "the bounds of reason and moderation."[19]

Hamilton's letter thus planted the seeds of suspicion in Washington's mind that something was afoot involving the use of the army for political ends and possibly intending an assault upon his character and authority. Perhaps even more influential in affecting his frame of mind, however, was a letter from Joseph Jones, a congressman from Virginia, dated February 27. He warned Washington that reports were circulating in Philadelphia of dangerous combinations in the army and that it had been said that "they are about to declare they will not disband until their demands are complied with." He had also heard that "there are those who are abandoned enough to use their arts to lessen your reputation in the army, in hopes ultimately the weight of your opposition will prove no obstacle to their ambitious designs."[20]

This letter, judging from Washington's later actions, appears to have confirmed his suspicions that the source of the agitation was in Philadelphia. He replied to Jones that when this letter arrived, there was "not a syllable of the kind of agitation in the camp" that Jones had mentioned.[21] Then Colonel Walter Stewart, a former aide to General Gates and now the inspector of the northern army, arrived in camp on March 8 from Philadelphia. He was apparently sent by the nationalists to draw to the officers' attention that the time to act to influence Congress was growing short and that a vigorous statement by the army was needed. Probably, he was not charged with approaching the Gates military family directly, because some of the nationalists—particularly Hamilton—distrusted Gates. Stewart, however, quite naturally turned to his old comrades as the group he could trust. Undoubtedly he convinced them that the army had only one recourse left to obtain a resolution of their claims before being disbanded.

The meeting was held in Gates's quarters on March 9 with twelve to fourteen officers present. Stewart, as the agent for the nationalists, was probably responsible for shaping the plans of the group in this meeting. It was first agreed that a public meeting of officers should be called and that an address should be written "setting forth the objects of the meeting, and preparing them to act in unison."[22] Armstrong, only twenty-four years old but already known for his skill with the pen, was designated to write the appeal to the officers. The first Newburgh Address was written by him, and it was circulated in the camp the next day, March 10.

The Gates group thus acted very hastily and very rashly, without first testing the sentiment of the camp or preparing the officers to receive their plans. There was virtual unanimity in the officer corps on the justice of the army's claims, but the consequences of their proposals would involve the army in politics, embarrass Congress, and possibly have even broader ramifications. They may have considered only the short-term benefits without properly reflecting upon the long-range effects. Even after this event, Gates seemed unaware of these hazards. He noted to Armstrong in June 1783 that the only object had been "that of getting the army to cooperate with the civil creditors, as the way most likely to obtain justice." Similarly, Armstrong asserted that only "some manly, vigorous Association with the other public Creditors" was desired.[23]

The crucial decision made in the meeting was that the appeal to the officers would be issued anonymously; thus, they left themselves open to criticism and misinterpretation of their motives. Washington's cooperation was essential to their plans, and if he opposed their actions they preferred to remain anonymous; but they assumed that their anonymity was the most likely way to obtain his support. This view is supported by Armstrong's mention later that Washington "was not to have been consulted 'till some later period," and that "Although the severe virtues of the Commander in chief gave small hopes of his countenance, yet they did not despair of adhering him in some measure to their views."[24]

In the Newburgh Address Armstrong spoke of "courting the auspices, and inviting the direction of your illustrious leader." Even the passage in the first Address widely viewed as attempting to weaken Washington's position, "suspect the man, who would advise to more moderation and longer forbearance," could be interpreted as applying generally to all timid souls. The Gates faction probably hoped that Washington would passively acquiesce in their game of pressuring Congress. They may even have believed that Washington would not oppose their actions for fear that he would be blocking an avenue of redress for the army, which might hurt his reputation. The Gates clique, in short, sought not to undermine Washington's authority, but rather hoped for his tacit support. Their approach was indirect, and their appeal for his backing was oblique. As it developed, their motives were misunderstood by Washington.[25]

The first Newburgh Address, entitled "To the Officers of the Army," produced an electrifying impact when it appeared in camp. Written in a crisp, vigorous style that has been frequently acclaimed, its contents have been just as frequently condemned. Timothy Pickering, who was in camp when the Address was issued, called it a "truly Junian" composition. Washington, although he denounced it, conceded that "The author of the piece is entitled to much credit for the goodness of his pen." John Fiske, the historian, wrote: "better English has seldom been wasted in a worse cause." Armstrong himself, with modest pride of authorship, commented to his son that the Addresses "had the merit of being well adapted to the occasion that called them forth, and this, by the by, is no small merit: but the language, though vigorous, is frequently incorrect."[26]

The primary purpose of the first Address was to call for a stronger statement to Congress, and secondarily to menace Congress. Most of the attention was concentrated on the few passages in the Address carrying out the latter motive, such as "Change the milk and water style of your last memorial . . . Assume a bolder tone, decent, but lively, spirited, and determined," and he advised that the new memorial should emphasize "what has been promised by Congress, and what has been performed; how long and how patiently you have suffered; how little you have asked, and how much of that little has been denied." The most seditious passage warned that if Congress failed to do justice, "the army has its alternative," namely, refuse to lay down its arms, and "courting the direction of your illustrious leader, you will retire to some yet unsettled country, smile in your turn, and 'mock when their [Congress's] fear cometh on.'" This passage was included for its shock value—the ultimate threat.

Evidence indicates, however, that the first Address was not intended as the beginning of a coup d'etat. Significantly, the camp was quiet and not in a state of agitation. If the Gates faction had been seriously contemplating a coup, they would have undoubtedly prepared the ground for the Address by circulating sentiments to shape the attitudes of those in camp. Apparently they only wanted the army to issue another, stronger protest to pressure Congress into resolving the army's grievances. Their actions, perhaps unwittingly, brought about a crisis that they never quite understood and a train of events that they had not anticipated.

When the first Newburgh Address was posted on March 10, there was a great consternation in the headquarters. Washington obtained a copy, and he obviously thought he saw through the scheme. Writing to Jones on March 12, Washington related that a state of agitation began "upon the arrival of a certain Gentleman from Phila.," obviously referring to Stewart. "It is generally believed that the scheme was not only planned but also digested and matured in Philadelphia," he added, "some people have been playing a double game, spreading at the camp and in Philadelphia Reports, and raising jealousies, equally void of foundation, until called into being by their vile artifices."[27] Although he may have suspected that the Gates group was cooperating with Stewart, Washington was clearly reacting to what he saw as a challenge to his authority and a scheme by a group outside the army to utilize the army for political ends.

It is equally clear that Washington believed that the first Newburgh Address was written in Philadelphia and carried to the camp by Stewart. According to David Cobb, one of Washington's aides, the view that Gouverneur Morris was the author was "I believe the unanimous opinion of Head Quarters." When the second anonymous Address appeared, Washington was forced to concede, as he admitted in a letter to Hamilton,

"The contents evidently prove that the Author is in, or near Camp." He undoubtedly still believed that Morris was involved. A month after the incident, he announced his suspicion to Hamilton that "to Mr. G.M. is ascribed, in a great degree the ground work of the superstructure which was intended to be raised in the Army by the Anonymous Addresser."[28]

In his mind Washington was prepared to meet a challenge to his authority. He believed there was an actual conspiracy, and he moved swiftly to suppress the threat. Accordingly, to rescue the officers "from plunging themselves into a gulph of Civil horror from which there might be no receding," he issued a general order on March 11, which he explained to Hamilton, "was done upon the principle that it is easier to divert from a wrong, and point to a right path, than it is to recall the hasty and fatal steps which have already been taken." In his general order Washington denounced the anonymous call for a meeting as an "irregular invitation," and he expressed his "disapprobation of such disorderly proceedings." At the same time, however, he called a regular meeting for Saturday, March 15, "to hear the report of the committee of the army to Congress," and to "devise what further measures ought to be adopted . . . to attain the just and important object in view." This gave him time to use his personal influence to counter the "dangerous tendency" of the Address, as he told Timothy Pickering on one tour around the camp.[29]

Washington's cool response led to a reaction against the Address. The Gates faction was undoubtedly shocked and perplexed by his reaction to a call for a meeting they conceived to be not unlike the earlier protest. They dared not challenge Washington directly; without his support or acceptance of their actions nothing could be done. One last futile effort was made to reclaim the initiative and enlist the support of Washington and the officers. Armstrong drafted a second Address, and it was posted in the camp on March 12. Stung by the criticism of the first Address, Armstrong asserted, "ye well know that it spoke a language which till now, had been heard only in whispers." As for the anonymity, he noted, "the best designs are sometimes obliged to assume the worst aspect." He asserted that Washington's general order should not be viewed as disapproval of the movement; he even suggested that Washington's call for a meeting was intended to "give system to your proceedings, and stability to your resolves." In any event, Armstrong concluded, "it cannot possibly lessen the independency of your sentiments," although the Gates group undoubtedly knew this was not the case. When there was no positive reaction to the second Address, the movement was given up. There is no evidence that the Gates group took any further steps to carry out their schemes.

Washington did not know it, but he had already won. There is ample evidence that he and his military family prepared carefully for a confrontation that never materialized. The meeting convened at noon, March 15, with General Gates presiding. Shortly after the meeting began, Washington arrived dramatically and asked to speak. He delivered a carefully prepared and eloquent speech to the assembled officers. He denounced the anonymous Addresses and in particular singled out the most vulnerable passages. He decried the intolerance of the anonymous author in advising the officers to suspect the views of those who counseled moderation. Further, the "dreadful alternative, of either deserting our country in the extremist hour of her distress, or turning our arms against it, which is the apparent object, unless Congress can be compelled into instant compliance," he exclaimed, "has something so shocking in it, that humanity revolts at the idea." He assured his officers that his efforts in their behalf would be unceasing, and he held out the hope that the army's desires would be met by Congress. To emphasize his point, he produced the letter from Joseph Jones to read to the officers. This led to the most memorable event of the meeting. Reaching for his spectacles, Washington, in an apparently ad-libbed comment, apologized that he "had grown gray in their service, and now found himself growing blind."[30]

Whatever resolve the officers might have had melted before the presence and presentation of their charismatic leader. After he withdrew, his lieutenants seized the initiative and engineered a series of resolutions through the docile assembly that expressed the army's confidence in Congress and the commander-in-chief and condemned the anonymous Addresses. Only Timothy Pickering raised his voice against these proceedings in the "general speechlessness of the assembly." He declared later that it was shameful that the officers "damned with infamy two publications which during the four proceeding [sic] days most of them had read with admiration, & talked of with rapture!"[31] By their silence, the Gates clique and the other officers who had "spoken of their discontent only in whispers," tacitly acquiesced, virtually forfeited any further action, and sealed the fate of their stillborn movement. Washington's devastating denunciation of this incipient agitation made association with the movement disreputable. Both the nationalists and the Gates group began to cloak their roles in this affair.

There was never any real danger that Washington would lose control of the army, or that the army would lose control of itself. Washington's reaction to the Addresses and his conduct during the entire affair has given historians the mistaken impression that some momentous crisis was averted. In fact, Washington was quashing a phantom conspiracy. Ironically, the rumors of the agitation at Newburgh had the predicted effect on Congress. Acting under the impulse of reports of trouble brewing in the army, Congress passed an act on March 22 providing for commutation pay of five years full pay for the officers, substantially the same as a bill they had defeated earlier.[32]

Washington eventually learned that he had overreacted. There is little doubt that he learned, at least in broad outline, the nature of the scheme to involve the army in politics, as well as those involved. Shortly after the event, he confronted Hamilton with the "suspicions" of the army that "the Financier [Robert Morris] is suspected to be at the bottom of this scheme." Hamilton did not deny that he and the Morrises were involved, but he asserted that there was no evil intent.[33] Washington replied soothingly that he supported the ends of the nationalists but not their means. "The Army was a dangerous Engine to work with, as it might be made to cut both ways," he stated. His fear was that some in the army would seek "immediate relief" from the states. This might have created divisions in the army which would have tended to "weaken, rather than strengthen the hands of those who were disposed to support Continental measures — and might *tend* to defeat the end they themselves had in view by endeavouring to involve the army."[34] Washington was correct, of course, and he proved himself to be a better politician than either the nationalists or the Gates clique. He bore no grudges against the nationalists, and in the years that followed Hamilton and the two Morrises were among his closest collaborators.

General Gates and those involved with him never really understood why Washington had reacted so strongly against their movement, but they were certain that the army had acted against its own best interests in denouncing the Addresses. Congress, they believed, now assured of no threat from the army, would continue its contemptuous policy toward them. The course of events seemed to bear out their predictions. On April 11, Congress proclaimed the official peace treaty ending the war. Nothing was said about disbandment, because Congress lacked the funds to settle the accounts. The army lingered in camp and awaited further action by Congress. Armstrong in Philadelphia reported on May 9 to Gates, who was now in Virginia, that "The intelligence from the army verifies all our predictions. The soldiers are loud and insolent, the officers broken, dissatisfied and desponding. The states obdurate and forgetful, & Congress weak as water and impotent as old age."[35] Finally, Congress authorized the troops to go home on furlough and most of the officers and soldiers left camp, without formality or ceremony, and with their accounts still unsettled.

As the army was disbanding there were many reports of threatened mutiny, and one did occur. A small detachment of Pennsylvanians, not a part of the main army, marched on Philadelphia on June 20 and held that city and Congress in fear for several days. Although the soldiers were belligerent, demanded the settlement of their accounts, and for a time even held Congress captive, they were eventually dispersed without bloodshed. The main consequence of this event was the removal of Congress from Philadelphia. Armstrong, in his bitterness, believed this a well-deserved humiliation of Congress. "The grand Sanhedrins of the Nation," he informed Gates, "with all their solemnity & emptiness, have removed to Princeton & left a state, where their wisdom has long been questioned, their virtue suspected & their dignity a jest."[36]

In Armstrong's letters to Gates there was no hint of any feeling that his authorship of the Newburgh Addresses had been improper. On the contrary, the events confirmed in his mind that they had recommended the proper action, and the failure of the army to take his advice had doomed them to their unpleasant fate. The closest he came to expressing remorse was in a letter to Gates on April 29, "I would have written again — had I not seen the impotence of the Army & the Assurance of Congress — they see our weakness & laugh at our resentments. My efforts, therefore, might have not only been unavailing, but injurious."[37] Although he had no real regrets about his role, he intended a political career and discretion made it wise to conceal his involvement. He did not conceal his role from his friends, however, and in this manner his authorship became fairly well known.

Washington, to his credit, did not forget that his denunciation of the Newburgh Addresses had laid a heavy stigma upon the motives of the author. Having learned that the real author was the younger son of his old friend John Armstrong, Sr., he was undoubtedly even more disposed to try to rectify whatever harm might result from his actions. Accordingly, in 1797, shortly before he left the presidency, Washington wrote an apparently unsolicited letter to young Armstrong that he was aware that his earlier harsh opinion of the Addresses might "be turned to some personal and malignant purpose." He then stated: "I do hereby declare, that I did not, at the time of writing my address regard you as the author of the said letters; and further, that I have since had sufficient reason for believing, that the object of the author was just, honorable, and friendly to the country, though the means suggested by him were certainly liable to much misunderstanding and abuse."[38]

Armstrong, perhaps because he did not desire to call attention to his authorship of the Addresses, did not make Washington's letter public for more than twenty-five years. He may have entertained the belief that the Newburgh incident would fade from public memory, but it continued to haunt him the rest of his life. Many public men of the time were prone to attribute a sinister, intriguing character to Armstrong, based in part on their knowledge of his authorship of the Addresses.

In retrospect, it is fair to say that the actions of Gates, Armstrong, and the others in their group may not have been wise, but they had no evil intent.[39] The Newburgh Addresses did not invite the army to turn its arms on the constituted authority. The threat was that they would not allow themselves to be disbanded. Even the Gates group recognized that their threat, to have any credibility, needed the support of General Washington. No other officer, not even Gates, had such support, love, and admiration. His perception that there was an evil intent behind the Addresses was sufficient to stifle the movement. The Gates faction understood that possibility, and undoubtedly they also understood that with the mood of the camp being apathetic, with discipline breaking down, only Washington could have roused the troops to any overt action. Even then it is highly unlikely that they could have been persuaded to attack the government and the people of the country for whom they had just won independence.

Finally, and most important, the federal system itself weighed against any prospective mutiny. Any group considering a mutiny would have to face not only the central government but thirteen state governments. With state loyalties stronger than any ties to a central government, it would have been difficult to predict loyalties among the troops. In view of these facts, it is hardly conceivable that the Gates group was seriously considering a coup, but it must be conceded that their bungled effort to use the army to influence Congress could have created a potentially momentous crisis.

2

POLITICIAN AND PATRICIAN

ACCORDING TO ONE STORY, a few days after Washington had so warmly condemned the Newburgh Addresses, Armstrong wrote to him "a severe and contemptuous letter . . . and the next morning waited on him and resigned his commission." Washington was quoted as saying to the young officer, "I am happy sir that you have no further occasion to exercise your talents."[1] This story is probably apocryphal, for Washington by his own later admission did not suspect the son of his old friend of being the creator of the disturbances in his camp.

In any event, Armstrong returned to private life after more than seven years of army life unmarked by promotion and little distinguished by military glory. "Whatever natural dispositions I may have to the *solemnity* of office," he wrote Gates shortly after resigning, "my last winter's experience has sufficiently corrected the mistake & left me convinced that pride and vanity are their own tormentors." Armstrong was fortunate, however, to move immediately from a military career to a political career. He successfully sought the appointment as the Secretary of the Pennsylvania Supreme Executive Council, an important position in the state government.[2]

Armstrong entered the new position with some misgivings. In a very revealing letter to his father he wrote:

> Party spirit rising high — interest pointing one way, inclination leading another. But was it necessary that I should mingle in the strife at all — that the second important step of my life should like the first, be made into the fire? Certainly no. As it now stands, I know not how to turn myself. The more I look forward into life the more I am embarrass'd in my choice. Law has its

promises, but not without extreme labor-drudgery. In this profession, as-
siduity itself will not do — to succeed you must be a Student for life. For
trade I feel myself entirely disqualified. I want the love of wealth that warms
the merchant's breast, & interests him in the acquisition of it. I want that
kind of industry that can pry into corners and draw lines, almost invisible,
between a good & a bad bargain. If I have anything speculative about me, it
exerts itself in another way & upon other subjects. What then am I to do? I
believe after all I could accept your proposal and go into the envied quiet of
a farmer's life. I may have industry eno' to raise hogs & horses.[3]

Armstrong's indolent habits and his conscious desire for a life of
ease are revealed in this letter. He never denied this fact. When Gates advised diligence in his new task, Armstrong replied, "I am aware of my
own indolence and how often it leaves me open and exposed to the curious eye of inquisitorial villainy. But, necessity will soon get the better of
nature and all its auxiliary habits. I already feel the force of method and
begin to adopt it with the whole family of dullness, merely because I find
them [sic] contribute so much to that ease I love."[4] Armstrong's lackadais-
ical attitude and his languid nature was a source of comment by many of
his contemporaries. Charles Biddle, the vice president of the Supreme Executive Council, for example, wrote: "Armstrong has very superior talents, but they are almost useless, he is so extremely indolent."[5] It must be
noted, nevertheless, that Armstrong accomplished a great deal in his long
lifetime — at least enough to call into question the complete accuracy of
this appraisal of his personality.

Despite his resolve to have nothing to do with political parties, the
1780s in Pennsylvania were characterized by hot political rivalry, and
Armstrong became identified with the conservative elements whose economic influence and social position gave them considerable power. John
Dickinson, the president of the Pennsylvania Executive Council and an
old friend of Armstrong's father, was a leader of this faction along with
Robert Morris.[6]

Armstrong's appointment was obviously related to the political maneuvering of this group. Timothy Matlack, the secretary of the Supreme
Executive Council, was abruptly removed by a resolution of the Pennsylvania Assembly on March 5, 1783, for neglecting to "keep accounts of
money received by him on behalf of the public, and also to pay the same
into the Treasury, according to Law." Matlack protested, and the Council
of Censors — Pennsylvania's unique way of reviewing the actions of the
Assembly — declared on December 15, 1784, that the Assembly had no
such authority to censure Matlack and annulled the resolution. Neverthe-

less, this did nothing to restore Matlack to his former position, and he still faced charges in the courts.[7]

As secretary of the Executive Council, Armstrong was charged with communicating the Council's decisions to the various public officials and seeing that they were carried out — for example, supervising the forwarding of supplies, ammunition, and equipment to the frontier to strengthen the forces there against the Indians. His duties also included supervising the collection of taxes, the running of surveys, the sale of state lands, the redemption of depreciated certificates, even the apprehension of the soldiers charged with the disturbances in Philadelphia.[8]

Armstrong also became deeply involved in the rival claims of Pennsylvania and Connecticut concerning the jurisdiction over the Wyoming Valley (in present-day northeast Pennsylvania along the east branch of the Susquehanna River), which had been held somewhat in abeyance during the Revolutionary War. In the summer of 1778 a combined force of British and Indians massacred about 150 settlers in this area. Most of the victims were from Connecticut, having settled there under the claims of the Susquehannah Company. Pennsylvania was sensitive to the sufferings of these people, but they were viewed nevertheless as interlopers who had no title or right to the soil. Consequently, when the war drew to a close, Pennsylvania called upon Congress to settle the question of ownership. Connecticut tried to delay the issue, but a hearing was held at Trenton, New Jersey, late in 1782, and the Commissioners ruled that the lands rightfully belonged to Pennsylvania.[9]

The settlement of jurisdiction resolved only one problem. The subject of soil rights presented an even larger issue. The Connecticut settlers were firmly resolved to stay on their lands and surrender none of their claims. Many had built homes, confident that their titles were secure, despite the fact that Pennsylvanians held rival deeds to the same land. Obviously, recognizing a Pennsylvania deed might deprive a Connecticut settler of his improvements on the land and confirm them to a Pennsylvania speculator. On the other hand, it was just as obvious that Connecticut speculators were the driving force behind the stubborn resistance of the Yankee settlers.

The harried leaders of Pennsylvania were faced with a nearly insoluable problem. The bitterness of feelings inevitably turned the situation toward violence. In the fall of 1783 the impatient Pennamites (a term used by the Connecticut settlers for the Pennsylvanians), led by Alexander Patterson, began systematically to harass the Connecticut settlers. Numerous assaults upon the Yankees occurred in May 1784. The Pennsylvania state officials clearly tried to do what was right. They brought indictments against forty-five Pennamites for rioting. As a further conciliatory gesture toward the Yankees, they removed the Pennsylvania troops from this area on June 11.[10]

The Yankees, however, led by John Franklin, responded with violence in retaliation for the May attacks. Pennamites fled to the old Fort Wyoming (renamed Fort Dickinson) in Wilkes-Barre. Two Pennamites were killed. The reports of violence prompted the Executive Council to call out a militia force of 300 infantry and fifteen Light Dragoons. John Boyd, a member of the Council, and Lieutenant Colonel John Armstrong, their secretary, were placed in command of the force. John Dickinson instructed the two commissioners to "convince the Insurgents that while we are determined to have justice rendered to all persons . . . we are also resolved to preserve peace and good order."[11]

Armstrong's friends were apprehensive. William Jackson wrote General Gates, "It is, I think, rather problematic whether he shall be able to accomplish his purpose." Although Boyd was joined with Armstrong in the command, he continued, "I apprehend our friend will be held the acting, consequently the more responsible of the two. I hope the business will terminate to his wish." The same fears were expressed by Armstrong's father. He wrote that he was sorry that John had gotten involved in the affair. Unwarranted acts had been committed by both sides, but he felt that some of the Connecticut claimants had rights and should be treated better by the government. He hoped for the best for his son, and he asserted, "not even the wisdom of Solomon could solve the issue to the satisfaction of all."[12]

Young Armstrong did not adopt a conciliatory attitude. Armstrong and Boyd added fuel to the controversy rather than quieting the situation. Despite reports from Wyoming that the Yankees had threatened the beseiged Pennsylvanians that if they did not surrender they would all be put to the sword, Armstrong and Boyd were frustrated in their efforts to gather their force. They reported from Easton on August 7 that not more than a third of those who had been called appeared at the place of rendezvous, and they were extremely poorly prepared. Designing individuals, they charged, had wickedly misrepresented the government's object. "We everywhere met the following Objections 'that it was [a] Quarrel of a Sett of Landjobbers that the whole Country was not worth the life of a single Man . . . that they were drawn forth not merely to support the laws but to exturbate the whole race of Connecticut claimants &c&c.'"[13]

While the force was forming, a report came that Connecticut settlers had attacked one of the advanced detachments of Armstrong's and Boyd's force on August 2 at Locust Hill, about twenty-three miles from

Wyoming, killing one and wounding three others. This attack reinforced their conception of the Yankees as the aggressors. On August 8 they rode to the fort with a force of about 400 with two goals in mind: to rescue the Pennamites under seige and to punish the Yankees who were guilty of the attack at Locust Hill. At the fort, they announced that the seige was over, and they asked for the submission of the Connecticut settlers to their authority. Their intermediaries were David Mead and Robert Martin, justices of the peace, who had previously tried to arbitrate between the two factions. The Pennamites spurned their efforts, claiming that Martin and Mead were partial to the Yankees.

The Connecticut settlers always maintained that Armstrong and Boyd gave a solemn promise upon their honor as gentlemen that no advantage would be taken of them if they surrendered their arms. Justice Martin later wrote only that he was assured by the Commissioners that they would "do complete justice without distinction of parties." It is quite probable that the justices misinterpreted Armstrong's and Boyd's attitude and imputed more to their statements than was warranted. Likewise, the Connecticut settlers placed more faith in the justices' promises than they should have. When they laid down their arms, Armstrong and Boyd and their force rode up to place the Yankees under arrest. Quite naturally, they felt betrayed. Martin and Mead were as shocked as the Yankees.[14]

It is highly unlikely that Armstrong and Boyd made any such promise, but in any event, it was an unfortunate and inauspicious beginning to their mission. If they had any sense of satisfaction that they had so easily restored order, they were soon disabused of it when word came that many of the prisoners had escaped or were released on bail. Martin and Mead served as the security for the Yankee leaders.[15]

Dickinson and the Council were now disposed to be conciliatory. Armstrong was asked to deal with a fine hand. On the one side he was to offer restitution of the land to those dispossessed Connecticut claimants at the risk of incurring the wrath of the Pennamites, and on the other he was to menace the Yankee insurgents with words, with little force to back it up. Nevertheless, Armstrong opened negotiations with John Franklin. On September 14 Armstrong informed Dickinson that those insurgents under arms, while refusing to submit to Pennsylvania authority, were not disposed toward violence.[16]

The Wyoming affair soon became involved in the domestic politics of Pennsylvania. Opponents of the government profited by championing fair play for the Yankees. This weakened Armstrong's hand, and delighted the Connecticut settlers, whose resolve was strengthened to persist until they ultimately gained their goals. The Council added two commissioners to join Armstrong and Boyd, but shortly after they arrived at Wyoming on September 26, a party of Connecticut settlers attempted to break into the public storehouses where the arms were deposited. They were repulsed, but in the process the dwellings of the commissioners were fired upon. Boyd and one of the other Commissioners narrowly escaped. As a consequence, the commissioners, citing "the dangers of assassination," left the next day. Shortly after their departure an attack by the Yankees upon the Pennamites began in deadly earnest, and two of the defenders were mortally wounded.[17]

The Executive Council reacted swiftly, and on October 5 they appointed Armstrong as adjutant general with the rank of brigadier general. This was a significant display of confidence in a young man only twenty-five years old. Presumably he had impressed the Council with his abilities, and possibly Armstrong's actions in Wyoming did not enter into their consideration. If it did, then the Council either did not understand the depth of feeling in Wyoming against Armstrong or, more likely, they were determined to coerce the Connecticut settlers into recognizing the authority of Pennsylvania and saw Armstrong as a hard-liner who would do just that. Dickinson, who was ill during this period, dissented. From his sick bed, he wrote the Council on October 5 that the militia call-out was unnecessary and unwise, would be extremely expensive, might provoke further violence, and would be construed by the public as waging war upon the Connecticut settlers. He also questioned the wisdom of Armstrong's appointment. "I am perfectly convinced at the uncommon merit of Colonel Armstrong," he wrote, but the appointment of the secretary of Council, "when it is well known that the settlers view him in the light of an enemy, are circumstances that may promote unfavorable constructions of the conduct of Government."[18]

Dickinson was offering sound advice, but unfortunately his conciliatory moves in the past had been tested and found wanting. Instead, the Council now opted for firm moves. Large rewards were offered for the apprehension of the Yankee leaders. The newly commissioned General Armstrong was again confronted with the reluctance of the militia to act against the Connecticut settlers. The Berks County militia, almost to a man, refused to serve. Armstrong was able to gather a force of only forty men to march into Wyoming. He nevertheless boldly marched in on Sunday, October 17, and arrested about thirty Connecticut men. The next day, reinforced by Patterson's men, Armstrong pursued Franklin and his followers to Kingston, but they occupied such a strong position that Armstrong was forced to retire. This circumstance thwarted, as he phrased it, "the happy prospect of exterminating the Banditti at once." With another hundred men, he asserted, he would have accomplished his objective.[19]

Armstrong attempted futilely to work out a cease-fire and to open a dialogue with John Franklin through one of the justices of the peace. Finally, on November 15, he admitted to Dickinson the failure of his mission. He was unable "to attempt anything offensive," and he concluded, "a line of meer defensive Conduct on the part of the State held out a promise of sooner bringing about the objects of the Government than one of a more active nature." He was not sanguine "in expecting any better Consequence" from this policy. Rather, he believed "further lenity . . . will be found unavailing," on a group of inflamed people that he characterized as "vagrants and desperadoes."[20]

When the militia withdrew, the Yankees began removing Pennsylvania families from their area. The Connecticut settlers received an unexpected offer of assistance from the revolutionary leader, Ethan Allen, in the summer of 1785. He promised to lead a small group of his Green Mountain Boys to Wyoming "to Vindicate . . . the rights of soil" of the Connecticut settlers. Whether Allen was acting out of interest for the Connecticut settlers, or out of his interest to acquire land is not clear. He did receive twelve rights in the Susquehannah Company, and he went to Wyoming and apparently tried to stimulate a statehood movement.[21]

The Pennsylvania Assembly sought in December 1785 to resolve the dispute by offering amnesty to those guilty of offenses against the state, providing they submitted to Pennsylvania authority. The Yankees met this offer with an attempt to bring in more Connecticut settlers and to set up new towns. In September 1786 the Assembly tried once more to soothe the trouble by creating a new county that would give the Connecticut settlers control over their area under Pennsylvania authority. The matter of private rights to the soil lingered in controversy for another twenty years.[22]

After his role in 1784, Armstrong had no further active part in the Wyoming controversy. He had contributed little to the resolution of the conflict, and his actions were probably detrimental. Even without his participation, however, it is unlikely that the situation would have been much different. Perhaps he acted out of misguided zeal, but his actions at least had the virtue of consistency. The vacillating approach of the Pennsylvania Council and the General Assembly, no matter how well-intentioned, aggravated tensions on both sides and satisfied neither. Armstrong's policy of repression failed, not only because most Pennsylvanians clearly had doubts about whether such a policy was right, but also because they did not have the inclination to force the resolution of an issue which favored one side over the other. As a consequence, the issue was prolonged.

The Wyoming affair led to a temporary decline in the political influence of the conservative-nationalist faction headed by Morris and Dickinson, but Armstrong was not affected in his two positions as secretary of the Supreme Executive Council and adjutant general of the Pennsylvania militia. He was frequently called the "boy general," and there is no doubt that he was extremely proud of his rank and title. Thereafter, for the remainder of his life, he preferred to be addressed by the title of "General."

With all the élan of youth, with rank and position beyond his years, an eligible bachelor and a witty conversationalist, and conscious of his superior talents, Armstrong had bright prospects for his future. He had taken up residence in May 1783 at the home of a Presbyterian clergyman, Daniel Jones, on Race Street. With him in the same lodgings was his friend, William Clajon, a much older man who had served during the war as General Gates's secretary and interpreter in the Northern Department.[23]

The worldly sophistication of young Armstrong was disturbing to the pious elder Armstrong. He urged his son to become fully informed of the doctrines of the churches, then he "must and ought to decide in favor of one Christian Society."[24] The injunction was not heeded by his son. Perhaps this was a reaction to an overbearing father whose piety bordered on religious fanaticism. Not until the very end of his life did Armstrong become a communicant of a church.

The problems of the government of the Articles of Confederation spurred a call from Virginia for a Commercial Convention at Annapolis in September 1786, and Armstrong was chosen by the Pennsylvania Assembly as one of its delegates. The convention adjourned after meeting only briefly and issuing another call for a convention to meet in Philadelphia the next May. Armstrong's political career advanced another step when the Pennsylvania Assembly appointed him as a delegate to Congress on March 24, 1787. His selection was welcomed by the nationalist group in Congress. James Madison, for example, informed Edmund Randolph, the Governor of Virginia, that Armstrong's appointment "throws that State into the right Scale."[25]

Armstrong began his service in Congress on April 18, 1787, thus following in the footsteps of his father, who had also served a term in Congress. He was presented immediately with a controversy affecting a state interest, namely the selection of the seat of Congress. This problem probably generated more debate than any other single issue during the history of the Congress. An attempt to move from the current seat at New York City to Philadelphia failed. Armstrong was only beginning to perceive the frustrations of participating in a government which few supported and which was at that very moment in the process of being replaced by the Constitutional Convention in Philadelphia. For some time Armstrong was the only representative from Pennsylvania present at Congress, but he affirmed that "no adjournment can or will take place," because it would give the impression of "an abandonment of the government under its present shape."[26]

Not until July 4 was there a quorum of seven states in attendance. Several important matters were taken up, including the establishment of a government for the western country, which was speedily passed on July 13, 1787. This was the famous Ordinance of 1787, largely the result of shrewd lobbying of the Reverend Manasseh Cutler of Massachusetts, representing a group of speculators from that state organized as the Ohio Company. Cutler was aided and abetted by William Duer, the secretary of the Treasury Board, who saw in the proposals of the Ohio Company the possibility of fostering a land scheme by his group of New York speculators, organized as the Scioto Company. Several congressmen were involved in this land scheme, as the two companies secured options to five million acres in the area of present-day southeastern Ohio.[27]

Armstrong was not involved in the machinations of the Scioto Company, nor was he apparently an investor. He knew William Duer through a mutual friend, Baron von Steuben, with whom Armstrong lived one winter in New York. He was certainly cognizant of the operations of the inner group involved in the Scioto Company. Besides Duer, he knew Daniel Parker, who later settled in France and with whom Armstrong renewed a friendship in Paris many years later, and Joel Barlow, who was to be named Armstrong's successor as minister to France.[28]

This group probably engineered Armstrong's appointment on October 16, 1787, as one of the three judges of the newly created Northwest Territory. The salary was low ($800 per year), but the prerogatives of his office and a position of status in the new territory offered political and social influence. After reflecting during the winter on the advantages and disadvantages, Armstrong resigned his position on January 21, 1788.[29] General Gates approved, and Armstrong replied, "I think with you it was right & that a little in society is much more desirable than a great deal in a desart." It was evident that ambition figured prominently in his decision to resign the judicial appointment, for which he had no particular training anyway.

What had changed the situation considerably, of course, was the writing of the Constitution and the creation of a stronger central government. The prospects of the new government, while uncertain, were nevertheless far more promising than those of the old one. Armstrong, as well as countless other ambitious men of the time, wondered what part he was to play in the new drama. "My standing at present," he wrote Gates, "considering my age, & that I have been oblig'd to make my way thro' very narrow & hostile politics, is as forward as I had any right to expect, & more so perhaps, when I consider how many with better pretensions, because with more collateral supports, I have left behind me." As for the careers opened by the new government, he noted, "I will neither conceal myself from view, nor obtrude myself upon it — & then if appointments come they will sit easy." He related that as a matter of fact, his friends in Pennsylvania had already "tho't of a place for me & mean to try their force in sending me to the new Senate," but as there were only two seats to be filled, he did not expect their endeavor to be a success. "The rich & the ag'd . . . will expect & most probably get them, & indeed so little am I set upon the success in the trial, that I scarcely feel a wish to cross them. My leading wish is to see them *well* fill'd."[30] He was merely being modest. He did expect to be chosen, but before that happened he fell in love. His courtship of Alida Livingston of New York diminished his prospects in Pennsylvania and ultimately altered the course of his political career.

Armstrong was now twenty-nine years old. The records do not reveal any serious romantic relationships prior to this time, although possibly there were some. His romance developed while he was living in New York in a boarding house at the corner of Nassau Street with Baron von Steuben. The old Prussian general, who had contributed so much to the success of the Revolutionary army, was in desperate financial straits and was then in New York to press a claim for a pension for his Revolutionary services. Armstrong shared expenses with Steuben. Steuben enjoyed Armstrong's youthful vitality. Writing to Colonel William North, Steuben related that at their house on Nassau Street he was near the church, the mayor, and the bishop, while Armstrong was near "the Play-houss, some B——— houses and blac[k] Sam [Fraunces Tavern on Broad Street, famed as the place where Washington bade farewell to his officers in December 1783]."[31]

Armstrong had probably known Alida Livingston for several years. The Livingston sisters visited Philadelphia often, their brother Chancellor Robert R. Livingston, the highest judicial officer of New York, was politically prominent, and their acquaintances were extensive. These particular Livingstons comprised a remarkable branch of a remarkable family. Their father, Judge Robert R. Livingston, a grandson of the First Lord of the Manor Livingston, had joined his estate with that of the Schuyler and Beekman Patents by a fortuitous marriage to Margaret Beekman, the only surviving child of Colonel Henry Beekman. The combined estate, with its seat at Clermont overlooking the Hudson River about 110 miles from New York City, amounted to perhaps 200,000 acres.[32] Alida was the tenth of eleven children, having been born on December 24, 1761. Edward, who later served as Mayor of New York City and Secretary of State, was born two and a half years later. With the death of Judge Livingston in 1775, the eldest son, Chancellor Robert R. Livingston, became the pater familias, but the real head of the family, and the dominant influence until her death in 1800, was Alida's mother, Margaret Livingston, referred to affectionately as "Mama."

The Livingstons traditionally spent the winter in New York City, enjoying the gay social life, to which they added a certain luster. Armstrong, the eligible bachelor, and Alida Livingston, the most attractive of the Livingston sisters, no doubt were occasionally guests at the same social affairs. It is almost certain that the romance began sometime during the winter of 1787–1788, even though Armstrong denied any romantic involvement to Gates as late as May 1788. "The report you allude to is unfounded," he wrote, "I'm not yet married, nor likely to be so." He may have been reluctant to express hopes that might be dashed. "The truth is that I'm too poor to marry a woman without some fortune & too proud to marry any woman, that I know, who possesses one. In this dilemma, 'till my circumstances change, or other objects present themselves, I must keep along in the cheerless solitary road I am in."[33]

A month and a half later he was Alida's guest at Clermont. By all accounts, she was an attractive, cultivated, gentle, and amiable young lady, to say nothing of the share of the Livingston-Beekman lands that would fall due to her. Yet she had reached her twenty-sixth year without marrying. This was no doubt primarily due to her relative isolation at Clermont and to a shortage of young men suitable to marry a Livingston. Her eldest sister, Janet, had married General Richard Montgomery, who had been killed during the Revolutionary War. Another sister, Margaret, had married Thomas Tillotson, a physician who had been surgeon-general of the Northern Department during the war. Yet another sister, Gertrude, had married General Morgan Lewis, later a governor of New York.

The visit to Clermont was a great success. During the next few months the exchange of letters revealed John's growing frustration with the delays and pettiness of the politics in Congress, which delayed a revisit to Clermont. Alida's cautious letters grew progressively warmer, and she was encouraged by Armstrong's own bolder confessions of love. His obvious infatuation did not escape the attention of his colleagues, as he noted to Alida. His enemies were industriously propagating "a belief that I had renounced Pennsylva[nia] & her interests & had in fact been quite a New Yorker."

His friends were unable to secure Armstrong's election as a Senator from Pennsylvania. His youth was cited, but he asserted to Gates that his New York connection was the real reason. They had reasoned that "G[eneral] A[rmstrong] is about to connect himself with N.Y. His property there will be greater than it is here — hence it follows that if we elect him — we in fact elect a Citizen of N.Y." This argument, he concluded, was powerful with men "who knew no lie but property & who felt no principle but interest." He admitted that "some envy and some prejudice mingled themselves with it, and excluded me from the Senate, where (notwithstanding my non-age) I should have else been seated by an allmost unanimous vote." This was written several months after the event, and reflects the bitterness he still felt at his exclusion from the Senate, which he had apparently set as his goal. He added, "a seat in the other house I would not accept. The Morris junto were the real authors of the opposition given me. By refusing to be their Fool I have made myself their enemy. But I have done with them & politics too — perhaps forever."[34] By the time this letter was written he had married Alida, he had quit politics, and he had decided to live in New York, but it is unlikely he had made this decision in October and November 1788. In fact, the Pennsylvania Assembly reelected him in November as a delegate to the expiring Congress.

Armstrong again visited Clermont during the winter of 1788, and he and Alida were married there on Friday, January 19, 1789. Despite the bride's ample dowry, there is reason to believe that this was a love match. There is no record of any marital differences, while there is abundant evidence of a deep affection and mutual respect that lasted until her death nearly thirty-four years later. Armstrong announced his marriage to his parents, which could not have come as any surprise to them. John's father wrote immediately to Alida's "Mama" expressing his pleasure, and incidentally, began an extensive correspondence between the old patriarch and the matriarch of the Livingston clan.

Although now linked by marriage to a prominent family of New York, Armstrong was still a delegate from Pennsylvania to Congress, but it never reassembled for lack of a quorum. He had spent nearly half of his young life in public service and he no doubt still anticipated some role in the new government. Around the middle of March, he set out for New York City, where the new government was assembling, obviously to discover what opportunities were open to him. He soon learned that the political winds were not blowing in his favor. His New York alliance excluded him from office in Pennsylvania, and his association with the Livingstons was a disadvantage, for the Chancellor and those associated with him were frozen out of the Washington Administration, largely due to the efforts of Alexander Hamilton.[35]

While in New York City, Armstrong wrote to Gates to inform him that he was married, and he also detailed in a bemused sort of way the bustle going on in the city. "All the world here and elsewhere are busy in collecting flow'rs & sweets of every kind to amuse and delight [Washington] in his approach and at his arrival & even Roger Sherman has set his head at work to devise some style of address more novel & dignified than Excellency." But Armstrong was pleased to note that there were still skeptics and wits. One caricature he described to Gates was called "The Entry." It represented Washington "mounted on an Ass & in the arms of his mulatto man Billy — [David] Humphreys leading the Jack and chanting Hosannas & birthday odes. The following couplet," he added, "makes the motto of this device: 'The glorious time has come to pass / When David shall conduct an Ass.'" The moral, according to Armstrong, was that "wit spares nothing — neither Washington nor God — and that the former like the latter will have something to suffer, and much to forgive."[36] Armstrong was in attendance on April 30, when Washington took the oath of office, administered by Chancellor Livingston.

Although he was disappointed in his quest for a political appointment, Armstrong had little reason to regret his failure to attain a position. He wrote Gates in July 1789, "The more I know of domestic life, the more I like it. My own little interests & those of my friends are the only ones that touch or affect me; & I now feel myself almost as indifferent to public measures, as you & Candida are to public men."[37] In September he and Alida visited his parents in Carlisle. While there he visited Philadelphia in December, apparently with the intention of finding a suitable place to live. From there he wrote Alida, "There is no part of your present property . . . that can be improved by our attentions, or injured by our absence." This statement no doubt deeply disturbed Alida, who hoped to remain in New York.

Mama Livingston had caused the Beekman lands to be surveyed and to be divided, supposedly equally, among the ten children, but the control of the bulk of the estate was held for a later reversion. Armstrong reminded Alida of the discontents among the children and that "your Mama may be called suddenly from you."[38] Perhaps Armstrong was sincere in his stated intentions of remaining in Pennsylvania, but more likely he was delivering a message to his wife: if her inheritance was not secured, he would stay in Pennsylvania. His letter animated Alida to jog her mother into making the reversion. On February 2, 1790, Alida received possession of approximately 25,000 acres, including about 19,000 across the Hudson River in the largely unsettled Hardenburgh Patent. The records indicate that Armstrong insisted that the title to the lands be transferred to his name. Mama and Alida acquiesced, and the transfer was made in June 1790.[39]

Assured of a position of status among the landed gentry along the Hudson River, Armstrong severed his ties with Pennsylvania and settled in New York. He gave up a political career that had been quite advanced and embarked on a new phase of his life. His concerns would no longer be for politics, but instead those of a landlord and a farmer — collecting his rents and planting and harvesting crops.

He settled into his new life with ease, and he was soon praising his newly adopted region, where on "the banks of this charming River . . . health, pleasure, convenience and society are all united." A son was born on May 19, 1790 at Clermont. The proud father informed Gates that Alida had acquiesced in his desire of prolonging "in my own descendants the memory of a father and a son for whom I ever felt the most disinterested attachment and sincere respect. He was accordingly named Horatio Robert Gates."[40] Armstrong was delighted to learn in 1790 that Gates had sold his farm in Virginia and had settled on an estate that he called "Rose Hill," approximately two and a half miles from the outskirts of New York City. (The site was on present-day Twenty-Fourth Street, between Second and Third avenues.)

In 1790 Armstrong bought a 400-acre farm in Rhinebeck Precinct (Dutchess County), and he moved his family into their new place in May. That next spring a second son was born in New York City on May 9. He was christened Henry Beekman Armstrong. With a growing family, Armstrong made plans to build a larger dwelling, but illness and poor health plagued both him and his wife during these early years of marriage. He referred to this often in his letters to Gates. Among his personal complaints were quinsy, a pain in the stomach that "had some of the character of that scourge of sinners, the Gout," and other maladies. He lamented to Gates, referring to his and Alida's illnesses, "We are not old — nor intemperate nor imprudent, nor, I hope ungrateful for any of the blessings of heaven; and yet this greatest of them all seems to be denied us." On another occasion he wrote of being struck by the ague, a violent fever reminiscent of his attack in North Carolina.[41]

The strain of accommodating himself to his new life also contributed to his sense of ill-being. First there had been the indecision accompanying his removal to New York, and then there was the matter of establishing his role in his own family and with the Livingston family. Alida, although a devoted wife, still tacitly accepted the guidance of Mama Livingston. Living at Clermont did nothing to salve his ego; hence his purchase of a farm, largely from his own funds. Their first home was small and dis-

Bust portrait of Horatio Gates after painting by Gilbert Stuart by H. B. Hall &
Sons, engravers. *Courtesy of the New-York Historical Society, New York City*

tinctly inferior to what Alida was accustomed to, and he soon drew up plans for a roomier dwelling. There were financial strains too. Most of his lands were non-rent producing. To meet his obligations, particularly to build his new house, he mortgaged some of his property and his mill on the Sawkill Creek to Alida's sister Joanna for nearly $4000. In addition, he attempted to sell some of his holdings, but his efforts were unsuccessful. Reflecting on his situation, he wrote to Gates in October 1792, "I know not whether there is any real calamity in being a little pinched at setting out in life. If the gripe is not too hard — it but awakens us to industry, and teaches better than any other instructor that wide distinction that wisdom makes between the use and abuse of property."[42]

In the winter of 1791, Armstrong was forced to borrow 300 pounds at 7 percent interest from his old speculator friend, William Duer. (A pound in New York was roughly equivalent to two and a half dollars.) In December 1792 Armstrong sold Duer 6000 acres for 1500 pounds, thus canceling his debt, and he received 600 pounds in partial payment from Duer. The subsequent bankruptcy of Duer, who spent most of the remainder of his life in prison, made the transaction a less than successful venture.[43]

These strains took their toll, and Armstrong despaired at times whether he should continue his life as a country squire. In April 1793 he complained to Gates of the fatigue of riding to his farm every day and conducting his business there while wintering in Clermont awaiting the completion of his new home. He noted that he had been afflicted with "some little nervous indispositions which vex and dispirit me." Of his indisposition he wrote, "much has been said, and much written, but little understood." He hoped it would pass; if it did not, he would not continue his country life.[44]

This state of depression passed, however, and by mid-May Armstrong's spirits had revived. His house was progressing and would be ready for occupancy by late fall. On November 11 he informed Gates that he would be moving into his "box" in a week or ten days. Although he was in fact very proud of his new home, by pretending that material possessions were unimportant, he revealed how important they were to him. There is little doubt that Armstrong often masked a basic insecurity with what seemed to strangers to be a cynical, haughty, or arrogant demeanor, and to his friends, a flippant, irreverent, or whimsical nature.

Once he had moved to The Meadows, as Armstrong called his new residence, he could finally say that he was established. He always had a particular fondness for farming, and he now applied his talents to the study of agriculture. These were happier times, as the vexations of the past year faded and a more serene pastoral life offered itself for the years ahead. His letters now spoke of the "country air," of where fish could be had every day, and lambs and chickens abounded, and of morning walks through valleys and by streams. Another boy was added in 1794 to their growing family. He was named "John" for his father and grandfather.

By 1794 Armstrong was already planning an even more handsome house on land he purchased south of him adjoining his small flour- and sawmill on the Sawkill Creek, a small meandering stream that flowed into the Hudson. An eye malady in the winter of 1794 led Armstrong to adopt the use of a pair of spectacles, courtesy of his brother-in-law, Edward Livingston. He had to rely on their aid the remainder of his life.[46] That winter also, Armstrong suffered the loss of his father. The old patriarch died at Carlisle on Monday, March 9, 1795.

In many respects, his father had been a self-made man. He had gained great fame as a military man, but he was essentially a surveyor and a farmer. The military life had never appealed to him, and his mediocre performance during the Revolutionary War had dimmed some of the luster of his military fame. A respected leader, his brief tenure as a delegate to Congress had taught him the compromises of principle that political life entailed, and as such, it was distasteful to him. A deeply religious man and convinced of the value of education, he had become one of the founders, with Benjamin Rush and John Dickinson, of Dickinson College in Carlisle, and he was a member of the Board of Trustees until his death. His eldest son, James, became a trustee in 1796 and remained one for thirty years.

The elder Armstrong had provided each of his sons with a good education. James became a physician, after studying with some of the outstanding physicians of the time, most notably Dr. Benjamin Rush. James married Mary Stevenson, daughter of the wealthy Dr. George Stevenson, in 1789. At least three of their children had been born before the elder Armstrong died. James was a dutiful son and had settled in the area of Carlisle. John, Jr., had early revealed an impetuous streak, but after a brief fling in Pennsylvania politics had apparently settled down, married, and become a farmer. His father may have regretted that John was not more religious, but he was pleased that his son had married a woman who was. Both sons had been profoundly influenced by their father's strong character, and his concern for them had not waned throughout his life. His will, after providing for the care of his wife, stipulated a share and share alike arrangement for his sons of a modest tract of western lands. John was named one of the executors of the estate, but he apparently left the handling of the family affairs to James.[47]

In 1795 Armstrong sought to sell some of his lands, by which he hoped to raise approximately 15,000 pounds. "Between you and me," he wrote Gates, "I have but one motive for selling and that is that I may pursue some of my litterary projects and attend a little more to public business and public objects, than I have for some years been able to do." The election for Governor that summer stirred within him some of the old instincts. He organized a group to prosecute violations of the suffrage. "If the late outrages be suffered to escape without prosecution," he wrote Edward Livingston, "the vile influence of debts and credits and dram shops will dictate nine tenths of the votes given in Rhinebec[k]."[48]

Armstrong was now well-established in his community. His mills were operating, and he was buying and selling land building up his rent rolls. He gave up The Meadows in 1795 to Chancellor Livingston, and he began building yet another house on his new land, which would establish him once and for all as a gentleman of some importance. While awaiting the completion of his grand house, the General and Alida lived in a barn that had been converted to their use. It was probably here that their fourth son, Robert Livingston, was born on March 20, 1797.[49]

These were satisfying years for Armstrong. His growing family was a constant source of pleasure to him. He took his duties as a parent seriously, particularly his children's education. When his house was completed, he noted with pleasure to Gates, "One apartment of it . . . you will like. It is a school-room for the boys."[50] He always delighted in reporting the academic progress of his sons, even to such things as the mastery of the alphabet. His care and attention was reflected, for example, when he fired a tutor in July 1798 and took over the task of teaching the boys himself. Further on in life, his concern for his children's education led to a decisive step in his career.

On November 16, 1797, Armstrong's mother died. James reported the death. He noted the long lapse in their correspondence and John's repeated promises of a visit. Mrs. Armstrong had left no will and her property was divided equally.[51] John again left the details of the settlement to James. Although the properties were jointly owned, the management of the estate fell to James, under whose hands it suffered.

Perhaps the lack of close family ties between the brothers can be attributed to their age differences. John was, however, invariably the one responsible for the lapses in correspondence between them. Despite James's residence in Carlisle, John revealed, perhaps unconsciously, his lack of attachment to his brother when he wrote to Gates, "the death of my last respectable parent leaves me but few motives for revisiting my native place." He had never shown any deep attachment to his mother. No

letter between them is known to survive, and references to her in his letters are extremely few. She does not appear to have had a very formative
influence over his life. Nevertheless, she was a strong-willed woman and
a leader of the women of Carlisle during the Revolutionary War.[52]

Armstrong's new estate, Mill Hill, so-called because of its location
on a high bluff overlooking the Hudson and its proximity to his mill on
the adjacent Sawkill, was imposing and spacious; quite satisfactory to
meet the needs of his growing family. The construction costs were about
$5000. He described the house as fifty feet square, containing "besides a
small pantry and hall, 12 rooms, four of which are 20x25 ft. each, 4
15x19, and four 12x9. These are exclusive of cellars, kitchen and servants'
rooms." Armstrong was the architect, and a Scotsman named Warner
Richards was the builder.[53]

In the late summer of 1798 a young friend and traveling companion
of Kosciuszko, Julian Ursyn Niemcewicz, visited this region. He stayed a
few days with Armstrong. "I was glad to meet General Armstrong,"
Niemcewicz recorded, "His character was truly republican. Because of his
intelligence, wit, grace, and pleasantness, all combined, he is held in universal esteem. He is, because of the strength and beauty of his style, one
of the best writers in this country." Niemcewicz added that Mrs. Armstrong, "Madam General," was by her virtue and pleasantness, worthy of
her husband. Niemcewicz was impressed with the setting of Mill Hill. He
was enraptured by the natural beauty of the region, which he characterized as "the best possible locale in the world." Armstrong's house was "not
showy . . . [but] comfortable." Most of the Armstrongs time, he noted,
was devoted to household care and especially to the education of their
four sons. The General's remaining time was devoted to study. "In this
way," Niemcewicz recorded approvingly, "all the moments are pleasantly
filled."

Niemcewicz was aware of Armstrong's friendship with Kosciuszko,
and he asked the General for his recollections. Armstrong's minute
knowledge of the details of the Revolution overwhelmed Niemcewicz,
who wrote, "There is probably no other officer or citizen in America who
knows more, both about the most important affairs, or the least detail or
anecdote of the war, the course of the government, or about the characters of the more important people." He added, "He knows everything and
he knows how to tell it eloquently with wit and charm. During the time of
the Revolution, as now, he was the severest critic of those in command of
the army and at the helm in public affairs." The latter statement referred
to the Newburgh Addresses which Niemcewicz condemned, but which
out of delicacy he did not mention to Armstrong.

Niemcewicz noted that along this beautiful river, "The trunk of the Livingston family is wide, it spreads its branches in all directions. All of these people are well-to-do, polite, related, closely knit in friendships and sentiment." He found them aristocratic but good-hearted people. They identified with the Republican party, but he noted that, "in truth they are simply dissatisfied with the government." He mentioned in passing their custom, which reminded him of Poland, of calling each other "not by name but by title, even the women." Such were his impressions, entirely favorable, of this little community in which the Armstrongs lived.[54]

The idyllic scene depicted by Niemcewicz was perhaps overdrawn, but Armstrong was a scholarly man, spending many hours in reading, writing, and meditation. After his initial enthusiasm for farming, he devoted more and more of his time to reading and study. From early life he had acquired a love of reading, and he was an avid collector of books. The breadth and depth of his reading was remarkable. Allusions in his letters reveal that he was familiar with most of the leading authors of the eighteenth century. References to Swift and Voltaire abound, but he cited Shakespeare enough to reveal a thorough knowledge, and he also cited Greek and Roman writers. His interests were primarily in drama, political and military tracts, history, and agriculture, but he aspired, after the eighteenth-century model, to encompass all knowledge.

Armstrong's erudition occasionally bordered on pedantry. In his extensive correspondence with Gates, he expressed freely his views on the nature of man and of their governments, the course of national and local politics, and foreign affairs. In his basic outlook, he was and always remained aristocratic. In his early years he was pessimistic about the prospects for the success of republican government, but in time he became more tolerant of the foibles of the masses and even stood eventually as a strong advocate of republicanism. This could hardly have been predicted from the content of some of his letters of this time.

He supported the government formed by the Constitution as a "step towards common sense and practicable Government," but it fell so far short of what he believed to be the situation and character of the country that he wrote, "I despair at once of both the stability and convenience of the Edifice." He held the view that "The philosophy that teaches the equality of mankind and the dignity of human nature, is founded in vanity and addressed to it alone." There was less consolation but infinitely more truth in the opposite doctrine, "that the many were made for the few, and that we are better govern'd by rods than by reason."[55] He disapproved of the French Revolution. The principle that the people had a right to change their form of government at pleasure, he argued, was "totally void of all foundation in common sense or common honesty; and is only a bill of rights for a den of robbers." Gates's position that "the many are generally right" was met by Armstrong's assertion that "the many of every Country are either weak or wicked," and that "in no Country are they fit to govern." Every state, he asserted, was governed by the invisible showmen who direct the course of governments, "an individual or Junto, more sagacious, more active, more bold and aspiring than the rest. This," he concluded, "is the aristocracy which is laid in human nature, and which no declaration of rights can obscure or invalidate."[56]

Armstrong's views generally agreed with the Federalist party, and his sympathies were with them. For example, he ridiculed the supporters of Governor George Clinton, who was the candidate for vice president. "I even now see his southern advocates pinning maxims upon republican equality and the rights of man with one hand, and with the other, lashing scores of poor devils before them, to the iniquitous task of the day."[57] The Livingstons, disappointed at not receiving suitable positions in the new government, had split with the Hamilton-Schuyler faction and were now supporting Clinton, but Armstrong remained stubbornly independent. He was no mere follower, and perhaps he felt the Chancellor overvalued his own talents.

It is an intriguing question whether Armstrong took up his pen in the election of 1792 and used it against his brother-in-law, Chancellor Livingston. This campaign was noted for its particular virulence and, in the style of the times, for large numbers of anonymous political tracts. The cloak of anonymity permitted much abuse. When the Chancellor wrote a pamphlet attacking his former friend, John Jay, who was running as the Federalist candidate for governor against Clinton, a mysterious antagonist entered the fray under the pseudonym of "Timothy Tickler." The attack upon Livingston was all too effective, and the Chancellor could not allow it to pass without response. Improbably, he decided that "Timothy Tickler" was John Jay. Signing himself "Aristides," he very intemperately denounced Jay. Livingston's biographer characterized this tract as "a decisive event" in his career. "Aristides had aimed his dagger at the bosom of John Jay, but had plunged it unerringly into his own."[58] Thereafter, the Chancellor began to disengage himself from state politics.

The author of "Timothy Tickler" has been widely alleged to be John Armstrong, who incidentally was also attacked by "Timothy Tickler." Contemporaries and recent authors have made Armstrong the culprit. So far as is known, Armstrong never responded to these charges, but he asserted to a friend in 1833 that it was incredible that he should have been considered the author.[59] There is evidence to the contrary however. In

1859, Friedrich Kapp, in a biography of Baron von Steuben, related a story told to him by John W. Mulligan, who as a young man had been a private secretary to the Baron and presumably spoke from first-hand knowledge. According to this story, Steuben was characterized as "a pensioner" in the first tract. Subsequently, the Baron called Armstrong and asked him who he thought the author was. Armstrong admitted that he believed Livingston was. Steuben then stated, "then, my friend, I rely on you for an answer." The next day "Timothy Tickler" appeared.[60]

This, of course, proves nothing. If Armstrong was the author, and it was done to avenge the honor of a friend, then did it have to result in the political humiliation of his wife's brother? It may be asserted that this result may not have been anticipated, but "Timothy Tickler" seemed to have been written to provoke just such an imprudent reply. On the other hand, the style is not clearly recognizable as Armstrong's, and there are several reasons why he would not have written this work. Obviously, the consequences of discovery would have resulted in his ostracism from the Livingston clan and thus by his neighbors, not to mention the effect it might have had on his marriage. There is no record of any hostility between Armstrong and the Chancellor during this period, and there is evidence of genuine friendship in later years. There may have been some lingering, latent ill-feeling related to the divisions of the Livingston lands among the children, but this possibility is too conjectural. Whether Armstrong wrote "Timothy Tickler," in short, must remain open until further evidence is presented.

Because Armstrong's Federalist leanings and the independence he displayed in shunning close political ties with the Livingstons were well known, the Washington Administration offered Armstrong the position of supervisor of the Port of New York in the spring of 1793. In making the offer, Washington apparently overcame any scruples he might have had about appointing the author of the Newburgh Addresses. Hamilton was probably responsible for the choice of Armstrong, no doubt anticipating that having a member of the Livingston family in the Administration might divide the clan politically. In making the offer, Hamilton admitted that the salary was low ($1300 gross pay), but he argued persuasively that the position would grow in importance. One drawback was that the supervisor would be required to be a resident of New York City.[61]

Hamilton would have found a member of the Livingston family to join the administration, no doubt, if he had a better position to offer. Armstrong was interested enough to inquire to Gates about the details of the job, but by the time Gates forwarded the information, Armstrong had decided not to accept the offer. He cited the expense of residing in New York City and the separation from his family as the reasons. To Gates, however, he dismissed the job as unimportant. "There is no great glory in boring some puncheons or gauging stills. It but requires very cheap, that is, very common qualities and qualifications too, to discharge these trusts." Alluding to Washington, he concluded, "There my correspondence with the great man has ended for the present — probably never to be renewed again."[62]

Despite his Federalist leanings, Armstrong advocated strong measures against the British for violations of American neutrality after their war with France broke out. He approved of James Madison's resolutions introduced before Congress in January 1794 calling for retaliatory duties upon British ships and merchandise. He may have been surprised to learn that his brother James, now a congressman from Pennsylvania, had come to the same conclusion about Madison's resolutions. Although nominally a Federalist, James wrote his brother, "I have taken a different part, and have been in favor of the most spirited measures. This I have done from a conviction that it is at once the surest and most honorable way of obtaining Peace." James also informed his brother that John Jay had been nominated as Envoy Extraordinary to Great Britain to attempt to resolve the differences. John Armstrong approved of Jay's mission, but his views were distinctly mixed when Jay's treaty was announced.[63]

Armstrong still remained aloof from politics, except for his brief fling in 1795 to correct electioneering abuses. It appears that he sought to avoid party affiliation. Indeed, it would appear that no political party could meet his exacting standards. The Livingstons continued to adhere to the Republican party, and their influence was, no doubt, a counterforce against his natural inclinations. His letters indicate an increasing dissatisfaction with the government and those associated with it. He was disgusted with the Federalist treatment of his old comrade in arms, Kosciuszko, who after leading a futile and abortive insurrection for Polish independence sought asylum in the United States in 1797. Republican Thomas Jefferson took the lead in securing back pay and military land warrants for Kosciuszko.[64] Armstrong's opinion of the Federalist Administration was also lowered by Edmund Randolph's, *Vindication*, an intemperate attack upon Washington because of Randolph's dismissal. Armstrong believed it presented a "wretched picture . . . of the executive of a great country." He was even more contemptuous of Hamilton's pamphlet exculpating his conduct while detailing a sordid affair with Maria Reynolds. Hamilton, he wrote, was attempting "to creep under Mrs. R's petticoats. A pretty hiding place for a national leader!" Interestingly, he also defended Monroe's pamphlet attacking the Administration after his removal as the American minister to France.[65]

Thus several factors explain Armstrong's conversion from a nomi-

nal Federalist to a staunch supporter of the Republican party. His growing
dissatisfaction with the men and the measures of the Federalist party, and
personal factors, such as the association with the Livingston family, no
doubt operated powerfully upon him. By the late 1790s, he was definitely
leaning in sympathy toward the Republicans. All that was necessary to
cause him to declare his allegience to them was for the Federalists to take
some action that outraged his sense of propriety and decency. That came
in the form of the Alien and Sedition Acts of 1798. These measures were
repugnant to Armstrong, and when he took up his pen against them, it
signified not only his break with the Federalist party, it also began a new
phase of his life.

3

SENATOR

THE INFAMOUS XYZ AFFAIR IN THE SPRING OF 1798, when French agents asked for a bribe from American representatives as the price for improving relations with France, caused a great outcry for war against France. The Federalist party, which was basically pro-British, capitalized on the situation by adopting not only measures of war but also repressive legislation designed to curb dissent and discredit their opponents in the Republican party, whom they considered pro-French. A Navy was created, a provisional army was authorized in the event of war or an invasion, and additional taxes were levied to pay for these measures. In addition, during June and July of 1798 the Federalists pushed through Congress the Alien and Sedition Acts. Aliens and immigrants, who were generally Republicans, were particular objects of these laws. The period of residence for naturalization was lengthened from five to fourteen years, and the President was authorized to deport or imprison aliens without a trial. Finally, fines and imprisonment were prescribed for anyone judged guilty of writing, publishing, or speaking anything deemed "false, scandalous, and malicious" against the government or an officer of the government. It may be, as many historians have asserted in recent years, that these measures were not as harsh as they appeared, but they were nevertheless perceived to be unduly severe and partisan at the time. Many foreigners, fearing prosecution under the Alien laws, fled the country. All the victims of the Sedition Act, notoriously, were Republicans.[1]

These Federalist measures prompted Armstrong to write an anonymous pamphlet late in 1798 in the form of a petition, ostensibly asking Congress to reconsider their actions, but in truth denouncing them. One historian aptly characterized Armstrong's work as "written with his usual ability and in his usual unequalled style of bitterness and severity."[2] A great deal of attention, quite deservedly, has been given to Jefferson's and Madison's Kentucky and Virginia Resolutions denouncing the Alien and Sedition Acts, but Armstrong's pamphlet was an equally strong attack on these acts and merits greater recognition.

Armstrong characterized the Alien laws as "obnoxious to a generous and free people," and "cruel, unjust, unnecessary, impolitic, and unconstitutional." It was the "superlative wickedness" of the Sedition Act "to convert freemen into slaves." The provisional army, he declared, was "a manifest outrage of the Constitution," because it gave powers to the president that belonged with Congress. He raised fears of a standing army, and interestingly, in view of his later opinions on this subject, he contended that "the wisdom of the ages, and our own experience" showed that the most "convenient, safe and efficient defense of any free nation is militia."[3]

The distribution of Armstrong's pamphlet in the counties of New York led to an unexpected development. Judge Jedediah Peck, a member of the New York Legislature, who circulated the pamphlet, was indicted on a complaint by Judge William Cooper, the father of the novelist, James Fenimore Cooper, for violation of the Sedition Act. Judge Peck was taken from his home in Cooperstown and transported as a prisoner to New York City. Peck's progress was a triumphant march of a martyr for the right of petition and the freedom of speech and press. As the historian Jabez Hammond wrote, "A hundred missionaries in the cause of democracy, stationed between New York and Cooperstown, could not have done so much for the Republican cause as this journey of Judge Peck."[4]

Despite his pamphlet, Armstrong remained aloof from Republican party matters. Then in a very fortuitous way he struck up a close friendship with a rising star in the New York democracy, Ambrose Spencer. Exactly how they met is not known, but it was sometime in January 1797. They were apparently attracted to each other immediately, and it began a warm and intimate friendship that lasted until Armstrong's death forty-six years later. In many ways they were very much alike. They were compatible intellectually, they were outspoken, opinionated, and they gave no quarter in partisan politics. They invariably agreed on political issues.

Spencer was a Federalist serving in the State Senate when he changed his allegiance in 1798. His reasons were obscure, but his opponents alleged that it was due to resentment in not receiving a desired appointment from Governor Jay. Spencer always denied the charges, but in any event he soon became allied with another young rising politician, De Witt Clinton, the nephew of former Governor George Clinton. In 1800 these two young partisans were elected to the all-powerful Council of Appointment, which controlled the patronage of the state. Clinton and Spencer curbed the influence of Aaron Burr in the Republican party of New York, they courted the Livingston interests, and they ruthlessly proscribed the Federalists, thus beginning the spoils system in New York. As one historian noted, "They swept the Federalists out of every office even down to that of auctioneer, and without regard to appearances . . . installed their own friends and family connections in power."[5]

Spencer may have influenced the election of Armstrong to the post of United States Senator on November 6, 1800, in the place of John Laurence who had resigned, although the Federalists were still in the majority in the New York Senate. The vote was unanimous in the Senate, and there were only two dissenting votes in the Assembly. It is probable, as one historian has speculated, that the Federalists remembered Armstrong's Federalist background and yielded to his appointment "as the least exceptionable Republican candidate for that office."[6] Armstrong, although associated with the Livingston family, still retained a degree of independence.

Armstrong arrived to assume his duties in the new national capital, just recently cut out of the wilderness, during the first week of January 1801. He presented his credentials, was sworn in, and took his seat on January 8. He took up board and lodging for himself and his servant (at $20 per week) in the same rooming house where many of the Republican leaders lived. Among them were President-elect Thomas Jefferson, Albert Gallatin of Pennsylvania, John Langdon of New Hampshire (an old friend), Samuel Smith and Joseph Nicholson of Maryland, and Abraham Baldwin of Georgia. Jefferson intrigued Armstrong the most. He was impressed by Jefferson's cordiality and learning, and he reported to his brother-in-law, Thomas Tillotson, "The nearer you approach Jefferson, the better you like him."[7]

Armstrong had arrived at a stirring time. The Federalists had lost power in the presidential election, but there had been an electoral tie between the Republican candidates, Jefferson and Burr. The decision had to be made by the lame-duck House of Representatives, where the Federalists had a majority. They could precipitate a crisis by blocking the election of Jefferson, or if they chose a less drastic course, they could attempt through legislation to retain as much power as possible. However, the Federalists were badly divided and had no clearly articulated goals or policies. President John Adams, bitter and disappointed by his defeat, was virtually isolated from his party. Armstrong observed on January 13 that Adams's movements were "altogether solitary, and even his secretaries are said to know no more of them than his footmen." The Federalists supported Burr, but Armstrong believed their real object was "to neutralize the election altogether and take the hazards of an interregnum." He predicted, however, that their plans would collapse and that they would content themselves with mischief, such as the Judiciary Bill which increased the number of Federalist judges, and the attempt to block the ratification of the Convention of 1800, which had settled the undeclared war with France.[8]

Armstrong was privy to party plans. He knew early in January, for example, that James Madison would be the secretary of state and Albert Gallatin the secretary of treasury. He also knew that Robert Smith and Henry Dearborn would become the secretary of the navy and secretary of war, respectively. Interestingly, General Gates recommended Armstrong to Jefferson for the post of secretary of war. Edward Livingston, who was then a member of the House of Representatives and was soon to become the Mayor of New York City, reported to his brother that Armstrong had a good chance for the position. There is no indication that Armstrong was approached about the position or that he ever solicited it. He had been accurately informed that the qualifications expected were those of a mere clerk, and for that reason alone the position would have had little appeal. In due course, he retracted his favorable impression of Jefferson. "Vigor does not seem to be the character of the man himself," he wrote Tillotson late in February, "and . . . his Cabinet will not be much calculated to supply his defects. A doctrine almost avow'd is, to leave everything in status quo." He added that "It has received my private and public reprobation and it shall continue to receive it."[9]

Despite his doubts about his party leader, Armstrong voted the party line faithfully. When the Federalists attempted to mutilate the Convention of 1800 "to furnish some occasion for its eventual rejection by Bonaparte," he proudly announced to Tillotson that the Federalists "are now (in despair of shaking our little Phalanx) treading back their steps, and opening the door to reconsideration." The Federalists did succeed in passing the Judiciary Act of 1801, but Armstrong had few apprehensions they would succeed in frustrating the election of Jefferson. "The actors on the other side are not all heroes," he wrote, "and when brought deliberately to choose between Jefferson and anarchy, they will not, they dare not hesitate." When it was all over, he dubbed the whole episode a farce. "If it was right on any ground to have opposed Burr to Jefferson, it was wrong to have stopped where they did," he wrote Richard Peters. The author of the Newburgh Addresses added, "There was a time when a little anarchy or a little usurpation — or something of that sort — would not have much affected my nervous system, but a wife and six children and some additional years have indisposed me very much for heroics. I could never be an indifferent, but I certainly would be a very quiet Spectator of such scenes."[10]

Near the end of the session Armstrong voted with the majority in a fourteen to thirteen vote to postpone the consideration of a proposed mausoleum to receive the remains of Washington. On one matter, Armstrong was disappointed that Congress did not vote to move the next session to New York City. He was disgusted with the disagreeable living conditions in the new capital, which was one of vast vistas and grand in conception, but at that time it was a swampy, dreary village devoid of any society and lacking in nearly all the essentials of shops, markets, and other amenities of life to relieve the tedium of members of Congress. As Henry Adams wrote, "Never did hermit or saint condemn himself to solitude more consciously than Congress and the Executive in removing the government from Philadelphia to Washington: the discontented men clustered together in eight or ten boarding houses as near as possible to the Capitol, and there lived, like a convent of monks, with no other amusement or occupation than that of going from their lodgings to the Chambers and back again."[11]

The Seventh Congress convened on March 4, and Armstrong, with others, was sworn in to begin a new term of office. Then the representatives and the senators assembled as a group and listened to Jefferson deliver his inaugural address and saw him sworn in as the third president of the United States. In the next few days Armstrong and the other congressmen began their trek back to their homes. His initial senatorial experience had not been pleasant. He did not enjoy the rigors of the legislative process. He did not participate in the debates, nor did he offer any recorded motions or resolutions. He was content to cast his votes, usually according to the dictates of party. Of course, in the easy, informal atmosphere of Washington the evenings were filled with political discussion, and there was ample opportunity for him to make his views known. It can be assumed, however, that the combination in Armstrong's personality of diffidence and arrogance did not endear him to his fellow senators. A close observer of Armstrong during this period, Albert Gallatin, perceptively discerned his limitations. In discussing with Jefferson the problem of rallying support for the anti-Burr wing of the Republican party in New York, Gallatin specifically exempted Chancellor Livingston and Armstrong as potential leaders. "The first is, in that state, only a name," he wrote, "and there is something which will forever prevent the last having any direct influence with the people."[12]

It was obvious in the fall of 1801 that Armstrong was having second thoughts about his new political career. He virtually shuddered at the prospect of returning to Washington. He wrote Edward Livingston in November 1801, "My day of grace is indeed almost out — but I shall be disposed to stretch it to the last of December, or longer if possible." He had seen recently some newly elected members of Congress who had been eager to get to Washington. "I take it for granted," he noted drily, "that they have formed some very rigid notions of duty — some very exalted ones of their importance, or some very false ones of the place." He added, "Three months experience however will in all probability, cure them of all these diseases." He also informed Gates that he would delay his departure for Washington. "A banishment of six months to Siberia would not be much more disagreeable, than a stay of the same length of time at that place — but my hope is, that the session will be a short one; and that, to myself, it may be still shorter than the others."[13]

Alida's illness and his own rheumatic ailment further delayed his departure. Finally, reacting to criticism from Burr and others that his delay was having a harmful effect on New York interests, he resigned his position. De Witt Clinton was chosen in Armstrong's place by the New York Legislature, which caused some Burr partisans to charge that some sort of bargain had been made to procure Armstrong's resignation, but Armstrong simply had no desire to continue in the position. His resignation was no great loss to the Republican party, but James Madison nevertheless expressed his regret to Gates. Armstrong's "great talents," he wrote, "are acknowledged I find by all parties."[14]

Thus Armstrong returned to private life. He had given up farming, and in the fall of 1801 he decided to sell Mill Hill and move his family into Clermont. The number of children had now increased to six. Their only daughter, Margaret Rebecca, named in honor of her grandmothers, had been born on March 22, 1799, at Clermont, and a fifth son, James Kosciuszko, was born at Mill Hill on June 17, 1801. A sixth son, Edward, was born at Clermont on July 21, 1802, but he died eight days later. Alida wrote her brother the Chancellor in October reporting the death of her son, and her grief was still apparent.[15]

Armstrong sold Mill Hill in 1802 to Mary Allen of New Jersey for approximately $10,000. After residing a year and a half at Clermont, he moved his family across the Hudson River to Kingston, and placed his children in the highly respected Kingston Academy. They rented a charming old stone house built in 1676, the so-called Senate House, because the Senate of the New York Provincial Congress met there in 1777. While at Kingston, Armstrong became embroiled in a controversy with Barent Gardenier, a Federalist lawyer in Kingston who had discovered Armstrong's authorship of the Newburgh Addresses. Armstrong responded by publishing a corrected copy of the Addresses "taken directly from the original draft." He was apparently more concerned about having the correct copy before the public than justifying its contents. The Washington letter of 1797 was not published, but it was displayed in the publisher's office and was authenticated by several gentlemen in the area familiar with Washington's handwriting.[16]

Armstrong still retained an active interest in state political affairs, particularly in curbing Aaron Burr's influence. He supported De Witt Clinton's efforts against Burr, suggesting that a victory for the Clinton faction over the Burr forces "prostrates him and his ambition forever, and will besides be a useful admonition to future schismatics."[17] Armstrong's letters to Chancellor Livingston, now in Paris, suggest that through Spencer he was privy to party strategy.

The big news in 1803 was the Louisiana Purchase, a magnificent bargain for the United States. The luster of this achievement was somewhat dimmed, or so Chancellor Livingston felt, by the fact that he had to share a part of the glory with James Monroe, who had arrived in Paris in time to take part in the negotiations. In his letters to the Livingston clan, the Chancellor made it clear that the Purchase was his achievement, that everything but the formalities was done before Monroe arrived. Writing to Alida, he commented, "I have no objections to sharing the laurels with my colleague, time will shew the share I had in earning them, and I wish my friends to be as modest upon the occasion as possible, but not, as they have hitherto done to pass me over in silence on every publick occasion."[18]

That same year, Armstrong's brother wrote that the Pennsylvania Legislature had proposed creating an Armstrong County in the area of the Kittanning Tract. James offered the state officials 150 acres to induce them to locate the county seat at Kittanning. They had accepted, and now he asked for John's power of attorney to turn over the deed. John complied, and Armstrong County was created with Kittanning as the county seat.[19]

In November 1803, in another turn of events, Governor George Clinton appointed Armstrong United States Senator from New York in the place of De Witt Clinton, who had resigned to become Mayor of New York City when Edward Livingston had resigned. There is no evidence that any bargain or deal was made. The appointment was probably a surprise to Armstrong, because Governor Clinton was not on friendly terms with the Livingstons. Indeed, he affirmed at a later period that he had appointed Armstrong despite his dislike of the Livingstons, because he believed him to be a man of integrity.[20]

Armstrong accepted quickly, attended to his affairs, journeyed to Washington, and arrived on the Senate floor on December 7, only a little over three weeks after receiving the letter of appointment. Exactly why he chose to return to a position that he had so disliked is difficult to determine. He had obviously retained a keen interest in political matters, and he explained to Chancellor Livingston that "the presidential election was approaching and measures were to be taken in relation to that object." He admitted, however, that "the Federalists have not the strength and the Republicans have not the inclination to exchange Mr. J. for any other person." That left the change to be made in the vice presidency, and it appears that Armstrong hoped to help bring down Aaron Burr.[21]

Washington had not changed much in two years, but under Jefferson a semblance of a social life had developed. Armstrong was occasionally a guest at Jefferson's dinners, which were pleasant, informal affairs with a few other senators and congressmen. Despite his aristocratic inclinations, Armstrong approved of Jefferson's decree that pell-mell would be the rule of etiquette in Washington, and he condemned Anthony Merry, the British minister, for taking offense at the practice.[22]

Armstrong attended to his duties in the Senate regularly, as indicated by the frequency of his votes, but as before he did not take an active part in the debates. He disliked the haggling and hair-splitting that often went on in the Senate chamber. He wrote Spencer that "the Old Congress was called a diplomatic college. The present Senate is, to my mind, much more so." His first recorded vote was with the Republican majority to send the Twelfth Amendment changing the method of electing the president and vice president to the states for ratification. This vote no doubt gave him great satisfaction because he viewed the amendment as being aimed at Aaron Burr. During this session Armstrong did not vote with the party leaders as regularly as he had during his first tenure, but with the overwhelming Republican majority in the Senate, a greater degree of independence could be exercised and tolerated. On one issue, however, where the party position was clear, that of the impeachment of Federalist District Judge John Pickering, Armstrong was absent on the crucial vote on March 12, 1804, to remove Judge Pickering. Presumably, he felt like many of his colleagues that the proceedings were, at the least, irregular.[23]

In late February 1804 Armstrong reported to Spencer, who had recently been elevated to the New York Supreme Court, that Governor Clinton had been selected by the caucus as the vice-presidential candidate. Burr had not received a single vote. Seeking to revive his political fortunes, Burr accepted a nomination as governor of New York. Armstrong's brother-in-law, Morgan Lewis, was nominated by the Republicans to run against Burr. In a hotly contested and bitter campaign, Burr was defeated by a three-to-two margin. This election effectively destroyed Burr's political career, and in the aftermath, he sealed his fate by killing Alexander Hamilton in their famous duel.[24]

Armstrong happily wrote Spencer that the results of the election gave "proof not only of the spread and ascendancy of republicanism, but what I estimate more highly, the soundness and sincerity of its professions . . . against the combined force of federalism and Burrism (putting all their machinery of misrepresentation into action against us.)"[25] These sentiments show how completely he had moved from his Federalist background to an identification with the Republican party and its philosophy.

The Clinton-Livingston alliance had always been unstable and within a year after the election of Governor Lewis the two groups were bitterly divided. Fortunately for Armstrong, he did not become embroiled in the intra-party dispute. President Jefferson selected him in May 1804 to replace Chancellor Livingston as minister to France. Why Jefferson and Madison selected him can only be conjectured. His association with the Livingston clan was obviously a factor, but the decision was probably based more on their estimation of the man. Despite his lack of diplomatic experience, Armstrong's knowledge of world affairs was extensive and he was noted as a scholar, which to men such as Jefferson and Madison was a valuable asset. Armstrong was also a skillful writer, an important qualification for a diplomatic post. Finally, he was sufficiently wealthy to afford the expense of the mission, he was cultivated, and he was experienced enough politically to represent American interests adequately at the French court.

Jefferson sought to remove any objections Armstrong might have to the job, particularly that of inadequate salary, a frequent lament of Chancellor Livingston. "A moment's reflection," Jefferson wrote, "will satisfy you that a man can live in any country on any scale he pleases." With a rank of minister, Armstrong would not be expected to entertain on a lavish scale. Livingston had not "had resolution enough to yield place there, and . . . he has taken up the ambassadorial scale of expense." Such expenditures, Jefferson concluded, procured only sunshine friends. Armstrong was urged to come to Washington for a briefing and that he should plan to leave for France as soon as possible.[26]

Armstrong frankly admitted doubts about his competence for the position in his letter of acceptance. He had no apprehensions of pecuniary loss or of a deficient salary, for he and his family had "long since found out the secret of living within our income, and have, on this head, no new habits to acquire," but he added, "Had my confidence in my own qualifications to discharge the highly important trust to be committed to me, been at all equal to my assurance of the competency of the sallary to discharge all my necessary expences, I should not have had a moment's hesitation on the subject."[27]

Obviously, Armstrong realized that the office might advance his political career, although the Louisiana Purchase would be a difficult act to follow. It is more likely, however, that his decision was based more on personal than political reasons. He explained to Edward Livingston, "Your sister's health and the education of my boys formed with me, the leading motive to this arrangement."[28] Alida's health had not been good for a long time due to a pulmonary complaint, and it was thought that a change of climate might help. Probably even more decisive to both John and Alida was the opportunity to educate their children in France. Chancellor Livingston no doubt also aroused their curiosity and excited their interest by his rosy pictures of life in Paris.

Armstrong wrote his friend Spencer, "How I shall acquit myself God knows, but I shall do my best." If he failed, his solace would be that he had not solicited the position, and that it had been "pressed upon my acceptance by such considerations and in such a way as left me no choice — the President himself taking the trouble of doing away every argument that my ingenuity, such as it is, was able to raise against it." Armstrong also wrote his old commander, General Gates, "I think it probable from my new destination, that after one meeting more, we shall part forever." After visiting Washington to receive his credentials and instructions, he would go from there to New York City where he would debark for France. He promised to see Gates then.[29]

Armstrong went to Washington the last of June. Jefferson, a former diplomat in France, named likely schools for the Armstrong boys as well as desirable locations to establish a residence in Paris. He also recommended to him the American consul in Paris, Fulwar Skipwith, as "a good-humored and rigorously honest man." Differences had arisen between Livingston and Skipwith, but lest Skipwith think that Armstrong had "succeeded to the animosities of the Chancellor as well as to his office," Jefferson wrote Skipwith, "No man thinks more for himself than Genl. Armstrong, and no man is less influenced by family partialities than him." Armstrong would operate "without the least tincture of prejudice from what has passed with his predecessor."[30]

Armstrong returned to New York City on July 13 to find it in a state of agitation after the death of Alexander Hamilton the day before, resulting from his duel with Aaron Burr. Armstrong reported to Madison that "The public sympathy is a good deal excited for Hamilton and his family, whether this is spontaneous or artificial I do not know, but it probably partakes of both characters." He noted that "the English interest" talked of erecting a statue to Hamilton. He also reported that he had taken passage on a ship to Nantes and would sail around the first of August.[31]

Alida and the children joined him, along with Alida's sister Joanna and Edward's son Lewis, both of whom intended to accompany them to France. While awaiting passage, news arrived that in May 1804 a new constitution had been adopted that elevated Napoleon Bonaparte to emperor of the French. Armstrong delayed his ship's departure until a new letter of credence could be forwarded to him "to avoid possible embarrassment." Lacking official notification and with the new style and title not precisely known, Madison furnished a blank letter of credence and commission to be filled in after he arrived in France in the style the French minister of foreign relations stated was proper. This arrangement, Madison asserted, "will be the strongest proof of the respect entertained here for the right of every nation to establish for itself what form of Government it pleases."[32]

One of the last details was to make arrangements for a talented young instructor at the Kingston Academy to follow them to France and assume the duties of private secretary. The Reverend David Bailie Warden was a young Irish revolutionary who had fled Ireland in 1798 and settled in America. His departure was delayed by the necessity of obtaining his citizenship. Armstrong left a letter certifying that Warden was to be his secretary, informing him that with this certificate and "observing the ordinary prudence of keeping your own secret," Warden should experience no difficulty in obtaining passports. He admonished Warden to "Loose no time in following me."[33]

After repeated delays, Armstrong and his entourage sailed for France around September 5. An uneventful voyage of thirty-five days brought them to Nantes on the night of October 10 in a "heavy and constant" rain. They were delayed a week in Nantes, and Armstrong complained that "the coronation engrosses everything." He had to pay an "exorbitant price for a most incommodious vehicle," and left with a part of his family while the rest followed in mail carts.[34] The trip from Nantes to Paris took the Armstrongs along the Loire River valley through the principal towns of Angers, Tours, Blois, and Orleans. Alida in particular was enthralled by the beauty of the country. "Imagine a combination of every object of delight that a country can possess," she wrote her brother Edward. "I was in a sort of extacy the whole way." From Orleans to Paris, however, the country was more open, flat, and less pretty. They arrived in Paris on October 29.[35]

After settling his family and enjoying a reunion with the Chancellor and his family, Armstrong called upon the minister of foreign relations,

Charles Maurice de Talleyrand-Perigord, on November 3 to present his letters of credence. It can be assumed that Armstrong was a little apprehensive meeting Talleyrand for the first time. Physically, Talleyrand was unimposing. He was short and he was lame from an accident that occurred in his youth. His features were unattractive and his disposition was haughty and cynical, but he could be ingratiating and charming when he chose to be so. This complex man also had a reputation, not unmerited, of being crafty and utterly without principle. Attesting to his political adroitness, he served in turn every French government over a forty-year span. He was now serving the emperor Bonaparte. Napoleon recognized Talleyrand's deficiencies, but he also recognized his abilities. Perhaps no man in France, with the possible exception of Napoleon himself, had his breadth of view of France's interests. Such a man could be exceedingly difficult to deal with, and Armstrong undoubtedly knew this well.

Armstrong had arrived in Paris a day late to have an audience with the emperor. Unfortunately, everyone in the government, including the emperor, was heavily involved in the activities preparing for the coronation, and there was little time available to schedule an audience. Finally, however, the emperor graciously consented to hold a private audience to receive Armstrong's credentials. Accordingly, at ten o'clock Sunday morning, November 18, Armstrong arrived at the Tuileries palace and was received according to the forms prescribed by the ceremonial and presented his credentials.

The letter of credence from Jefferson to Napoleon characterized Armstrong as "one of our distinguished citizens," expressed the desire to "cultivate the harmony and good correspondence so happily subsisting between us," and beseeched the emperor "to give full credence" to whatever Armstrong may say on the part of the United States. Armstrong then addressed the emperor, presenting his respects and assurances of the cordial friendship of the government and the people of the United States for France. The general thrust of his remarks was summed up in his statement congratulating the French people "on the exercise of a principle to which the Republic I serve owes at once its existence and prosperity," namely "the right of every nation to modify its government according to its own will." He assured Napoleon that the United States saw in his elevation to emperor "the most exalted tribute to those virtues and talents which equally signallize your Imperial Majesty, the country you govern and the age in which you live."[36]

No doubt Napoleon approved of the sentiments in Armstrong's address. He expressed his satisfaction at the appearance of the General, who he hoped "would be the means of still further strengthening the ties of amity by which the countries were so happily connected." The audience was concluded, and Armstrong withdrew.[37]

Armstrong now entered officially into the duties of his office. "I am not sure that in this first step," he wrote to Madison alluding to his address to the emperor, "I shall have given all the satisfaction I could wish. On your side of the Atlantic it may be supposed that I have gone too far, while on this it is thought, that I have not gone far enough." He believed that it accommodated "the feverish sensibility" of the French government while showing "a becoming respect for the political sentiment of our own."[38] His first effort may be considered a satisfactory beginning of a diplomatic career that was destined to last nearly six years. These were to be eventful years, for Europe, for American-French relations, and also for Armstrong.

4

MINISTER TO FRANCE

T HE CITY OF PARIS, where the Armstrongs would reside for the next six years, was, like the government, undergoing change. It was being transformed into a capital city befitting an empire, with new buildings and monuments rising, streets being paved, and broad boulevards being laid out. A triumphal arch was being built in the Place du Carrousel opposite the center gate of the Tuileries palace and another just beyond the barrier of the Champs-Elysées. A splendid new veterans hospital, les Invalides, was finished, and a boulevard had been extended across the spot where the Bastille stood to the iron bridge on the Seine, opposite the botanical gardens. "Thus," Alida marveled, "whilst one of the most extraordinary men in the world is executing the greatest projects, the smallest are not neglected."[1]

Paris had a population of approximately 550,000 and a circumference (including ten of its suburbs) of about eleven miles. An immense population swarmed around the center, or the old city. The suburbs were more spacious and the streets were wider, but many of them were only then being paved. A more pleasant aspect of the city were the many beautiful gardens and the seventy-five public squares.[2] Paris was exciting, but Alida complained that it was a much more expensive place to live than New York City, and that "the climate of Paris is much too wet to be pleasant," but she confessed to her sister, "I find Paris a more agreeable residence than Kingston." Armstrong was equally satisfied. He wrote Ambrose Spencer in June 1807, "My situation here is in many respects more agreeable than I had expected it to be." The resources of Paris, he noted, were "so multitudinous and varied, that one must be very strangely constructed, if he does not meet with something adapted to his taste, habits, principles and purse." It furnished "so many means of making the most of this life, that I no longer wonder at the sort of magic it exercises over those who have once tasted its enjoyments." The most objectionable feature of Paris, he informed another correspondent, was "the dreadful state of morals that prevails here."[3]

Alida's health improved, but ironically, her husband was the one who was chronically ill. He suffered a series of debilitating illnesses during his stay in Paris. He was afflicted by rheumatism, recurrent attacks of his old malarial fever, and an unusual amount of sickness arising from his weakened condition. This chronic ill-health undoubtedly affected his personality and may account to some extent for his generally morose disposition. There is a hint that the French government traced his splenetic notes to this cause. On one occasion they even suggested to their minister in the United States that he should hint to the American government that they should send a minister in better health.[4]

In addition to their own children, the Armstrongs brought Edward Livingston's six-year old son, Lewis, whose mother had recently died. He stayed with them their entire six years in France. Soon after their arrival in Paris the boys were placed in a school in Nantes. The importance of this experience was expressed by Alida to her eldest son Horatio: "Remember my dear son that great expectations will be formed of you, after having had the advantages of an education in France . . . I am in hopes you will not disappoint these expectations. Regard the present moments as the most important in your life. By a proper use of them you may obtain acquirements that may stamp a value on your character forever after."[5]

In the summer of 1805, the boys were transferred to a school at Pont Le Noz near Blois. They were unhappy there and when the Armstrongs visited them in early August they brought the youngest, James Kosciuszko, back with them. Shortly thereafter they transferred the other boys to a pension, or boarding school, in Paris. This school was deemed too rough, and in December 1805 the boys were moved again to a pension in the Faubourg St. Germain. While the cost of education in the new school and in France generally was very high, Alida noted that the curriculum included such attainments as "dancing, fencing, drawing, foreign languages, &c." Margaret was also placed in a school, but she resided with her parents. Alida's only regret was that the children's religious education was being neglected. "Were they Catholic," she noted, "that would not be the case." John and Robert proved to be the best students, both winning first prizes in 1807 and repeating in 1808. Their father's attention to their studies was not indifferent. For example, while traveling in the south of

France in 1808, he dispatched a stern note to his secretary, David Bailie Warden, to pass on to his sons. "Say to John & Robert that I am well pleased with them," he wrote, "to Henry, that I very much regret to hear that his attention to his studies is so indifferent and to Horatio, that I have a rod in soak for him."[6]

In their first two years in Paris the Armstrongs lived on the left bank of the Seine at the Hotel de la Guiche on the Rue de Regard. In late 1806 they established themselves for the remainder of their stay in a large house nearby owned by Daniel Parker, an old acquaintance, which had been formerly the residence of Joel Barlow. This place, No. 100 Rue de Vaugirard, was situated about a mile from Pont Royale and was then in one of the most tranquil and pleasant quarters of the city. Alida wrote Edward in April 1807 of the pleasant surroundings for the children. "We have a most delightful garden for them to play in, which is beginning to be gay with blossoms."[7]

The Armstrongs did not go into society often, particularly in the early years of their residence in Paris. As their circle of friends widened in later years, they were more active socially. They did not attend court often, due to Armstrong's poor health and limited financial means. They were by no means impoverished, but they very prudently tried to live within their income. As Alida informed Edward in January 1806, "Mrs. Chancellor will tell you how impossible it is in Paris to live on nine thousand dollars, and have any money to spare." She admitted that she did not go often to court because "The expense of an exhibition there is continually increasing." She told of a "lady of distinction," who was said to have been "handed out of the circle by the master of ceremonies, who observed that she was plainly dressed." But Alida noted in amazement, "She was dressed in spangled velvet!" This incident had occurred before the latest glorious campaign, and she added, "there is no knowing what dress will be tolerated now."[8]

Armstrong received a signal honor from the emperor in 1807. The artist Jacques Louis David was commissioned to paint a scene of the coronation and could allot space on the canvas for only five members of the diplomatic corps. Napoleon selected Armstrong as one of the five. Alida took advantage of Armstrong's sitting for the artist to look at the unfinished painting, which was on a canvas of thirty by nineteen feet.[9] Armstrong's portrait may be easily discovered in this famous painting, now displayed at the Louvre.

Paris afforded the Armstrongs a very pleasant society of French, English, and Americans. They saw Lafayette frequently. Armstrong's old companion, Kosciuszko, also visited briefly in Paris. Several prominent

"The Coronation of Napoleon Bonaparte," by Jacques-Louis David, now in the Louvre. General Armstrong is marked by arrow. *Photograph in Rokeby Collection, courtesy of Mrs. Richard Aldrich and sons, Barrytown, New York*

French families, including Marbois, entertained the Armstrongs at their country places. Among those Alida mentioned as friends were Baron Dreyer, the Danish Minister; Madame de Pappenheim; Count Waldbourg and his wife; and a circle of American friends, which included the De Forests, Robertsons, and Daniel Parker. The latter was notorious for his speculations and financial manipulations, but he was also a very

"The Coronation of Napoleon Bonaparte," detail. Armstrong is at top row, center of photograph. *Photograph in Rokeby Collection, courtesy of Mrs. Richard Aldrich and sons, Barrytown, New York*

charming, considerate, and wealthy man. Armstrong had known Parker in the 1780s when he was involved with Duer and Barlow in the Scioto Land Company scheme. Parker came to Paris in 1787, began speculating in American bills, and through contacts among French officials and shrewd manipulations during and after the French Revolution, he amassed a considerable fortune. Parker apparently considered himself an unofficial representative of the Americans in Paris. He had an elegant home on the Rue du Montparnasse, was the owner of several large hotels in Paris, including Armstrong's residence, and was the owner of two elegant chateaus in the country. The Armstrongs often visited Parker at his favorite country seat at Draveil, a small village on the Seine about twelve miles above Paris. On the road to the estate was a field of maize or corn, planted primarily for ornamental and nostalgic reasons. The furniture, decorations, and everything in the house and around it was in the very best taste. Parker's estate contained more than 1100 acres and he employed approximately 200 persons in agriculture, superintended by an Englishman. About 100 acres were reserved as a magnificent park. Alida told her sister after a visit there in June 1807 of his "bergerie" or sheepfold. It was circular in form with a court in the center and was "capable of containing one thousand sheep in a comfortable manner." Alida's interest in Parker's sheep was no idle fancy. The Armstrongs were to bring back to America some fine Merino sheep, thus helping to introduce this breed into the United States.[10]

No doubt the Armstrongs visited many of the other attractions of Paris, such as the cathedral of Notre Dame and the Tuileries palace. It is likely that the Armstrong boys insisted upon seeing the emperor review the troops in the Place du Carrousel, which he did on Sundays from ten o'clock to noon when he was in Paris. They probably also toured Versailles, which one observer described as a "deserted castle," because Napoleon never used it.

Despite his scholarly interests, Armstrong did not associate with the many scholars, scientists, artists, and literary figures in Paris, which was reputed to be the first city in the world as a school of the physical and mathematical sciences and the fine arts. Among the many interesting members of this community was Benjamin Thompson (Count Rumford), the eccentric former American Loyalist who was famous for his discoveries in physics, and John Vanderlyn, a Kingston, New York, native of Dutch descent, who came to Paris in 1807 after studying painting in Rome. Vanderlyn was soon commissioned to paint portraits of General Armstrong and Alida and a profile portrait of the General which was reproduced as an engraving in Paris. Rembrandt Peale also painted Armstrong's portrait in Paris and eventually accompanied the Armstrongs home in 1810.[11] Armstrong's secretary, David Bailie Warden, took full advantage of the scholarly opportunities in Paris, engaging in a wide variety of literary and scientific studies. He was highly regarded and well-known by many French scientists and belonged to many of their societies.

The Armstrongs were privileged to reside in Paris during one of its most brilliant eras. The incredible feats of Napoleon Bonaparte awed his contemporaries as much as they do people today. The Armstrongs watched in fascination as Napoleon's obsessive ambition reordered the map of Europe. His actions inevitably made Armstrong's ministry eventful. One of Armstrong's first problems was how to expedite the payment of the $3,750,000 authorized by the Louisiana Purchase to satisfy claims of American citizens against France arising primarily from maritime violations. A bitter and acrimonious dispute had developed between Livingston and the three-man American Board of Commissioners, which ruled on the validity of the claims. The claims convention, drawn up primarily by Livingston himself, unfortunately had been too hastily and loosely drawn. In order to satisfy the shortcomings, Livingston, as one author noted, "was willing to go further in what might be called the creative interpretation of it."[12] The Board insisted upon their complete independence, even implying that Livingston could not be impartial because his brother, John R. Livingston, was one of the largest claimants.

The major problem was greed. Although the sum involved was relatively small, it unleashed the forces of venality and corruption, as a swarm of claimants sought to press their bloated claims upon the convention. The ambiguities of the convention left ample room for maneuvering by American-European mercantile houses, ostensibly excluded from the process, but they were determined to press their claims nevertheless. Worse, the agents in the French bureaus, who were to make the final decision on the payment of the claims, were hardly paragons of virtue. The process for the admission of claims was too complicated and prone to chicanery. It became evident very early that the sum allotted was too small, and thus some claimants sought to undermine the claims of others in order to increase their own share.[13]

It would have taken a personality and a temperament far different from Armstrong's to have avoided becoming embroiled in the Parisian-American politics. At stake was more than honor; money was involved. If necessary, this sniping, bickering group of agents and merchants were willing to defame any reputation that stood in the way of making good their claims. It is just as well that this is a little-noted chapter of American history, for it does little credit to any of the principals involved.

When Armstrong assumed his duties, the board's service was near-ing its end. He did experience one minor sample of the priggishness of the board. What Armstrong believed to be a routine request for a copy of an opinion on a particular case was only grudgingly given by the board. In doing so they noted pointedly, "we do not wish it to be understood that by this act, which we consider irregular, we are to be supposed connected in any manner with steps that have been or may be adopted in relation to the American claims, after the expiration of our duties here."[14] There is little doubt that Armstrong was relieved to see the duties of the board at an end.

Armstrong's brief time in Paris had not yet taught him the necessity of acting with extreme caution in all matters involving the claims, nor was he yet able to judge the reliability of his informants. This inexperi-ence cost him dearly in the matter of the *New Jersey*. On voyage from Canton, China, to Philadelphia, this ship was captured on February 13, 1798, in the Caribbean by a French privateer. On June 5, 1798, it was con-demned as lawful prize by the Tribunal of Prizes at Santo Domingo. The vessel and the cargo were subsequently restored to agents of the owners on July 5, 1798, after they deposited $203,050, the value of the vessel and cargo. There the matter rested until 1803. The appeal on behalf of the un-derwriters of the *New Jersey* was apparently not prosecuted until that time. The American Board of Commissioners held up the admission of the claim in part because these appeals had not been exhausted. The French Council of Liquidation also rejected the claim for numerous rea-sons, including the lack of a proper invoice, lack of proof of abandon-ment to the underwriters (the owners having reacquired title to the vessel), and their belief that the ship and cargo were partially or alto-gether British property.[15]

This latter question brought Armstrong into this tangled affair. Marbois, the minister of the treasury, applied for information relating to the *New Jersey*, and Armstrong responded on December 5, 1804, that he had no information that Philip Nicklin and Robert E. Griffith, the own-ers, were an English house or that the cargo was loaded at English facto-ries at Canton. On the contrary, he noted that the American Board of Commissioners recognized the *New Jersey* as American property. Arm-strong then unwisely made a gratuitous offer of "much verbal informa-tion which furnished strong presumptive evidence . . . that the Jersey was partially or altogether English property." Improper as this reference to an unsubstantiated claim was, he compounded his error by further stating that it was probable that "no loss was sustained by the ostensible claimants," and that "the present claim is pursued, not on account of the ostensible owners, but of the insurors." He elaborated, with a certain lack of clarity, "If these insurers were American, they have been amply paid in their profits which in 1797 were equal to 200 per cent per an[num] on their capital, and if English they cannot come within the provisions of the treaty."[16]

Armstrong's motives in writing this letter were in the aftermath ascribed to some base reason. It may be surmised, however, that he believed that the *New Jersey* claim would exclude many deserving claimants. Writing to Madison a few weeks after the ill-fated letter to Marbois, he stated that accounts already settled had nearly depleted the entire sum, and many equitable cases which had been rejected for want of form only might be excluded. "Unless we should enlarge this margin," he added, "by rejecting other cases of more doubtful character which may have been admitted, the redress will necessarily be very limited." Madison's instructions, in fact, charged him to protect "the rights of all claimants by combating injurious misconstructions of the instrument, and by favoring the most equitable distribution of its benefits."[17]

Armstrong's letter was certainly indiscreet and ill-advised, but the fury it unleashed was all out of proportion to the nature of the indiscretion. On January 2, 1805, John R. Livingston wrote Armstrong from New York City that his letter had been published in the papers, which "the merchants and underwriters are making a great noise about to the injury of your Reputation." If Armstrong chose "to publish any explanation to qualify it in any respect the sooner it is done the better." To his credit, Armstrong had recognized his mistake and had moved to correct it long before the hue and cry excited in the United States had crossed the Atlantic. He retracted his statement that Nicklin and Griffith were probably an English house in a letter to Marbois on January 5, 1805. On January 21, for the record, he wrote to the agents of Nicklin and Griffith, Peter Samuel Dupont de Nemours and John M. Delagrange, that the documents they had submitted to him had removed any doubts that the *New Jersey* and her cargo were American property, and that they might avail themselves of this information "in the further prosecution of your claim as agents for Messrs. Nicklin and Griffith, and the various Insurance Companies whom you represent."[18]

The French still objected to the *New Jersey* claim, but in consultation Marbois and Armstrong agreed to admit the claim for its full proportion of the marginal fund. Armstrong maintained later that but for his efforts, the claimants "never would have received a single cent." He did admit to Madison, however, "It is true, that Mr. Marbois and I differed somewhat concerning the proportion. He would have given 330,000 francs, whereas I thought that 300,000 [$55,000] were quite as many as fell to its share." He explained: "You will think as I did, I have no doubt, when I inform you, that there are many claims amounting to more than three millions, as sound in point of principle, less objectionable in point of form and better recommended by the pecuniary circumstances of the Claimants, for which I have not yet got a single sous."[19]

Armstrong undoubtedly believed that he had done more than justice to the claims of the *New Jersey*, which had been questioned by the American Commissioners, rejected by the French Council, and had yet received $55,000. Nevertheless, the agents of Nicklin and Griffith, Dupont and Delagrange, paving the way for a claim against the American government, resorted to a deliberate campaign of character assassination designed to establish the fact that the rejection of the entire *New Jersey* claim was due exclusively to the unwarranted interference of Armstrong. On July 25 Nicklin and Griffith submitted a memorial to Madison detailing their grievances against Armstrong. They alleged, falsely, that the American Commissioners "did not hesitate to admit it," and that the French Council was just as favorably disposed, but Armstrong's letter had led to the rejection of the claim and the effect produced was such that "the recantation of the minister himself could never eradicate." They also alleged that in the joint negotiation of Marbois and Armstrong, the latter "retained the extraordinary idea that indemnity for maritime spoliation, was not due to American underwriters who had paid a loss to the original American owner."[20]

The inference that Armstrong had asserted that the rights of the insured did not pass to the insurers had been widely proclaimed in America. That had never been his view, but the repetition of it convinced the underwriting community that this was indeed his position. Madison, reflecting the concern of the Administration, even informed Armstrong on August 25 that it should be distinctly understood that the president's opinion was that American underwriters were entitled "to the benefit of the Convention where they have paid the loss of the original owners, citizens of the United States."[21]

Armstrong responded that the difficulties of the *New Jersey* had not arisen from "the causes to which they have been ascribed." He explained that his objection was not to all insurors, merely to the insurors of the *New Jersey*, who had presented no evidence that they had paid the claim. "You will readily perceive that in all of this," he concluded, "there is not a single syllable pointed at the rights of insurers 'who have paid the loss of the original insurors.'" But the campaign of invective initiated by Nicklin and Griffith was such that President Jefferson personally wrote to Armstrong in February 1806 citing the "terrible tempest" and advising him to respond to these charges, in order to "place you where you would wish to be in the public favor."[22]

Armstrong heeded Jefferson's advice. On March 9, 1806, he enclosed the documents relating to the *New Jersey*. "If we did not know . . . that to fix an error upon me would be one means of bolstering up their pretensions," he declared to Madison, "we should be entirely at a loss to account for such a flood of feeble calumny & impudent falsehood as has been let off on this subject."[23] John Randolph of Roanoke, the eccentric Virginian now in open opposition to the Jefferson Administration, perceived in the *New Jersey* business an opportunity to attack the "corruption" of the Administration. On March 6 he lashed out in the House at the handling of the French claims in general and at Armstrong in particular. He asserted that there were "hundreds of cases even worse" than the *New Jersey*, because the United States was "represented abroad by unfaithful, dishonest agents." The claims money, instead of being paid "to *bona fide* American citizens" had gone instead "into the pockets of renegadoes, and the bureaux of Paris . . . the traders in neutral character have divided the spoil with the harpies of the French bureaux."[24]

A Senate Resolution on March 3 called for the documents relating to the *New Jersey* case, an apparent Administration effort to get all of the facts out before the public. In the meantime, however, the Senate dealt another blow to Armstrong's reputation. Jefferson had designated him to join with James Bowdoin, the Minister to Spain, in a joint commission to negotiate in Paris with Spanish emissaries for the acquisition of Florida. Bowdoin was approved easily, but Armstrong's nomination was vigorously opposed. All the pressure the Administration could muster produced only a tie vote on March 17 of fifteen to fifteen. It took the vote of Vice President Clinton to confirm the appointment. John Quincy Adams, who opposed Armstrong because of the Newburgh Addresses, recorded in his diary that he considered Armstrong's appointment "one of the most disgraceful acts of Mr. Jefferson's administration."[25]

Reports of Randolph's speech and the near rejection by the Senate reached Armstrong late in May. He set to work at once to respond to his critics and to answer the charges against him in the *New Jersey* case. Madison denied Armstrong's request for copies of the correspondence of the Board of Commissioners relating to the *New Jersey*, but he stated that Randolph's charges were not regarded by the executive, and he added by way of reassurance, "there has been no failure either of justice or friendship on our part."[26]

Armstrong's pamphlet defending his conduct was published in Philadelphia in October 1806. Although it was strongly written and severely denunciatory, it was generally well received. Benjamin Rush, the eminent physician, reported to former President John Adams that although he had not read the pamphlet, "It is said to be well written." He added that John Randolph was "the subject of a good deal of abuse in it."[27] The case against Armstrong had been built upon false premises and innuendo in the first place, and he had little difficulty in putting down the major charge against him of opposing the claims of underwriters. He argued that as minister he had "combatted and controlled the many extravagant doctrines set up by the French treasury," as well as those of the many claimants, including Dupont and Delagrange, who were "Like the Dutch spice merchants, they would have trampled upon Christ himself had He been placed between them and their percentage."[28]

Armstrong also bitterly answered Randolph's charges, which he asserted "insinuates offences, but specifies nothing." Armstrong subjoined a list of those to whom payments were made to prove the falsity of his charges that the money had not been paid to Americans. Armstrong gloated and wrote savagely, "Should it not provoke a return, you will have to thank your *castrato* voice and *pathic* countenance; which, as they degrade you below the character of a man, may be supposed to place you below the notice of a Gentleman." He added tauntingly, "Let him . . . assign the worst of motives that his sickly jealousy or habitual depravity can suggest . . . as far as the present Minister at Paris may be implicated by his charges, we despise them all."[29] So far as is known, Randolph made no reply nor were Nicklin and Griffith awarded any additional compensation for their claim. Too many charges had been hurled at Armstrong, however, to assert that his pamphlet cleared his reputation from the suspicion of corruption, but it did add to his reputation as a caustic, polemical writer of the first rank. Neither Jefferson or Madison ever recorded any reaction to the pamphlet, but they could not have been displeased to see the facts of the *New Jersey* affair brought out, and it must have delighted them to see John Randolph so deservedly chastised.

The claims required a great deal of Armstrong's attention during the first two and a half years of his ministry. He worked very closely with Francois de Barbe Marbois, the minister of the treasury, a charming, industrious, and honest bureaucrat, who had negotiated the sale of Louisiana for Napoleon. Their relations were very cordial despite the constant vexations and the myriad financial details that had to be arranged. At one point early in 1805 Armstrong wrote Madison, "Of all the business I have ever been concerned in, this has been the most troublesome, and I have often and sincerely regretted that those who had the honor of making the

Convention, had not also the vexation of executing it." Little did he realize then that the claims problems would occupy him for two additional years.[30]

In the hundreds of claims awarded, many similar to the *New Jersey*, obviously there were those who were not satisfied with their share and believed that their claims were handled unfairly. For example, on May 20, 1807, Armstrong wrote Madison that a Mrs. Stewart, a ship-owner, was returning to the United States 20,000 francs richer, but unhappy because she wanted twice that much. Her claim, he explained, was accepted when there was only 108,000 francs left in the fund, and there were three others all recommended by him. He proposed to divide that sum among the four, but soon learned that Mrs. Stewart was intriguing with another claimant to get the other two rejected. Armstrong actually received a proposition to that effect from the French treasury. Believing that the other two were more worthy, he had recommended against it. "Mrs. Stewart thinks I have done her a personal injury and will probably so represent it," he wrote, "so apt are we to forget the obligations of truth & justice in the pursuit of money." One of the two she wanted rejected, he added, was "litterally a beggar."[31]

Finally, on June 28, 1807, Armstrong announced the impending conclusion of "this tedious and disagreeable business," which demanded so many delicate and sensitive decisions that no matter how carefully made were certain to be assailed. His reputation had been damaged, perhaps not beyond repair, but his handling of the claims left a legacy suggesting that not all of his decisions were disinterested, that less deserving claimants had been favored, and even that he had benefitted personally and financially. It is impossible to say today if there is any validity to the many accusations. Most, if not all, were without substance and can be attributed to a sense of injury and ill-treatment on the part of the accusers. Few understood the enormous pressures bearing upon him by conflicting forces. His compromises with the French government on some claims, for example, were often dictated by the simple fact that an obstinate insistence on his part would have jeopardized any payment, and he believed that a portion was better than none at all. His decision in giving proportional shares was based upon his desire, as well as his instructions, to distribute the claims as broadly and as equitably as possible. Undoubtedly, as he admitted, out of the over five hundred claims there may have been abuses, but he always denied knowledge of them.[32]

One of the most unseemly squabbles relating to the claims erupted between Armstrong and Fulwar Skipwith, the commercial agent of the United States and consul at Paris. Essentially, the problem was broader than the personalities of the two men, it involved a conflict between the roles of the two officials, and in the case of Skipwith, a blurring of personal interest and official duties. Skipwith was a native of Virginia, born in 1765. As a youth he saw combat at Yorktown. He was appointed consul general by President Washington to the French island of Martinique in 1791, where he served for two years. In this position he displayed an imperious nature. He was hot-tempered, irascible, and proud. In 1794 he went to France as James Monroe's private secretary, and in 1795 Monroe designated Skipwith the consul-general in Paris. Following Monroe's recall by President Washington and the worsening of relations between the United States and France due to the XYZ affair, Skipwith was left as the sole commercial and diplomatic agent in Paris. Among his duties were settling commercial claims for French spoliations. No distinction was ever apparently made between Skipwith's official duties to forward the claims of American citizens and his service as agent for nearly 200 claimants, for which he normally received 5 per cent. His chief rival was James Swan, an American merchant, and a personal as well as business foe.[33]

Armstrong remained on good terms with both the Swan and Skipwith factions until 1806. By this time Swan was losing in his effort to cover his debts and was soon to be imprisoned. Presumably because he hoped Armstrong might forward his claims, Swan and his confidential agent, Michael O'Mealy, paid court at Armstrong's residence with much greater regularity. This caused much consternation among Skipwith's friends, particularly Isaac Cox Barnet, a former member of the American Board of Commissioners, then acting as Skipwith's deputy and agent while Skipwith was on a brief visit in America on business. Barnet and O'Mealy, in fact, came to blows in March 1806 in front of Armstrong's residence. Barnet maintained that he was in an official capacity and asked for support from Armstrong, who declined, saying that he did not want to become involved in personal matters. Shortly afterwards, Barnet had O'Mealy arrested, but Armstrong soon appeared and got O'Mealy released claiming Barnet was not acting in an official capacity. O'Mealy was made to pay a fine.[34]

Skipwith returned to Paris late in April 1806 and found that his personal claims had been recalled for revision due to error. He suspected Swan was behind the action, but he especially blamed Armstrong for permitting his claim, which had passed through liquidation, to be recalled. Armstrong, for his part, noted that there was nothing in the Convention that prevented the French from recalling claims to the Council of Liquidation on the suggestion of error.[35] Relations between Armstrong and Skipwith had been amicable. Skipwith had even defended Armstrong's actions in the *New Jersey* case while in the United States. All of this meant nothing, however, and Barnet's account of his fight with O'Mealy and Armstrong's ostensible support of O'Mealy, no doubt further convinced Skipwith that Armstrong had sided with Swan.

Skipwith wrote a very menacing letter to Armstrong on July 24 warning, "if I do not find justice where I have a right to expect it, I shall carry my remonstrance to the feet of my Government & present to its view my aggravated injuries." Armstrong, as Skipwith should have known, was not a man easily threatened. He brushed off the letter by stating that it was of little or no concern to him what Skipwith thought of his conduct. If he wished to complain, then he must specify the irregularities. On August 14, responding to Armstrong's taunt that he specify charges, Skipwith wrote a long, indiscreet letter which led ultimately to his downfall. He complained of corruption in the Treasury Department and the Council of Liquidation, and he asserted, "Many of the claims settled & paid in favor of Mr. James Swan, ought never, from their character and nature, to have been paid out of the funds provided by the Convention." Armstrong forwarded this letter to the new minister of the public treasury, Mollien, and he called for the investigation requested by Skipwith. An investigation was undertaken, but it dragged on for over a year. In the meantime, Armstrong deemed it necessary to write another pamphlet defending himself from Skipwith's accusations. While he wrote, Skipwith bombarded Madison with charges that Armstrong was conspiring for his ruin.

Jefferson and Madison must have been appalled to learn that their minister in Paris was involved in another unseemly controversy so soon after the *New Jersey* affair. Armstrong forwarded copies of his pamphlet to Jefferson and Madison. To Jefferson he wrote that "defence, both on public and private grounds, became necessary, and I have (fortunately I hope) been able to make one in the very terms of my motto — non verbis sed factis." He characterized Skipwith's attack to Madison as "the most weak and wicked, unprovoked and unexpected, that ever was made on a public officer." Through all this acrimonious dispute both Jefferson and Madison refrained from taking a position. Skipwith, for example, complained on September 11, 1807, that he had not received a single line from Madison in seventeen months.[37]

On November 7 the Council of State's report, approved by the emperor, was announced. Skipwith was accused of abusing his powers by using his influence to have certain claims adopted, and because of his "public and scandalous accusations" against French authorities and the minister of the United States, the minister of exterior relations was requested "to demand from the American Government, the recall of this agent."[38] Skipwith had permitted his anxiety over the diminution of his income and his passionate rivalry with James Swan to warp his judgment. His reckless charges ultimately led to a thorough scrutiny of his cases, which revealed some extremely questionable, if not criminal, practices. It is difficult to escape the conclusion that he brought all of his problems upon himself.

Skipwith made a last desperate effort to salvage his reputation. On February 23, 1808, he wrote the minister of exterior relations, Champagny, begging him not to request his recall. "Surely his Majesty's Government is not bound to avenge the injuries of Genl. Armstrong in his official relations with Mr. Skipwith." His plea was to no avail, and he submitted his resignation to Jefferson on March 8, 1808.[39] He left France in September 1808. If he had any information to incriminate Armstrong, he did not use it to demand a congressional investigation of Armstrong's conduct after he arrived in the United States. Perhaps he remembered the results of his last demand for an investigation. The Armstrong-Skipwith controversy thus died. Armstrong had won another round with an antagonist, but it was a hollow victory, for once again suspicions had been aroused about his integrity, and those who would believe the worst of him had one more reason for doing so.

5

MINISTERIAL POLITICS

A MATTER REQUIRING EVEN MORE OF ARMSTRONG'S TIME AND ENERGY than the claims business during these early years of 1804–1807 was pressing American interests over the boundaries of the Louisiana Purchase. Livingston and Monroe had failed to secure specific boundaries for Louisiana, and their subsequent efforts to gain a more precise definition was met by Talleyrand's cynical comment to Livingston, "You have made a noble bargain for yourselves, and I suppose you will make the most of it." The Americans were thus seemingly invited to claim as much as their scruples would allow and the weakness of their neighbor Spain would permit. As Henry Adams expressed it, Livingston and Monroe found that "having been sent to buy the east bank of the Mississippi, they had bought the west bank instead, that the Floridas were not a part of the purchase," but they conceived the extraordinary idea "that France had actually bought West Florida without knowing it, and had sold it to the United States without being paid for it."[1]

This position at least had the merit of providing the basis for negotiations with Spain, or even, if the United States had been so inclined, the pretext for war. While not averse to utilizing the occasional threat of war, Jefferson and Madison preferred to win West Florida by diplomacy.[2] Madison, for example, confidently informed the French minister to the United States, Turreau, that "when the pear is ripe it will fall of its own accord." They adopted the Livingston-Monroe interpretation of the boundaries of Louisiana, for they ardently desired West Florida (that is, the region now comprising the southern portions of the states of Mississippi and Alabama below the thirty-first parallel) for many reasons, political, strategic, and commercial. Despite the fact that Louisiana and West Florida were distinct colonies under Spanish control with different governors, Jefferson and Madison concluded upon review of the treaties of 1763, 1783, and 1795, that the limits of the Louisiana Purchase included West Florida to the Perdido River. This policy had the unfortunate result of poisoning relations with Spain, enmeshing the United States in the machinations of Napoleon, and contributing to domestic discord and division.

It is difficult to tell how sincerely Jefferson and Madison believed in these pretensions, but they expressed their opinions so fervently and so often that it can be readily imagined that they were convinced by their own rhetoric. The success of this policy, however, depended upon the cooperation or at least the sufferance of France. When Spain became an ally of France by declaring war on Great Britain, it soon became clear that France, despite Talleyrand's whimsical suggestion, had no intention of permitting the Americans to fashion the treaty to suit their pleasure. France now supported the Spanish contention that West Florida was not included in the Louisiana Purchase. Livingston's opinion, as he informed Madison, was that "France wishes to make our controversy favorable to her finances."[3] When Armstrong arrived in Paris, he joined with Monroe, who was on his way to Madrid to press the American claim, to write the French asking for their aid in obtaining Florida. No response was forthcoming. Monroe and his family attended the coronation of Napoleon as emperor on December 2 in the company of the Armstrongs, then he left for Madrid on December 8, still without official word from the French, but with sufficient unofficial information to indicate that his chances for a successful negotiation were virtually nil. Talleyrand finally wrote to Armstrong on December 21, declaring that the American claim to West Florida was totally unfounded.[4]

The American leaders and their diplomats could never quite comprehend the French motives. They were convinced that France needed American trade desperately, and that it would be foolhardy to alienate the United States and even drive them to seek an alliance with Great Britain. Furthermore, as a last resort the United States could simply seize West Florida. Thus, they laid the French position to a pecuniary reason, and the long history of bribes, corruption, and jobbery in the French capital lent substance to this view. Although officially in his position only a month, Armstrong felt qualified to warn Madison that France was "determined to convert the negotiation into a job." Repeated intimations had been made to him that if certain persons could be gratified, the negotiations could be brought to a favorable end. He indicated that his responses had uniformly been "that it was quite impossible that the measures of a nation like this could ever be influenced, much less determined, by the considerations that would equally dishonor them to offer and the United

States to hear." He believed the choice of the United States was between an immediate accommodation or a delay which could take advantage "of any new crisis in the fortunes of France and Spain." There was another alternative, however, and it was one he preferred, namely "an effort (which cannot fail) to do the business at home." Armstrong thus expressed in his maiden letter an attitude that seemed to infect all of Jefferson's diplomats, the preference for Napoleonic measures. Madison was pleased by Armstrong's rebuff to the French agents, and he congratulated him for his "just and dignified" response. Jefferson was more perceptive and noted that Armstrong was already forgetting the temper of his country and catching the hue of those around him.[5]

Monroe's mission was a failure. After nearly four months of negotiations with Cevallos, the Spanish minister of state, and with Manuel Godoy, the prince of peace and the real negotiator, the Spanish remained obdurate. Armstrong's conversations with Talleyrand led him to conclude by early spring that the French policy was to procrastinate and prolong the negotiations. He wrote Monroe on May 4, "You will in fact be a couple of oranges in her hands, which she will squeeze at pleasure, and against each other, and that which yields the most will be the best served, or rather the least injured." After reflection he now believed there was only one course which would have the double advantage of getting everything the United States wanted without a war with Spain or the mediation of France: "It is simply to take a strong and prompt possession of the northern bank of the Rio Bravo [Rio Grande], leaving the eastern limit in status quo. A stroke of this kind would at once bring Spain to reason, and France to her rescue, and without giving either room to quarrel. You might then negotiate, and shape the bargain pretty much as you pleased."[6]

Removed from the temper of Europe, Madison persisted in believing that the best interest of France should be to serve the interests of the United States. He wrote Armstrong that the part France was taking on the side of Spain was "not a little extraordinary." If the French were indeed attempting to convert the negotiations into a pecuniary job, they must eventually despair of success and "yield to the obvious policy of promoting equitable arrangements between Spain and the United States." The French should also open the trade of their islands in the West Indies to the United States. There was a hint of a future policy when he concluded, "The time is not distant when the United States with a reduced debt, and surplus of revenue, will be able, without risking the public credit, to say with effect, to whatever nation they please, that they will shut their trade with its colonies in time of war, if it be not opened to them equally at all times."[7]

Jefferson's refusal to use military means to achieve diplomatic ends, while laudable, did have drawbacks. The French, realizing that the United States did not intend to use military force, treated the American representatives with greater contempt. In a world that seemingly only understood force, it was a constant frustration to American diplomats that their superiors expected diplomatic triumphs with only words. Armstrong stated his case as clearly and candidly as he could. Acknowledging his preference for vigorous action, he reflected:

> Hints of this kind have so frequently escaped me, that you may perhaps begin to suspect, that I have caught a little of the influenza of Europe. This however is far from being the fact. It is here that a man of any tolerable degree of sense & soberness will soonest perceive how little is the good conferred, and how great & lasting are the mischief inflicted by war; but it is also here that he best discovers that in nine cases out of ten of national insult or injury, the motives to their perpetration have partaken more of the cowardice that believes it has nothing to fear, than of the intrepidity that fears nothing – & he will hence conclude that national, like personal spirit, is not only our best support under actual hostility, but our most substantial protection against it.[8]

Monroe, after breaking off negotiations with Spain, came to the same conclusion. He returned to Paris and joined Armstrong in urging Charles Pinckney, the minister to Spain, to advise James Bowdoin, who had been designated as Pinckney's replacement, to decline treating with Spain until Madison had reviewed the results of Monroe's negotiations.[9]

Curiously, despite advice to take a strong stance, Jefferson now proposed to turn the controversy into a French job. The place to settle it was Paris, he argued to Madison in October 1805, "through Armstrong, or Armstrong and Monroe as negotiators, France as the mediator, the price of the Floridas as the means." He added cynically, "We need not care who gets that, and an enlargement of the sum we had thought of may be the bait to France." The Cabinet was sounded on November 12, and it was decided to employ Armstrong in this extraordinary business. The sum that he would be permitted to dangle before the French was $5 million.[10]

Ironically, within a week a letter arrived in Washington from Armstrong telling of a conversation with a French agent that Spain could be made to part with the Floridas if certain concessions were made: that Spain and France would receive commercial privileges in Florida; the Rio Colorado was to be the western boundary; thirty leagues on each side was to remain unoccupied forever; Spanish claims, excluding French spoliations, were to be paid by bills on the Spanish colonies; and $10 million would be paid by the United States to Spain. Armstrong objected that the United States would be giving up three points in controversy, a fourth was advantageous to Spain, and ten million dollars was too much for the barren province of East Florida. The agent stated in response that he saw "where the shoe pinches" and lowered the sum to seven million dollars. Armstrong replied that he could say nothing, but he promised to forward the proposal to his government. He observed that the note was in Talleyrand's handwriting. The scheme was for the United States to menace Spain to force them to seek the good offices of France. If this failed, the United States should send a note to the French government seeking their mediation to avoid a rupture between the two nations. Armstrong did not encourage the agent to believe the United States would accept the offer, but he nevertheless believed the offer was genuine. France was on the eve of a renewal of hostilities, he noted, and "all possible means of raising money are tried" and this was one of the expedients.[11]

Jefferson presented Armstrong's letter to his Cabinet on November 19, and they very agreeably conceded every point required by France, but they held firmly to the sum of $5 million.[12] The Jefferson Administration thus committed itself to the dubious course of playing the French game. As it developed, almost any other course would have been better. No immediate instructions were forwarded to Armstrong; Congress was to convene in a few weeks and its support was deemed necessary to execute the policy.

In the meantime, in Europe, James Bowdoin, when he learned that Monroe's negotiations had broken off, had retraced his steps from Spain to join Monroe in London. He explained to Monroe that he did not wish to change the public impression of what had happened in Spain (effectively a cessation of relations). Bowdoin was the son of a famous governor of Massachusetts, but he was otherwise undistinguished except for his wealth. Monroe sought to dump his unwelcome guest on Armstrong. On September 2 he announced to Armstrong Bowdoin's imminent arrival in Paris. It might have a "good effect" as it would be an act of conciliation to France and it might induce them to preserve friendly relations with the United States and foster a settlement with Spain. They had decided to send George W. Erving, Bowdoin's secretary, to Madrid to serve as the secretary of the legation.[13]

Armstrong obviously did not want Bowdoin in Paris. He hastily wrote Monroe arguing against the wisdom of the move. Nevertheless, Bowdoin arrived in Paris on November 1. Armstrong greeted him coolly. His arrival created an awkward situation of whether the two ministers should cooperate in any subsequent negotiations arising from the secret proposals, and it also created problems of precedence and etiquette, as Bowdoin's role and official status had to be worked out.[14]

Erving wrote from Madrid that he attributed Armstrong's reserve to base motives. He informed Bowdoin that he had been so apprehensive, "I have very candidly opened my mind to Mr. Monroe." Bowdoin obviously agreed. He complained that he had to "skrew & wire-draw" to obtain any information, and that only the day before Armstrong had promised to give him a copy of the secret propositions "under the very particular injunctions that I should show them to no one!" Armstrong, who was ill at this time, merely reported to Madison on December 22 that Bowdoin had arrived, and that he intended to remain there until he received instructions.[15]

Bowdoin sought Monroe's advice, while Armstrong, apparently unaware of this correspondence, was writing Monroe at the same time implying that Bowdoin was extremely gullible. Soon after his arrival, Armstrong wrote, "the old project was dressed up for him; put into a Spanish habit, made to affect great shyness of French interference. . . ." He was told that there was a plan for France to take the Floridas in payment of a guarantee of a balance due by Spain, and if the United States did not act promptly with generous proposals, an auspicious occasion would be lost.[16]

Bowdoin was indeed gullible, and he acted foolishly. He was approached by a Spanish agent, or as Bowdoin styled him, an "agent of an agent." As a result, he asked Erving to inform Godoy that it would be to Spain's benefit to keep France out of the controversy. Incredibly, he authorized Erving to communicate to Godoy the secret propositions made to Armstrong, believing that this would "have great weight with him in inducing an adjustm[en]t of our disputes without the interference of this government." If Godoy was agreeable, Bowdoin would go immediately to Madrid and settle the treaty.[17] The spectacle of these two amateur diplomats duped by Spanish agents and presuming to outwit the likes of men such as Talleyrand and Godoy has an air of unreality. Undoubtedly, both men were well-intentioned, but by attempting to by-pass the French and craftily maneuver Godoy, they revealed their innocence as diplomats.

Godoy stored the information for later use, but he made no move to negotiate. Finding no field to exercise his talents in writing a treaty with Spain, Bowdoin turned to Monroe and suggested that if a treaty was to be written with England, he was available. He next pressed Armstrong to write the French that if they would intervene, the United States could resist Great Britain and "take part in the war." Armstrong opposed this idea, but Bowdoin planned to go to Prussia to present this view in person to the emperor, until he was dissuaded from this rash act by Daniel Parker.[18] At the same time, Bowdoin was writing Jefferson that the secret propositions to Armstrong had encouraged jobbery and speculation. He also wrote Madison that waiting for instructions had completely tied his hands and placed him in a disagreeable situation "between duty and etiquette." Duty prompted him to measures his judgment approved, but etiquette restrained him "for the sake of keeping up a friendly correspondence with Genl. Armstrong." He noted that he had been presented to the emperor and had been very graciously received, but he added, "I have not yet seen M. Talleyrand or been introduced to him, altho' it is more than six weeks since Genl. Armstrong and I sent him our cards."[19]

Armstrong was caught in a delicate situation. He had received no instructions for more than six months, none to the propositions he forwarded to his government in September 1805. The French government continually pressed him for an answer, and Bowdoin could not understand Armstrong's reluctance to act. The instructions had been delayed by the obstinate resistance of John Randolph to the Two-Million Bill, which was finally passed and was signed on February 13, 1806. The Randolph schism was followed by the fight over Armstrong's nomination for the joint commission with Bowdoin. Jefferson and Madison must have wondered if playing the French game was worth the price, morally, politically, or financially. Nevertheless, the instructions went forward to Armstrong and Bowdoin, dated March 13, and they arrived in Paris on April 28.[20]

These instructions authorized negotiations along lines of proposals now eight months old. Moreover, the circumstances had now radically changed. Napoleon had through a series of brilliant victories secured control over Europe, his treasury was no longer depleted, and he now supported Spain's desire to hold on to the Floridas. Further, he could act with impunity, certain that the United States would not turn to Britain because of their recent depredations upon American commerce. The American negotiators were permitted to pursue the elusive hope that the negotiations would begin once the preliminary arrangements were made. Armstrong, in exasperation, demanded to know the reason for the change in the French attitude.

Talleyrand, to cover the French reversal, replied that Erving had communicated the secret propositions to Godoy, causing Spain to complain that France was attempting to usurp Spain's sovereignty by putting her provinces on sale without her knowledge. Talleyrand thus deftly evaded the question and turned Armstrong's wrath upon his colleague. Armstrong promptly reported Bowdoin's indiscretion to Madison. "You

may readily imagine my confusion and astonishment at this discovery,"
he wrote. "I had confided the propositions to Mr. Bowdoin under the
most solemn injunctions of secrecy . . . Could I believe," he added, "that
a man to whom his country had committed so high an office could so fla-
grantly violate a trust so sacred?" He added, "how am I to behave to a
man who has outraged my confidence in the very first step I have taken
with him?" For the sake of harmony, however, he would attempt to work
with him, but there could henceforth be no degree of confidence between
them.[21]

The split between Armstrong and Bowdoin at the very beginning of
their joint commission was unfortunate but, in view of their previous
relations, hardly surprising. Just when Armstrong had good reason to
suspend relations with Bowdoin, he was forced to cooperate with him.
Bowdoin, now endowed with an official status, could and did expect to
be treated with greater deference. He informed Armstrong that he expected to be consulted on correspondence with the French relating to
Spanish affairs. Armstrong replied that he had the right to confer exclusively with the French government, and he reminded Bowdoin that his
duties would not begin until the Spanish authorities were willing to enter
negotiations. Since no Spanish representatives had been appointed, and
since Bowdoin was not accredited to France, he concluded, "it leaves us
exactly where we were." Bowdoin accepted this interpretation, but he
complained to Monroe about his "extraordinary situation" working with
a man "in whom I have no confidence; & whom, for obvious reasons, I
cease to visit," and who, he continued, "has shown a reserve towards me
better suited to an enemy of the U.S., than one of their ministers."[22]

From Bowdoin, Erving, and Skipwith, reports flowed to Monroe in
the summer of 1806 accusing Armstrong of betraying the trust of the
American people in collusion with unscrupulous agents of France, Spain,
and corrupt American merchants in Paris. He reacted by writing Jefferson
warning him of the apparent lack of cooperation between Armstrong and
Bowdoin. There appears to have been a concerted campaign of invective
aimed at Armstrong by a small, noisy faction centered in Paris. By failing
to placate this faction, and avoid the aspersions cast upon his character,
Armstrong paid a dear price. Even more questionable, however, are the
actions of his enemies, who embarked upon a course of character assassination because they believed that Armstrong's failure to support them
meant that he was also failing to support the best interests of the United
States.[23]

Early in the summer of 1806 the negotiations appeared to be about
to begin. Talleyrand, apparently convinced of the emperor's sincerity,

pressed Godoy to bring about direct negotiations. Armstrong learned on June 28 from Erving that Spain had appointed Don Eugenio Izquierdo to negotiate. However, in an abrupt change of policy, Napoleon severely chastised Talleyrand for his haste. This start-stop policy was mystifying to the Americans, and perplexing even to Talleyrand who, at the same time the Spanish negotiations were taken out of his hands, was made Prince of Benevento by Napoleon. The Spanish, learning of Napoleon's change of policy, returned to their obstinate, temporizing course.[24]

Bowdoin became convinced that somehow Daniel Parker, who was "daily closeted" with Armstrong, was behind the failure of the negotiations to begin. Reasoning from the totally false premise that "the Emperor is well disposed to having our affairs satisfactorily adjusted," he concluded that it was not in the interest of the stock-jobbers and their confederates for the negotiations to succeed.[25] Bowdoin had divined the outcome of their negotiations, but he had misconceived the reason. Cut off from contact with the French government, ignored by Armstrong, besieged by mercenary agents preying on his naiveté, surrounded by carping, bitter men like Skipwith and Barnet, it is not surprising that in his frustration and his ignorance of the true nature of affairs, he arrived at his mistaken conclusions.

Finally, on October 10, Armstrong announced to Madison the probable failure of the joint commission. Izquierdo's powers had been suspended or recalled, and the emperor had left for Germany to begin a war with Prussia.[26] Finding nothing further to require his presence in Paris, the Armstrongs departed on a four-week vacation into the Normandy region as far as Dieppe. Alida wrote her brother Edward that they saw a countryside "resembling some parts of our own, fine orchards and excellent grass lands."[27] Bowdoin meanwhile wrote Erving, "As soon as this business with Spain is finished it is my intention to return home," and he added disgustedly, "My debut has not been either flattering or pleasing to me; it has perfectly satisfied me by proving to me that the situation of a minister is neither a source of pleasure or profit; it will not afford the first because deception & deceit characterize those with whom you must associate, & the latter because the allowance of govt. will not more than half pay the necessary expenses."[28]

During this period Bowdoin received a report that Izquierdo was to obtain a grant of from three to six million acres in Florida for a minimal purchase price, and with Parker and Armstrong would form a company and divide the spoils. Bowdoin was so confident that he had finally uncovered proof of the corruption of Parker and Armstrong, that he hounded Erving in virtually every letter in the next few months to un-

Alida Livingston Armstrong with her daughter Margaret Rebecca, later Mrs. William B. Astor, attributed to John Vanderlyn, ca. 1809. *Rokeby Collection, courtesy of Mrs. Richard Aldrich and sons, Barrytown, New York*

cover the documents in the Spanish archives. Erving was unable to do so. Nevertheless, Bowdoin was so certain of the truth of his information that, incredibly, he presented his charges to President Jefferson.

Bowdoin disavowed any responsibility for the failure of the negotiations, which he laid to the corruption of Armstrong. He submitted a sworn statement by an Irish Catholic clergyman, Charles M. Somers, who was employed as a translator of French and English in Paris. This statement, dated February 5, 1807, and attested by Skipwith, told of a land speculation scheme involving Parker, O'Mealy, Izquierdo, and a few Frenchmen, to acquire three million acres in Florida with possession to take place after the United States took control of the territory. The document of cession would be sent to Madrid and would be antedated to preclude charges of fraud or collusion. Somers claimed that his source was O'Mealy. Armstrong's name was not mentioned except in a postscript where it was noted that an acquaintance was known to exist between Armstrong, Parker, and O'Mealy. Bowdoin explained that he enclosed the Somers document so that the president might "guard against the schemes & strategems of a sett of men, who by some means or other, have had but too much influence in our foreign affairs!" Despite the inability of Erving to find any evidence to support the statement, and notwithstanding the questionable wisdom of relying upon hearsay and the veracity of the original source, O'Mealy, Bowdoin presumably believed the document incriminated Armstrong in the scheme, despite the fact that it only mentioned that he knew the individuals involved. He concluded his letter by expressing his strong desire to return home.[29]

It does not appear that Bowdoin's letter made much of an impression upon Jefferson. He endorsed the letter as received in June and noted, contrary to Bowdoin's claim that he had received no letters from the president, "mine, 1806–July 10, 1807–Apr. 2." If we may take this as any indication, the charge that most upset the President was that of being a faithless letter-writer. Jefferson did not even bother to inform Madison of the allegations, nor did he, in his reply to Bowdoin, mention the Somers statement. He accepted Bowdoin's request to be recalled, and then, delicately, he noted, "with real grief," the misunderstandings between Bowdoin and Armstrong, but he added, "We are neither qualified nor disposed to form an opinion between you. We regret the pain which must have been felt by persons both of whom hold so high a place in our esteem."[30]

Bowdoin's effort to blacken Armstrong's reputation thus failed. Armstrong learned of these charges in May 1810. He asked for an explanation from Somers, who admitted that "being much *questioned*" by Bowdoin regarding Armstrong's knowledge about speculative activities,

he had added a postscript "in which I mentioned your name" but only relating Armstrong's acquaintance with Parker and others. Armstrong also
elicited a letter from Daniel Parker, who declared that "nothing forbade
me from buying from the King of Spain what certain[ly] belonged to him
& what of course he had a right to sell." But he also asserted that the details of the Somers deposition were "entirely false."[31] Armstrong asked
Madison for copies of the correspondence intended to implicate him in
land speculation. "I venture to say in advance, that I will cover with infamy the fabrication of this calumny," he wrote. "They are assassins, and
deserve no pity." Madison refused, stating that policy dictated that confidential messages were not released without the assent of the party making
them, but he added, "I need not say that no evidence of that sort, whatever might have been its particular complexion, would have been permitted either by Mr. Jefferson or myself, to withdraw a particle from the
perfect confidence felt by both in your honor & integrity."[32]

During the fall of 1806, after Spanish forces in Texas engaged in a
series of provocative maneuvers along the disputed border, Armstrong
attempted to use these actions as a pretext for French officials to reopen a
dialogue, but no response was received. Jefferson's and Madison's rhetoric in 1807 suggested a stronger policy toward Spain. Ironically, Armstrong, who had always advocated tough measures against Spain, was
now renewing the request for the interposition of the emperor. He proposed essentially to trade off a part of the claim to Texas in return for the
Spanish surrender of West Florida. Nothing came of this approach; and
Talleyrand, with whom Armstrong corresponded, was soon on the way
out. He was replaced by the minister of the interior, Champagny, who
was characterized by Armstrong as "a highly respectable man."[33]

The appointment of Champagny, new developments in Europe,
and the virtual state of war existing between the United States and Great
Britain as a result of the *Chesapeake-Leopard* affair on June 22, in which a
British ship fired upon and captured an American man-of-war, all gave
Armstrong the hope that the situation might soon be resolved. On August
15, he reported a conversation with Napoleon in which he "adverted to
the outrage committed by the Leopard on the Chesapeake. 'This,' said he,
'is most abominable, they have hitherto pretended to visit merchant-
vessels & that they had a right to do so, but they — even they have set up
no such pretension with respect to armed ships. They would now arrange
it by giving up a right or usage which never existed!! But they will arrange
it. They are afraid to go to war with your country.'" Following this remarkable conversation, Champagny invited Armstrong to dinner. He
promised a new exposition of the Berlin Decree touching on the United
States, and he indicated that the emperor had given fresh instructions to

the French ambassador at Madrid relating to the United States controversy with Spain. "The promptitude with which this last measure was taken," Armstrong wrote hopefully, "is the best illustration of the temper and policy which led to its adoption."[34]

Taking advantage of the apparent favorable mood of the French, Armstrong pressed his long-standing demand for a French opinion on the western boundary of Louisiana. Champagny responded by enclosing copies of the French treaties relating to Louisiana, which were not wholly satisfactory. Armstrong viewed this as a positive step, but he decided to await information from the State Department because the "business with Britain" might dictate new directions. The instructions coming across the Atlantic, in fact, directed a suspension of the negotiations due to the possibility of war with Britain. Madison even suggested that if a treaty had been negotiated, it might be renegotiated to reduce the price in view of the obvious advantages to Spain of a probable war between the United States and Great Britain.[35] Madison obviously had a totally unrealistic view of the situation. The possibility that Britain might seize the Floridas in the event of war with the United States, suggested to him that this might "stimulate Spain to an immediate concurrence in the plan of adjustment proposed by the U. States, and on another, prepare her and her ally for any sudden measures of fair precaution which the approach of war with Great Britain may prescribe to this Government."[36] Madison could give no news to guide Armstrong relating to any United States action regarding the *Chesapeake* affair. He was instructed to act according to his own best judgment. There was a hint, however, that war with Britain might not occur.[37]

Thus if one were to characterize the foreign policy of the United States in the fall of 1807, at least as far as it involved Armstrong, it would have to be described as indecisive or undetermined. With the possibility of war with Great Britain looming on the horizon, the controversy with Spain was temporarily shelved and the joint commission was terminated. Before the news of this termination arrived in Paris, however, the steadily deteriorating relationship between Armstrong and Bowdoin reached its climax. Bowdoin asked Armstrong to procure a card of introduction from the master of ceremonies so that he might pay his respects to the emperor on his birthday on August 15. Armstrong was unable to procure a card of introduction because it was announced that only ministers accredited to the emperor would be received that day. Bowdoin angrily complained to Armstrong that he had presented him in his private and not in his official character, and he asserted that Armstrong had constantly refused to introduce him to Talleyrand.[38]

Provoked, Armstrong replied that he knew of no lack of protection; Bowdoin had not been molested, and he had enjoyed the civilities of the court. Bowdoin may have been addressed in his private character rather than "His Excellency, James Bowdoin, Esq., Minister Plenipotentiary and Extraordinary to His Catholic Majesty." If this style of address was among "those forms of *significance* and *character*" which Bowdoin stated were highly "important to the government we represent," then Armstrong added, "Mr. B. himself cannot be more afflicted at this omission than I am."

Bowdoin was not permitted to make court at the last diplomatic audience, and Armstrong had explained why, but Bowdoin "with his characteristic delicacy and good manners, places the order of his Majesty . . . to the account of Gen. Armstrong, and would insinuate that it was *particular* in its operation." Armstrong insisted that "If Mr. B. would dismiss the ear-wigs that now approach and even monopolize him, and who knew even less than himself, and particularly if he would enter but once a week into any well-instructed society in Paris, he would get over his misconceptions and other errors into which he is now constantly falling both with regard to the French nation, the French government, and even the conduct of his own colleague."

Armstrong reminded Bowdoin that he had twice sought for Bowdoin an introduction to Talleyrand, despite his knowledge that Bowdoin was attempting to open a secret official correspondence with Talleyrand. Furthermore, Armstrong wrote mockingly, in fact "Mr. B. *has been actually introduced to this minister, nay that he introduced himself*," at a public audience, heedless of the indications of impropriety. "If it were possible for Mr. B. to have forgotten this extraordinary *introduction*," Armstrong wrote with malicious pleasure, "it is quite impossible that he could forget the still more extraordinary *reception* it met with. To have lost sight of the one would argue a total want of memory; but to have forgotten the other would demonstrate the absence of everything in the human character worth having." After handling Bowdoin so roughly, Armstrong expressed the hope that Bowdoin would "hereafter look out for some new subject upon whom to discharge the irritations of ill-health or ill-humor. He is completely weary of being the subject of either."[39]

Despite the severity of the chastisement, this did not end their correspondence. When Armstrong forwarded Champagny's reply regarding the western boundary of Louisiana, Bowdoin felt constrained to answer, noting as he did that he had received Armstrong's "ill judged, unauthorized & I might say, abusive letter."[40] Having learned from Erving that there was no disposition on the part of Spain to enter negotiations, he immediately began making plans to leave Paris. It was with a great sense of relief, he informed Erving, that he left that "scoundrel" Armstrong who had made his stay "as disagreeable to me as a worthless corrupt fellow could make it . . . I thank God I have done with him, & I hope forever."[41] Armstrong left no record of his feelings at the departure of his former colleague, but they can be readily imagined.

Bowdoin's departure came when American affairs were, relatively speaking, in a state of suspension. The next few months would reveal the American response to the *Chesapeake* affair, and Napoleon would soon disclose the next steps in his plan for the domination of Europe. In due course, he would also make known what role he envisioned for the United States. Armstrong could not know it, but he was about to enter upon the most important and the most arduous and difficult years of his ministry.

GÉNÉRAL JOHN ARMSTRONG

John Armstrong, Jr., by John Vanderlyn, ca. 1808. This profile was reproduced as an engraving in Paris. *Courtesy of Frick Art Reference Library and Rokeby Collection, courtesy of Mrs. Richard Aldrich and sons, Barrytown, New York*

6

DEFENDER OF NEUTRAL RIGHTS

THE RESUMPTION OF WARFARE between Great Britain and France after
1803 gradually brought about a renewal of violations of American
neutral rights by both nations. As the belligerents turned increasingly to
economic retaliation, the United States shipping became whipsawed
between them. French policies toward the United States were just as ca-
pricious and rapacious as those of the British, and Armstrong vigorously
defended American neutral rights during these crucial years of 1804 to
1810. The French suffered stinging rebukes from his pen, and his letters to
his superiors in Washington, some of which found their way into print,
fully apprised the American government and the American people of the
true nature of French policy.

The British court decision in the *Essex* case in the summer of 1805
brought a renewal of British seizures of American vessels engaged in trade
between France and her colonies. Armstrong wrote Monroe that the seizures were "not to be regretted," if they brought the British to "a full &
clear acknowledgment of the principle we contend for." Monroe replied
that the French, with their navy destroyed and their commerce severely
restricted, would perceive that the United States alone was left to combat
British policies. "I should suppose," he wrote, "that it would hasten to compromise our business with Spain to leave us free to support our neutral
rights."[1] This was a reasonable assumption, and the corollary proposition
would be that it was in France's interest to favor American commerce and
neutral rights. This belief, in fact, permeated American attitudes and
policies throughout this period. French policies contrary to this premise
constantly confounded American leaders. Armstrong was also imbued
with this idea, but his close proximity to the actual situation brought him

to a realization much sooner than his government that the French policy was essentially hostile. But he did not adhere consistently to this view. Rationally, he believed that the French would eventually realize the folly of their policy, and they very deftly offered the hope from time to time that their disastrous policy would be altered.

The first French violations occurred in the spring of 1806. Four American ships were seized for trading with Britain. Armstrong protested and demanded that the French disavow this conduct. "Of the other foreign ministers who had the same ground of complaint with myself," he explained to Madison, "but one (the minister of Denmark) is disposed to examine and repel the principle put up. . . . Those of Prussia and Portugal are contented with a mere remuneration of the pecuniary loss." Great Britain, he reported, was about to be excluded from all commerce with northern Europe. American trade would thus become more valuable to the British, and he argued, "the present becomes a precious moment for putting our rights, not merely out of reach of injury, but out of that of insult also."[2]

This letter reveals two further corollaries to American foreign policy assumptions during this period — namely, that other countries were not disposed to resist the anti-neutral pretensions of the belligerents and the United States thus stood virtually alone, and second, that the French policies would require Britain to moderate or even to reconcile their policies toward the United States, in short that it was in Britain's interest to favor American commerce and neutral rights.

The idea that advantage might be gained from both powers by stressing their mutual interests with the United States was beguiling. It was self-evident that the United States must remain aloof from involvement in European affairs. Madison, for example, instructed Armstrong in the spring of 1806 that should a congress of neutrals be called, he was to reject politely any effort to bind the United States to an agreement, although he was authorized to express the deep interest of the United States in the success of their efforts.[3]

These assumptions were still operative when Napoleon issued the Berlin Decree in November 1806, establishing a paper blockade of the British Isles. The British retaliated with an Order in Council in January 1807 closing trade to neutrals between ports owned or occupied by the enemy. American shippers obviously could not conform with both measures without incurring the wrath of one or the other belligerents, and national honor dictated conformity with neither. It was the French policy, of course, that occupied Armstrong's interest and time, and he moved to seek a clarification from the French of the effects of the Berlin Decree upon American commerce. It should be noted, however, that the British policies were not unimportant in these dialogues between Armstrong and the French. Napoleon and his officials invariably followed the relations between the United States and Great Britain with great interest, and quite often they justified their actions by citing the British example.

At first the Berlin Decree did not disturb the existing commerce between France and the United States. A favorable decision of the Council of Prizes in the case of the *Hibernia*, the first case of capture under the decree, Armstrong informed Madison in March 1807, "cannot fail to give satisfaction to the trading part of our community." He succeeded in obtaining three concessions: that those American ships not having knowledge of the rule were exempted; those not coming directly from a British port to a French port were not affected; and those coming directly but involuntarily would not be condemned and would be held in sequestration until a decision could be reached by the emperor.[4]

Events took a more ominous turn in the summer of 1807. Strengthened by victories in Prussia and the Peace of Tilsit with Russia, only Denmark and Portugal held out from Napoleon's extension of his Continental System to all of Europe. Pressure was immediately applied to coerce them into conformity. That the French did not immediately attempt to bring the United States into the system can be attributed to the *Chesapeake* affair, which had aroused a war fever in the United States. By the end of August, Denmark and Holland had been coerced into enforcing the Berlin Decree in their ports. On September 24, Armstrong informed Madison that the Berlin Decree was now going to be enforced against Americans. The two great rivals of Europe, he noted, seemed to be striving not only to see "which one should do us the most harm but which should most injure itself, in the measures pursued in relation to us!" He suggested what was shortly to become the policy of the United States, an embargo, which would not only secure "your present safety and future strength," but also teach the belligerents a lesson of how important a regular commerce was to them.[5]

Armstrong attempted to stave off the implementation of the new French policy, but he also sent a circular to all the U.S. consuls in Europe warning that the decree was about to be literally executed and that it would be prudent for all American vessels to return to the United States.[6] His diplomatic efforts did not alter the intentions of the French. In early November the Council of Prizes ruled in the case of the *Horizon*, which had shipwrecked on the French coast, that the part of the cargo of British manufacture was good prize under the Berlin Decree. Armstrong characterized this as "the first unfriendly decision of that body," and he protested strongly, employing his very considerable talents for polemics. His legal-istic and sarcastic language utterly demolished, at least to his satisfaction, the arguments of the council.

Napoleon was equal to the challenge. "Reply to the American min-ister," he wrote Champagny on November 15, "that since America suffers her vessels to be searched, she adopts the principle that the flag does not cover the goods." Since Americans permitted the British to violate their neutral rights, then she must submit to the same by the French. Napoleon admitted, at least to Champagny, that the measure was "unjust, illegal, and subversive of national sovereignty," as Armstrong contended, but his motives were revealed when he continued, "it is the duty of nations to re-sort to force, and to declare themselves against things which dishonor them and disgrace their independence."[7]

Armstrong's frustration was manifest in his letter to Madison on November 15. The United States was to be "invited to make common cause against England, and to take the guarantee of the Continent for a maritime peace which shall establish the principle of *free ships, free goods.*" He advised against such a step. "Will we not by connecting our-selves with this vast combination, be compelled to pursue objects far be-yond, and perhaps very different from our own?" He reiterated his advice to institute an embargo, and he recommended the seizure of Canada, and for good measure, the occupation of the Floridas. Such grandiose advice was worthy of Napoleon himself, but Armstrong assured Madison that if these measures were "executed with promptitude and spirit, they would do more to preserve inviolate your peace and happiness than all the parchment and diplomacy of both hemispheres."[8]

On December 17, 1807, Napoleon announced the Milan Decree, de-claring that any neutral ship searched by a British vessel or which had paid any duty to the British government would be confiscated upon enter-ing a port under French control. Armstrong's reaction to this "extraor-dinary decree" was restrained. "Whether it be meant to stimulate Great Britain to the commission of new outrages, or to quicken us in repelling those she has already committed, the policy is equally unwise," he de-clared, and he added that "not a single man of consideration" in Paris ap-proved of it.[9]

Armstrong's suspicion that the French policy was to induce the Americans to go to war with Great Britain was verified by Napoleon's re-sponse to his protest against the Milan Decree. Napoleon declared that he was "ashamed to discuss points of which the injustice is so evident"; that he had no doubts that the United States would declare war on England be-cause of her order of November 11, and that he regarded war as being declared "from the day when England published her decrees." Consequently, American vessels were to be sequestered, "to be disposed of as shall be necessary according to circumstances." Champagny's letter of January 15, 1808, to Armstrong, which was widely published in the United States, did not noticeably soften the bluntness of the language. His Majesty was ready to consider the United States as associated with those powers defending themselves against England, and he added that American vessels would remain sequestered until a decision was made by the United States.[10]

Napoleon thus blatantly detained millions of dollars of American shipping as both a threat and an inducement for the Americans to declare war on England. Although he opposed any form of alliance, Armstrong nevertheless sounded out the French on how far they were willing to go in the event of war between the United States and Great Britain, particularly in permitting the Americans to occupy the Floridas. Napoleon was willing to offer that bribe, and accordingly, on the evening of February 3, Armstrong was visited by Marbois, who gave such assurances.

Armstrong was unwilling to accept mere verbal promises and, for the record, he prescribed the terms necessary for American friendship. He prefaced his remarks by noting that French policies had done little to promote the views of the emperor. The British had violated American rights, but he reminded the French that the United States had no treaty with the British as it did with France, "a treaty resulting from the most liberal and enlightened policy . . . stipulating the broad principle, that free ships make free goods; a treaty sanctioned with the name and guaranteed by the promise of the emperor himself 'that all its obligations should be inviolably observed.'" If the French did indeed wish better relations, he concluded, they would release all American property held in violation of existing treaties and forbid any future outrage of their provisions.[11]

Champagny responded that the emperor still regarded the principles in the treaty "as sacred," but France could not be the only country acknowledging these principles. British violations of these principles, in fact, were considered "as a new motive for union between France and America." In the column of this letter, which he forwarded to Madison, Armstrong commented sarcastically, "In the moment when they make such fine promises about maritime rights, they take care to secure a retreat from their performance. Make an alliance tomorrow," he declared, "the depredation on your property will not cease." The Danish alliance had not raised the sequestration of Danish property. He concluded that "they mean to go on with the sales of the property captured at sea or seized in the ports. This may amount to forty mill[ion]s of francs."[12]

In a separate letter he wrote Madison skeptically, "With one hand they offer us the blessings of equal alliance against Great Britain; with the other they menace us with war if we do not accept this kindness; and with both they pick our pockets with all imaginable diligence, dexterity, and impudence." He urged his government to select an enemy, but in any case "do not suspend a moment the seizure of the Floridas." A week later he wrote that Napoleon had declared to his Council that the Americans "should be compelled to take the positive character either of allies or of enemies." There had been additional confiscations of American vessels. It was clear that the emperor had taken his ground, and Armstrong added, "I cannot be wrong in concluding that you will immediately take yours."[13]

The next few months were extremely busy. Corrupt French agents condemned cargoes illegally, and American sailors were held virtual prisoners until the issue of condemnation or liberation was resolved. Armstrong was besieged with requests to do something to alleviate the plight of these unfortunate men, but there was little he could do except to ask in the name of humanity for better treatment or their release. His concerns and responsibilities extended to all of Europe. He was the only American representative of ministerial rank on the Continent. Reports of outrages flowed into him from American consuls in all parts of Europe: from Hamburg, Amsterdam, Italy, Denmark, Spain, and even from North Africa. He carried on an extensive correspondence with these consuls, and he also corresponded on a multitude of matters with many French officials, including not only Champagny and Decres, the minister of marine, but also Gaudin, the minister of finance; Regnier, the minister of justice; Fouche, the minister of police, and other minor French officials. In addition, Armstrong used other individuals from time to time to forward his views, including Talleyrand, Marbois, and Lafayette, the Dutch ambassador, Ver Huell, and the Danish minister, Baron Dreyer.

Armstrong finally received instructions from Madison around April 1, dated February 8, with an addendum of February 18, officially announcing the passage of the Embargo Act. Madison gave no explanation of why he waited two months to give notice of the enactment of the embargo. Written before he had knowledge of the Milan Decree, Madison's concern was directed at the changes portended in the French policy by the *Horizon* case. Armstrong was "to superadd," to whatever protest he may have made already, "a formal remonstrance in such terms as may be best calculated either to obtain a recall," or cause American rights to be respected. Armstrong complied by writing a formal complaint, even though he had, as he informed Madison, written at least twenty notes relating to different cases arising under them.[14]

Madison asserted that France would "be a sufferer" from the effects of the Embargo Act, and that the inconvenience felt from it might "lead to a change of . . . conduct." France did change their policy as a result of the embargo, but it was not such that Jefferson or Madison, or even Armstrong, would have predicted or desired. The embargo policy suited Napoleon, and it had the virtue of permitting him to continue to plunder American commerce. The Bayonne Decree was issued on April 17, "to seize all American vessels now in the ports of France, or which may come into them hereafter." Armstrong was informed that "no vessel of the U.S. can now navigate the seas, without infracting a law of the said States, and thus furnishing a presumption that they do so on British account, or in British connexion." He commented cynically, "This is very ingenious."[15]

Early in June, Armstrong received the notice of the American rejection of the overtures for an alliance made by the French five months earlier. The time lag in communications was painfully obvious. Perhaps because he realized these instructions might be out-dated, Madison announced that this packet of letters was being brought to Europe in an American vessel specially employed for this purpose and therefore exempt from French seizure. A special messenger, John Martin Baker, would carry any messages from William Pinkney, the minister in London, or from Armstrong back to the United States. Such a means of communication was long overdue and was infinitely preferable to the haphazard method by which the government or a minister entrusted correspondence to virtually any ship or person who might be traveling to the desired destination. Henceforth, better communications resulted, but there were still problems, such as an important event occurring a few days after the departure of a communication ship. Unforeseen problems also arose. Baker, for example, arrived in Paris penniless. Armstrong had to advance him 2880 francs, although he admitted to Madison that it was not entirely regular, but he asked, "what could I do? I could not suffer a messenger of the U.S. with a wife and three children, to starve in the streets of Paris."[16]

There is a suspicion that Armstrong's ostensible lack of communication was a primary reason for this effort by Jefferson and Madison to improve their contact with their ministers. In a private letter to Armstrong on May 2, Jefferson closed by stating, "One word of friendly request, be more frequent and full in your communications." It is difficult to understand how Jefferson arrived at this view, but he expressed it even to other correspondents.[17] The problem seems to have been delays in communication, not a lack of correspondence. For example, five letters, with several enclosures, were received from Armstrong at the State Department on March 26, one of them dating as far back as November 15. Letters apparently piled up at the docks until a passage could be found. On May 2 Madison acknowledged four more letters with an additional dozen and a half letters relating to Armstrong's correspondence with French officials. Many were long and full of information. Jefferson's complaint was thus hardly valid, and it is even more difficult to reconcile the statement of Madison's biographer that Armstrong's letters were "skimpy," due to his "habitual laziness."[18] Actually, it was Armstrong who had a right to complain of a lack of communication. In a critical six-month period from November 7 to May 2, Madison wrote Armstrong only one letter.

Armstrong reported to Madison that the emperor accepted the refusal of the proposed alliance "with at least apparent good temper." Changes, however, were taking place in Europe that would materially alter the political situation. On June 15 Napoleon's brother Joseph was crowned king of Spain. Armstrong was now informed that the United States had no right to occupy the Floridas without the knowledge and consent of the king of Spain, and his protests about the predatory seizure of American vessels were met by the irrelevant allegation that many vessels arriving in French ports were English ships flying the American flag. Armstrong admitted to Madison that this was true, but he added that many American ships were also arriving in France in violation of the Embargo Act, some even with fraudulent French papers.[19]

Armstrong could offer only one solution — military action by the United States. On July 28, in a long letter to Jefferson, he asserted that with Europe consumed in "its fires and follies," the United States had the justification and the opportunity to "make our own boundaries." Jefferson, however, had to deal with the political realities at home. Armstrong's recommendations were simply too extreme. Interestingly, Jefferson did consider for a time the possibility of capitalizing on the situation in Europe. He wrote to Madison on August 12 that "a moment may occur when we may . . . seize to our limits of Louisiana as of right, & the residue of the Floridas as reprisal for spoliations," but he added that Congress must approve. He guessed that Armstrong's advice would change when he learned of the uprising of the Spanish people against Napoleon's armies, which had occurred in May. He also expressed his irritation that Armstrong couched his recommendations "so much in the buskin, that he cannot give a naked fact in an intelligible form."[20]

Disgusted by his inability to modify French policies and beset by his old health problem of rheumatism, which had failed to respond to the waters of Rivoli, Armstrong decided in early August to take his physician's advice and visit the baths at Bourbon d'Archambault, about 150 miles from Paris. The court had been at Bayonne since April and was not expected back in Paris until autumn. Prior to leaving for the baths, however, Armstrong tried a different and interesting approach, namely that France convert their trade laws to municipal regulations. France could even require American vessels to take a return cargo equal to the value of the imports. Whether the cargo went voluntarily to England, thereby turning the balance of trade against them, or involuntarily, increasing the prospect of war between the United States and England, France's interests would be served. This was an ingenious argument, but it is probable that when Armstrong departed Paris he expected it to be ignored like so many other such appeals. There is evidence, however, that it generated a great deal of discussion among Napoleon's advisors.[21]

While at the baths Armstrong received Madison's instructions to protest the burning of American vessels "in terms which may awaken the French Government to the nature of the injury and the demands of justice." This lack of appreciation of what his minister had been doing for months must have been discouraging to Armstrong. Another letter, dated July 22, revealed how completely Madison misunderstood the true position of France. "If France does not wish to throw the United States into the war against her," he wrote, ". . . she ought not to hesitate a moment, in revoking at least so much of her decrees as violate the rights of the sea, and furnish to her adversary the pretext for his retaliating measures."[22]

Armstrong responded that it would be unwise to try any new experiments at the moment, based on the "ill success of my past endeavors, which have hitherto produced only palliations, and which have latterly failed to produce these." From the "most authentic information" he had learned that "the Emperor does not, on this subject and at this time, exercise even the small degree of patience proper to his character." Lest he be charged with refusing to comply with his instructions, he added that he did not interpret the instructions as requiring him to provoke the increased irritability of the emperor.

Two days later he wrote a long, confidential letter to Madison designed to disabuse him of his misconceptions. "We have somewhat overrated our means of coercing the two great belligerents to a course of justice," he wrote. "The Embargo is a measure calculated, above any other, to keep us whole and keep us in peace, but beyond this you must not count upon it. Here it is not felt, and in England (in the midst of the more recent & interesting events of the day) it is forgotten." Armstrong exaggerated, but his intent was to show its limitations and the error of relying upon the embargo to alter the policies of the belligerents. The emperor, he continued, would first wish for a state of war between the United States and England, but he preferred the embargo to any other policy but war.

Armstrong proposed the experiment of an armed commerce. "There is much, very much besides that we can do," he wrote, "and we ought not to omit doing all we can because (among other reasons) it is believed here, that we cannot do much, and even, that we will not do, what we have the power of doing." He concluded emotionally, "For God's sake let your measures be such, as will correct this erroneous estimate both of your power and your spirit."[23]

In the next month and a half Armstrong took a long, leisurely vacation. Leaving the baths early in September with his wife and two youngest children, Kosciuszko and Margaret, he toured through southern and eastern France. They stayed briefly at Clermont and Lyons and then journeyed on to Geneva. Armstrong was unimpressed with Lyons, which he described as "physically an interesting place & once was morally; but," he added, "who delights to look at poverty & palsy? — the two characteristics of French manufactures & commerce." He was delighted with Geneva, calling it "much the most agreeable part of France we have seen." Early in October he returned to Paris through the Champagne and Burgundy regions, "to see it in the vintage," arriving on October 14.[24]

During Armstrong's absence French officials approached Captain Nathan Haley, who was in Paris carrying messages from the United States to Armstrong, to discover how Americans would react to a policy of restriction. Haley obviously consulted Armstrong upon his return, and the two drafted a letter to Champagny, roughly following Madison's instructions to Armstrong and reiterating many of the ideas expressed earlier by Armstrong. Then almost as if he desired to prejudice his case, Armstrong sent a strong protest note on October 20 condemning the burning of American ships on the high seas. It can be presumed that he wished to make it perfectly clear to the French that any change of policy must also be accompanied by a willingness to compensate Americans for previous injuries. It was not within the purview of his instructions to ask for anything less. Besides, as he realized, events in Europe, and not words, would ultimately determine the future course of France's policies toward the United States.

Napoleon was at that moment conducting discussions with the emperor Alexander of Russia, attempting to shore up his continental system; another of the occasional offers of peace had been sent to England; and the insurrection in Spain presented great problems to Napoleon.

Because Armstrong expected further Napoleonic triumphs, he was very pessimistic. Adding to his gloom, no reply was forthcoming to his overtures through Haley, and Champagny told him that the emperor was too busy to consider American affairs. On October 25 he wrote morosely

John Armstrong, Jr., by Rembrandt Peale, ca. 1808. *Courtesy of Independence National Historical Park Collection, Philadelphia, Pennsylvania*

to Madison, "I do not longer see a public reason for keeping a minister here. Neither general law nor particular treaties have any obligation with France. If the President is of my opinion, he will recall me in the spring."[25]

Armstrong pinned his slender hopes for a change in French policy upon the Russians. Count Nicholas Romanzoff, chancellor of the Russian Empire, was in Paris late in 1808, and Armstrong attempted through Andre de Daschkoff, who had been designated as the Russian minister to the United States, then in Paris, to approach Count Romanzoff to forward American views. Daschkoff was unexpectedly noncommittal, and Armstrong enlisted his colleague William Short, who had been appointed the American minister to Russia and was also in Paris, to approach the Count directly, but this met with an equal lack of success. These initiatives failing, Armstrong surmised that "no change is to be looked for in the system adopted by *this* government."[26]

Early in 1809 Armstrong set out to enlighten his superiors on the true nature of the French policy. The embargo had proved to be a failure, politically, economically, and diplomatically. Domestic tranquility was disturbed; a fractious Federalist opposition was revived; the embargo had seriously crippled the nation's economy, and had failed to coerce the belligerents to modify their policies toward the United States. On February 16 he strongly urged the repeal of the embargo. "Has it not produced some effects at home of a character less friendly than could have been wished?" Why protect the mercantile part of the community when they were not disposed to take care of themselves? "Why annoy these gentlemen with protection?" he asked cynically. He advised throwing open the trade of the United States to all but France and Great Britain. Interestingly, Congress was debating such a measure, and on March 1 they repealed the Embargo Act and replaced it with the Non-Intercourse Act which reopened trade with all but France and England.[27]

Armstrong had always recommended an aggressive policy to his government, but he must have startled the newly elected President Madison and his new secretary of state, Robert Smith, in the spring of 1809 by recommending war with both France and England. He explained this seemingly perilous course as the only effectual way to preserve the union and secure it. A war with either nation exclusively "would paralyse half of your enemies — whereas a war with both will put into motion every drop of American blood and will be followed by many other useful consequences," including turning them to "the less profitable, but more secure and independent channels of useful manufactures." He acknowledged the audacity of his idea of "waging war with the two great Champions of the Universe at the same time and single handed," but he asserted that the war with France "would be nominal (a meer war of words and paper)," and it would gain the Floridas. War with England would be more serious, but England would be routed from Canada and Nova Scotia.[28] Neither Madison nor Smith ever responded directly to this letter. No doubt they did not take Armstrong seriously. In any event, by the time his letter had arrived an ostensible arrangement, the so-called Erskine Agreement, had been negotiated with England, which made Armstrong's recommendations appear ludicrous. Nevertheless, his argument that war would not only serve the nation's interests but also revive national spirit was one that would be heard with increasing frequency in the years ahead.

French policy slowly began to shift early in 1809 to a trade by exception (or licensing) policy. To revive their failing economy, the French offered to release the embargoed American vessels under bonds which amounted to licenses. Armstrong called it a "mere trick" and advised his consuls to urge the owners and agents not to incur the obligations. Since French laws declared that a British license denationalized ships, he protested that it was inconsistent to require a neutral to an act that subjected it to capture.[29]

News of the Non-Intercourse Act and subsequently the Erskine Agreement, apparently resolving the differences between the United States and Great Britain, caused Napoleon to further reconsider his policies. Armstrong was approached by the counsellor of state, M. d'Hauterive, who opened discussions looking toward a more favorable interpretation of France's commercial decrees toward the United States. However, when the news arrived that the British had disavowed the Erskine Agreement, the negotiations were dropped. Armstrong cynically dubbed the repudiation of the Erskine Agreement "a true specimen of modern diplomacy," and contrary to the actual fact, he believed "the late change in the Emperor's language in relation to our commerce, was a change in language only."[30] For a time he feared that the news of the Non-Intercourse Act might cause his expulsion, because it was also accompanied by the anonymous publication (probably by Federalists) of some of his letters to his government, entitled *Suppressed Documents*, which were circulated in France. It would have done much mischief, he declared to Madison, if his standing with the French government "had not been personally good." "I have no fear that anything I have said, or shall say, can be disproved," but he added meaningfully, the English doctrine of libel was also that of potentates "who have unlimited power to punish offences against it."[31]

Despite his abrasive personality, there is ample evidence to substantiate Armstrong's claim that his standing with the French government was good. He had established cordial relationships with many French officials. He had worked long and successfully with Marbois on the claims business, and the two men became good friends and the families frequently visited each other. Armstrong also established a nearly similar relationship with Talleyrand. Even when Talleyrand was no longer an official of the French government, Armstrong continued to visit him and solicit his advice. Talleyrand, it should be remembered, supported Armstrong against his colleague Bowdoin by rejecting Bowdoin's imprudent attempts to communicate unofficially with the French government. Armstrong also had friendly working relationships with Fouche, d'Hauterive, and even with Napoleon's brother Joseph.

Armstrong's pugnacious disposition, however, forbade the ingratiating obsequiousness so often practiced by diplomats. In truth, as one contemporary noted, no minister in Paris "adventured anything quite so daring in the very teeth of the tiger."[32] He insisted that the French government receive the unvarnished facts. At times he might have achieved greater success by engaging in the diplomatic game of "thrust and parry," but to Armstrong this was a waste of time. In the end it always came down to the basic facts, and he perceived, probably correctly, that "playing the game" only allowed the French to procrastinate and manipulate diplomats to their advantage.

Early in his ministry the French, as previously noted, became exasperated with Armstrong's health problems and hinted to his government that he should be replaced by a minister in better health. There is no other evidence of displeasure during these early years, and it has been noted that Fulwar Skipwith accused the French government of taking Armstrong's side in their dispute. Nevertheless, despite his belief that the French took no offense at the publication of the *Suppressed Documents*, Armstrong took the precaution of demanding his passports and detaining a communication vessel briefly on the possibility that it might cause his expulsion.

The French, however, were not particularly outraged by the Non-Intercourse Act, and they could hardly have been surprised that Armstrong harshly condemned their actions in his letters to his government, considering the tone of his letters to them. Far from asking for his expulsion, Champagny, speaking for his government, urged Armstrong to stay on as the American minister. Armstrong responded that he would "remain here 'till spring," and continue to work "to open & smooth the road between the two powers to an amicable adjustment of their differences," but he grumbled to Smith, "I would have better consulted both my own honor and that of my own government, by redemanding my passports."[33] In the months ahead Armstrong's representation of the American position severely strained his "good standing at the Court."

In the United States the publication of the *Suppressed Documents* actually disproved the Federalist charges of a pro-French bias on the part of the Jefferson Administration, and Armstrong's credit with the American people rose as a result of his vigorous letters. On the negative side, the letters no doubt gave the British assurance that no rapprochement was in the offing with France.

Late in 1809 Armstrong learned of the problems of American commerce in Holland, and being informed "by several respectable houses of commerce there that my personal application to the King might be attended by useful effects," he decided on a visit to Amsterdam. He left Paris on July 28, accompanied by his wife and sons Horatio, Henry, and Kosciuszko. Due to extremely bad weather and a leisurely pace through Antwerp, Rotterdam, and the Hague, they did not arrive in Amsterdam until August 15. Armstrong met with the minister of foreign relations, Roel, on August 18 and submitted the protest of the United States against the depredations of French cruisers off the coast of Holland. The next day he had a private audience with King Louis, Napoleon's brother. The king was sympathetic, but he informed Armstrong that there was little he could do. Privately, Armstrong told Madison that the king promised to instruct his ambassador at Paris "to make common course with us, in resisting French depredations and in endeavouring to bring about a change in the councils and conduct of his brother."[34] Armstrong returned to Paris on September 4, perhaps believing that he had secured an ally in his resistance to Napoleon's system. This did not prove to be the case, however, for within six months Napoleon had obtained Louis's pledge of submission. When that promise was broken, however, Louis was forced to abdicate and Holland was annexed to France in July 1810.

When Armstrong returned, a letter from Champagny, dated August 22, awaited him. In effect, it stated that France would not allow her allies a trade (authorized by the Non-Intercourse Act) that she may be excluded from, but if England revoked her blockading Orders, then France would withdraw her decrees.[35] Armstrong still believed the proper answer to be a war with both belligerents. In a letter to Senator Samuel Smith, the brother of Robert Smith, Armstrong asked, "How long shall we submit to this system of indignity and injustice?" He added, "Some measure of stronger character than any you have yet taken, must be adopted, or we shall become a proverb of weakness & irresolution." He expressed the same sentiments to former-President Jefferson. "It has been much doubted," he wrote, "whether it was in the nature of man, when slapped on one cheek, to turn the other to the blow? If we submit much longer," he added drily, "we shall settle the controversy, but we shall certainly not be gainers by doing so." He reminded Jefferson that he had urged war with both belligerents, and he asserted, "Every hour assures me of its correctness."[36]

During the next few months, contrary to Armstrong's expectations, there seemed to be a disposition on the part of several French officials to improve relations with the United States. He did not completely comprehend the reasons for this change of attitude but he nevertheless cooperated with them, as well as with the Dutch, Danish, and Russian representatives in seeking a modification of Napoleon's Continental System. Armstrong's exact role in this movement is unclear. There are some hints, however. On October 25, the day Napoleon arrived in Paris, Armstrong wrote Smith that he had written d'Hauterive an informal note impersonating a Frenchman, "to save appearances."[37]

Despite hints of a reevaluation of Napoleonic policies, Armstrong remained pessimistic. He was upset that Champagny's letter of August 22 was published in the Paris journals shortly after it was given to him, because it would "operate as a direct invitation to G.B. to maintain her system and to the northern powers &c. of the continent, to that of France." The French had also seized additional American ships. "How does this differ from a state of war on the part of France?" he asked disgustedly, "In nothing excepting that she permits me & others to remain here witness of her outrages."[38]

The hostility of the French system toward the Americans, as well as its inanity, Armstrong thought was revealed in an account he gave Smith on November 18. According to his information a cotton-spinner near Paris petitioned to import 600 bales of American cotton, but he was rejected. What was so extraordinary was that "Portuguese" cotton, well-known to be English, was admitted without difficulty. In early December he reported that American property in Spain was about to be declared British goods and a French agent would be the exclusive purchaser of the merchandise. He dubbed this "a specimen at once of the violence and corruption which enter into the present system."[39]

Thus two contradictory aspects of French policy were evident in the fall of 1809. On the one hand, Armstrong was aware that discussions were taking place in the French Cabinet pointing toward an amelioration of the restrictive Continental System, while on the other hand there were hints, supported by actions, that indicated an even harsher system. In fact, both forces were operating simultaneously. The emperor's inclinations preferred the latter, but there was abundant evidence that his restrictive system had a harmful effect upon the French economy and, ironically, benefited England. A modification of the system had already taken place with the use of special licenses, "to which," Armstrong informed his government, "(I am sorry to add) our countrymen lend themselves with great facility."[40]

As Armstrong noted to Smith, many in France had a vested interest in retaining the old system. The emperor did give serious consideration, however, to the admonitions of his advisers, and he instructed Champagny (now the Duc de Cadore) to draw up a report on how "to get out of the position in which we find ourselves." Unfortunately, at the very moment when the French policy was in a state of flux, Armstrong came to the conclusion that it had hardened into overt hostility toward the United States.

He was thus in a black mood when Jean-Baptiste Petry, an aide to Cadore, approached him on January 18, 1810, requesting a written memorandum stating the terms the United States required for a treaty. Armstrong undoubtedly treated this approach too lightly, for he confined his reply to two brief points, both of which were unsatisfactory to the emperor. The first point stipulated the restoration of all sequestered property; the second granted the concession that any ship, on proof that it had paid tribute to England, would be liable to confiscation, but otherwise commerce would be placed under no restraints. Napoleon had asked the terms for negotiation, not the terms for his surrender. In his most imperious manner, he denounced Armstrong's note to Cadore. "You must see the American minister," he wrote, "It is quite too ridiculous that he should write things that no one can comprehend." The note was perfectly clear, but perhaps if it had been written in Armstrong's native language, it might have been more explanatory. "I prefer him to write in English," Napoleon asserted, "but fully and in a manner we can understand. It is absurd that in affairs so important he should content himself with writing letters of four lines." He directed Cadore to send a dispatch to the French minister in the United States, Turreau, to let the American government know that it was "not represented here; that its minister does not know French; is a morose man with whom one cannot treat; that all obstacles would be raised if they had here an envoy to be talked with." He added, "Write in detail on this point."[41]

By the time this note was delivered, Armstrong was on the point of departure for home. There is no evidence that he was treated any differently in his public or private capacity, or that he realized that he had incurred the emperor's wrath. The question remains whether Armstrong's obstinate attitude, in view of the subsequent failure of the negotiations, was responsible for that failure. The issue was not Armstrong's personality, nor his lack of knowledge of French (in truth, he was more fluent than the emperor's note indicated), it was simply that any concession or moderation in policy had to be made by the French. Armstrong was tired of being asked what the United States wanted. He had long since made that clear. What disturbed the emperor was that Armstrong was unwilling to accept anything less than a restoration of American ships and cargoes, restitution for those illegally seized, and a return to free and open trade. These terms were just (in fact, Madison thought them too conciliatory), and as Armstrong said at one point in the negotiations, "a treaty, in any form, which did not provide reparation for the past, as well as security for the future, would neither be accepted by me, nor ratified by the President and Senate."[42]

The emperor, forced to choose between the loss of $6 million and the prospect for future plunder, or the improvement of relations with the United States, chose the former. Armstrong was informed on March 10 that "His Majesty has decided to sell the American property seized in Spain, but the money arising therefrom shall remain in depot." This message provoked a response, which Armstrong himself characterized as "in a temper . . . which could not be softened without encouraging the belief that we no longer dared to speak the truth."[43]

This letter, a summation of American complaints and an effective rebuttal to the untenable positions stated by Cadore, was published in full in the United States and was well received both by his government and by the American people. However, Armstrong's arguments had no impact upon Napoleon. Cadore was directed to explain that France could certainly do to the United States what they did to France. "I cannot recognize that she should arrogate the right of seizing French ships in her ports without putting herself in the case of incurring reciprocity."[44] On March 23 Napoleon signed the so-called Rambouillet Decree, which ordered the seizure and sale of all American vessels that had entered the Empire since the past May 20, 1809. By this stroke he laid his hands on several million dollars of American property and, typically, it was retroactive in its effects, was executed secretly, and was not announced until later, on May 14. Once again a reevaluation of French policies had emerged as one more step in the ever-increasing violence toward American commerce.

Armstrong wrote Madison on May 25 that the Rambouillet Decree was less the result of the Non-Intercourse Act itself than its "non-execution." Napoleon stated to Armstrong in conversation that the act had been violated openly "much to my prejudice and greatly to the advantage of British commerce." The allusion was obviously to the supposed active American participation in the British license trade. As a matter of fact, Armstrong supposed the same thing was occurring in France. Suspecting many Americans were lending themselves to the use of French licenses, Armstrong directed a young American from Boston, Leonard Jarvis, to tour the French ports seeking American violators. His final report to Armstrong on May 18, however, indicated that he could find almost no Americans involved in this trade.[45] Ironically, although many Americans were undoubtedly involved in the license trade with both the British and the French, much of the activity was actually between the belligerents themselves. Sylvanus Bourne, the U.S. consul at Amsterdam, commented on the enigmatic conduct of the two belligerents: "It has the appearance of a combination between them to our injury, for while their measures are calculated to prevent us from trading with either, they daily are in the habit of granting licenses reciprocally to trade with each other."[46]

By the summer of 1810 the French system was clearly evolving from a policy of exclusion to one of licenses. Napoleon, finally convinced that it was necessary to revive commerce and stimulate manufacturing, created a Council of Commerce, held numerous meetings, and "issued decrees and orders by dozens." He also proposed to open a limited trade to American vessels, which were to be permitted to bring certain desired products into French ports and to take out cargoes of French production of equal value.[47] It is amazing that Napoleon, after announcing his Rambouillet Decree seizing all American vessels touching the ports under his control, could conceive that Americans might be enticed to enter his ports again under special licenses. Undoubtedly, he believed they would, and Armstrong apparently also believed some American merchants would place their interests above their country's.

Early in July Armstrong received an English newspaper that published a copy of the so-called Macon's Bill No. 2, passed by Congress on May 1, repealing the Non-Intercourse Act and removing all restrictions on American trade. There was a proviso that if either England or France revoked their measures violating neutral rights, the United States would reimpose non-intercourse against the other offending nation. Although this was unofficial, Armstrong submitted it to Cadore, who replied that the notice being unofficial, it could not become the basis for any government proceeding. Armstrong failed to see the potential of this measure and the consternation it caused in the French government. He recognized that removal of the restrictions was favorable to England, but he believed the consequences would be to give the Rambouillet Decree "full scope & activity" and "invite new or prolong old aggressions." Only time would tell, and he advised Smith, "We must therefore resort to patience, the only remedy in incurable cases."[48]

In fact, Macon's Bill No. 2 was an abdication of the effort to maintain neutral rights. The prospect was that American merchants would simply follow the path of least resistance, conform to the British measures, and abandon efforts to trade with France, especially in view of the predatory Rambouillet Decree. Obviously a new strategy was called for, and Napoleon, in the midst of altering his system to revive French industry, was faced with only two practical alternatives. He could give up his Berlin and Milan decrees and readmit American trade, or he could pretend to give them up and attempt to maintain his licensing system. The third option of taking further retaliatory measures, as Armstrong anticipated, was clearly unwise.

Again, however, as during the earlier negotiations, Armstrong infuriated Napoleon by refusing to give him the slightest room for maneuvering. He denounced the French proposals for a licensing of American trade, and he refused to discuss the Macon's Bill No. 2 until he received instructions from his government and an official copy of the law, which was not until early August. He had received no instructions since early January, those of December 1, 1809. The "patience" exhibited by Armstrong was incomprehensible to the emperor, who was anxious to sound the terms of the Americans but was met with silence instead.

The imperial wrath was aroused again. Napoleon instructed Cadore to write the French ambassador at St. Petersburg to tell the American minister, John Quincy Adams (who had been chosen minister when Short was not confirmed by the Senate), "that we have here an American minister who says nothing; that we need an active man whom one can comprehend, and by whose means we could come to an understanding with the Americans." Adams was duly informed. He was told "they did not impeach his integrity; but he was morose, and captious, and petulant." They also complained that "he never shows himself; and upon every little occasion, when by a verbal explanation with the minister he might obtain anything, he presents peevish notes." It was implied that relations between the United States and France would improve if someone else represented the United States in Paris. Adams passed off these complaints. Armstrong's offense, he declared, "is omitting to go to Court, and presenting notes too full of truth and energy for the taste of the Emperor Napoleon."[49]

Faced with the stony silence from Armstrong, and stimulated by rumors reaching Paris on July 27 that the United States Congress had been called into special session, possibly to declare war on France, Napoleon decided to act anyway. A letter was drafted and, with corrections by the emperor, was presented to Armstrong bearing the date of August 5. This document, famous as the Cadore Letter, announced that the Berlin and

Milan decrees would cease to have effect after November 1, "it being understood that, in consequence of this declaration, the English shall revoke their orders in council, and renounce the new principles of blockade, which they have wished to establish; or that the United States, conformably to the act you have just communicated, shall cause their rights to be respected by the English."[50]

Despite the vague phraseology, there was no doubt in Armstrong's mind that this letter announced a significant victory for American diplomacy, and it confirmed the correctness of his advice so frequently given to his government. He wrote Madison privately that the change was due to reports that reached Paris on July 27 that Congress had been called into extra session for the purpose of declaring war on France. It created a great excitement, he related, and he was asked repeatedly if the report was true. His response, perhaps hopeful, was that the report was probably true. "To these circumstances, light as they appear, is owing the revocation." It proved that France did not want war with the United States, and having followed a policy that lost character, money, and impoverished her people, "she would now return to a degree of justice, moderation and good sense." He warned, however, that he feared France would "content herself by coming within the mere letter of your law & instructions. That is — she will revoke her decrees, and make her seizures a subject of future negotiations." Whether this Cadore Letter was sufficient for Madison to fulfill the provisions of the Macon Bill No. 2 was for the president to decide. He also reported that the Council of Commerce was on the verge of adopting new tariff duties of not less than 50 percent of the marked price of the article. He had suggested to French officials that this would discourage rather than encourage trade, and worse, would lead to smuggling. Nevertheless, the Trianon Decree was adopted. Armstrong added that the licensing system would continue and that he had no hope for any changes.[51]

After forwarding the official copy of the Act of May 1 on August 8, Armstrong did not address a single note to the French government in the next twelve days. Puzzled by his silence prior to the Cadore Letter, they were now just as mystified by his lack of response after the letter. Cadore assumed that Armstrong did not wish to open before his departure "those difficult questions which he forsees must rise between the two governments, in order to arrive in America without having seen the fading of the glory he attaches to having obtained the Note of August 5."[52]

Many historians have agreed with Cadore — which judgment, of course, accepts as fact that Armstrong did foresee the difficulties and, thus, attributes a certain deviousness to his actions. However, it is just as probable that Armstrong was simply waiting for the other shoe to drop.

The Cadore Letter announcing the repeal of the Berlin and Milan decrees was unanticipated and arose from unknown motives that Armstrong could only ascribe to a desire for peace with the United States. Perhaps he was waiting a decent interval to see whether the further concession of a restoration of American property would be forthcoming. Then came Napoleon's birthday (August 15), which was treated as a national holiday, and no business was transacted during this week. No further magnanimous gesture was indicated to Armstrong at the diplomatic audience. Instead, Napoleon declared that American cannon should talk if England did not follow his example and repeal her orders in council.[53]

Accordingly, on the following Monday morning, August 20, Armstrong wrote Cadore two letters, one protesting the attacks of French privateers upon American commerce, and the other asking for "a full explicit and written declaration" of the treatment American commerce was "destined to meet in the ports of France &c. both *before* and *after* the 1st of November next, and whether the seizures in Spain are to be regarded simply as sequestrations (and open of course, to future negotiation) or as confiscations, and beyond the limits of compromise?" "I am sorry . . .," he wrote Secretary of State Smith, "that there does not yet appear to be the smallest disposition to make reparation for the past wrongs, tho' they are careful to employ terms, which do not exclude the hopes that some reparation may be made." This definitely implies that he had communicated verbally with French officials on this subject. It is thus difficult to reconcile his activities with Henry Adams's summary: "he wrote home no report of any conference with Cadore, he expressed no opinion as to the faith of the Emperor's promise, made no further protest against the actual reprisals, and required no indemnity for past spoliations."[54]

In fact, Armstrong expressed doubts about the fulfillment of the emperor's promise and even suggested a possible postponement of the implementation of the provisions of Macon's Bill No. 2; he fully informed his government of the details of the tariff policy in the Trianon Decree, and sent a copy of the decree; he indicated that the licensing system would continue; he sought clarification of the status of American commerce after the Cadore Letter; and, while offering little hope, he suggested a solution to the problem of reparations. All of these facts were available to Madison before he issued his proclamation of November 2 instituting non-intercourse with England. These facts hardly sustain the statement of Madison's biographer that "Armstrong's delay forced the President to make his first basic decision in the dark, with misleading indications of French policy before him."

In truth, these letters from Armstrong arrived only one day before the issuance of the proclamation, owing not to Armstrong's inaction but rather to French red tape and lagging communications.⁵⁵ Immediately upon receiving the letter from Cadore, Armstrong sent two copies of the letter to Pinkney in London and a third, with some details, "*directly* in a fast sailing schooner by M. Jarvis." Unfortunately, Leonard Jarvis's ship, the *Spencer*, was held up by a succession of difficulties at Bayonne, including, it was reported, abnormally low tides. As a consequence, Jarvis did not land in New York City until October 30, and he arrived in Washington late in the evening of November 1. The nearly simultaneous arrival of Jarvis and the packet of letters on the *Hornet* still offered Madison the opportunity to stay the issuance of the proclamation but, significantly, he did not.⁵⁶ The historian, Roger H. Brown, has argued that Madison saw the opportunity in these circumstances "to produce concessions from Great Britain, [and thus] the United States would no longer be confronted with the alternatives of war with both belligerents or submission."⁵⁷ If that is true, and it is certainly plausible, then Armstrong's actions one way or the other made little difference.

On the other hand, Armstrong did not press for a clarification of the qualification expressed in the Cadore Letter: "it being understood (bien entendu)." It became a crucial question whether this was an actual or conditional repeal of the Berlin and Milan decrees. Madison's proclamation presumed the actual repeal, but his opponents charged the conditions were precedent and cited evidence of continued French violations of neutral rights. Armstrong obviously saw that the letter could be read either way, but he chose to believe that France was offering the Americans a diplomatic weapon to use against the British and that it would be unwise to press for a clarification. Thus he assured Pinkney on September 29 that the conditions were not dependent on the actions of the British, but offered the alternative of action by the United States. "It necessarily follows," he wrote, "that the conditions are not *precedent*, as has been supposed, but *subsequent*, as I represent them." He sent this letter to Jonathan Russell, the charge d'affaires, to forward to Pinkney, and explained, "Whatever you and I may think and say to our government, we ought, as I believe to impress both this government and that of England, with a belief, that we repose full confidence in the promises made to us by the Emperor and of course, that we count certainly on the extinction of his offensive decrees and of all Executive and other measures growing out of them, after the first day of November next." He added confidentially, "With this rule in your eye you will read and understand my letter to P." He hoped that Pinkney would press this distinction of the Cadore Letter with that of the statement by Lord Wellesley that England would withdraw their orders only upon proof that the French decrees were repealed and neutral commerce was restored to complete freedom.[58] Thus Armstrong's failure to press for a clarification was based upon the belief that the United States must presume the fulfillment of the pledge and maintain that posture to both the French and the British. If Madison later came to this same conclusion, then Armstrong's position was not only prescient but also useful.

Armstrong spent his last days in Paris seeking clarification of French intentions. He warned his government about being too sanguine. "By the way, " he wrote Smith on September 10, "the system of which these decrees make a part, is fast recovering the ground, it had lost, & I should not be astonished, were it soon to become as great a favorite as formerly."[59] This sounded like the old, familiar refrain, and it was. Finally, on September 15, leaving Jonathan Russell in charge of the legation, Armstrong left Paris with his family. Ten days later he arrived at Bordeaux to await passage on the ship *Sally* for his return to the United States.

7

RETURN TO POLITICS

BEFORE HE LEFT FRANCE, Armstrong became involved in one more of his seemingly endless controversies. This involved his former personal secretary, David Bailie Warden. Due to problems in getting his citizenship papers, Warden did not arrive in Paris until late 1805 or early 1806. During this period before Warden's arrival, Armstrong employed Nicholas Biddle, the son of an old Philadelphia friend, Charles Biddle, as his secretary. Young Nicholas served faithfully for a year and then departed on a grand tour of Europe.[1]

Warden was a closer family friend, and although he did not serve as a tutor for the Armstrong children, he did watch carefully over their academic progress. His differences with Armstrong arose out of his desire to fill the positions of consul and agent for prize cases after Skipwith's dismissal in 1807. Somewhat surprisingly, Armstrong did not favor the pretensions of Warden as Skipwith's replacement. He explained to Jefferson in July 1808, "My poor friend Warden writes to you and asks you for the appointment of consul for this place. I could not promise to do more than send his letter. He is an honest and amiable man, with as much greek and latin and chymistry and theology, as would do for the whole corps of consuls—but after all, not well qualified for business." He suggested that "the man for this place ought to be a man of business, as well as a gentleman."[2]

This letter smacked of snobbery, and indeed it must have been difficult for Armstrong to accept the idea of a mere secretary and a resident of his household as a semi-independent American official. Nevertheless, he did appoint Warden to the positions temporarily. Warden quickly tangled with Isaac Cox Barnet, who refused to turn over the registers of the consulate office on the grounds that they were given to him in his private capacity by Skipwith, and he would not return them unless Skipwith told him to do so. Armstrong's opinion of Barnet was expressed contemptuously to Madison in November 1807: "This man really has not sense enough to feed turkies." He suspended Barnet from his duties as consul at Havre on June 3, 1809, and wrote to Smith to explain that the cause arose not only from the withholding of the Registers, but also because Barnet was in the habit of giving passports out of his own district in direct contradiction of Armstrong's orders. Barnet in turn claimed that he acted out of his consulate to secure the release of American prisoners because Armstrong was not doing his job.[3]

The Federalist press in the United States picked up this issue, and William Coleman in particular attacked Armstrong in the columns of the New York *Evening Post* for not making an effort to release American prisoners in France. Warden, in Armstrong's defense, responded in the columns of William Duane's Philadelphia *Aurora* refuting the charges. For his efforts, Warden was denounced by the Federalists as a tool of Armstrong, a "vagrant preacher," and a "zealot attached to French politics."[4]

Armstrong could not have been displeased by Warden's defense, and he exhibited a confidence in him by leaving him in charge of the legation in 1808 during his absence of nearly two months and again for three weeks in 1809 while he was in Holland. But the relationship cooled in the spring of 1810 when Warden learned that Armstrong had recommended against his permanent appointment as consul. Although he was "not yet an open enemy," Armstrong wrote Madison, "[he] soon will become such. This I regret because in discharging what I believed to be my duty to the public, I did not intend to injure Mr. W." He added, "The injury if there was any . . . was incidental, and not to be avoided but at the expense of a duty to the state." He stated that he was pleased to learn that Jonathan Russell had been chosen to replace Warden.[5]

Warden admitted later that he was hurt at losing his place. He also believed he had qualifications superior to Russell's. Armstrong offered Warden appointments at Havre or Bordeaux, but these he declined as inferior positions. Armstrong then offered to procure him an appointment in South America. Warden accepted and prepared to return to the United States with Armstrong. However, when Russell arrived in Paris late in August 1810 it was announced that he would become charge d'affaires, and Warden asked to be retained in his position at least until the next spring.

Armstrong, however, learning of charges made by Warden against him to an American in Paris named Seth Hunt, challenged him to state whether he had any charges to make relating to either Armstrong's private morals or public duty. If not, then he demanded a statement to that effect. Warden replied at length, denying the statements attributed to him; but Armstrong had asked for an explicit denial, and he repeated his demand. Warden responded that he could not censure Armstrong's private conduct and, he continued, "With your ministerial acts I have nothing to do, except those which may regard me in my present delicate situation." He asserted that he had the means to protect himself, but "unless you become my enemy, I cannot be yours." He expressed the desire to preserve their friendship, and added that if Armstrong gave his, then Warden would gladly reciprocate, and the support of his friends would be given also.[6]

Armstrong interpreted this letter as tantamount to blackmail and decided to replace Warden immediately. Ironically, in casting about for a successor he selected a friend of James Monroe, Alexander McRae, who had only recently arrived in Paris armed with a letter of introduction from Thomas Jefferson. McRae soon clashed with Warden, when Warden delayed turning over the books and documents of the consular office. Even when he did, McRae accused him of failing to give up the papers relating to prize cases.[7] This was the situation when Armstrong left Paris. Perhaps this controversy could have been avoided, for there was seemingly no principle involved. Rather, the dispute was the outgrowth of Armstrong's belief that Warden was simply not competent for the job, and Warden's conviction that he was. It seems evident that Armstrong provoked the final split in order to justify replacing Warden.

Armstrong's career in France thus ended the way it began. From the *New Jersey* case to the Warden affair, he had been almost continuously engaged in controversy. Obviously, his duties involved more controversy than most diplomatic posts would — and he undoubtedly met with more adventurers, speculators, and unscrupulous men than was the lot of most ministers — but it does seem that he almost invited assaults upon his character. Certainly, some attacks during the *New Jersey* affair, particularly Randolph's assault, were unprovoked and unwarranted. But in his feuds with Skipwith, Bowdoin, Barnet, and Warden, his stubborn refusal to yield or to give any quarter only invited prolongation of such disputes. Armstrong lacked to a great degree any spirit of conciliation or toleration of the faults of others. As such, he fell short as a person, and as a consequence, he severely limited the potential of his career.

Before departing for America, Armstrong exercised himself to harass an old enemy — at least in the opinion of Aaron Burr, who had arrived in Paris in February 1810 to peddle his scheme for the separation of the western states from the United States. Finding the French government uninterested, he was still detained by a mysterious failure to receive permission to leave the Empire. Describing himself as a "prisoner," Burr laid the blame on the machinations of Armstrong, "who has been, and still is, indefatigable in his exertions to my prejudice; goaded on by personal hatred, by political rancour, and by the natural malevolence of his temper."

There is evidence to verify Burr's belief. Armstrong was reasonably certain that Burr would make a presentation to the emperor and that he would be able to gain access to the document. "No man is weaker in the choice of his friends and confidants," he told Smith. By his own admission, Armstrong warned Fouche against Burr. Later, he noted with some relief that Burr's memorial to the emperor "displays no marks of talent and is far from possessing the degree of plausibility of which the subject is susceptible." When Armstrong departed for America, Burr was still languishing in Paris.[8]

Armstrong left France satisfied that he had performed his duties to the best of his abilities. The news of the Cadore Letter preceded him and he considered that greatly to his credit. Moreover, he had learned from several sources that his strong letters to the French government defending American neutral rights had been well-received in the United States, and one correspondent even suggested that he would be chosen governor of Pennsylvania.[9]

After being delayed in Bordeaux for nearly three weeks due to the tax troubles of his ship, Armstrong and his family finally sailed for the United States in mid-October. The passage, as he described it, "was short, but boisterous — 31 days from land to land." Left unsaid was the frightening experience that occurred at their first landfall near New London, Connecticut. The *Sally* in a gale struck a reef off Montauk Point. William Lee, the consul at Bordeaux, who accompanied the Armstrongs back to the United States, reported the vessel "beat over the reef into deep water, with the loss of her rudder only, but lay the whole night afterward in a most perilous situation, expecting every moment to go to perdition."[10]

When the Armstrongs arrived in New York City, his reception, as he told Russell, was "highly flattering." "I am a great favorite with both parties," he continued, but he added, "This cannot from its own nature, be of much duration." Two days later, Armstrong was honored by a dinner with Governor Daniel D. Tompkins, and that evening when they attended a play, the audience greeted Armstrong with "three cheers and three claps."[11] Such a welcome was undoubtedly extremely pleasing to Armstrong, unaccustomed as he was to receiving adulation in any form. From Philadelphia came even more flattering news. One correspondent urged him to move to Pennsylvania and run for governor, assuring him that there would be no problem on the point of eligibility and that he would be supported "by a great and overbearing interest." Another asserted that while some were for making Armstrong governor, he was for making him president of the United States. Yet another announced that the prominent citizens of Philadelphia were planning a public dinner for him when he visited that city on his way to Washington.[12]

Armstrong was thus confronted with some very enticing possibilities. His natural inclination was to return to the pastoral serenity of farm life, but the lure of ambition and high—perhaps the highest—office pulled in the opposite direction. "Our future destiny is not, as you know, in our keeping," he wrote his brother-in-law Chancellor Livingston, "What mine may be is very doubtful." He had written William Short, however, that he was coming to Philadelphia for the purpose of possibly establishing himself there, "for I am really sick of the unsettled life I have latterly led."[13] This suggested that he had an interest in claiming the governorship of Pennsylvania.

Armstrong arrived in Philadelphia on December 9. "Nothing can exceed the cordiality with which I have been received here by all parties," he wrote Alida, "They no doubt have overrated my services, but I cannot overrate their politeness & friendship." The *Aurora* reported that a "sumptuous entertainment" was given, and the dinner was attended by a "very large and respected assemblage of citizens." It was particularly noted that the gathering included an equal number of gentlemen "who have too long been habituated to regard each other as political opponents, [but] they all appeared on this happy occasion to bury in oblivion, past differences of opinion." The dinner was presided over by the old revolutionary patriot, George Clymer. The guests drank "with honest enthusiasm" seventeen toasts, plus several more volunteers, including one to "General Armstrong and the spirit of the late mission to France."[14]

From Philadelphia, Armstrong journeyed to Baltimore and again he was given "a public & very splendid entertainment." He arrived in Washington on December 20. He reported to Alida that he was treated very civilly both by the president and his ministers, and he commented that the president's wife, Dolley, was a charming hostess. "She plays her part very graciously & very well." His most important objective was to settle his accounts, including a claim for an additional $9000 for services in settling the claims relating to the Louisiana Treaty and for his negotiations with Spain. The Chancellor's and Monroe's were not yet settled, and he was determined to attend to his business until it was finished; a duty which occupied him until January 24, 1811.

The Warden controversy marred what was otherwise a heady and triumphant return to America. Warden arrived in Washington before Armstrong, and he made a powerful impression. He had very shrewdly called upon Jefferson at Monticello, who was moved to take up his pen in Warden's defense. "He is a perfectly good humored, inoffensive man, a man of science & I observe a great favorite of those in Paris, and much more a man of business than Armstrong had represented him," Jefferson wrote Madison. He hoped Madison would find some post for him.[16]

Madison did not press Armstrong for the particulars of the Warden affair, and Armstrong made no effort to prejudice any of his senatorial friends against Warden. Rather, he was urging the appointment of Russell as his successor and presumably did not consider the Warden business worth his attention. Only belatedly did he comprehend that Madison was seriously considering reinstating Warden. When Madison informed Armstrong of this fact, it brought a prompt and indignant response from Armstrong. He characterized Warden as "an imposter in everything, and as deficient in capacity, as he is in fidelity." Madison and other respectable men might think favorably of Warden's character, but Armstrong asked, "Who . . . can know his character and habits better than myself? With me he has lived nearly eight years in an intercourse of daily business — six of these under my roof and at my table, and I scruple not to declare it as my solemn conviction, that he is unworthy of both public and private trust." He accused Warden of scattering an "abundance of falsehoods." There must be numerous native born citizens willing to fill the consulate at Paris, he contended, and if not, he wrote, "God help us, for our national intellect must in that case be smitten with barrenness." In conclusion, he pointed out to Madison the essential issue: "if Mr. Warden be reinstated, you pass an indirect censure on my conduct in removing him, and, of course, impose upon me the necessity of shewing the grounds on which I acted."[17]

Such a threat was not to be taken lightly. The initial enthusiasm that had greeted Armstrong's return had waned somewhat, but he was still popular. There was no identifiable core of Armstrong followers, but Madison could hardly overlook the receptions accorded Armstrong in New York City, Philadelphia, and Baltimore. Superficially, there was little to be gained by reappointing Warden. Madison had never even met him before, while as secretary of state he had directed Armstrong's activities and had continued him as the minister to France. By reappointing Warden, as Armstrong noted, Madison would repudiate his own representative and to some extent reproach his own Administration.

It seems likely that this was a politically motivated decision. Warden's reappointment was approved unanimously in the Senate. Such remarkable support for a minor official barely known to the vast majority, repudiating the actions of the minister who had represented American interests in France for six years, would seem to indicate that the Administration took the precaution to line up the party in support of their decision. Undoubtedly it was a slap at Armstrong, and Warden was only a pawn in the game. Armstrong's sudden emergence as a potential governor of Pennsylvania, or as a vice-presidential candidate, was no doubt disconcerting to Madison and Gallatin and other party leaders. James Wilkinson, who was in Washington at this time, wrote to a friend predicting that "Armstrong may take the White House this time two years if things are well managed." The Warden incident was well-calculated to curb Armstrong's political ambitions. Armstrong recognized by early March 1811 that he had fallen from grace. He wrote Russell, "What I recommend, is not done, & what I disapprove, is certainly done. Such is my standing with the Court."[18]

Madison and the other party leaders perhaps counted on Armstrong's peculiar personality and reputation for disputation to offset any charges that he might make against the Administration, and they may even have welcomed such an attack. One is reminded of the statement made by Gallatin several years earlier that "there is something which will forever prevent him having any direct influence with the people." Gallatin was personally an enemy of Armstrong, whose popularity with the Duane faction in Pennsylvania and the Smith faction in Maryland, Gallatin's particular enemies, would tend to explain the Administration's hostility toward Armstrong.

Madison informed Jefferson that he had no doubts that "the ground on which we stand is sufficiently firm to support us with the nation, ag[ain]st individual efforts of any sort or from any quarter." Jefferson replied that Armstrong was "cynical & irritable & implacable. Whether his temper or his views induced his dismission of Warden, his persecution of him now will render public benefit by the development of his character." He was certain the public would approve of the appointment. Madison responded that Armstrong had "entangled himself in such gross inconsistencies," that he might not execute his threat to vindicate himself.[19]

Whether this was the actual reason or not, and it seems unlikely, Armstrong wisely chose not to engage in a pamphlet war with the Administration. He had been approached by the anti-Administration leaders soliciting his support. The Duane faction, the Smiths of Maryland (Robert and Samuel), and the Clinton forces in New York all sought his adherence to their cause. Armstrong was certainly hostile to the Virginia domination of the Republican party, but he always believed that schism would only strengthen the southern control over the party. He did not encourage their separatist tendencies. Undoubtedly, he felt betrayed by Madison, for he had always believed that he had loyally and faithfully executed the wishes of the Jefferson and Madison administrations.[20]

In the fall of 1811 Armstrong purchased a farm along the Hudson River, about three miles south of his old farm at Mill Hill. His new estate of approximately 728 acres had a large front on the river, and here he planned to build another fine mansion. He christened his new farm, "La Bergerie," a French term meaning "sheep walk" or "sheep-fold," a whimsical play upon the fact that he had brought Merino sheep from France and intended to raise them on his farm. He wrote to one correspondent jestingly, "I hope this will not be considered a proof of French influence."[21]

Armstrong's return to farming did not dull his active interest in politics. He resumed his correspondence with Ambrose Spencer who, although a judge on the New York Supreme Court, was quite active and an influential force in New York politics. Armstrong was still an advocate of war and he complained to Spencer in 1811 that Napoleon had undone all of the arrangements of the past August. There was not spirit enough in the government or the nation to employ war as the remedy, he lamented, "We are a nation of Quakers, without either their morals, or their motives." When the Federalists in the Twelfth Congress appeared to support Republican war measures, Armstrong wrote one correspondent, "This course is certainly the true one for the Feds and they behave like idiots, when they oppose or obstruct it. A war will give them another chance of ascendancy and I know not anything else that will do so."[22]

Armstrong was disappointed when James Monroe replaced Robert Smith as Secretary of State, a step many considered preliminary to Monroe's succession to the Presidency. Neither the western, middle, or northern states, Armstrong argued, would consent to take a third consecutive president from Virginia, and he hoped Virginia herself would take steps to prevent this from happening. Whether his concern about the perpetuation of the Virginia dynasty was expressed because of a latent ambition for the presidency is conjectural. There were others in New York besides himself who had even stronger ambitions, among them De Witt Clinton and Daniel D. Tompkins. It was rumored in the spring of 1811 that Tompkins would go to the War Department, "with a reversion of the presidency, when Monro [sic] and Madison have done with it," but Armstrong doubted whether Tompkins would "lend himself as a crutch to this tottering edifice . . . I think better both of his patriotism & wisdom. He cannot enlist as a Virginia Satrap."[23] The rumor was unfounded, but Armstrong remained skeptical of the statesmanship of the two Virginians. The only war looming on the horizon, he believed, would be "with the red man of the West and with them there must be war for various reasons, one of which is however abundantly sufficient, viz. an increased western influence." The spread of territorial governments would allow Virginia to "furnish governors pro-tem & leaders in future & thus everything will go well at home." Spencer agreed, and on one occasion in the spring of 1812 he wrote, "That you are a much injured man, I know & I have uniformly expressed my opinion that there was great blame in the President, in not availing himself of your talents at a time like the present. The policy at Washington," he continued, "is governed by mean & paltry motives — they are jealous of you & may little men be always so."[24]

The preparations for war by the national government in the spring of 1812 gave Armstrong some hope, and they had a direct impact upon his family. His second son, Henry, was appointed a captain. Armstrong approved, but he urged Horatio in vain to refuse a commission "to study politics & our politicians." He lamented "the decaying strength of republicanism throughout the country," and he was alarmed by De Witt Clinton's ambition to oppose Madison in the forthcoming presidential election. "The effect will be to perpetuate, not to put down, the policy of the South," he wrote Spencer, and New York would be placed "in the light of Burr's faction." The way to put a Northerner in the presidency was to adopt the practices of the Southerners by placing able representatives in Congress, moving with the rise and fall of public sentiment, and combatting their opponents by increasing their own strength. Lest he be characterized as a schismatic, Armstrong consented to allow Spencer to commend him for a position in the army, but he added, "Your discretion must . . . be well exercised & there must be no defeat."[25] Shortly thereafter he received a discreet "feeler" from Secretary of War William Eustis, undoubtedly with Madison's approval. Armstrong made it clear in reply that he would accept nothing less than a separate command, which he thought not unreasonable, for he pointed out that Generals Hull, Bloomfield, and Pinckney all held ranks inferior to his during the Revolutionary War. Governor Tompkins resolved the problem by suggesting to the influential congressman from New York, Peter B. Porter, that Armstrong be appointed to command the defenses of the Port of New York and her dependencies. He was assured that Armstrong would accept such a command if it were independent. Accordingly, on July 7, the secretary of war informed Armstrong of his appointment as brigadier general in the regular army, and on July 20, he was assigned the defense of New York harbor.[26]

Armstrong's desire for the position was based less on ambition than his sincere conviction that the country must be supported in time of war, for Congress had declared war upon Great Britain on June 18. His acceptance of a commission disappointed the anti-Administration faction headed by De Witt Clinton, who charged he had been "bought off." The rift between Clinton and Armstrong was followed by a split between Clinton and Spencer, who was Clinton's brother-in-law. Spencer was angered by Clinton's acceptance of Federalist support. One of these supporters, Solomon Southwick, the editor of the Federalist Albany *Register*, launched an attack upon Armstrong, claiming he had intrigued for public office. Armstrong replied that "Those which have been conferred upon me . . . have been spontaneously given." He also denied that he had ever written or printed any censure against Madison or his Administration.[27]

Armstrong's rebuttal was hardly a model of candor, but his sincerity and support for his cause was shown in a private letter to William Duane. Because of his hatred of Gallatin, Duane had threatened to support Clinton if Gallatin was not dropped as secretary of the treasury. Armstrong warned Duane that he must not become an agent for the policies of the Federalists and the Clinton faction. "I neither did nor could hesitate," he wrote, "I rejected their overtures, and have once more taken the field in support of principles, which are, I hope, common to us both." He added that "there will be a fair expression of the republican sentiment at the next session of the Legislature, and that this will be decidedly against any man or any measure, whose policy identifies itself with that of federalists and federalism."[28]

During the campaign, Spencer produced a ten-page pamphlet attacking Clinton. The last two pages of the pamphlet, entitled "The Coalition," were contributed by Armstrong, identified as "a man of the most distinguished talents, services and probity." Armstrong's assault was savage. He accused Clinton of "learning from an enemy," meaning Burr, who instead of modestly and patiently waiting for the call of his country "must precipitate that event by artifice and intrigue." He asserted that Clinton was surrounded by "sycophants and tools. . . . To this shrine repair pilgrims of every political sect and description, and all are equally welcome. They form together the brotherhood of Hope, and the only test of communion is submission to his will, and the belief in his infallibility." He closed uncharitably, "Nor are his private better than his public morals. The rubrick of his face shows the nature of his religion and the deity he worships."[29] Despite Spencer's and Armstrong's efforts, New York was carried by Clinton in the election of 1812.

Armstrong assumed his new duties in New York City late in July. A little while later he published a short (71 pages) book entitled *Hints to Young Generals*, signed pseudonymously, "By an Old Soldier." More than a mere handbook, it compressed a great deal of useful information on strategy and tactics with rules and principles both for offensive and defensive operations. Armstrong borrowed liberally from the writings of the eminent French military thinker, Major General Antoine H. Jomini, whose first book was published in 1804. He thus helped to introduce the concepts of Jomini, whose ideas influenced American military thought for the next fifty years. In particular, Armstrong emphasized concentration of forces upon a point, a rule that he and other American generals did not always follow. Armstrong was pleased with its reception, and he noted to Alida that "This work did not employ me above 3 or four days."[30]

Armstrong's conduct of the defense of New York harbor displayed a certain vigor, but his recruiting policies soon brought anguished cries from Gallatin, who complained to acting Secretary of War Monroe early in December 1812 that Armstrong's plan for 5000 volunteers for the defense of New York to be in constant pay was unnecessary and all out of proportion to other objects, and his plan of raising volunteers for the local service would destroy the recruiting service.[31]

Armstrong's lavish hand was stayed, but his activities at least showed some energy and did not escape notice. With the reverses suffered by the American army in the fall of 1812, particularly the fall of Detroit and the failures on the Niagara frontier, his name was prominently mentioned to command on the northern frontier in the place of General Henry Dearborn. When William Eustis resigned as secretary of war in the face of mounting congressional pressure on December 3, 1812, Armstrong was also mentioned for that post. Despite his support for Madison in the recent election, Armstrong's background of political enmity against the Virginians and his well-known ill-tempered disposition did not appear at first to favor his selection. In the end it fell to him almost by default. William Crawford and Henry Dearborn declined. Monroe was assigned the post temporarily, but he refused to take it permanently because he desired a military command, and according to Gallatin, because of "its horrors and perils."[32] Governor Tompkins of New York was considered, but objections were raised to his lack of military knowledge. Gallatin offered to take the post himself rather than give it to Tompkins. Reluctantly, Madison was forced to consider Armstrong, who at least possessed the qualifications of military knowledge and experience. Also having a New Yorker in the Cabinet would help secure the support of that important state. Monroe objected to Armstrong's appointment, but he promised to "harmonize with him to support the Administration," and Gallatin indicated that he was willing to work with Armstrong. Armstrong's appointment was urged by many public figures. Richard Rush, for example, asserted that "General A. is, as things stand, our very best man for the war office . . . All agree he has genius and energy."[33] Armstrong's strategic ideas of concentration of effort were generally acceptable to the Administration, and he had shown vigor in his command of the defense of the Port of New York. Years later Madison explained his reasons for appointing Armstrong:

> It was not unknown at the time that objections existed to . . . [Armstrong] as appeared when his nomination went to the Senate, where it received the reluctant sanction of a scant majority. Nor was the President unaware or unwarned of the temper and turn of mind ascribed to him which might be uncongenial with the official relations in which he was to stand. But these considerations were sacrificed to recommendations from esteemed friends; a belief that he possessed, with known talents, a degree of military information which might be useful; and a hope that a proper mixture of conciliating confidence and interposing control would render objectionable peculiarities less in practice than in prospect.[34]

Madison offered the position to Armstrong on January 14, 1813, and Armstrong quickly accepted. However, he was confirmed by the Senate only with difficulty by the narrow margin of 18 to 15. He was attacked not on grounds of competency, but rather on old charges of favoritism in settling American claims against France and his authorship of the Newburgh Addresses. The appointments of Armstrong and William Jones, who was chosen Secretary of the Navy at the same time, were greeted with general public approval.[35]

Armstrong certainly realized the pitfalls of the War Department, for he informed Spencer, "The office to which I am destined is full of drudgery & environed by perils. If the results of its management be fortunate, there will be little praise, and if unfortunate, extreme censure." He also knew that the Cabinet was filled with men who hated him, and he was undoubtedly aware that Madison had selected him of necessity and not by choice. He had no illusions about his prospects. "I have to execute other men's plans and fight with other men's weapons," he wrote Spencer. He went into the War Department "reluctantly and with diffidence, and purely to exert whatever knowledge and talent I possess, to rescue our arms from their present fallen condition." He noted that already he was being assailed "by personal & by party malevolence," alluding to the attacks upon the Newburgh Addresses, "which it seems my enemies will not permit to sleep." Spencer replied, "I was perfectly apprised that nothing but a conviction of the necessity, would have induced you to accept an office of such complicated duties, so deranged, so sunk, as is the war office." He added, however, "I differ with you as to the result, & I cannot but believe that you will retrieve our affairs & pluck our drowning honor from the deep—in which case the gratitude of your country will reward you for all your toil & labours."[36]

Jefferson also congratulated Armstrong. "Whatever you do in office," he began, "I know will be honestly and ably done, and although we who do not see the whole ground may sometimes impute error, it will be because we, not you, are in the wrong; or because your views are defeated by the wickedness or incompetence of those you are obliged to trust with their execution." The perils of the office seemed evident enough. Few Cabinet officers in American history have ever undertaken so important a task with so little support.[37]

8

SECRETARY OF WAR

WHEN ARMSTRONG ASSUMED OFFICE on February 5, 1813, the War Department was in a state of flux, despite the fact that the war was now in its eighth month. Much of the confusion and disorganization was due to the inadequate and tardy legislation of Congress. Many supply departments, for example, were created hastily on the eve of the war and did not begin functioning until after the war had actually broken out. A Quartermaster Department was authorized on March 28, 1812, as was the office of the Commissary General of Purchases, and the Ordnance Department was not created until May 14, 1812. A Commissary General of Purchases could not be found until August 8, and consequently Secretary of War Eustis was obliged to perform most of the duties of supply when the war broke out. Unfortunately, the supply functions frequently overlapped or they duplicated each other's work, requiring the secretary of war to arbitrate, thereby adding to his burdens.

Overwhelmed by a variety of other responsibilities and lacking sufficient personnel to assist him, Secretary Eustis unfortunately lacked the administrative ability to cope with the situation. William Crawford, a future secretary of war, characterized Eustis as a man who "instead of forming general and comprehensive arrangements, for the organization of his troops and for the successful prosecution of the campaign, consumes his time in reading advertisements of petty retailing merchants to find where he may purchase one hundred shoes or two hundred hats."[1]

Eustis clearly needed military advisers and agencies permanently located in Washington to assist him in managing the army. With an increasingly complex task, he had only the assistance of Daniel Parker, the chief clerk, and seven clerks. Madison urged Congress in April 1812 to create two assistant secretaries to relieve the secretary of some of the details of the office, but Congress defeated the plan arguing that it was too expensive, that it tended to vest too much power in that department, and it was hinted that Madison was merely seeking to create sinecures. Eustis could hardly exercise any close surveillance over his subordinates or over the army. At the outbreak of war the only sections of the War Department in Washington to assist him were the Paymaster and Accountant offices. The Ordnance Department was added in July 1812. Other officials were located elsewhere, such as the quartermaster general, who was assigned to the principal army, as was the adjutant and inspector general. The commissary general of purchases was located in Philadelphia.[2]

James Monroe, as acting secretary of war, presented to the Military Committee of the Senate in December 1812 a project for the Army General Staff. Apparently drawn up by Colonel William Winder, it was much improved by the suggestions of Albert Gallatin. The General Staff Bill was finally passed on March 3, 1813, nearly a month after Armstrong came into office. There is no indication that Armstrong offered any changes, although he was consulted in the final stages of the bill. The adjutant and inspector general with the rank of brigadier general was assigned to the principal army, and the act specified the number of deputies and assistant adjutants and inspectors authorized in the army. The numbers of deputy commissaries of Ordnance, and deputy and assistant quartermasters, were increased. A Hospital Department was authorized, to be headed by a physician and surgeon general, and to include an apothecary general. The secretary of war was given responsibility for preparing general regulations to define and prescribe the respective duties of the various departments.[3]

Congress also created on March 3, 1813, a superintendent general of military supplies to perform the much-needed task of keeping centralized accounts of all military supplies. He was to reside in Washington and be responsible to the secretary of war. Armstrong added to his staff in Washington on March 18 an inspector general and an assistant adjutant general, and he added an assistant topographical engineer on April 12.[4] These offices, in addition to those already in Washington (accountant, paymaster, and ordnance), at least offered Armstrong a reasonably adequate staff, although it fell short of being a general staff. As constituted, it was essentially a housekeeping staff.

The "Rules and Regulations of the Army of the United States," compiled under Armstrong's direction, and announced on May 1, 1813, laid down the rank of regiments and officers, rules with regard to promotions, and the duties of different staff departments, clarifying their responsibilities in minute detail, and many other matters with regard to army business, including technique and etiquette. One historian has said of these regulations: "The War Office has seldom performed a more valuable practical service to the army than in the publication of these 'Rules and Regulations' of 1813, which may be described as a fair epitome of the present elaborate work known as the Army Regulations."[5]

The number of general officers was increased on February 24, 1813, to eight major generals and sixteen brigadiers. Madison and Armstrong selected six new major generals: James Wilkinson, Wade Hampton, William R. Davy, Morgan Lewis, Aaron Ogden, and William Henry Harrison. The two senior major generals were Henry Dearborn and Thomas Pinckney. Except for Harrison, who was forty, the major generals were old men without much vigor. The new brigadier generals added some youth to the top commands. Among those appointed were: Zebulon Pike, George Izard, Duncan McArthur, Lewis Cass, Benjamin Howard, William Winder, and Thomas Parker. Except for Howard and Parker, who were Revolutionary veterans, the average age was thirty-six.[6] Congress did not create a lieutenant-general to command the armies. The ranking officer, Dearborn, commanded the Northern Army, but he had no general control over any other force than his own.

Armstrong divided the country into nine military districts and placed a regular military officer in command of each, complete with a staff. It was clear, however, that except for those on the northern frontier, these districts were established primarily for providing better organization for defense. These divisions further fragmented the military commands, but it soon appeared that Armstrong intended to exercise military as well as civil control over the commanding generals of the various districts, for in every respect he treated them strictly as military subordinates. This was quite an undertaking for a man generally considered to be indolent and less than assiduous toward his duties. In truth, Armstrong did not meticulously devote his energies to details. An insight may be gained into his administrative habits in a series of letters from Edward Ross to his uncle, David Parish, the wealthy financier of Philadelphia. Young Ross came to Washington in March 1813 to solicit a commission in the army. Armstrong promised to do something for him, but in the meantime he prevailed upon him to assist with some secretarial work. With no private secretary, Armstrong had to answer and copy every evening a disagreeable number of letters upon a variety of subjects. Ross noted Armstrong's imperturbable nature, and he related an incident when a rider arrived from Baltimore reporting that the city was in imminent danger of attack. Armstrong took it calmly, but Secretary Jones was alarmed and made plans to go to Baltimore. "So many false allarming letters arrive here daily," Ross wrote, "that one does not know what to believe."[7]

Ross was given numerous small duties to perform, such as making models of a new uniform, purchasing a horse for Armstrong (for $172), as well as a saddle, bridle, and a leopard skin. He also rented a house for Armstrong (for $500 per year), and he asked his uncle to procure a pair of number-nine concave spectacles to replace Armstrong's which were broken when a drunken hack-driver had fallen off his hack and the horses bolted, forcing Armstrong to leap for safety, breaking the glasses in the process. "He never says what he means to do and always gives very short notice," Ross wrote, and he added, "Many more such curious commissions I have daily to execute, which are all out of the way nor do I know what he will be at and what I really have to expect." Armstrong enjoyed having young Ross around him. He said that Ross made him laugh so much that it inflamed his eyes, but Ross argued that the inflammation was due to Armstrong's frequent rubbing of his eyes with a silk handkerchief. Ross was thrilled being in the midst of important preparations and in the presence of prominent persons. He recounted to his uncle a visit with Armstrong to the French Minister, Louis Serurier. He listened in rapt attention for three hours to a conversation about many important subjects, including hints of future operations. Armstrong procured for Ross a commission as a captain of the light dragoons on April 23, 1813, but the Senate negated the appointment on July 29.[8]

Armstrong's biggest task when he took office was to address supply problems. Provisions for the army were supplied in three ways: food was provided by civilian contractors; the Purchasing Department in Philadelphia supplied arms, ammunition, clothing, and accoutrements; and the Quartermaster Department was authorized to buy riding horses, pack horses, teams, wagons, and forage. Any article, however, in case of emergency, could be purchased by the quartermaster or deputies at the order of the commanding officer. Transportation of supplies was the chief business of the quartermaster. With the reorganization in the spring of 1813, Armstrong was able to place a quartermaster staff in each of the nine military districts, complete with deputies and assistants and their subordinates. Each quartermaster in his district was, however, virtually autonomous. Morgan Lewis's successor as quartermaster general, Robert Swartwout, gave all his attention to his own district, and there was no coordination, except as the Secretary of War might occasionally direct.

The supply system functioned very poorly in the campaign of 1812, particularly the contract system for troop subsistence. Bids were received for rations, but if contractors thought they might lose money by meeting the terms of their contracts, they would often shift the responsibility for feeding the army to the commissaries, who had to purchase rations that were usually much more expensive than the price fixed with the contractor. Along the northern frontier, the commissaries often competed with the British army's Commissariat Department for food. Sir George Prevost, writing to his superiors in England in August 1814, admitted that "two thirds of the Army in Canada are, at this moment, eating Beef provided by American Contractors, drawn principally from the States of Vermont and New York."[9] Contractors who failed to meet a requisition were theoretically responsible for the additional cost to the government to make up the deficiency, but actually they were never held to this clause of the agreement. The contractors were widely criticized by many officers. The redoubtable Andrew Jackson, to give just one example, repeatedly asserted that the Creek War could have been terminated in a few weeks if the contractors had not failed to provide provisions. Nevertheless, the War Department continued to rely on this system, chiefly because Congress believed it to be the most economical.[10]

The procurement and distribution of all other supplies of the army (except for the few items to be purchased by the Quartermaster Department) were centralized in Philadelphia under the commissary general of purchases, Callender Irvine. He was responsible for buying clothes, equipment, military stores, arms, ammunition, medicine and hospital supplies, and instructing the quartermasters concerning the transportation of such articles. In July 1813, Armstrong informed him that thereafter his department would be responsible for the safekeeping and distribution of the goods purchased, because of complaints of waste and misapplication of government property and the lack of accountability by the Quartermaster Department. Six issuing commissaries were established with instructions to receive goods from the commissary general of purchases or his deputies and distribute these items to the regimental quartermasters.[11] Accountability, however, due to the pressures of war, was hardly regularized by these efforts. Many officers, for example, were forced to obtain articles where they could, and they never reported the matter further. The want, the waste, and the inefficiency in supplying the armies was an important reason for their many failures. Armstrong, shackled with an inefficient system, only tried to make it more efficient. His efforts did not get at the root of the problem of decentralization.

The many failures of supply would not have been as glaring had sufficient funds been available. On March 5, 1813, for example, Secretary of the Treasury Gallatin warned President Madison, "We have hardly money enough to last till the end of the month." Fortunately, Gallatin managed to arrange with three wealthy Americans, David Parish, Stephen Girard, and John Jacob Astor to complete a $16 million loan. The War Department was allocated $13,320,000, with expenditures not to exceed $1,480,000 per month.[12] This limitation on expenditures acted as a brake upon the military operations, and seriously hampered the War Department in its planning and conduct of the 1813 campaign. Congress authorized $25,000,000 in 1814, but by September, when Armstrong left office, only $10,000,000 had been raised, and the country was verging on bankruptcy. Congress failed to provide a solid foundation for revenue and relied instead upon loans. It adopted a half-way system of taxation, permitted the specie to escape from the country, refused to establish a national bank, and yet expected the war to be carried on with vigor.[13]

Throughout his administration of the War Department, Armstrong gave the most careful attention to his financial limitations. In fact, it is conjectural whether he did not sometimes lose sight of the objects to be gained for concern over their cost. For example, faced with the critical shortage of funds, he arbitrarily cut almost all expenditures for coastal defense fortifications. As might be imagined, this was an unpopular decision, but Armstrong did not waver. Ironically, however, his dismissal from the War Department, as we shall see, was due in part to his failure to provide fortifications for Washington.

Armstrong also refused to pay for unnecessary militia calls, even when state governors pleaded that emergency situations had not permitted regular procedures to be followed. Governor James Barbour of Virginia, for example, grumbled after Armstrong's refusal to pay for the militia called out to protect Norfolk early in 1813, that in the future the states might merely content themselves with coldly complying with the letter of their duty. Instead of "generous and unsuspecting confidence" in furthering the wishes of the government, it would beget "the close suspicion of the miser, who before he acts demands solid and unquestionable pledges."[14] When Armstrong left office in the fall of 1814, Governor Isaac Shelby's militia force of over 5000 men from Kentucky, which had been so important in bringing about the successful western campaign of 1813, had not yet been paid. Ostensibly the reason was lack of funds, but in reality the delay was also due to Armstrong's objection to the excessive cost of the force. The militia had cost about $300,000 more than a regular force, because it had enough officers for twelve regiments, but in reality had shown less bayonets than four regiments of regulars.[15] To Armstrong, who had pressed so hard for a regular force in the West, the cost was hard to accept. Nevertheless, in areas where invasion was threatened, Armstrong's reluctance to sanction calls for militia was incomprehensible and just as unpopular as the failure to provide funds for fortifications.

Armstrong has not been given any recognition for his creditable management and allocation of the meager sums allotted to the War Department. Beset by demands for more funds, he was forced on many occasions to choose between two equally critical needs. Based on his strategic views he consequently applied the largest portion of War Department funds to the Northern Army and cut back the expenditures in the West. He explained to William Duane in March 1813, "Had I let them go on, as I found them (with every man's hand among them in the public coffers) the game would have been up for want of means, before a single stroke had been made, useful or creditable to our arms."[16] Even the amounts given to the Northern Army brought complaints from General Dearborn of insufficient funds. Armstrong wrote to Quartermaster General Swartwout that the general had "altogether lost sight of the State & usages of the Treasury." He asserted that he had only $1,400,000 per month with which to "subsist, pay, equip, cloathe, & move five or six Armies of Regulars & Militia." Swartwout would be supplied as means were available, but he added, "economy must be your alpha & omega as well as mine."[17]

Expenditures for the Northern Army were particularly heavy in the late summer and fall of 1813 preceding the abortive invasion of Canada. Armstrong went to the front himself in a vain attempt to coordinate the campaign. In order to ensure success, he asked Madison for increased funds so that "nothing would be permitted to check the impulse given to the campaign in the last stage of it." Madison complied, writing to the secretary of the treasury that "no other expenditure, not essential to the life or what is next to it, the credit of the Government, can be equally urgent." An advance on War Department funds was arranged, but success, at least in this case, was not commensurate with the amount expended. In 1814 the major portion of the War Department funds were again allocated to the Northern Department. In the Southern Department, the Creek War called for increased expenditures, but the success of the Northwestern Army released funds from that department. Armstrong was again forced to hoard the money carefully and use it selectively. The want of funds severely hampered operations. American arms gave a better account of themselves in 1814, but no decisive, tangible gains were made.

In summary, Armstrong at least followed a consistent policy in allocating War Department funds. His strategy of war called for the reduction of Canada, and this naturally led him to concentrate his meager resources in that effort. As a result, serious hardships were felt by troops in other sections of the country, and practically the entire coast lay open and unprotected from incursions of the enemy due to a lack of fortifications. Armstrong may be criticized for occasional rigidity, and even for error in failing to provide funds for critical needs, but it seems equally clear that

Congress, by failing to provide adequate funds for the war effort, must bear the major responsibility for the ill-fed, poorly clothed, inadequately equipped condition of the troops.

Just as vexing as the problem of keeping an army in the field was the problem of getting one there. At the outset of the war Congress authorized a force of 36,700, but when Armstrong took office in February 1813 the regular army was at scarcely half the authorized strength, only 18,945. On January 29, 1813 Congress authorized twenty additional regiments to be enlisted for one year instead of the usual five years, which raised the aggregate authorized to 57,351, but the force in service rose to only 27,609 in June and 34,325 in December. Even these figures are misleading, for Armstrong admitted to the chairman of the House Military Committee on January 2, 1814 that the actual effectives for the entire northern frontier was only 8012. Obviously, short-term enlistments hampered efforts to raise a regular force (one year's service being preferable to a five-year enlistment), but public apathy and personal preferences for the easier service of the militia were also reasons for the failure to recruit an adequate army.[19]

Prior to the war recruiting was the responsibility of the regimental commanders, but the service was revamped by establishing recruiting districts and by placing a field grade officer in each, reporting directly to the War Department. They received their instructions and bounty and premium money from the War Department. This centralization of the system did not notably increase the number of recruits, nor did Congress's timid increases in bounties alter the lack of zeal of Americans for military service. Armstrong, as noted, made a strong effort to force General Harrison to rely upon a regular force. The effort was unavailing, however, for westerners showed a strong disinclination for the regular army, and Armstrong reluctantly permitted Harrison to use militia for his campaign of 1813, which was, incidentally, very successful. Armstrong nevertheless considered the militia extremely wasteful, poorly trained, and unreliable. As a measure of the failure of the recruiting system, 30,000 militiamen were called into service during 1813.[20]

Following the failure of the campaign against Canada in 1813, an obviously disappointed Armstrong proposed to Madison the drastic resort to conscription as the only means of raising an army competent to win the war. Such a measure, he argued, would "immediately fill our ranks and enable us to finish the war (without again calling on Militia) in one Campaign. The public mind is I think prepared for vigorous measures and this should be made the foundation stone." Secretary of the Navy Jones and Secretary of State Monroe both opposed this plan as politically dangerous. Monroe, who personally distrusted Armstrong, asserted that it would "ruin the Administration," and he urged Madison to dismiss Armstrong.[21] Madison, nevertheless, permitted Armstrong to submit his plan to Congress. Armstrong did so, justifying his plan as having "the sanction of revolutionary wisdom and energy — it produced that army which achieved our independence." Congress, however, undoubtedly for political reasons, shied away from the Revolutionary wisdom. Conscription was denounced by the Federalists and Armstrong was assaulted, particularly by Monroe's friends. Instead, Congress merely raised the bounty. Although authorized 60,000 men, the regular army averaged about half that number in 1814. When Armstrong left office in September the effective regular force on the northern frontier was only 7500. At that time, he was even considering a proposal to raise a black regiment in Philadelphia.[22]

The events of 1814 bear out Armstrong's belief that regulars offered the best hope for a victory. In the South, the heart of General Jackson's force was the small Thirty-ninth Regiment. In the North, regulars led by Generals Brown, Scott, and Gaines won several victories on the Niagara Peninsula. On the other hand, the most notorious example of the incapacity of the militia was the debacle at Washington, which the British burned in 1814. Interestingly, even Monroe, who had opposed conscription, after he replaced Armstrong as secretary of war in September 1814, recommended conscription to Congress. However, Congress was pathetically divided and fearful of such a measure and merely doubled the land bounty and authorized the enlistment of minors.[23] Had the war not ended, the country faced the prospect of entering the 1815 campaign with 30,000 regulars and six-month militia, which experience had shown was not enough. It would be difficult to say what effect conscription would have had on the war's outcome, but Major General Emory Upton, the noted historian of American military policy, stated unequivocally, "Had Congress, on the 11th of January [1812], declared that all men owed their country military service, and decided to raise the Army immediately, by volunteering or by draft, to 35,000 men . . . it scarcely admits of doubt that after six months' training and discipline this force could have occupied Canada and ended the war in a single campaign."[24]

Armstrong's relations with his commanders were frequently stormy. At least two generals resigned in protest against his high-handed actions. Many of the problems stemmed from a long-time War Department practice of transmitting orders directly to posts, without delaying them by sending them through the hands of the commander. The commanders were often sent a duplicate of the orders, but Armstrong obviously abused the practice. Expeditions were sometimes set on foot within departments without official notice to the commanding general of the district. General Dearborn, barely a week after Armstrong took office, reminded the secretary, "It has been usual for the commander of an Army to issue his orders through the Adjutant General of that Army, and not to receive orders *from him* or through him."[25] General Wilkinson, before going to the northern district in the fall of 1813, took the specific precaution of getting an agreement with Armstrong that all orders would pass through the commander's hands first, and the secretary of war would forbid all correspondence from Wilkinson's subordinates. Nevertheless, Wilkinson complained later that proper channels were often ignored, and there was a lack of subordination due to the secretary's interference. "For Gods sake and the good of the Service," he wrote Armstrong, "send us no more orders into the District, to Contractors, Quartermasters or Apothecaries, which do not pass through the regular, and only proper channel."[26]

Armstrong justified his actions by asserting that prior practice authorized his conduct and that following the chain of command would have led to interminable delays. His broad view of his powers, however, gave little thought to the impact of his actions on his commanders. They resented his communications with their subordinates, which they contended weakened their authority. General Flournoy, who commanded the Seventh Military District at New Orleans, resigned in June 1814, and he gave as one reason that private orders from the heads of departments at Washington "in the hands of every staff officer in the District, and in many instances in the hands of officers of the line and some cases to Captains of Companies — of which orders I know nothing, until they are produced to counteract some of *my* orders, have produced such a state of insubordination, that I can no longer command the district."[27]

Armstrong denied this charge, and the offense may have been inadvertent. This was not the case, however, in the affair involving General Harrison. In February 1814 Harrison complained of Armstrong's breach of military etiquette in countermanding Harrison's order to Brigadier General Benjamin Howard to march to Detroit. Armstrong answered aggressively that "As a general principle it cannot be doubted but that the Government has a right to dispose of the Officers of the Army as they may think best for the public interest," and he asserted, "Had it been sent through you to General Howard, the objects of Government might have been hazarded by the delay which would have necessarily attended this mode of transmission."[28] Harrison acquiesced, but his patience was finally exhausted by another incident shortly afterwards.

Armstrong informed Harrison on April 25, 1814, that he had ordered Major A.H. Holmes at Detroit to lead an infantry force against

Mackinac. Colonel George Croghan, Holmes's superior, however, refused to allow Holmes to leave until he received orders from Harrison. Croghan wrote Harrison, "were I a general commanding a district, I would be very far from suffering the secretary of war, or any other authority, to interfere with my internal police."[29]

Harrison had already decided to submit his resignation, and he did so on May 11, 1814. Armstrong was amazed by the furor, and he wrote Madison, "Are the orders &c. of the War Dept. to be sent to every Col. in the army before he will consent in an expedition directed by the government?" Madison conceded that the orders to Major Holmes were proper, "the case forbidding delay," but he also noted that it might have been better to have sent the orders through Colonel Croghan.[30] The essential problem in this case, as well as in many others like it, was communication. Armstrong's grand conception of his office did not permit the little compromises so necessary to secure complete cooperation.

Armstrong not only assumed many of the prerogatives of a military commander, he also indicated that he did not intend to be a mere agency for communicating policy to the various commanders. There is the notable example where he actually went to the northern front to forward the operations of the Northern Army. This decision generated much discussion in the Cabinet. Gallatin accepted this step, commenting to Madison, "His military views are generally more extensive, and for this year's operations appear to me more correct, than those of General Dearborn." Monroe, however, opposed Armstrong's plan, arguing that it would combine the powers of the president, of the secretary of war, and a lieutenant general "in hands where it is most dangerous," and wound the credit of the Administration and leave the War Department without someone to direct the general movements of every other army. He added, "As soon as General Armstrong took charge of the Dept. of War I thought I saw his plan [to keep the control over the military operations in his own hands]. I anticipated mischief from this, because I knew that the movement could not be directed from this place — I did not then anticipate the remedy which he had in view."[31]

Monroe was upset because his plans had backfired and created a potential rival. Prior to Armstrong's appointment, he had contemplated taking a military command, first in the West after Hull's defeat, but the selection of Harrison by the Kentuckians caused him to cancel these plans. He next thought of supplanting General Dearborn on the northern front, but Secretary Eustis's resignation forestalled that plan, and he took the War Department PRO TEMPORE. He refused to take the War Department permanently, apparently believing he would be offered the com-

mand on the northern front. In stepping aside, however, he had opened
the way for Armstrong to enter the Cabinet. Armstrong, in a move perhaps calculated to cool Monroe's military ambitions, offered to nominate
Monroe as one of the new major generals just authorized by Congress,
but with the understanding that he would serve under General Dearborn.
Monroe declined the nomination, and he never forgave Armstrong for
excluding him from command. Armstrong, for his part, thought it ludicrous that Monroe should want the command, for he believed Monroe
"knew nothing of war & was without military experience."[32]

Despite Monroe's objections, Madison was disposed to try "conciliating confidence," and he agreed to allow Armstrong to proceed to the
front. Monroe's opposition to Armstrong eventually extended to actual
interference in his conduct of the War Department. In the summer of
1813, prior to leaving for the front, Armstrong had to await the arrival of
General Wilkinson from the south, who was on his way to assume the
command of the northern army after General Dearborn was replaced.
When Wilkinson arrived in Washington the last of July, Monroe contacted Wilkinson and offered his advice on the manner of conducting operations on the northern frontier. This highly irregular conduct was done
secretly, as is indicated in Wilkinson's reply to Monroe. "Your ideas, offensive & defensive," Wilkinson wrote, "are in my Judgment sound." He
added confidentially, "Your confidence is as sound as my Honour which is
all I have—I shall speak to you on the subject of your project before I go
& with permission will borrow some specific Ideas from it, which without
permission I will not record even in memory." There is circumstantial evidence that earlier that summer Monroe also approached General Wade
Hampton before he went to the northern front. Thus when Armstrong
left Washington for the front early in August, Monroe was in friendly
communication with both of his major generals on the northern front.[33]

Armstrong was absent from the War Department for more than
four months, and he did not return to Washington until Christmas Day.
While he was absent, Monroe attempted to undercut the authority of the
Secretary of War and even to assume control over the War Department.
Madison, who had been seriously ill in June and July, found it necessary
to retire to his home in Virginia early in August, where he remained for
nearly eleven weeks. Daniel Parker, who was left in charge of the War
Department, was instructed to consult the president or the secretary of
war when time allowed before making any important decisions. In case of
emergency, when time could not be lost, Parker was to consult with Monroe verbally. Monroe did not hesitate to assume responsibility plainly not
intended for him, and he soon arranged for all the military correspondence of the War Department to be routed to him for review.[34]

When Madison returned in October, Parker informed him of Monroe's actions, and the President asked Parker to tell Monroe to call upon him the next day, presumably to explain his actions. However, Monroe left the city the next morning, and the angry Madison went personally to the State Department and ordered the correspondence to be brought to him, which he then sent over to the War Department. Parker described the event later to John Quincy Adams, who recorded in his diary: "He was more in a passion than Parker ever saw him at any other period of his life, and gave it very distinctly to be understood that he thought that Mr. Monroe had been meddling with the affairs of the War Department more than was proper."[35]

Armstrong's return to Washington late in December signalled a period of intensifying rivalry between the two men. Monroe not only denounced the conscription plan (previously noted), he also accused Armstrong of promising promotions and preferment to many officers; exciting resentment against the president; and furthering a corrupt system in the Quartermaster Department of New York. He asserted to Madison that he had been able to persuade some congressmen to drop efforts to investigate by what authority Armstrong exercised his duties on the northern front during the last campaign only because he convinced them it would appear to be an attack upon the President. He warned that if Armstrong was not checked, he would "ruin not you and the Administration only, but the whole republican party & cause." He concluded that Armstrong "wants a head fit for his station & indolent except for improper purposes, he is incapable of that combination & activity which the times require. My advice to you therefore is to remove him at once." There was little to fear politically from such an action. "He has as you well know few friends & some of them cling to him as I suspect either from improper motives or on a presumption that you support him."[36]

Madison was determined to bear with Armstrong as long as possible. Perhaps Armstrong did not understand this conciliatory disposition and only viewed it as weakness. That he had few friends was certain. He confided in a conversation with John W. Taylor, a New York Representative, on January 12, 1814, that he was "determined either to have at the head of the army men in whom he can rely & to have a competent army or to resign his office." Madison, he continued, must "act with decision or give up the country." Taylor noted that Armstrong was "mortified that his conscription project was not adopted."[37] Rufus King, a leading Federalist, reported that Armstrong was "on a poise whether he is to have the fair support of the President or not." Whether out of anger or frustration, Armstrong, through an intermediary, contacted the Federalists seeking "an understanding with the Federalists in Congress." They were told that "he desired nothing on their part in respect to himself; that he was willing to cooperate ag[ains]t Virginia, leaving men and things to take their course when the Presidential Election comes on." He was rebuffed. The Federalists had little reason to trust him, and they were convinced he would soon fall from office. King, writing to Gouverneur Morris, thought it was strange that Armstrong should still have ambitions when his plans had already "proved so lamentably deficient . . . and only to be accounted for by the good opinions he entertains of his own Powers." He believed Armstrong's "scheme for a Lieutenant Generalship" would probably bring forth General Harrison for that position. He concluded that Armstrong "were he skilled in the Chaldean Dialect, would understand the Mene Tekal written on the Walls of the War Office. He must, I think, go down."[38]

In order to explain the failure of the northern campaign of 1813, Armstrong encouraged and eventually got a request from Congress for a report on the causes of the failure. The report was presented to Congress on February 2, 1814. One historian has asserted that Armstrong, "by skillful selection exculpated himself and threw the blame impartially on Generals Wilkinson and Hampton, letting each of them strike down the other."[39] Undoubtedly this was Armstrong's intention, but there was enough material included to indicate that he had meddled far too much in the affairs of both generals. While Armstrong escaped the brunt of the criticism, one Federalist stated after reading the report, "whose fault this was seems not to be determined," but it proved "how badly every operation was contrived, how wretchedly executed, and the jealousies, and insubordination of the officers."[40]

One of the major problems of the army in 1813 had been the lack of vigorous leadership in the top commands. By 1814 most of the older officers had been removed from positions of command, and Armstrong began to promote and place younger men who had proven themselves in the 1813 campaign in these positions. He was a good judge of military ability, and his recommendations advanced many men of unquestioned ability who were destined to have distinguished careers in the army. On January 21 and February 21, the president sent to the Senate the names of two new major generals, George Izard and Jacob Brown, and six brigadier generals, Alexander Macomb, T.A. Smith, Daniel Bissel, Edmund P. Gaines, Winfield Scott, and Eleazer W. Ripley. These men represented a new generation of military leaders who gave a far better account of American arms. The average age of the brigadiers, for example, was only thirty-three. Adding General Andrew Jackson, who was appointed major general in the spring of 1814, the average age of the nine new appointees was thirty-six. The appointment of these younger men over officers senior to them in rank reflected Armstrong's view that the best men should be advanced without regard to seniority. Madison must also be given credit for recognizing the merit of these men and for resisting the inevitable political pressures to alter the list.[41]

The question of the appointment of a lieutenant general to command the army was raised again in the spring of 1814. Representative William H. Murfree (North Carolina), a Monroe supporter, rose in the House of Representatives in January to attack Armstrong's recent absence from the War Department and asserted that he had assumed the role of commander-in-chief. Murfree introduced a resolution directing the Committee on Military Affairs to enquire into the expediency of empowering the president to appoint a lieutenant general. That Monroe was to be the lieutenant general was obviously the purpose of the resolution. Monroe revealed in a letter early in March 1814 to his son-in-law, George W. Hay, "I still think that we may save everything, and terminate the war with honor, provided proper measures be adopted . . . Whether I ought, in connection with them to take any other status, is not clear." He asked whether a statement disclaiming any desire for the presidency might allay suspicions of his intentions. Monroe had pondered such a statement since the past September. This must have amused his friends, for his desire for the presidency was obvious, but in any event they recommended against this course. Hay remonstrated strongly against making this "proposed declaration." Instead, he believed Monroe should threaten to leave the Cabinet unless he was allowed to have his just weight. However, the Murfree resolution was tabled, ironically because many feared Armstrong would be appointed the lieutenant general.[42]

The rivalry between Armstrong and Monroe did little credit to either. Instead of attending to their duties, they were, as one Cabinet colleague noted, "full of zeal . . . running for the Presidential purse intent only on each other." Neither was apparently able to concede the possibility of good intentions on the part of the other. Each sought to check the actions of the other lest he undermine the Republican cause or render the nation incapable of winning the war. Monroe, for his part, despite his obvious dislike of Armstrong, denied even to his closest confidant, George Hay, that he had any personal quarrel with Armstrong, "but that his removal was due to the public feeling & hope."[43]

It became obvious in the spring of 1814 that Madison was losing confidence in his secretary of war. He had given Armstrong virtually a free hand in the conduct of the War Department, and there is no doubt that Armstrong abused this privilege. Madison now gave indications that he was shifting from "conciliating confidence" to "interposing control." The reasons for his change of attitude are obscure. He was recovering his health after a series of illnesses, and perhaps he was in a vigorous mood. He may also have been disenchanted with the failures of the 1813 campaign, or it may have been simply an accumulation of grievances over Armstrong's high-handed methods. Possibly Monroe may have pressed his case as Hay suggested and threatened to resign. Many people believed Madison either too timid to control Armstrong or too easily manipulated by him. General Wilkinson asserted later, "I had long known that the poor President was a nose of wax in his fingers," and he added, "I am indeed shocked when I take a retrospect of the evidence of the terror in which that minister kept more than one great man at Washington."[44]

In May 1814 Madison read in the *National Intelligencer* that the War Department had published a register of officers retained when four regiments were consolidated into two. Madison wrote Armstrong, "You must have inferred more from my communications than I could have meant to convey by anything in them on the subject." Presidential responsibility, he pointed out, could not be satisfied without "weighing well the whole proceeding."

Armstrong also overstepped his bounds with regard to the resignation of General Harrison and the appointment of Jackson as major general in the regular army. Armstrong first suggested a regular appointment for Jackson. The vacancy created by Hampton's resignation, however, could not be filled until Congress convened, so the best course would be to make Jackson a brigadier and give him a brevet of major general and assign him to command the Seventh Military District. Madison agreed on May 17. Then on May 20 Armstrong wrote that Harrison had resigned, but he did not enclose the letter or give any reason for the resignation. Madison suggested to Armstrong on May 24 that Harrison's resignation would enable them to send a major general's commission directly to Jackson, but he stated, "I suspend a final decision, however, till I see you, which will be in two or three days after the arrival of this." Two days earlier Armstrong had written Jackson that there was no vacancy for major general, but now instead of waiting for Madison's arrival, he wrote Jackson that Harrison's resignation had created a vacancy, "which I hasten to fill with your name." (If Armstrong intended that it appear to Jackson that he was the source of the appointment, Jackson did not construe it as such. He acknowledged the appointment "made by the President.") Thus when Madison arrived two days later, he discovered that Armstrong had not only accepted Harrison's resignation, he had also appointed Jackson to the vacancy.[46]

Madison accepted the *fait accompli*, but this incident spurred him to increase his surveillance and exercise greater control over the War Department. On June 15, for example, he requested all War Department correspondence of recent months with Generals Harrison and Jackson, and since May 1 with Generals Izard, Brown, and Gaines. He broadened the scope by asking in August for the correspondence with the northern generals.[47] A number of directives began to flow to the secretary of war. Some were concerned with such minute details that they might be termed "meddling"; others were sound. For example, Madison noted the lack of communication between the commanders on the northern front and the lack of coordination with the naval commanders, and he suggested developing a cypher for confidential messages. Armstrong, chafing under Madison's scrutiny, misunderstood the thrust of Madison's comment. He replied that Generals Izard and Gaines were fully informed of General Brown's movements by letters from the secretary of war. Madison noted on this letter, "It remains that no instruction to correspond *among themselves*, appears to have been given or presumed."[48] Madison was also piqued when Armstrong released a list of officers recommended by General Brown for brevet promotion before Madison had signed them. Madison wrote angrily to Armstrong, "The Secretary of War will not in future permit commissions to be filled up in the office until it be ascertained that the appointments are approved."[49]

The accumulation of a mass of derogatory data resulted in a letter of reprimand on August 13, 1814. Madison criticized Armstrong's high-handed and independent actions and proceeded to lay down rules which would guide the secretary's conduct in the future.[50] The reprimand was deserved, but there is perhaps no better testimony than this letter of reprimand to the fact that Madison had been remiss in not exercising good control over the War Department. The nature of the conduct of that office will be the subject of the next three chapters.

9

THE CAMPAIGN OF 1813

LITTLE WAS ACCOMPLISHED MILITARILY on the northern frontier in 1812. On the Niagara peninsula both General Stephen Van Rensselaer and General Alexander Smyth proved to be incompetent. Van Rensselaer made an ill-conceived and unsuccessful attack upon Queenston Heights. He was replaced by Smyth, who wrote ringing pronouncements about what he was going to do, but he did nothing. General Henry Dearborn made one feeble thrust toward Montreal, but his troops stopped at the New York border, and the army went into winter quarters. It was obvious that before Canada could be successfully invaded, armies had to be raised, trained, and supplied, as well as provided with adequate leadership. A sound strategy also had to be developed, and control had to be gained over Lakes Erie and Ontario. Armstrong had written Secretary of War Eustis on January 2, 1812, noting the strategic importance of the lakes, and he recommended gaining the ascendancy over them in case of war.[1] When the war began, however, General William Hull's expedition to Detroit and his operations from there failed, in part because no effort had been made to secure control over Lake Erie, and he was too far separated from his source of supply.

Armstrong also noted in his letter to Eustis the strategic importance of Montreal. In office, however, his view had altered somewhat. His plan for the campaign of 1813 presented to the Cabinet on February 8, 1813, focused on Kingston and the destruction of the British ships stationed at the head of the St. Lawrence. York (present-day Toronto) and the ships being built there would be the second object, and Forts George and Erie at each end of the Niagara Peninsula, the third.[2] He was no doubt influenced by exaggerated reports of the enemy strength at Montreal, but Kingston was perhaps second in value to Montreal in overall strategic significance. The naval historian, A. T. Mahan, wrote that "no other harbor was tenable as a naval station; with its fall, and the destruction of shipping and forts, would go the control of the lake, even if the place itself were not permanently held." The enemy would be deprived of water communication and "could retain no position to the westward, because neither reinforcements nor supplies could reach them." The capture of Kingston, he concluded, "would have settled the whole campaign and affected decisively the issue of the war."[3]

The Cabinet approved Armstrong's plans, and on February 10 he wrote General Dearborn at Albany. He estimated that Dearborn would have approximately seven thousand men at his disposal, and his staff, particularly in the Quartermaster and Hospital departments, would be increased. The time for the movement would be governed by the opening of Lake Ontario to navigation, usually about April 1. Colonel Peter B. Porter, commanding near Buffalo, was ordered not to take any offensive action unless assured of success, and the Deputy Quartermaster General of the Northern District was instructed to begin construction of one hundred ships, each capable of carrying forty men and their baggage and provisions. On February 12 general orders were issued directing all officers and soldiers on furlough and belonging to the army corps serving on or near the Niagara River to report to their corps immediately.[4]

Armstrong's efforts to get the expedition underway were commendable, but he soon revealed a fatal flaw in his character — indecisiveness. His initial letters were directed toward the primary objective, Kingston, but only five days after writing Dearborn, he wrote again suggesting the idea of diverting some of the force to Ogdensburg on the St. Lawrence to confuse the enemy. A week later he reversed his instructions to Colonel Porter, giving him contingent orders to take his force across the frozen Niagara River and attack Fort Erie, where information indicated the enemy force was small and weak. Fort George at the other end of the Niagara might also be attacked, but he left that up to Porter's judgment. On February 24 Armstrong suggested a further alteration to Dearborn of the mode of operation. A movement led by the newly promoted General Zebulon Pike up the St. Lawrence in sleighs might seize Kingston. This maneuver might force General George Prevost, the British commander, to divert a large force to save Kingston, opening his supply lines to attack and weakening his defense of Montreal. After this apparent change of strategy, however, Armstrong informed Dearborn on March 4 that "the hints I gave in my last as to a change of plan were for your consideration, choose between the alternatives."[5] His equivocal orders were obviously

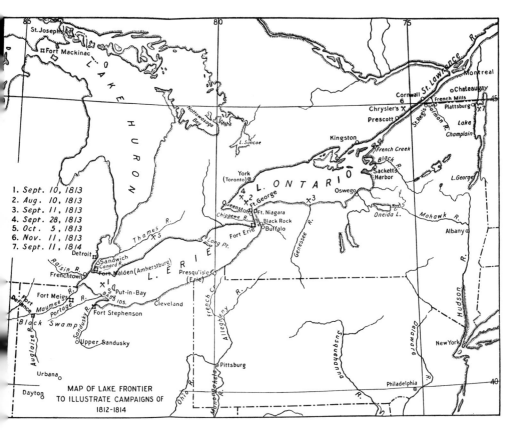

1. Sept. 10, 1813
2. Aug. 10, 1813
3. Sept. 11, 1813
4. Sept. 28, 1813
5. Oct. 5, 1813
6. Nov. 11, 1813
7. Sept. 11, 1814

MAP OF LAKE FRONTIER
TO ILLUSTRATE CAMPAIGNS OF
1812-1814

From A. T. Mahan, *Sea Power in Its Relations to the War of 1812* (New York, 1903; New York: Greenwood Press, 1968) I:370.

confusing to his commanders. Worse, weak commanders used the vagueness of his orders to avoid taking action. Some perhaps believed that his equivocation was an attempt to cover himself in case of failure, but the truth is probably that Armstrong simply often lacked a firm commitment to his objectives.

The British altered Armstrong's arrangements when they crossed the St. Lawrence from Prescott on February 23 and captured Ogdensburg. General Dearborn, fearing this was the prelude to an attack upon Sackett's Harbor, the American naval base on the northeast coast of Lake Ontario, ordered Pike and his men to move from Lake Champlain by sleighs to Sackett's Harbor. He also directed troops from Greenbush (near

Albany) to reinforce the post, and he hurried there himself to conduct the defense against what he supposed to be a large force massing at Kingston, which was only thirty-six miles away. Armstrong discounted any danger arising from the British action, and he professed to see some advantage. It would serve to mask the movement of troops to Sackett's Harbor and might draw Prevost from Montreal westward to a country "where subsistence is both difficult and doubtful & leaving us at the same time an opportunity of enterprising on his convoys & his Rear." However, on second thought, he noted that such actions might induce the enemy to reinforce Kingston, and it might be advisable to revert "to the first plan of waiting until you can approach your object by water." He reminded Dearborn that Kingston was the primary objective, but he added that now would be a good time to cross the Niagara River to attack Forts Erie and George.[6]

Armstrong expressed a cautious optimism to Ambrose Spencer on February 28. "The wonder & wishes of the public will be gratified if *my orders be executed*," he wrote, and he added, "They have been given on more than one point." He was even more sanguine when he wrote William Duane on March 16. "My plans of Campaign are made, and if they can be executed, we shall, I think, do something." General Prevost had drawn his whole disposable force to Kingston. "It is where I wish him to be," he continued, "The country is exhausted, and his sustenance will be doubtful, and his place d'Armies one hundred miles in his rear. If we have legs and Arms and a particle of head to direct these, we may weave a net for his Knightship, strong as that thrown around Burgoyne."[7]

Dearborn wrote Armstrong on March 3, that he expected an attack by Prevost with between six and eight thousand men within forty-eight hours. On March 9 he expressed some doubts whether they would attack, but the movement of the enemy would in any case "effectually oppose the movements contemplated on our part." Five days later he announced that the enemy had undoubtedly abandoned the idea of attacking Sackett's Harbor. There had been no likelihood of any attack, for Dearborn had greatly overestimated the size of the British force at Kingston. These exaggerated reports, nevertheless, convinced him that any attack upon Kingston would be unwise. In this view he was supported by the commander of the American fleet on Lake Ontario, Commodore Isaac Chauncey.

Dearborn therefore seized upon Armstrong's letter of March 4, which allowed him to choose the alternative modes of attack, and he informed the secretary that a council of principal officers, including Commodore Chauncey, had unanimously decided not to attack Kingston until the lake should be open to navigation around April 15. A few days later Dearborn wrote that he and Commodore Chauncey, after "mature deliberation," had decided to alter Armstrong's plan so that instead of attacking Kingston first, Commodore Chauncey would take ten or twelve hundred troops under General Pike and capture York, proceed and capture Fort George, and then mass the force for an attack upon Kingston.[8]

Armstrong accepted the alteration of his plan of campaign by stating that it "would appear to be necessary, or at least proper." If he really understood the critical strategic importance of Kingston, he would not have acquiesced so easily. Conceivably he believed the diversion westward would be quickly and easily effected without detriment to the assault on Kingston. There are hints that he was anxious for a victory to impress public opinion. He cautioned Dearborn to use a large force and leave nothing to chance. "If our first step in the campaign, and in that quarter from which most is expected, should fail," he wrote, "the disgrace of our arms will be compleat. The public will lose all confidence in us, & we shall even cease to have any in ourselves." He urged the use of the troops defending Sackett's Harbor, for he thought the enemy would be unlikely to attack there. "How then would it read in a newspaper," he asked, "that we had lost our object on the Niagara for want of Troops, while we had another brigade at Sackett's Harbor doing nothing?" On April 8 he directed Dearborn to lead the expedition.[9]

While preparations were underway for the attack on York, Armstrong turned his attention to the West. After the Hull disaster, William Henry Harrison, the governor of the Indiana Territory and the hero of the battle of Tippecanoe, was commissioned a brigadier general by President Madison and given command of the Northwest Army. The humiliation felt in the West after Hull's surrender led to calls for an immediate expedition to retake Detroit. The Administration, also anxious to recover lost prestige, placed almost unlimited means at Harrison's disposal. Despite some misgivings, Harrison began to organize the campaign. Heavy rains in the autumn, however, precluded the movement of guns, materiel, and provisions toward the staging area at the Maumee River rapids at the west end of Lake Erie. Confusion, lack of organization of the supply departments, and disease added to the physical difficulties. By December 1 not a troop or a supply wagon had reached the rapids, and the expenses mounted alarmingly.[10]

Harrison, to his credit, recognized that a successful expedition was nearly impossible in the winter months, and even if he accomplished his objective, it could hardly be maintained without control of Lake Erie. However, instead of delaying the expedition until spring, he attempted to shift that decision to the War Department, temporarily headed by James Monroe, who also declined for political reasons to assume that responsibility, despite the project's excessive cost. A disastrous defeat of a force led by Brigadier General James Winchester on January 21 at Frenchtown on the Raisin River, however, eventually led to the termination of this winter campaign which had wasted over a million dollars.[11]

That was the situation when Armstrong took office. He gave first priority to the affairs on the northern frontier, but he read the correspondence between the War Department and the West, and he also received further information and advice from Governor Isaac Shelby of Kentucky, Governor Return J. Meigs of Ohio, and Senator Thomas Worthington of Ohio. On March 5 Armstrong wrote Harrison approving the end of the campaign, and indicating that he should not engage in any offensive measures except for continuing demonstrations against the British post at Fort Malden to keep up the enemy's alarm. He explained, "we shall very soon be in motion on the Niagara and the St. Lawrence," and until Fort Malden could be approached by water, Harrison was to keep his present ground. War vessels were being built at Presque Isle which would hopefully be able to operate by the middle of May. Boats were also being constructed at Cleveland for the transportation of troops. Also, three of the twenty new regiments recently authorized by Congress would be assigned to Harrison's army. Additional calls for militia should be avoided, and Harrison was urged to encourage the recruiting of the regular regiments. Should there be a "want of force" to maintain his position, Harrison should "retire to the frontier settlements" and interpose the wilderness between himself and the enemy.[12]

Armstrong did not bother to explain that the funds at the disposal of the government were nearly gone, and that Secretary of Treasury Gallatin had placed severe restrictions upon military expenditures. Armstrong was, however, appalled at the waste that had occurred in the West, and he was determined to bring it under control. Harrison was limited to twenty thousand dollars per month. Protests from the West were not long in coming. Harrison asserted that the force contemplated was too small. He doubted the new regiments could be raised, and they would be raw recruits and very little superior to militia. He suggested "a large auxiliary corps of Militia," citing the "disinclination to the service which appears to prevail in the western country." Governor Shelby supported Harrison, who was concerned that he would not have enough troops to garrison the posts along the frontier where there was more than half a million dollars of government property.[13]

Harrison's distress was manifest in his letter to Armstrong on March 27. "I must confess," he wrote, "that the Idea never occurred to me that the Government would be unwilling to keep in the field at least the

semblance of an army of Militia until the regular troops could be raised."
He disclosed that he had already called for 1500 militia from Kentucky to
replace the militia being discharged in order to protect the artillery and
valuable stores at the Maumee Rapids. He asked for authority to call out
another 1500 men from Kentucky to protect Fort Wayne and other western posts. He warned ominously, "if any disaster happens to any of the
posts for the want of troops to protect them, the popularity of the administration in the western country will receive a shock [from] which it will
never recover." Other western correspondents, Richard M. Johnson,
Duncan McArthur, and Thomas Worthington, expressed essentially the
same view. Armstrong probably expected such an outcry, for he was not
much concerned by what he felt were "artificial alarms." He wrote Samuel
Huntington of Ohio, for example, that there would soon be a regular
force "competent to the whole service of offence or defence in your quarter," leaving the militia "to their civil pursuits."[14]

On April 9, fearing an attack on the post of Fort Meigs at the rapids,
Harrison requested an additional 1500 men from Governor Shelby as reinforcements. "It is necessary upon every military principle," he wrote,
"that our force should be treble theirs; at present it is inferior." Then he
wrote Armstrong, "I was sure that my doing so would meet your appro-
bation, when you should be informed of all the circumstances that produced such disobedience."[15] Armstrong at first discounted the probability
of an attack. But new information led him to caution that Colonel Henry
Procter, the British commander, might attack Fort Meigs. He added,
however, "He can neither bring into the field nor keep in it more than two
thousand effectives." Armstrong assured General Lewis Cass on April 28,
"I have no fears with regard to fort Meigs," and he concluded sarcastically, "I cannot but believe that under any circumstance you will be competent to your own defence, & that the spirit and patriotism of the West
are not so far exhausted, as to permit two thousand enemies of any kind
or color to disturb you either long or materially."[16]

On the very day that Armstrong wrote Cass, Procter was advancing toward Fort Meigs, and he began the seige on April 30 with a force of
approximately 2400 regulars, militia, and Indians. Harrison was prepared. A stiff battle occurred on May 5 when General Green Clay, leading
about twelve hundred Kentucky militia reinforcements, walked into a
trap. About 600 of his men were killed or captured. The fighting that day,
however, was not decisive, and Procter gave up the seige on May 9.[17] Fortunately for the Americans, Procter's attack came too late, for had it occurred earlier in April with the post practically without defenders, he
would undoubtedly have been successful. Armstrong perhaps did not un-

derstand that but for the exertions of General Harrison another disaster might have befallen the Northwest, and he would have been chiefly responsible.

Armstrong was still determined to force Harrison to make the effort to recruit a regular force rather than relying on the easier, and more expensive, way of calling out the militia. He had a low opinion of Harrison and had recommended him for promotion to major general unwillingly, as he indicated in a letter to Duane. "Harrison is an artificial General — but the West and South, were only to be satisfied by his appointment, and our's is, you know, a Government of opinion." Harrison had no higher regard for Armstrong, and he did not personally approve of Armstrong's plan for future operations, but he wrote on April 21 that it was "no doubt the best that could have been devised in the event of the promised naval success and a prosperous issue to the Recruiting business." He added, "My measures will therefore be entirely directed to the prosecution of the campaign in that way."[18]

Armstrong's intolerant attitude toward the West is well revealed in a remarkable letter to William Duane on April 29. He alluded to the waste of funds in the West, particularly by Kentucky. Every man was to be on pay, he asserted, alluding to the large scale militia drafts and the discouraging recruiting results. He also noted the exorbitant prices charged for supplies. For the West, he believed, "The war is a good thing, and is to be nursed." He was determined to break down this system. He had cut the size of Harrison's force, as well as his expenditures, and he would embark him at the foot of the rapids and carry him directly to Malden. The West was protesting. "They have so long governed the Governor," he wrote, "that they now think they have that authority jure divino." Governor Shelby, he continued, wanted 15,000 men for the campaign, "and that they must be mounted like Asiatics, and to do what? To take a work defended on three sides by pickets! To fight an enemy, not more than two thousand, of all colors and Kinds!" He urged Duane to use the pages of the Aurora to expose these abuses.[19]

Armstrong believed Harrison was interfering with recruiting. Early in April Harrison had ordered Brigadier General McArthur to report to Fort Meigs to assist in its defense. McArthur and Brigadier General Cass had been assigned recruiting duty in Ohio, charged with raising two new regiments of the Northwestern Army (the Twenty-Sixth and Twenty-Seventh). Enlistments were lagging when Harrison gave his order to McArthur. Governor Meigs and Senator Worthington, as well as McArthur and Cass, all protested to Armstrong that the order would deal a blow to the recruiting service. Armstrong quickly delivered a reprimand to Harrison, noting that he had twice detached officers from duties assigned by the War Department. Henceforth, no general officer commanding a district could take an officer from duties assigned him by the War Department. Harrison replied that considering the circumstances prompting him to give the orders, he did not feel the rebuke was merited.[20]

Enlistments did not meet Armstrong's expectations. Colonel Thomas D. Owings, recruiting the Twenty-Eighth Regiment in Kentucky, enlisted about 700, Cass raised about the same number, and McArthur recruited less than 500.[21] By the middle of July, adding these recruits to the regulars of the Seventeenth and Nineteenth Regiments already with Harrison, but vastly understrength, and those of the Twenty-Fourth Regiment marching from Illinois, Harrison could count on no more than 3000 regulars, considerably less than the 7000 authorized. It was obvious that Armstrong's "experiment" of relying upon regulars rather than militia had failed. He attributed this to ill-will and lack of effort on the part of Harrison and the other westerners, but Harrison had already pointed out the chief reason, namely a disinclination among westerners for infantry service in the regular army.

One interesting group which eventually assisted the regulars was a regiment of mounted volunteers led by Congressman Richard M. Johnson of Kentucky. On February 26, 1813, Armstrong authorized Johnson to organize and hold his regiment in readiness. He apparently intended this force for defense along the frontier, but when Fort Meigs was attacked, Johnson called out his troops and Harrison accepted them into service. Armstrong eventually approved of this decision, and a very important force was added to Harrison's invading army.[22]

Armstrong did not really understand the feelings of the people of the West. His instructions and policies were frequently abrupt, peremptory, and ill-advised. In broad outline, his decision to cease all offensive activity until control of the lake was gained may have been correct, but his apparent assumption that the war and events in the West would stand still was not only frustrating to westerners but also clearly wrong. Where a certain amount of flexibility was desirable, he was rigid and unyielding. Several of the important decisions, such as Harrison's call-out of militia for the defense of Fort Meigs and the use of Johnson's Volunteers, were taken in defiance of Armstrong's orders or without his authorization. Actually, it seems clear that Armstrong paid little attention to the affairs of the West. His primary focus was riveted to the events along the Niagara and St. Lawrence frontiers, where unfortunately his instructions were anything but peremptory and dogmatic. Instead they took on the character of vacillation.

Thus Armstrong had accepted meekly a most fundamental alteration of strategy by Dearborn. He not only accepted the change, but he began to alter future planning based on the certainty of the success of Dearborn's expedition against York and Fort George. On April 19 he wrote
Dearborn that the success of the expedition might cause Prevost to lose
hope, abandon Kingston, and concentrate his forces at Montreal. If not,
then Dearborn was to proceed after the expedition to destroy the communication between Montreal and Kingston, and assail Kingston by a joint
military and naval operation. If Prevost abandoned Kingston, then Montreal should be approached down the St. Lawrence rather than by the
Lake Champlain route which presented a much stronger defense from
assault.[23]

This was typical of many of Armstrong's letters. Instead of a realistic appraisal of the various factors, including the possibility of failure, he
appeared to be engaged in wishful thinking. He was certainly expecting
too much if he believed American successes at York and on the Niagara
Peninsula would induce the British to surrender the remainder of their
line of defense west of Montreal. If that was why he allowed Dearborn
and Chauncey to divert the campaign westward, he was sadly mistaken.
The success of the expedition did not meet expectations, and it resulted in
a delay of the campaign on the St. Lawrence — ultimately, as it developed,
a fatal delay.

The expedition began auspiciously enough. York was captured on
April 27, but the success was marred by a magazine explosion which killed
Brigadier General Pike, one of the most promising young officers in the
army. On May 27, Fort George was taken, but the incompetence of American leadership was painfully revealed in the series of reverses that followed. Dearborn was ill, and General Morgan Lewis, who was the acting
commander, delayed until June 1 sending a force in pursuit of the British.
Generals William Winder and John Chandler, who led this detachment,
were surprised by the British and both were captured in the confusion.
General Lewis then retreated to Fort George.

Armstrong was clearly upset by the turn of events, and he wrote
Dearborn, "There is, indeed, some strange fatality attending our efforts. I
cannot disguise from you the surprise occasioned by the two escapes of a
beaten Enemy — first, on the 27th Ulto., and again on the 1st instant." He
added that "Battles are not gained when an inferior enemy is not destroyed. Nothing is done while anything that might have been done is
omitted." There was yet to be another disaster. On June 24 an American
detachment of nearly 600 ventured out of Fort George and was ambushed
by Indians and a small force of British regulars. The whole detachment

surrendered to a force only half its size.[24] Although Dearborn was not directly responsible for these failures, his lack of leadership was obvious.
He was too ill to command and on July 6 Armstrong removed him from
his command. Madison agreed only reluctantly to take this step because
of Dearborn's political connections.[25]

While the Americans were engaged on the western end of Lake Ontario, the British, despite Armstrong's expectations, launched an attack
on a virtually unprotected Sackett's Harbor at the eastern end. On May
27, the same day the Americans captured Fort George, the British appeared
before a small detachment of regulars and New York militia commanded
by Brigadier General Jacob Brown. The British assault did considerable
damage, but the American defense was well-conducted by Brown, and
the British retired. Brown was rewarded with a commission of brigadier
general in the regular army.[26]

One persuasive argument that Dearborn and Chauncey had used in
convincing Armstrong to alter the campaign plan, was that the capture of
York would assure "complete command of the Lake." Nevertheless, Sir
James Yeo and the British fleet assumed mastery over the lake on June 3.
Armstrong conjectured that the appearance was temporary and to facili-
tate a "general retreat to Kingston." He wrote Dearborn on June 19, "We
count upon very soon hearing of an action on the lake between Chauncey
and Yeo." Chauncey, however, decided not to contest the British control
over the lake until his new ship, the "General Pike," was launched at the
end of July.

The military effect was to frustrate Armstrong's plans, because the
army could not move. His indecision was reflected in a bewildering array
of alternatives presented to General Lewis. If the British won control of
the lake, troops would have to be carried from Sackett's Harbor to Niagara and "endeavour to make a stand for the Peninsula & the country
west of it." Or Lewis's force could join Hampton's on Lake Champlain and
"seize some point below, which shall cut the Enemy's line of communication." Another possibility would be presented if Prevost detached too
freely from Kingston and left it without protection of the fleet, "a fine
blow might be struck from Sackett's harbour." Two days later he suggested that if Yeo took shelter at Kingston when Chauncey reappeared,
troops from Sackett's Harbor might reinforce those at Fort George and
jointly assault the British under General Vincent at Burlington Bay (at the
western end of Lake Ontario). Another alternative, and the one he preferred, was to bring the troops from Fort George to join those at Sackett's
Harbor, and from there launch an attack upon Kingston. The combined
strength of the Americans would be 7000, while the enemy force would be

only about 4000. "Could a successful attack be made here," he added, "the fate of the Campaign is decided — perhaps that of the War." A week later, apparently assuming an attack upon Kingston was decided upon, he informed Lewis he had ordered Hampton "to push his Head Quarters to the position held by our Army the last campaign on Lake Champlain." At the same time he ordered General Boyd at Fort George to take no offensive action.[27]

General Lewis was not anxious to undertake any offensive operation. He reported to Armstrong on July 5 that the British force was superior, that his troops were undependable and "eternally intoxicated," and besides he did not believe Chauncey would be on the lake before the first of August. On July 23 he reported, based on "indubitable authority," that large reinforcements had arrived at Quebec, and he believed the force opposing him would amount to 12,000 regulars in the next week. "I am completely satisfied," he wrote, "that the British Force in Canada is much larger than has been supposed." Lewis's reticence and the ease with which he could believe the grossly exaggerated reports on enemy strength marked him as being of the same stripe as Dearborn. It was obvious that aggressive and competent leadership was lacking on the northern frontier. General Porter, who commanded a militia force at Fort George, wrote Armstrong that it was "impossible to remain quiet & witness the ruin of the country." He complained that "The general officers plan nothing unless it be for their own safety; & what has been done, has been at the instigation of inferior officers." He argued that unless Armstrong himself or General Wilkinson, "or some other officer of more talents & experience than any we have had is sent in, we shall never take Canada."[28]

As Porter wrote, General James Wilkinson, who had played a key role in the southern theater, was slowly making his way to Washington to receive his instructions before proceeding to the northern frontier. When the war began most Americans had looked to the Canadian frontier, but many Southerners coveted the Spanish territory of Florida. Spain was at peace with the United States, but she was a nominal ally of the British. President Madison and Secretary of State Monroe were particularly anxious to obtain Florida, and in October 1812 Madison authorized Governor Willie Blount of Tennessee to call out 1500 militia for the intended conquest of Florida. The response was rapid, and by December 10 Major General Andrew Jackson of the Tennessee militia had raised 2000 men whom he pronounced ready to place "the American eagle on the ramparts of Mobile, Pensacola, and Fort St. Augustine." Major General Thomas Pinckney, whose command included Georgia, was informed that a force would be placed under his command adequate for the "reduction of St.

Augustine." General Wilkinson, commanding at New Orleans, was instructed to prepare to take possession of West Florida.[29]

Congress, however, balked at an offensive war against Spanish territory and authorized only the occupation of West Florida, to which the
United States at least had a dubious claim. When Armstrong took over
the War Department, his first task was to dismiss Jackson's force, which
was no longer needed. On February 5, the day he took office, he wrote a
curt letter to Jackson stating merely that the reasons for embodying the
corps had "ceased to exist," and they were therefore dismissed. Jackson's
march had been halted at Natchez by Wilkinson who had no desire to
have this force placed upon his short supplies, nor was he anxious to see
his old enemy Jackson in his district. The reason he gave the War Department, however, was that he could not predict the consequences of 2000
undisciplined militia removed from the social restraints in which they
were bred "turned loose on this licentious community, made up of all
kinds, countries, and colors." More to the point, he observed that Governor Blount had sent 2000 men and a major general instead of 1500 men
under a brigadier general. Jackson would out-rank Wilkinson, and thus
take precedence in command. Nevertheless, Wilkinson promised that he
would harmonize with Jackson for the public good. He even advised
keeping Jackson's force in service despite their expense because of the discontent which would arise from their dismissal.[30]

Wilkinson at least anticipated the political consequences of dismiss-
ing Jackson's troops. He received a copy of Armstrong's letter to Jackson
before it was received by Jackson. "The order will come like a thunder
clap on Jackson," Wilkinson predicted to Armstrong, and he added, "I
have considered it my duty to soothe him by a complimentary letter."
Jackson's reaction to the War Department order was reported to Wilkinson: "When the Genl. read this he flew into a passion & damned himself if
he would disband them till he had marched them back to Tennessee and if
the Q. Master and contractor would not furnish them with the needful
provisions he would take it."[31]

Jackson wrote to Armstrong that his brave men deserved a "better
fate" than being dismissed "eight hundred miles from home, deprived of
arms, tents, and supplies for the sick," and he informed the secretary that
he was going to march his men back to Nashville where he expected the
troops to be paid, and the necessary supplies furnished by the agents of
the government, after which he would dismiss his force. Governor Blount
shortly afterwards advised Armstrong that he had called upon the contractor and paymaster to provide for Jackson's men, and in case they
failed to do so he would borrow the money from the Nashville bank. He

added that he assumed the government would sanction his measures, as the object was to promote the public good.[32]

Armstrong, unaware of the furor created by his letter, had written more fully to Jackson in the meantime that the troops were to be provided for and marched back to Tennessee where the paymaster was directed to have funds available for their pay. Had he been more precise in his original letter, the anger aroused would have been avoided. The incident, however, should have been instructive, for it marked Jackson as a strong-willed and aggressive man. Armstrong, if he recognized these traits, at any rate failed to accept Jackson's offer "to support the Eagles of our country at any point ordered by the constituted authorities."[33]

While the invasion plans against East Florida were called off, Wilkinson took possession of West Florida as far as the Perdido River. Mobile surrendered on April 15. Although he conducted himself creditably, the accumulation of grievances against him in Louisiana forced Madison to replace him. Senator William H. Crawford of Georgia had warned Madison on March 3 that the two senators and representatives from Louisiana would be driven into opposition to the Administration unless Wilkinson was removed. Wilkinson was aware of the effort to remove him, and he wrote Monroe early in February "my Constitution will not bear a northern Climate, and . . . I do conceive my Rank & Service give me claim to a separate Command."[34] This letter was received two days before the order of March 10 calling him north, and this was undoubtedly why Armstrong wrote him a personal letter on March 12 to soften the blow. Alluding to their common service under General Gates, Armstrong wrote, "Why should you remain in your land of cypress when patriotism and ambition equally invite you to one that grows the laurels?" The men of the North and East wanted him, while those of the Southwest were less anxious to have him among them. "I speak to you with the frankness due to you and to myself," he concluded, "and again advise, come to the North and come quickly! If our cards are well played, we may renew the scenes of Saratoga."[35]

Wilkinson's appointment was accompanied by a promotion to major general. Due to his absence in West Florida, he did not receive Armstrong's order until May 19. His reluctance to come north was revealed in his reply that the late receipt of the order would expose him to a "sultry, fatigueing, dilatory journey, and retard my arrival on the theatre where I am destined to take a part." He did not depart New Orleans until June 10, and his progress was indeed dilatory. He did not arrive in Washington until July 31, nearly five months after Armstrong's order was given.[36]

When Wilkinson arrived in Washington, he was designated to replace Dearborn. He also received his instructions and Armstrong's latest thoughts on a plan of campaign. Armstrong anticipated American naval ascendancy on Lake Ontario, and thus the time for increased activity was near (in fact the *General Pike* was ready for service on July 20). Armstrong proposed to move the forces at Fort George to Sackett's Harbor for an attack upon Kingston, which he pointed out would be returning to the original plan of campaign. Then, typically, he began offering alternatives. He suggested that a simultaneous movement might also be made from Lake Champlain toward Montreal, which might become an actual attack if the enemy weakened the post to save Kingston. Another alternative was to occupy a point on the St. Lawrence at Madrid (Hamilton), approximately twenty miles below Ogdensburg, and then move in concert with General Hampton against Montreal. In any event, the commanding general would elect the best plan according to circumstances.[37]

The man to whom Armstrong now entrusted the fate of the northern campaign had, to say the least, a tarnished reputation. Wilkinson's passion for intrigue ran from the Conway Cabal through the so-called Spanish Conspiracy in Kentucky in the 1780s, when he became a pensioner of the Spanish as Agent 13, down to his involvement in Burr's Conspiracy. He had retained his high positions despite several courts of inquiry and, as recently as 1811, a court-martial. His military reputation was more impressive. He had served under General Anthony Wayne against the Indians during the 1790s (while at the same time intriguing to replace him), and in length of service, Wilkinson had more than any other officer in the army.[38]

When Wilkinson had the temerity to suggest an alteration in Armstrong's plan, it gave a portent of a future unhappy relationship between the two men. He recommended that if the forces were not immediately competent to attack Kingston, operations should begin around Fort George while Hampton menaced Montreal. Once victorious on the western end of the lake, he would move like "lightning" to attack Kingston, and after reducing it, move downstream and form a junction with Hampton and reduce Montreal. Armstrong answered with a long, finely reasoned letter, designed obviously to demolish the fatuous reasoning of his general. Wilkinson's proposal to carry operations westward of Kingston would leave the strength of the enemy unbroken, and as long as they kept their line of communication open to the sea they could reinforce their defenses or renew the war in the West. Kingston, therefore," he wrote, "as well on grounds of policy as of military principle, presents the first & great object of the Campaign." Kingston should be attacked directly, or lacking the force, indirectly by seizing and obstructing the line of communication and drying up sources of supply. This strong affirmation of the campaign objective was compromised, however, when he suggested some ideas on an alternative plan, previously presented, of making a feint against Kingston and marching against Montreal. Wilkinson expressed contempt for this letter later as "a pleasant work, to a minister in his closet, and quite easy of execution, on paper; where we find neither ditches, nor ramparts, nor parapets, nor artillery, nor small arms."[39] In truth, Armstrong had an equivocal mind which was capable of allowing him to see the right policy, but not to hold it with any conviction.

Armstrong informed Wilkinson that he would soon join him at the front in order to "furnish with promptitude whatever might be necessary." It soon became apparent that one of his main functions would be to keep two bitter enemies, Wilkinson and Hampton, appeased so that they would cooperate during the campaign. Both had been assigned to the North to augment General Dearborn's staff, but Dearborn's removal made Wilkinson the senior officer and thus the commander of the district and Hampton's superior. Wilkinson was determined to establish his control over Hampton, who commanded in the Lake Champlain region. Armstrong had informed Wilkinson that Hampton would operate "cotemporarily with you & under orders in prosecution of the plan of Campaign which has been given to you." Armstrong told Hampton that his command was intended to be distinct and separate, and that only in joint operations would the principle of seniority operate. Hampton accepted reluctantly, as he indicated to Armstrong later. "You did not affect to force [it] upon me, although I saw very clearly I was to expect no other."[40]

As soon as he arrived in his district, Wilkinson ordered Hampton to furnish the returns of troops and his status on supplies. Hampton quickly wrote to Armstrong to reaffirm his separate and distinct status or accept his resignation. He had correctly interpreted Wilkinson's intention to subordinate him to his control or to drive him from the service. Wilkinson wrote Armstrong that unless Hampton followed orders "he should be sent home."[41] Armstrong informed Hampton that the operations planned would create a situation in which the seniority rule applied. He noted that the commands could be separate and distinct without being independent, and he added that it had not been his intention to make a junior officer serving in the same district independent of a senior. He had meant only that the physical separation would place Hampton's command beyond the immediate supervision of the senior officer. He reassured Hampton, however, "I shall be with you throughout the campaign, & I pledge to you my honor as a soldier, that your rights shall not be invaded." Hampton replied, "Your letter has locked the door upon me . . . The close of the campaign must open me a passage should I not find a shorter route in the course of it."[42]

Wilkinson meanwhile wrote Armstrong from Sackett's Harbor that if all went well he would be ready to move by September 15, and he should be in possession of Kingston by September 26. Armstrong, now in Albany, reported this to Madison on August 28, and he informed him that he had been busily arranging for a militia levy, forwarding supplies, and attempting to appease Hampton. He left Albany the next day for Sackett's Harbor and arrived there in mid-September. Wilkinson was at Fort George speeding up the movement of troops, but while there he became ill and for a while nothing was done. Armstrong remained optimistic, and he reported to William Duane on September 18 that Wilkinson was recovering and the troops would soon be in motion.[43]

At about the same time, the good news arrived of Oliver H. Perry's victory on Lake Erie, which meant that Harrison would soon be in action in the West. Lieutenant Perry had taken command in March 1813 at Presque Isle (Erie, Pennsylvania), where the ships were being constructed. With great exertion and some luck, he managed early in August to join the four ships built at Presque Isle with the five vessels from Black Rock (on the Niagara River) without British interference. He was faced with a serious lack of seamen, but Harrison made up the shortage with some of his men. Perry met the enemy on September 10, and he won a complete victory, thus opening the way for the enterprise against Canada.[44] Harrison was short of troops, but as previously noted, Armstrong modified his position to permit the use of militia for the Canadian expedition. Governor Shelby was called upon for 2000 men, and Governor Meigs of Ohio for two regiments of militia. Harrison expected to raise at least 4000 militia to make up the complement of 7000 intended for the expedition against Fort Malden.

For the next six weeks Armstrong manifested no interest in the events in the Northwest, and he wrote no letters of advice. On September 27, 1813, Perry's ships and the troop boats constructed at Cleveland carried a force of approximately 4500 men to a point about three miles below the town of Amherstburg. The British had already abandoned the town and Fort Malden. Harrison informed Armstrong that he had no hope of catching the enemy "as he has upwards of 1000 horses and we have not one in the army." However, Colonel Johnson's mounted regiment, which had gone around by land, joined Harrison in Detroit on September 30, and the pursuit began in earnest on October 2. On October 5 they caught the British, and at the Battle of the Thames, fought mostly by Johnson's regiment, the Americans won a complete victory.[45]

Harrison returned to Detroit on October 9. The militia departed for home, but Harrison still had a force of about 2500 regulars. He intended to send a detachment westward to reduce Mackinac and St. Joseph's, but Armstrong directed him, instead of pursuing the Indians into their "woody and distant recesses," to carry his main force down the lake and approach the British at Fort George from the rear. Harrison moved to Buffalo with about thirteen hundred men, arriving there with General McArthur on October 24.[46]

Unfortunately, the gains in the West were not achieved in time to affect the developments along the St. Lawrence. Harrison's movement to Fort George was for defensive reasons, and on November 3 Armstrong directed Harrison to send his regulars to protect Sackett's Harbor, despite his protests that this would leave Fort George practically defenseless. Harrison received permission to return to the West, but perhaps hoping to clear up some of the misunderstandings, he asked for an interview with Armstrong. They met for the first time in Albany, but the interview was unproductive. Indeed, on his way home Harrison made an oblique attack on Armstrong's scheme of conscription. At a public dinner held in his honor in Philadelphia, he volunteered a toast which began by stating: "A sentiment is gaining ground unfriendly to republicanism and injurious to the nation, and knowing from my own experience, that the sentiment is not well founded," he then offered a toast to the militia of the United States.[47]

Meanwhile, Wilkinson was reluctant to assault Kingston. From Fort George he suggested a sweep of the western end of Lake Ontario, taking possession of Burlington, which he believed would capture as many as three thousand enemy. Armstrong, patiently awaiting Wilkinson's arrival at Sackett's Harbor, advised him that if Kingston was seized, "all above perishes, because the tree is then girdled," and he asserted, "The main object must be prosecuted." Wilkinson then suggested a feint against Kingston and moving down the St. Lawrence against Montreal.[48] Armstrong was becoming exasperated, not only by Wilkinson's incomprehensible suggestions, but also by the delay occasioned by the futile activities of Chauncey on the lake. He wrote to Madison that he was trying to convince the Commodore that Yeo would continue to refuse a battle, and that instead the fleet should be used for "convoying our troops immediately to this post & thus enabling us, to go to our particular object." The delay forced Armstrong to halt the movement of General Hampton from Lake Champlain at Four Corners (approximately forty miles from Plattsburgh), until further advised. Armstrong was still hopeful, and he informed Madison on October 4 that Wilkinson was moving from Fort

George with 3000 troops. "The weather is uncommonly fine," he added, "and of the general issue of the campaign we have everything to hope."[49]

Wilkinson arrived at Sackett's Harbor on October 4, and again he urged that Kingston be passed by and the main attack made upon Montreal. Armstrong disagreed; his mind was fixed upon Kingston. Wilkinson again became very ill, and this prompted Armstrong to note sardonically in his next report to Madison, "This climate seems to be very unfriendly to our commanding generals." He seriously considered taking command of the army himself. On October 19 he hinted to Madison that the attack on Kingston would be called off. The enemy had been reinforced and would no longer he found "naked & napping." Hampton's force could be brought to join those at Sackett's Harbor, but that would produce delay and "compel us to abandon the other and better object below."[50] Heretofore, Hampton's force had not been considered necessary for the reduction of Kingston, and now Armstrong realized that the season was too late for an attack upon Kingston. They had been idly waiting for nearly a month to cooperate against Montreal, if such a contingency developed. Armstrong might be credited with foresight in having a force adequate to obtain a secondary object if the first was unobtainable, but it seems equally clear in retrospect that the failure to use this force of four thousand men against the primary object eventually resulted in neither object being gained.

Armstrong still believed that by prompt and efficient action Montreal could be gained. He argued to Wilkinson on October 19 that Montreal was a "safer and greater" object, which "if seized now, will save one campaign." It would sever the enemy line of operations, "it restrains all below, withers and perishes all above itself." Wilkinson resented Armstrong's interference, and he showed his pique by announcing that he had changed his mind. He now preferred to make the attack on Kingston, and he used Armstrong's arguments to buttress his case. He also demanded that Armstrong must "by the authority of the President, direct the operations of the army under my command particularly against Montreal."[51] Armstrong replied that Wilkinson's instructions gave him the alternative and that he was not at liberty to change the ground of those instructions, because "the only effect of this would be to substitute my opinion for yours." Armstrong undoubtedly recognized that his presence agitated the General, and the same day he answered Wilkinson he wrote Madison, "I shall forbear my visit to Canada until a future day."[52]

It is perhaps too easy to attribute the worst possible motives to Armstrong's actions at this critical juncture of the campaign. He had assumed the role of coordinator between Wilkinson and Hampton, and now at the moment when cooperation was most essential he removed himself from that role and became merely an interested spectator. He may have felt, as he informed Hampton, that the rule of seniority now applied, but a wiser man would have known that throwing the two enemies upon each other would not work. Armstrong obviously had some doubts about his authority to accompany the army, and he may have feared some criticism. He may also have sensed the failure of the expedition, as many have charged, and wished to disassociate himself from that failure. However, it is unlikely that he believed he could escape fully the responsibility for the campaign.

Hampton, for his part, had been fretting about the adequacy of his supplies, and nearly every letter to Armstrong repeated the same refrain about the "rawness" of his troops. Late in October he crossed the border toward the St. Lawrence to be in a position to effect a junction with Wilkinson's force. Hampton's ineptitude was revealed when he was repulsed by a smaller British force in the battle of Chateaugay. Informed by the quartermaster that orders had been given by Armstrong to build huts on the Chateaugay River below the border, Hampton wrote Armstrong on November 1 that a war council unanimously decided to return to camp at Four Corners in "fulfillment of the ostensible views of the Government." "The campaign," he added, "I consider substantially at an *end*," and he submitted his resignation."[53]

Armstrong's order of October 18 to Quartermaster General Swartwout directing the building of huts perhaps merited this interpretation by Hampton, for it could be reasonably deduced that the secretary did not expect the army to reach Montreal. Wilkinson claimed later that he was not informed of the order. Armstrong defended his action to Madison as merely a contingency. "The failure of the enterprise was a possible event & being such was guarded against. It showed only wisdom and foresight. If we got to Montreal, we but lost the labor . . . If we did not get to that city — a covering for the army was provided."[54] His explanation is plausible, but even if his order did proceed from good motives, it offered a pretext to General Hampton to do nothing, and this was detrimental to the success of Wilkinson's expedition.

Armstrong's withdrawal as an active participant did not become known to Wilkinson until he was actually ready to depart on the expedition. He believed Armstrong intended to travel by land down the river in order to maintain contact with the army. Armstrong informed him on October 30, however, that "bad roads, worse weather, and a considerable degree of illness, admonish me against receding further from a point where my engagements call me." He then directed Wilkinson to "Give

Hampton timely notice of your approach, and of the place and hour of junction." Wilkinson received this order reluctantly, noting that Hampton had "treated my authority with contempt, & has acted exclusively under your orders. I wish this Information could come from you, that I may be saved the hazard of a second insult." He added, "You may however rest assured, that in this case my feelings shall be silenced, and that I will humiliate myself to make the most of this Pretendce."[55]

Hampton, meanwhile, proceeding as if the campaign were over, was undoubtedly surprised when he received a letter from General Wilkinson calling upon him to effect a junction of forces. He declined to join Wilkinson, citing his shortage of supplies and Wilkinson's request to bring a "two or three months supply." He ignored Wilkinson's statement that lack of provisions "should not prevent the progress of the expedition." Hampton could not admit to his personal enemy that he had thought the campaign was over, was preparing to place his army in winter quarters, and was thus unprepared to join Wilkinson's army. He explained this to Armstrong. He had sent off the cavalry, artillery, and provision teams to Plattsburgh for subsistence. "General Wilkinson had no spare transportation for us," he noted, "and the junction would have reduced the stock of provisions to eight or ten days for the whole. The alternative was adopted under the impression of *absolute necessity*."[56]

Wilkinson's force had suffered a check on the way down the St. Lawrence at Chrysler's Farm (November 11), and it was obvious that he was reluctant to make the assault upon Montreal. Hampton's letter offered the pretext to call off the attack, as well as an opportunity to shift all the blame upon his old enemy. He replied to Hampton that the refusal to join his force "defeats the grand objects of the campaign," and the next day (November 13) by a general order, he proclaimed that the army would be compelled to retire because of the "extraordinary, unexampled, and it appears unwarrantable conduct of Major General Hampton in refusing to join this army."[57]

Meanwhile Armstrong had gone to Albany. Arriving there on November 8, he wrote Madison a series of optimistic letters. When he received Hampton's letters, he immediately, by express, ordered him to make a movement to join Wilkinson or to detain the enemy on the south side of the St. Lawrence while Wilkinson passed in the rear and seized Montreal. He noted to Madison that the jealousy and misunderstanding between Wilkinson and Hampton would make it necessary to part with one of them when the campaign was over. As late as November 14, despite all appearances to the contrary, Armstrong was still optimistic. He informed Madison that Hampton was on the move and Prevost would be compelled to stand and fight or fall back to defend Montreal. On November 19, however, he reported, "you will find in the enclosed letters the probable termination of the campaign on the St. Lawrence."[58]

The failure of the campaign was followed by efforts of the individuals involved to cast the blame on the others. Wilkinson blamed Hampton and advised Armstrong to have him arrested. Armstrong declined and Wilkinson gave the order himself. Hampton, however, left his army and proceeded to Washington to defend himself where he had powerful political friends. Armstrong at first believed Wilkinson, and not Hampton, was chiefly responsible, but he later threw the blame on both equally.[59] All three were, of course, to blame for the failure of the campaign. The two American forces probably amounted to twice the number of defenders on the other side, but their numerical superiority was never brought to bear upon a single point. Even when the junction of the forces was planned for the assault upon Montreal, the merger did not take place due to a lack of liaison and the ineptitude of Hampton. Wilkinson was ill and unaggressive. He arrived at Sackett's Harbor on August 20, but the force was not collected and ready to move for nearly two and a half months. Armstrong's efforts to prod Wilkinson were ineffectual and probably harmful, because his presence was resented by Wilkinson.

Armstrong must, however, bear the major share of the blame, for he was primarily responsible for the planning and coordination. Instead of directing a build-up of men and supplies and firmly establishing a single objective, he gave the commander a choice of three plans and placed two widely separated armies on the front commanded by two men who were personal enemies. He assumed the responsibility for coordination, but he divested himself of that function at the critical moment when his services were most needed. Hampton admittedly was ignorant of the fact that Wilkinson intended a movement down the St. Lawrence, and when advised by Wilkinson, he was incapable of acting.

The failure of the campaign was a blow to the hopes of the Administration. Late in September, Madison had written William Wirt expressing the hope that a victory would stifle "the Censorious adversaries and criticising friends of the Administration." By the end of October, with prospects of a victory dwindling, he wrote Armstrong, "In the worst event, I hope an intermediate establishment between Kingston & Montreal can be secured." Even that limited objective was not obtained.[60]

Armstrong apparently felt it necessary to remind Madison that despite the recent failure, the campaign of 1813 had some successes. On November 25 he wrote a summary of the year's military events, noting that several enemy attacks had been successfully repulsed, while Americans had been successful in attacks on York, Fort George, Erie, and Malden.

Detroit had been recovered, and the Indians subdued in the West. Additionally, several battles had been fought on the borders of the St. Lawrence, "though not accomplishing their special objects, reflect the highest honor on the discipline and prowess of our soldiery and offer to us the best assurance of eventual victory."[61]

Armstrong's summation of the conduct of American arms on the St. Lawrence is questionable, but his evaluation of the 1813 campaign, as it developed, was premature. The British at least were not through for the year. They began actions early in December on the Niagara frontier, inadequately defended by only a few hundred New York militia. Fort George was abandoned (on December 10) by their commander, Brigadier General George McClure. Before retreating, he burned the near-by town of Newark, and this act brought swift retaliation by the British. On December 18, they crossed the Niagara River and surprised the American force at Fort Niagara, killing sixty-seven Americans. This was followed on December 29 by the assault and burning of Black Rock and Buffalo, with the destruction of all the public stores and American boats located there. General Lewis Cass, passing through Buffalo a week after this attack, described the ruins of Buffalo as "a scene of distress and destruction such as I have never before witnessed." He criticized the commander of Fort Niagara, but he also asserted that the militia "behaved in the most cowardly manner. They fled without discharging a musket."[62]

The failure of the militia was not an uncommon occurrence in the War of 1812, and indeed this was why Armstrong was at this time urging the president and Congress to adopt conscription to do away with the necessity of relying upon them. Yet even though convinced of their worthlessness, Armstrong had confided the defense of the whole Niagara frontier exclusively to militia. Harrison had warned on November 11 that the militia force would be inadequate to protect Fort George. Armstrong did call upon the governor of New York on November 25 for 1000 militia, but only to replace those of McClure's force whose terms were up.[63] The people of Buffalo paid dearly for Armstrong's miscalculation.

In his report to Congress, Armstrong included a letter from Colonel Winfield Scott stating that "it is difficult to conceive how one or two hundred men could have been suddenly dislodged from its block-houses, even by a force of one or two thousand assailants." Scott undoubtedly referred to regular soldiers, an advantage not enjoyed by McClure, who declared in his defense, "The militia will do to act with Regulars, but not without them, in spite of all my exertions to insure subordination, my late detachment ultimately proved to be very little better than an infuriated mob."[64]

The British justified their unusually severe actions because of Mc-

Clure's burning of Newark. McClure acted apparently under a mistaken impression. After burning the town he wrote Armstrong that it was done "in conformity with the views of your Excellency disclosed to me in a former communication." In sending this letter to the president, Armstrong wrote in the margin, "not true. My letter authorised it only in case it should be necessary to the *defense* of Fort Geo. In that case the measure would be justifiable." As the British had asked whether the burning of Newark was committed by authority of the American government or was the unauthorized act of an individual, Madison ordered Armstrong to have Wilkinson "say frankly to Prevost, that the Burning of Newark was the effect of a misapprehension of the officer & not an order from the govt."[65]

Thus the campaign of 1813 ended on a note of humiliation, and on the northern front the events of the year left the situation in a little better condition at the end than it was at the beginning. The gains on the Niagara Peninsula were wiped out; the major British posts of Kingston and Montreal had been threatened but not attacked, and no American force yet seriously threatened on the St. Lawrence, the vital link of communication between these two posts. Armstrong's original strategy presented to the Cabinet was sound, but it was soon altered by the timidity and specious reasoning of General Dearborn and Commodore Chauncey, as well as by the indecisiveness of the secretary himself, who lacked the firmness of his convictions. A spring and summer were wasted on military activity on the Niagara Peninsula which reflected little credit on the military leadership. An autumn was wasted organizing an expedition that should have begun in the spring, and it began in the winter when it should have ended.

The unique experiment of the Secretary of War going to the front must be counted a failure. There is nothing to indicate that Armstrong performed any creditable function which he could not have performed in Washington. Many activities, such as forwarding supplies, issuing calls for troops and issuing tactical orders were more properly the duties of the staff officers or the commanding general. His most important function, that of maintaining liaison between Wilkinson and Hampton, was the least creditable and unjustifiable from the military viewpoint. That he failed to perform that duty at the critical juncture of the campaign, was one important reason for the failure of the expedition against Montreal. In the final analysis, he did little that was useful, much that was unnecessary, and a few things that were actually detrimental.

10

THE CAMPAIGN OF 1814

ARMSTRONG'S PUBLIC DUTIES delayed the completion of the splendid house he was building on his estate along the Hudson River. He had started construction in the spring of 1812 on a site about a half-mile from the river. Because of the undulations of the land and the position of the woodlands, the river could be seen only in glimpses from this location. The front of the house did not even face the river, the orientation being north-south. One tradition states that the site was chosen because of an "inexhaustible spring" nearby, but it is nowhere to be seen today. The house was built against and somewhat into the southerly slope of a rise, apparently to shield the inhabitants from the "icy northern blasts." This gave the house a unique tri-level feature, in that from the back entrance one had to go either up to the second floor or descend to the first. Because the house was built on a rocky shelf, there was no basement; the kitchen and the other service rooms were evidently in wings attached to the basic structure.[1]

In Warner Richards, a master carpenter of Scottish origin, Armstrong found a skilled craftsman to carry out the plans of the stately mansion. Richards was not only the builder, but he was also the master joiner who executed all the fine interior wainscoting and moulding by hand. He was at work on the window cases in October 1812, indicating that the work on the house was well underway by then. A farm account book from this period notes the arrival of a large number of bricks, no doubt for the interior walls and chimneys of the house. Although work on the house continued during the war, Armstrong's preoccupation with other matters delayed the completion until 1815.[2]

The war also affected the Armstrongs personally in another way.

Four of their sons served in the War of 1812, with Henry, who rose to the rank of lieutenant colonel at the age of twenty-two, having the most distinguished career. He participated in the battles of Queenston Heights (where he was wounded) and Stony Creek. Horatio was a major, but he served primarily only as a courier. After graduating from West Point, where his father had procured an appointment for him, John served briefly as an aide-de-camp to General Jacob Brown. Robert, who was also appointed to the Military Academy and graduated near the war's end, saw no action. He did, however, retain his commission and made the army his career. Kosciuszko, perhaps because of his youth, refused an appointment to West Point and remained with his parents.[3]

Armstrong's personal concerns were small compared to the damage the failures of the 1813 campaign did to his public reputation. He must have paused to reflect on the strange fate that gave him a surfeit of incompetent generals, and he must have pondered the irony that the most impressive gains came in the theatres to which he gave the least attention. This generalization, however, must be qualified if applied to the South, where the war was prosecuted with less success than might have been expected had the War Department rendered more assistance. Actually, little fighting had been expected in the South. When Brigadier General Thomas Flournoy replaced General Wilkinson in command of the Seventh Military District (encompassing the States of Louisiana, Tennessee, and the Mississippi Territory) on May 26, 1813, most of the regular troops in his district had been given orders to march to the northern front. Flournoy protested, but Armstrong informed him, "We have no reason to believe that the Enemy's attention will be turned toward your Command during the present summer." Flournoy was advised to fill his regiments and avoid lending his influence to any faction as Wilkinson had.[4]

Although Armstrong was not concerned about the safety of New Orleans, disturbing reports began to reach him about a civil war raging among the Creek Indians (residing primarily in present-day Alabama) and its possible effect on American settlements along the southern frontier. General Wilkinson, while on his way northward in 1813, wrote that the Creek war party was very numerous, and he advised that if some demonstration was not made in behalf of the well disposed, "we may eventually be obliged to make some sacrifice of blood & treasure, to extinguish the flame which appears to be on the eve of bursting forth."[5] Similar letters prompted Armstrong to halt the march of the Third Regiment to the northern front, and the governors of Georgia and Tennessee were asked on July 13 to raise a force of 1500 men and to correspond and cooperate with each other. General Thomas Pinckney, Commander of the

Sixth Military District (the two Carolinas and Georgia), was advised that "if the agents of Spain at Pensacola are seen to give it nourishment & support, it will be an act of War on their part, which may at least leave us at liberty to strike at Pensacola, & thus to seize a point which from local & other circumstances, is, in my judgment, essential to the safety of our frontier on the Gulph."[6] Armstrong's prompt response thus may have had another motive. The force raised might be used to conquer East Florida. The offer of Russian mediation and the subsequent mission sent to St. Petersburg had placed a barrier in the way of projects to seize East Florida, but the cooperation of the Spanish with the Creeks would be sufficient to remove that barrier.

Southerners were by no means unanimous in their belief that the Creeks intended hostility toward the whites. Benjamin Hawkins, the Creek Indian Agent, still referred to the disturbances as a civil war, but by late July he was warning of a meditated attack. He still did not blame the Spanish. "It is reduced to a certainty," he wrote, "that the civil war which has raged for sometime among the Creeks originated with the British in Canada." The Spanish became involved, however, when a group of Creek warriors visited Pensacola in the middle of July. The Spanish governor received them politely, but he gave them only a small quantity of powder and bullets. On their way back to their villages, the Indians were attacked by a group of Americans who had learned of their visit to Pensacola. The Indians fought off their attackers, but this incident at Burnt Corn on July 27, 1813, was, as Henry Adams wrote, "regarded by the Indians as a declaration of war by the whites." On August 30, the Creeks attacked Fort Mims (about forty miles north of Mobile) and massacred over 250 of the inhabitants, including women and children. The Fort Mims massacre aroused the whole country, and the militia force called out earlier by Armstrong now faced a war with the hostile Creeks.[7]

The organization of this force was slowed by the lack of cooperation between the governors of Georgia and Tennessee. Armstrong had failed to mention where or how the troops were to be supplied. The problems and misunderstandings were complicated by the fact that Armstrong departed for the northern front on August 10, leaving the department in the hands of the chief clerk, Daniel Parker. The two governors had interpreted Armstrong's letter of July 13 differently. Governor David Mitchell of Georgia had issued a call for militia upon receipt of the letter, but Governor Willie Blount of Tennessee did not believe that he had been given that authority, and he merely alerted his militia. Governor Mitchell informed the War Department that due to Governor Blount's interpretation, he would increase the Georgia force to 2500 men, and he urgently requested information on how funds and supplies were to be furnished. Parker answered early in September that instructions and funds had been sent to the contractor, and that additional funds would be placed at the disposal of the governor.[8]

Governor Blount, after learning of the Fort Mims massacre, wrote the War Department asking if the letter of July 13 was intended as authority to call out the troops. He complained particularly about the lack of instructions and information.[9] Armstrong's departure for the North thus came at a crucial time for the southern front. The lack of guidance and coordination by the War Department severely hampered the campaign against the Creeks.

Still without instructions, Blount and the Tennessee legislature decided to authorize a force of thirty-five hundred men in addition to the fifteen hundred already called for the service of the United States. Madison accepted the additional force into public service, explaining to Armstrong that it was thought best to deliver "a decisive blow" before the British or Spanish could render the Creeks much assistance. Armstrong, following these events from the northern front, disagreed. "After so much unaccountable sluggishness," he wrote, "Tennessee is pouring out thousands. How shall we pay them? I think it would be well to admonish Gov. Blount that our calculations were made with strict regard to our means — and that the amount of the requisition (1500) is as many as we can pay & feed." Madison was not persuaded. He noted that the period of service of the militia would be short. Governor Blount had already been reminded to avoid all waste.[10]

Armstrong could not, and did not, exercise much control over the policy in the South. On September 26, after being informed that the Spanish had burned some blockhouses on the American side of the Perdido River, he urged Madison to act immediately to take Pensacola. Madison was sympathetic and this action would have met with enthusiastic approval in the South, but he doubted that he had the authority to act without congressional approval. There was no shortage of troops, but there were problems of supply and there was a want of cooperation and coordination among the various forces around the Indian country. Five thousand volunteers from Tennessee under Major Generals Jackson and Cocke were operating separately in northern Alabama. In early November Jackson and his men won two decisive victories, but they could not follow up their advantage because of a lack of supplies. The Georgia militia was inactive until late November, when General John Floyd led a raid into the Indian country, but they soon returned to defensive positions. Brigadier General Ferdinand L. Claiborne of the Mississippi volunteers raided up the Alabama River, but without cooperation and supplies, he was forced to retreat. Thus four expeditions were made into the Indian territory in 1813 from four directions without successfully ending the war.[11]

The lack of direction from the War Department and the lack of a military commander to coordinate the actions of the various forces obviously contributed to the ineffectiveness of the campaign against the Creeks. A problem of command had plagued the operation. Madison had named Governor Mitchell commander, but he was satisfied to hold a defensive position along his frontier. If Armstrong had been at the War Department, it is doubtful that such a political appointment would have been made. By early October Madison was having second thoughts about his selection of Mitchell, whose term of office was approaching an end. As Brigadier General Flournoy would be subordinate to the Tennessee commander, Major General Jackson, Major General Pinckney of the Sixth District was informed on October 18 that his command would be extended to the Seventh District for the purpose of the campaign against the Creeks. General Pinckney arrived in western Georgia in late November to assume his command, and there was hope that the campaign would receive a more positive direction in the South as well as in the North in 1814.[12]

The failures of the 1813 campaign obviously necessitated a reevaluation of the strategy and mode of operation for the forthcoming campaign of 1814. Armstrong informed President Madison that the primary emphasis for the coming year should be to gain control over Lake Ontario and Lake Champlain before further offensive operations. An increase in naval means, he wrote, would "be essential to the only plan of campaign we can persue with effect."[13] The success of Perry on Lake Erie might be repeated on Lakes Ontario and Champlain.

Armstrong expressed very strong ideas about operations in the West in 1814. Asserting that the enemy would attempt to use the British settlements along the Thames as a base to reestablish their communications and control over the Indians, he declared that the cheapest and surest method would be to "convert them into a desart." Friendly Indians should be conciliated, assured of their boundaries, and then let loose against the inhabitants along the British frontier. The example of the enemy justified this mode of warfare. "All the horrors brought to our firesides," he wrote, "ought to be carried to theirs." Various individuals in the West, including Generals McArthur and Cass, had recommended using Indians against the British and even destroying disaffected settlements, and so had Governor Tompkins, with "prior notice to the inhabitants." President Madison, however, thought Armstrong's measures too harsh, and instead Harrison was directed to make prisoners of male British settlers who might be disposed to do harm.[14]

Despite Wilkinson's suggestions for an offensive thrust and occupation of a place on the St. Lawrence, Armstrong ordered him to withdraw to a safer position into winter quarters to await spring before taking any offensive action. He was, however, authorized to take minor actions to harass the enemy. Political pressure was also building to retaliate for the British attack on the Niagara Peninsula. Armstrong was concerned about an attack on Sackett's Harbor and he reasoned, "Some activity on our part is the surest method of keeping down their enterprises." Governor Tompkins, however, warned that something more than diversionary movements was expected. "Be assured, Dear Sir, that something must be done, & that speedily and effectually, or the confidence of the citizens of this quarter of the United States, in the government, will be lost." Tompkins suggested attacking Kingston or Prescott, and if that was not approved, he asked for 2500 regulars and he would raise 5000 volunteers and attack Burlington or York. He asserted that he could easily raise the volunteers in ten days; such were the excited feelings of the people of New York.[15]

Wilkinson continued to submit schemes. One was for a three-pronged attack of two thousand men each from Chateaugay and Plattsburgh to cooperate with four thousand from his camp at French Mills to seize a position on the St. Lawrence. A little over a week later, however, he reported that his subsistence was very low and that he might be compelled to retire from his position on the Salmon River. Then, incredibly, he offered to "endeavour to find quarters for them in Prescott & Kingston." Two days later he reported that Governor Tompkins favored attacking Prescott and Kingston, but he now preferred an attack upon Montreal.[16]

Despite the pressure from Governor Tompkins and the posturing of General Wilkinson, Armstrong was determined not to be rushed into any project. On January 20 he ordered Wilkinson to withdraw to Plattsburgh and to detach General Brown with two thousand men to Sackett's Harbor. The quartermaster general was directed to provide huts for four thousand men at Plattsburgh and for two thousand at Sackett's Harbor. Madison assumed the delicate task of explaining the government's inaction to Governor Tompkins. Acknowledging Tompkins' suggestions, he asserted that troops could not be spared from the other armies and that there were other objects to be kept in view. "Sackett's Harbor and the stake on Lake Champlain have an essential and constant claim to attention," he wrote, "If, besides making the former safe, Kingston can be attacked, or even seriously threatened, the effect will be salutary every-where."[17]

Armstrong insisted to Wilkinson that ordering the troops into win-ter quarters would not interfere with any "well digested project" of attack-ing enemy posts on the St. Lawrence during the winter or early spring. Detaching troops for the defense of Sackett's Harbor was not expected to produce a counter movement by the enemy. If Kingston was not rein-forced, Brown might even "avail himself of the ice, & with the aid of Commodore Chauncey, carry Kingston by a coup de main." Thus the same note that characterized Armstrong's letters the previous year was manifested again. After choosing to place the army into winter quarters and wait until the spring to renew the offensive, he informed Wilkinson on January 30 of a project against the enemy in their winter quarters on the Niagara Peninsula. Colonel Winfield Scott would command a force of about five hundred regulars, twenty-five hundred volunteer militia, and five hundred Indians. Wilkinson's feelings toward Scott were not much different from those toward Hampton, and his first knowledge of Scott's independent command came from Scott himself. Wilkinson revealed his disgust to Governor Tompkins, but Tompkins was not impressed. Wilkinson was "wonderfully tenacious of his authority," Tompkins in-formed Armstrong, and he was full of plans, but Tompkins added, "I pre-dict that he will venture but little if he can help it."[18]

It is not clear why Armstrong changed his mind and decided on an offensive operation on the Niagara Peninsula. Just a week before, Madi-son, presumably expressing the attitude of the War Department, had in-formed Tompkins that troops could not be spared for such a project. Mili-tarily, Scott was certainly a capable officer, and it offered some hope of success without committing the regular army in great force. Armstrong may also have viewed it as a prudent step politically. It would forestall any ill-advised project of the New York militia acting without the sanction of the War Department. Armstrong informed Governor Tompkins on February 3 of the project "to dispossess the Enemy of the Country be-tween Lakes Ontario & Erie." At the least, he informed Tompkins, the enemy would be compelled to retire from Fort Niagara, or if he attempted to maintain it, he would have to weaken his defenses below and "abandon the hope of reestablishing himself at any point on the River Thames, or western part of Lake Erie."[19]

While the newly promoted Brigadier General Scott prepared to make a demonstration on the Niagara frontier, Armstrong was con-fronted with a thorny question of rank and precedence on the southern frontier. General Pinckney's appointment, as has been noted, was made primarily because a major general of the regular army was wanted to command instead of a militia officer who outranked Brigadier General Flournoy in whose district the Creek campaign was taking place. Flournoy was to give his attention to the other areas of his district. Pinckney, however, took the position that he was commander of both the Sixth and Seventh Districts. Flournoy protested, but Armstrong declined to decide between the pretensions of the two generals, except to honor Flournoy's earlier request to be relieved of his command.[20]

Fortunately, the bickering between Flournoy and Pinckney did not affect the outcome of the campaign. In January Generals Jackson and Floyd launched movements into the Creek country intending to form a junction, but the effort was premature, and both were compelled to withdraw before they could join. Then, on March 27, Jackson won a bloody and decisive battle at Horseshoe Bend, and by April 15 he effected a junction with the Georgia force. General Pinckney joined the two armies on April 20 and took command. Two days later he advised Armstrong that the Creek resistance was at an end. He urged that commissioners be quickly appointed to make the treaty arrangements with the hostile Indians. He also allowed General Jackson to dismiss some of his troops, and he announced that he would soon go back to the sea coast and relinquish command of the Seventh Military District to General Flournoy.[21]

The Creek War was terminated successfully, and the task of writing the treaty fell to General Jackson, who was appointed a major general in the regular army in late May and assigned command of the Seventh Military District replacing General Flournoy. Flournoy wrote a bitter farewell letter to Armstrong. He complained particularly of Armstrong's failure to resolve the conflict with Pinckney, who had acted in an "insufferable manner" and without the "respect due from one officer to another." He charged that the War Department's frequent correspondence directly with officers under his command had "produced such a state of insubordination, that I can no longer command the district." Armstrong blandly disavowed any misconduct, expressed his regret about the controversy between the two generals, and he stated that it appeared to have arisen out of misconceptions.[22]

In the North changes were taking place too. On March 24 Armstrong relieved Wilkinson of his command and announced a Court of Inquiry on charges of misconduct during the expedition the previous autumn. While this letter was making its way north, Wilkinson moved four thousand troops across the border. Their advance was blocked on La Cole Creek by a strongly fortified mill. A small British force of fewer than five hundred men successfully repelled the American force, and Wilkinson ordered a retreat and retired back to Plattsburgh. Armstrong's letter unfortunately arrived too late to spare approximately 150 American casualties. The inquiry was postponed when Wilkinson demanded a general court martial, but he was relieved of active command which was given to Major General George Izard. General Hampton was permitted to resign on March 16, and thus two of the men responsible for the debacle the previous fall were removed from active command. Generals Dearborn and Lewis were also placed on an inactive status. Then on May 11, as a result of an accumulation of grievances, General Harrison submitted his resignation. The campaign of 1814 would thus be placed under new leadership, and in most instances far more capable hands.[23]

One of the promising new leaders was General Jacob Brown. Brown, at Sackett's Harbor, had discretionary authority to attack Kingston, and on February 28, based on information that Kingston was weakly defended, Armstrong ordered him to cross the ice and capture the post. However, as usual Armstrong qualified the order by cautioning that before the expedition was undertaken there should be "practicable roads, good weather, large detachments (made westwardly) on the part of the enemy, and a full and hearty co-operation on the part of our naval commander." If the enterprise was agreed upon, Brown was to use an enclosed letter designed to mask the object. This letter directed him to detach a brigade to assist General Scott on the Niagara.[24]

Armstrong had so qualified the circumstances for the attack upon Kingston that Brown was easily persuaded that he had an alternative. There was no reason why Armstrong should not have been more explicit, nor any reason to have a cover letter. The tactic backfired, and once again as in 1813 the thrust of the American forces went westward, away from Kingston and Montreal. Undoubtedly, Armstrong had intended Brown to have the alternative of either attacking Kingston or not, but Brown was convinced by Commodore Chauncey that the plan proposed in the cover letter was an alternative to attacking Kingston. Brown thus directed 2000 men to Niagara. Armstrong commented later that the two commanders, "by some extraordinary mental process, had arrived at the same conclusion — that the main action (an attack on Kingston) being impracticable, the ruse (intended merely to mask it) might do as well, and should be substituted for it."[25]

Brown was apprehensive that he had mistaken the meaning of the letters. On March 21 he wrote that his force was too small to attack Kingston. He went to Batavia, and as the instructions in Armstrong's second letter had directed, announced he would await further orders. Then, almost as an afterthought, he wrote, "If I have misunderstood your instructions it must be my misfortune." Upon reflection, he became convinced that he had misunderstood Armstrong's order, and he hurried back to Sackett's Harbor. Arriving there, he was again convinced by Chauncey that his first understanding was correct. Brown reported to Armstrong that he was now happy again, for he had been "the most unhappy man alive." Governor Tompkins was also confused. He reported to Armstrong, "Gen. Brown proceeded to Geneva, from whence on the 21st, he wrote me an unintelligible letter about retrograding. On the 24th he wrote me from the *Harbour*, that in a few hours he would return to his troops . . . & would then proceed to Niagara in earnest."[26]

Brown's second understanding was no better than his first, but he escaped humiliation when Armstrong accepted his movement as an alternative to the attack on Kingston. "You have mistaken my meaning," Armstrong began, directing Brown's attention again to his letter, but he added that if Sackett's Harbor was not endangered by this movement, then "go on and prosper. Good consequences are sometimes the result of mistakes."[27] Once again Armstrong failed to adhere to a consistent policy, and once again American forces were diverted westward where Armstrong knew that any success would have little or no impact upon the outcome of the war. His actions may be interpreted as a desperate hope that a victory might be won to boost the morale of both the armed forces and the public.

Brown's troops went to Buffalo where General Scott began drilling them in the hope of converting them into a disciplined unit. Brown apologized to Armstrong for misunderstanding his instructions. He returned to Sackett's Harbor where he reported he had fifteen hundred men for its defense. Armstrong had in the meantime, fearing an attack, rushed additional militia to that post. By late April American forces on the northern front were still holding defensive positions. General Izard's army on Lake Champlain was much diminished by sickness and expiration of enlistments. Armstrong advised Izard that additional reinforcements would be sent to him, but he warned that they would be composed chiefly of recruits and would require great attention. Having written this, he authorized Izard to attack the enemy posts in front of Montreal.[28]

Thus far no comprehensive plan of campaign had been drafted. Operations had largely reflected a reaction to the circumstances, with little view of any over-all objective. The amazing example where Armstrong allowed Brown to divert 2000 men to the Niagara Peninsula after he had ordered an attack on Kingston was not unlike the previous year when he allowed Dearborn to carry the operations westward. Armstrong's original plan for the campaign of 1814 had been to concentrate a large force near Lake Champlain and operate from there against Montreal or some point on the St. Lawrence.[29] Events on the Niagara Peninsula, however, which he conceived to be the prelude to enemy operations either toward the Thames and Detroit or possibly against Sackett's Harbor, forced him to alter his plans. He dispersed the force, placed the army in a defensive status, and decided to wait until spring. Thus his concern about Brown's movement toward the Niagara was not that it upset any strategic considerations, but that Sackett's Harbor was left unguarded.

On April 30 Armstrong finally presented to the president a plan for the campaign of 1814. He assumed that little was to be expected from Commodore Chauncey, that control of Lake Ontario would not be gained, and that any operation could not depend on the fleet. However, Armstrong believed that the advantage of control over Lake Erie could be used to transport troops against the rear of British positions on Lake Ontario, particularly Burlington and York. This, however, was the limit of the utilization of the control of Lake Erie, and Armstrong must have realized that any prolonged activity on the shore of Lake Ontario without control of that lake would expose the army to great danger, a point that Madison raised. His project seems to have been offered for want of any better idea. At least Detroit and Malden would be protected, the enemy's communication with and control over the Indians would be reduced, and the British might be forced from the Niagara Peninsula. Yet Armstrong himself had said earlier that operations west of Kingston, even if successful, left the strength of the enemy unbroken; that it merely wounded the tail of the lion and would not hasten the end of the war. The conclusion must be that he was willing to accept control over the Niagara Peninsula as better than nothing, and unless control of Lake Ontario was won, this was all he reasonably expected in 1814. As he related to General Brown, "If you can best the Enemy out of the Peninsula, or compel him to withdraw from it, and establish yourself at York — you will do well." In the event Chauncey was able to meet Yeo and win control over the lake, he added, "I do not despair of your taking Kingston before the campaign ends."[30]

Madison replied that the 6000 to 8000 man force Armstrong contemplated raising was "greater than I had relied upon; and if employed towards Burlington bay & York can not fail to have a salutary effect in different directions." As Armstrong's plan would call for the use of ships the secretary of navy intended to use on Lake Huron, Madison indicated that the two secretaries should resolve the differences. In fact, Armstrong argued very cogently that the Lake Huron expedition was useless. "Take Mackinaw," he asked, "and what is gained but Mackinaw itself?" On May 7, acting upon the assumption that his plan had been approved, Armstrong wrote General Brown enclosing his April 30 letter to Madison. He asserted that this was the outline of the plan of campaign, and he ordered Brown to quicken the pace in assembling troops. Madison, however, had not approved the plan, and the secretary of the navy had not given up his project, which would carry with it a large part of the Detroit garrison which Armstrong intended to use on the Niagara Peninsula.[31]

Armstrong nevertheless continued to act as if his plan had been approved. On May 25 he laid out in great detail to General Scott the course he was to pursue, the essence of which was that everything depended upon who controlled Lake Ontario. If Chauncey was beaten or unable to assist Scott's force, then Scott should instantly retreat back to Lake Erie. This was an open admission that the fleet was essential to the success of the expedition; that without it a retreat should be ordered immediately. This was realistic, but what gives it an air of unreality was the inability of Armstrong to recognize that by his own reasoning the force should not be ordered to advance at all without first having the support of the fleet. The implication that Scott was to lead the expedition caused Brown to draft an angry letter to Armstrong demanding an explanation.[32]

Meanwhile, Armstrong's whole strategy was being called into question at Washington. On June 3, shortly after returning to Washington from his home in Virginia, Madison called a Cabinet meeting for June 7, "to decide on the plan of campaign." The Lake Huron expedition was approved, which would divert about 800 to 1000 troops that Armstrong had intended to use. It was also decided that fourteen or fifteen boats would be built at Sackett's Harbor for use on the St. Lawrence to intercept water communication between Montreal and Kingston. General Izard would make demonstrations toward Montreal to divert the enemy from operations westward, and possibly break up the enemy's connection with Lake Champlain. Armstrong's project to attack Burlington "preparatory to further operations for reducing the Peninsula, & preceding towards York, &c.," was approved, dependent upon Chauncey winning control of Lake Ontario.[33]

Armstrong explained to Brown that the expedition was contingent upon the success of the American fleet on Lake Ontario. Brown should in the meanwhile keep his troops occupied, and Armstrong asked, "why not take Fort Erie & its garrison, stated at 3 or 400 men?" Thus in this casual way Armstrong set on foot an expedition that was to lead to some of the fiercest fighting of the war. Brown, unlike previous commanders on the northern frontier, was not hesitant to act. He quickly assembled a force of approximately 3500 men. On July 3 they crossed the Niagara River and assailed Fort Erie, which was taken that day. Then they marched on to

Chippewa, about sixteen miles below, where on July 5 they defeated the British led by Major General Phineas Riall. Brown marched on to the rear of Fort George, but as he reported to Armstrong, the enemy would not engage and stayed near their works. The British, however, began massing their forces and reinforcements began arriving. Brown was compelled to retire, and on July 25 he fought a desperate and bloody battle at Lundy's Lane. Both sides suffered heavy casualties, and Generals Brown and Scott were both wounded severely. The Americans withdrew to Fort Erie where Brigadier General Edmund P. Gaines, due to the wounds to Brown and Scott, assumed command on August 5. The British began a seige of Fort Erie which dragged on into September. That was the situation when Armstrong left office.[34] The fighting had been creditable to American arms, but it produced no decisive results, as Armstrong had foreseen a year earlier. There was hardly an excuse for the campaign except as a testing ground for the bright, young military leaders who finally showed that Americans could fight. It was however too late to alter the course of the war.

In the West the Huron expedition commanded by Lieutenant Colonel George Croghan assaulted Fort Michilimackinac late in July, but it failed and Croghan led his force back to Detroit. Brigadier General Duncan McArthur, who replaced Harrison as commander of the Eighth Military District, was discouraged in his effort to organize a force to join Brown on the Niagara Peninsula. He wrote Armstrong in mid-June that he was "almost entirely destitute of information and instructions relative to the affairs of the district." He even went so far as to offer his resignation, but Armstrong persuaded him to delay this action until the campaign was over. Finally, McArthur got his force of approximately a thousand men ready to move from Cleveland to Buffalo late in July. By this time, however, the battles of Chippewa and Lundy's Lane had been fought and Brown's force had taken a defensive position in Fort Erie.[35]

McArthur was concerned that not only was his movement too late, but that in the meantime the British might cross over to Detroit while Croghan and the fleet were away and reestablish their control. As a precaution, before he left to join Brown, he called for 1000 militia from Kentucky and 500 from Ohio to march to Detroit immediately. On August 8, 1814, after joining Brown, he wrote Armstrong that Brown agreed Detroit should be reinforced. A portion of his force returned to Detroit along with McArthur. The fears proved groundless. Armstrong was not worried about an attack on Detroit, but he was concerned about the continued unrest on the frontier. He believed the only way to keep the frontier quiet was to sweep the British settlements along the Thames with five thousand mounted men and Indians. If the war continued, he informed McArthur, that measure must be adopted. "It was my plan for the present Campaign," he added, "but was thought a policy of too much severity."[36] That was Armstrong's last official letter dealing with western affairs.

In the South Jackson was worried about the remnants of the Creeks and Seminoles and about the rumors of a British force hovering on the southern coast. He urged that someone be appointed immediately to run the boundary as soon as the treaty was entered into. "This is suggested from a full conviction," he wrote, "that [there is] no time like the present (when the *past* is fresh on their minds) to receive ample remuneration for this war." Armstrong discounted the reports of a British naval force on the southern coast. "Having permitted the months of April, May & June to escape without effort, on their part, it is not presumable, that they will attempt much during the hot & sickly seasons." Nor did he believe the Seminoles would be disposed to enter the contest now, when they had not taken part when the issue was doubtful. Jackson was ordered to discharge the force "as early as may consist with the interests of the Public." As usual, Armstrong was concerned about the expense entailed in keeping a large militia force in the field, particularly when it was not fighting.[37]

Jackson still believed an Indian threat remained, and that a reduction of the militia might encourage the Creeks to renew their efforts, particularly if they were given assistance by the British and Spanish. On June 27 he asked if the government would approve an attack upon the Indians who had taken refuge in East Florida if it could be proved they were being fed and armed by the British. If the government approved, Jackson continued, "I promise the war in the South has a speedy termination, and the British influence forever cut off from the Indians in that quarter." Armstrong replied that "if all the circumstances stated by you unite, the conclusion is inevitable. It becomes our duty to carry our arms where we find our Enemies." He noted, however, that it was not believed the Spanish wished to break with the United States nor encourage Indian activity from their territory. "If they admit, feed, arm & cooperate with the British and hostile Indians," he added, "we must strike on the broad principle of self preservation. Under other & different circumstances we must forbear."[38]

Jackson wrote Armstrong on July 24 that the capitulation of the Indians would be signed in a few days, and he noted that by his instructions he was ordered to dismiss the militia. He asked to be advised "whether it is the *order* of the President that this post be left defenceless and a frontier of eight hundred miles open'd to the incursions of Frances, McQueens [Creek leaders], and other Maurauders, who may be excited to mischief by British influence and Spanish intrigue." He was particularly concerned because the Creeks, once the terms of the capitulation became known, might be "excited to a spirit of hostility." Jackson had forced the Creeks to submit to a harsh treaty (signed on August 9) which appropriated approximately two-thirds of their lands — most of the southern and western half of Alabama. The treaty was written with chiefs representing only about one-third of the Creeks. Most of the hostile Creeks had fled to East Florida, and Jackson had every reason to expect that the treaty might lead the Indians to renew hostilities before submitting.[39]

Armstrong had instructed General Pinckney to maintain a garrison at Fort Jackson and other posts along the Georgia frontier, and Pinckney wrote Armstrong on August 11 that Jackson had misunderstood the orders. At any rate, Jackson was ordered on August 20 not to abandon Fort Jackson. Also, Governor Blount was ordered to hold 2500 men in readiness in the event the rumors of a British landing were true. Jackson, typically, had not waited. After receiving definite proof of a British landing at Pensacola early in August, he called out the Tennessee militia and informed Armstrong of that fact on August 25.[40]

The day before, Washington had been burned by the British, and the aftermath of that incident led to Armstrong's removal from office. For over a month Jackson was without instructions, and he ran affairs in his district as he pleased. He indulged his desire to strike at the Spanish, and he occupied Pensacola on November 7. Then he went on to conduct the defense of New Orleans, for which he gained lasting fame. Unlike the other theatres of war, Armstrong never developed a strategy for the South, nor did he interfere to a marked extent with the commanders. They were allowed to conduct their own affairs, and with men such as Jackson he could not have done better.

On the Lake Champlain frontier, however, Major General George Izard complained not of neglect but of interference. When Izard took command in the spring of 1814 his forces were demoralized and depleted. Although he was the ranking officer in the district, his position was not unlike that of Hampton in 1813. Armstrong explained that "Territorial limits of command are found inconvenient." Izard would have his own command, Armstrong related, and "when two or more Divisions unite, the senior officer will necessarily command."[41] Armstrong might as well have created a separate district. There was no coordination between Izard and Brown, except when Armstrong acted as the intermediary.

Armstrong's plan of April 30 did not even include Izard's force in his strategy. Presumably they were to threaten Montreal and prevent a large enemy force from detaching westward. In truth, the outcome of the struggle to win control on Lake Champlain would largely dictate any activity by Izard. The American naval commander, Lieutenant Thomas Macdonough, was confronted with a situation similar to Perry's on Lake Erie, namely a lack of seamen. General Izard directed his commanders to support the needs of the navy, but his order aroused much discontent. "The circumstance of taking soldiers from our Ranks to man the Navy is in every respect a very unpleasant one," Izard reported on June 10, "It is not only unjust to the Individuals, but mortifying to their officers." Armstrong asked him to cooperate. He agreed the calls were too frequent and were producing a considerable diversion from the field, but he was anxious that the issue of control over the lake be decided. If Macdonough won or if the enemy failed to engage the American fleet, Izard was instructed to seize and fortify Rouse's Point, thereby closing the entrance to the lake. If Macdonough was beaten, Izard was to adopt the best defensive plan he could.[42]

After the June 7 Cabinet meeting, Armstrong directed Izard to establish a post on the south bank of the St. Lawrence, strongly fortified, and garrisoned by a force of 1500 men. The order was contingent upon the American fleet winning control of Lake Ontario. Izard was ordered additionally to select a position on Lake Champlain to exclude the enemy flotilla. These and other letters from Armstrong to Izard during this period were perhaps unnecessarily detailed. Izard was overly sensitive, and he was offended by the tone of the instructions. On June 3 he wrote a private letter to Armstrong inquiring, "What Degree of Responsibility I am to have in the Exercise of my Functions as Commander of an Army of the United States." He protested "the imperative tone in which Instructions are frequently sent to me from the War-Office, and against the minute Detail with which my Operations are dictated." He was "ready to receive the Orders of my superiors," but he added that if the secretary of war had a different conception of his authority, then he was prepared to resign his command. Izard alerted his friend Monroe by sending him a copy of this letter. Izard complained that Armstrong's orders "need not assume the style of lectures from a pedagogue. Although young as a General," he continued, "I am too old to be schooled so repeatedly in anticipation of my not knowing what to do in contingencies to be easily foreseen." He concluded by requesting Monroe to "take the proper method of representing my conduct to the President before it can receive a colouring to my disadvantage." Armstrong undoubtedly deduced that Izard was in friendly correspondence with his rival, and this no doubt greatly influenced his attitude toward Izard. His response to Izard, if any, cannot be found. It is interesting to note that Madison later called specifically for this correspondence with Izard when he was investigating Armstrong's conduct of his office.[43]

By the end of July Izard had a force of approximately 5000 men. He did not think that it was competent, however, to conquer and hold any important part of the country. He offered instead to give support for the forces on the Niagara Peninsula by moving to the St. Lawrence and threatening the rear of Kingston. Armstrong claimed on July 30 that he had anticipated this suggestion on July 27. Strangely, however, he forwarded a copy of the July 27 letter on August 2. Izard was directed to march to Ogdensburg, leave a two-thousand-man force there, and proceed to Sackett's Harbor to cooperate with Commodore Chauncey in attacking Kingston. If Kingston was considered invulnerable, two thousand troops were to be taken from Sackett's Harbor to Burlington Bay to cooperate with General Brown against the British.[44]

When this letter was received, however, the situation had changed considerably. Izard hastily informed Armstrong on August 11 that the enemy force in his vicinity was now superior to his and daily threatened an attack. He speculated that the only reason they had not yet attacked was because of their caution and the expectation of reinforcements. "I will make the movement you direct, *if possible,*" he stated, "but I shall do it with the Apprehension of risking the Force under my Command, and with the Certainty that everything in this Vicinity but the lately erected works at Plattsburgh and on Cumberland Head will in less than three days after my Departure, be in the Possession of the Enemy." Izard no doubt recalled his pledge of June 3 to execute any project the government directed, but he nevertheless wanted to place it on the record that he had warned Armstrong of the precarious situation that would result by the execution of the order. "It has always been my conviction," he continued, "that the numerical Force of the Enemy has been underrated," and he asserted that his army had kept a much larger British force in check for many weeks.[45]

Armstrong was not persuaded. Several times in the past his commanders had grossly overestimated the strength of the enemy, and he undoubtedly suspected that Izard was guilty of the same fault. His attitude was revealed in a letter to General Brown early in the summer of 1814. The problem, he asserted, stemmed from giving credence to the "wild reports" of informers. "It is by duping animals of this kind & sending them to us, " he wrote, "that the British Army in Canada have done half their work & prevented us from doing a tenth part of our own. Dearborn believed . . . [in March 1813] that the British Army at Kingston amounted to Eight-thousand men!" Thus Armstrong, despite Izard's report, wrote confidently to General McArthur on August 6, "The reports of great detachments having arrived from England are much exaggerated." He was wrong. British regulars, veterans of Wellington's Army, were arriving almost daily. By the end of August, the British force within twenty to thirty miles of Izard amounted to approximately 16,000 men.[46]

When no order came from the War Department canceling his movement, Izard resolved against his better judgment to comply with his orders. He warned as he did so, however, "I must not be responsible for the consequences of abandoning my present strong position." On August 29, still believing an attack was imminent, he marched westward with approximately four thousand men. On September 3 Sir George Prevost crossed the boundary with eleven thousand men. The assault on Plattsburgh, commanded by Brigadier General Alexander Macomb with about fifteen hundred men, began on September 11 and coincided with an attack of the British squadron on the American fleet. Fortunately for the Americans, Macdonough defeated the British fleet, and Prevost gave up the seige of Plattsburgh and returned to Canada, or else another disaster would have befallen the Americans.[47]

If the British had been successful, Izard would have shared in the criticism that would have certainly fallen upon Armstrong's head. Armstrong's attention was obviously focused upon the Niagara Peninsula. Not only had he directed McArthur to reinforce Brown on the Niagara at the risk of the western posts, but as part of the same strategy he had directed Izard toward the Niagara, hazarding the loss of the posts on Lake Champlain. He went so far as to assert to Izard on August 12, "it has become good policy on our part to carry the war as far to the westward as possible, particularly while we have an ascendancy on the Lakes." It is ironic that Armstrong, who had recommended Montreal as the major objective in 1812, and Kingston in 1813, concentrated the American forces on the Niagara Peninsula in 1814. Lacking control of Lake Ontario, he apparently believed the peninsula offered the only hope for the success of American arms. Nevertheless, success on the Niagara would not have had a conclusive impact on the outcome of the war, while capturing Kingston or Montreal would possibly have had a decisive effect. Armstrong recognized this, and he can be criticized for constantly allowing American operations to be carried west of the vital supply artery, the St. Lawrence. That was the single most significant failure of the war.[48]

11

THE WASHINGTON AFFAIR

The arrival of the british fleet off the American coast in the spring of 1813 caused great excitement and alarm along the seaboard. Armstrong, newly appointed secretary of war, reported to William Duane that the whole coast was "demanding defence, at a hundred points," but at best the War Department would be able to fortify only the most prominent points. The British were active particularly in the Chesapeake Bay area, and they made occasional raids along the coast, accompanied by much destruction of private property and outrages upon the defenseless inhabitants. An exception was on June 22, 1813, when an attack upon Norfolk was repulsed.[1]

The prospect of further incursions prompted Armstrong in the summer of 1813 to propose additional defenses along the coast. His interest was short-lived, however, and, as noted elsewhere, most of the funds for fortifications were diverted to other needs. Armstrong was, in fact, convinced that fortifications were much too expensive in proportion to their military usefulness. In response to a plea from General Dearborn in the spring of 1814 for additional defenses, Armstrong bluntly stated: "If New York and its neighborhood, with a population of 100,000 souls — the defences already made, and 1800 or 2000 Regular troops, are not a match for 4 or 5000 British assailants we may as well give up the game at once." He also observed, "If the present rage for fortifications was yielded to, there would be no end to them. The truth is that one generally begets a supposed necessity for another."[2]

In a similar manner, Armstrong resisted demands for fortifications for the defense of Washington. Major General John P. Van Ness, commander of the District of Columbia militia, reported that he frequently brought up the matter of the defenseless situation of the District, but Armstrong "appeared rather indifferent, and expressed an opinion that the enemy would not come, or even seriously attempt to come to this District." Van Ness noted that the lack of defensive works caused "great anxiety, inquietude, and alarm [in] the District and surrounding country." In fact, a deputation from Alexandria, Washington, and Georgetown came to Armstrong early in May 1813 urging a more efficient defense for the District, particularly at Fort Washington, below the capital on the Potomac. Consequently, Armstrong sent Colonel Decius Wadsworth of the Ordnance Department to examine the fort and make recommendations. Wadsworth reported on May 28 that "an additional number of heavy guns . . . and an additional fort in the neighborhood, are both to be considered unnecessary."[3]

Nothing further was done in 1813. In the early summer of 1814, however, Armstrong was approached by a committee of bankers who renewed suggestions for increased defenses and recommended building an additional fort below Fort Washington. Armstrong answered that "a small work would be unavailing, and that, to erect one of sufficient size and strength, was impracticable, for want of money." The bankers then offered to loan the government $200,000 on condition that it be used to defend the District. The offer was accepted, and the money was to be paid into the Treasury on August 24, ironically the very day Washington was captured by the British. As Armstrong noted, "The events of that day put an end to the business, and at the same time furnished evidence of the fallability of the plan, had it even been executed, by showing that no works on the Potomac will, of themselves, be sufficient defence for the Seat of Government." He continued, "The considerations which governed my own opinion on this subject . . . were, that to put Washington *hors d' insulte*, by means of fortifications, would, from physical causes, among which is the remoteness from each other of the several points to be defended, have exhausted the Treasury; that bayonets are known to form the most efficient barriers; and that there was no reason, in this case, to doubt beforehand the willingness of the country to defend it."[4]

Lack of money certainly governed Armstrong's actions. Had the government not been verging on bankruptcy, some fortifications would undoubtedly have been built, if merely to satisfy the anxious citizens of the District. Nevertheless, even though Armstrong believed bayonets were "the most efficient barriers," the lack of funds limited even the utilization of this expedient. Armstrong was reluctant to incur the expense of militia calls to defend the District. Essentially, he believed that Washington was relatively safe because it offered no military objective of great importance. Even when the British entered the Patuxent River in August 1814, he was still not concerned. General Van Ness asserted to Armstrong that the enemey intended to strike a serious blow. His reply, according to Van Ness, was "Oh yes! by God, they would not come with such a fleet without meaning to strike somewhere, but they certainly will not come here; what the devil will they do here?" Van Ness disagreed, and Armstrong countered, "no, no! Baltimore is the place, sir; that is of so much more consequence."[5]

Armstrong's attitude, to say the least, disturbed the people of the District. Evidently he never attempted to explain to them, except to the committee of bankers, that the lack of funds limited expenditures for fortifications. Public confidence in Armstrong was rapidly declining, and he must have realized that he would be blamed if Washington was attacked. In fact, early in July 1814, William Tatham, a consultant for the War Department's topographical branch who had studied the area about Washington, wrote "My belief is, we *cannot* defend Washington, because Congress have such a mistaken notion of *public* economy that they will not allow us the where-with-all!" He warned prophetically, "Thus, I foresee, if they are in a condition to make a push from the enemies fleet, as policy will direct them to do if we are not the peculiar favorites of heaven, the result will be that, we shall fail; and popular clamour will shelter the real pittiful cause, by an abuse of John Armstrong, for being less than omnipotent."[6]

Increased activity by the enemy in Chesapeake Bay in the spring of 1814 led to a call-out of the District militia for a short time in June. This alarm, along with the arrival of the news from Europe of the fall of Napoleon, prompted Madison to call a Cabinet meeting on July 1 to discuss measures for the defense of Washington. A new Tenth Military District was created on the Potomac, and on July 2 Brigadier General William Winder was chosen to command. He was to have a force of approximately three thousand, of which about a thousand were regulars. Additionally, ten thousand militia were to be held in readiness by the neighboring states for a call from Winder.[7]

Armstrong had little to do with these plans. He reported later that these measures were "prescribed by the President." Nor did he approve of Winder's appointment, who was chosen because he was a native of Maryland and a relative of the governor of that state.[8] Considering his strained relations with Madison at this time, Armstrong's statement is plausible. He may even have suspected that his rival Monroe, who was outspoken in his belief that the District needed more protection, was in reality behind these actions. Armstrong's conduct during this period tends to indicate that he believed the responsibility for the defense of Washington was as much the president's (and the secretary of state's) as his own. Madison's aggressive attitude and Armstrong's passive role are in striking contrast to their previous roles.

Armstrong and Winder quickly clashed on the best way to utilize the militia. Winder suggested that the militia "should be called out for one, two or three months," but Armstrong argued, according to Winder, "that the most advantageous mode of using militia was upon the spur of the occasion, and to bring them to fight as soon as called out." If that was indeed the argument used by Armstrong, then he was being less than honest. Undoubtedly the real reason was his old objection to the expense of unnecessary calls. He had resisted a similar suggestion from General Van Ness that the Washington militia be called out on a rotational basis until the danger passed. Armstrong believed they should not be paid unless they were fighting — a position he had taken to limit Harrison's militia calls.[9]

Winder obstinately persisted. On July 9 he again recommended a militia call of 4000 men to be placed in the best positions for defense to retard the advance of an enemy movement. "Should Washington, Baltimore, or Annapolis, be their object," he wrote, "what possible chance will there be of collecting a force, after the arrival of the enemy, to interpose between them and either of those places?" Sufficient numbers of militia, he argued, "could not be warned and run together, even as a disorderly crowd, without arms, ammunition, or organization, before the enemy would already have given his blow."[10]

Winder's arguments apparently had no effect on Armstrong, who would have done well to have heeded them. Instead, he instructed Winder on July 12 to call for militia only "in case of actual or menaced invasion of the District," to avoid unnecessary calls, and "to proportion the call to the exigency." Armstrong had some basis for his position. The militia had responded effectively to alarms in the past. In June 1814, for example, when the British appeared at the mouth of the Patuxent River about forty miles below Washington, the Georgetown and city militia had swiftly mobilized and marched to the river, but the British retired down the bay and the militia was dismissed. At that time Madison supported Armstrong's ideas on the utilization of the militia. He wrote to Governor Barbour of Virginia in June 1814 that the question was whether the militia should be called out immediately under an uncertainty as to the objects of attack, or whether they should be held for an immediate call to the states under attack. An immediate call, he contended, would waste resources, exhaust the means, and hazard everything. The task, he concluded, was to discover the objects of the enemy; then apply the resources and militia effectively.[11]

On July 17 the British reappeared on the Patuxent River. At the call of General Winder, three companies of the Washington militia were promptly dispatched. When they reached Woodyard, about ten miles from the city, he halted them after receiving information that the British were again retiring down the river. Rather than utilizing this force to prepare defenses or for other purposes, Winder dismissed them even, as he admitted, while still unsure of the intentions of the enemy. He explained his decision in terms which Armstrong undoubtedly approved. "The facility with which they can turn out and proceed to any point, renders them nearly as effective as if actully kept in the field; and the importance of them individually of attending to their private affairs, decides me, even in doubt of the enemy's probable movement, to give this order."[12]

Until this time, and for some time thereafter, Winder was busily engaged in travel about his district, occasionally accompanied by Tatham, informing himself of the topographical advantages of the area. His letters indicate that during the whole month of July he rarely stayed in one place more than one day. There was really no reason for him to engage in this incessant activity. The War Department provided him with a series of topographical reports of the Tenth District prepared by Tatham, which should have been very useful to him.[13] His constant movement allowed no time for the organizational activity which demanded his attention. On July 23 he designated Bladensburg, four miles north of Washington, as the rendezvous point for the Maryland militia, and he asked that arms, ammunition, tents, camp equipment, and other supplies be deposited there. Although he had commanded the Tenth District for three weeks, he confessed, "I have no knowledge where these articles are in store, nearest that point, nor under whose charge they are." He did not inspect the regular detachments of the Thirty-Sixth and Thirty-Eighth Regiments for the first time until July 27, and it was not until August 1 that he established his headquarters in Washington.[14]

The War Department was also remiss in giving Winder staff support. Except for an aide and the assistance of Tatham, Winder had no staff. An assistant adjutant general was finally assigned on August 16, and an assistant inspector general was named on August 19.[15] It was apparent that Armstrong rendered assistance only when it was asked for, and during the whole period he presumably offered no advice. This is all the more remarkable, when his past inclination to interfere with his commander's activities is recalled. Possibly he felt constrained by the knowledge that Madison was then investigating his conduct, which resulted in the reprimand delivered on August 13. Also, since Madison had assumed the initiative in organizing the defense of the District, Armstrong may have believed he was somehow divested of the responsibility for its protection.

Armstrong's remarkable indifference to the affairs of the Tenth District was contrasted with Madison's interference in Winder's business. One example was when the lower shores of the Patuxent River were plundered by the enemy late in July 1814, and the people became "extremely importunate with both the Secretary of War and the President" for aid and protection. Winder hesitated to put a force so far down the river, which would expose it to the danger of being cut off and reducing the protection of Washington and other places. "But the President, in conversation," Winder related, "told me that their situation required aid, and directed me to move the detachments of the Thirty-Sixth and Thirty-Eighth down."[16] The British had already withdrawn and the first week of August was wasted by an exhausting march for the troops, and Winder lost still more valuable time.

When Winder returned to Washington, he learned that instead of 3000 Maryland militia which he had expected to assemble at Bladensburg, only one company had appeared. He hurried to Baltimore to speed up the raising of a force, but on August 13 he informed Armstrong that "after all shall be assembled, . . . they will not exceed one thousand men." Winder also called for Pennsylvania to send a regiment, but he learned that due to a reorganization of the militia the state would not be able to send any troops to meet their requisition.[17]

Only 250 men were at Bladensburg when information was received on August 18 that the British had again entered the Patuxent with a very large squadron of ships and had landed a force of 4000 to 4500 at Benedict. The British were undoubtedly unaware of the disarray of their foes. In fact, their primary objective was Commodore Joshua Barney's flotilla, which was drawn for safety up the Patuxent. Once cornered, however, Barney blew up his flotilla on August 22. That object obtained, Rear Admiral George Cockburn, the British naval commander, persuaded a reluctant Major General Robert Ross, the British military commander, to attack Washington.[18]

The British menace created a great flurry of activity in Washington. Calls for militia were sent out to Viriginia and Maryland, and all the militia of the District were ordered out *en masse*. Winder reported to Armstrong pessimistically, "The result of all these operations will be certainly slow, and extremely doubtful as to the extent of force produced." Monroe offered to take a troop of cavalry and scout the enemy. Despite his lack of qualifications, he was provided a force of twenty-five to thirty dragoons, and he left on his mission about mid-day on the nineteenth. Armstrong approved this force only under orders from Madison. Monroe hardly made a good scout because he dared not venture too close to the enemy for fear of capture. He failed to take any field glasses, and he even had to borrow pen and paper so he could make his reports. At best he gave only exaggerated estimates of the size of the enemy force.[19]

Madison, with whom Monroe corresponded, did what he could to assist in the arrangements for the defense of Washington. Armstrong also aroused himself from his lethargy and began to offer advice to Winder. On August 19 he advised that, "If the enemy's movements indicate an attack on this place, means should be taken to drive off all horses and cattle, and remove all supplies of forage, and etc., on their route; a moment is not to be lost in doing both." He added, "For this purpose the whole of your cavalry may be pushed into the neighborhood of the enemy without delay." On August 22 he suggested placing Barney's seamen (about 600) at Nottingham, on the Patuxent River approximately twenty miles from Washington, at the rear of the enemy threatening their communications.[20]

Years later Armstrong recalled, citing the journal of Colonel Allen McLane, who served as a volunteer aide to General Winder during this period, further advice to Winder on August 23. Deducing from the size of the enemy force and the equipment they brought with them that if they did attempt to attack Washington, it would be "a mere Cossac hurrah, a rapid march and hasty retreat," he recommended two modes of operation: either harass the flanks with repeated attacks, or retire slowly before the enemy to Washington where the Capitol and the houses around it could be utilized to place artillery to break the advance of the enemy. As the enemy was unprepared for seige and investment, he would gain nothing and endanger himself. Armstrong preferred the second plan.[21] The conversation may well have taken place. Armstrong rarely ever proposed a single mode of operation, and his advice frequently, as in this case, was based on the assumption of an ideal situation and not on the circumstances at hand.

In the state of confusion that existed, the harassed Winder could not think of diversionary tactics, nor of splitting his force, nor of falling back to Washington and inviting the assault of the enemy. He related to the House Committee that by August 22 "A doubt at that time was not entertained by anybody of the intention of the enemy to proceed direct to Washington." Yet by his own account he sent out troops that evening to check on rumors that the enemy was moving toward Annapolis. By August 22 General Ross had marched his troops about twenty miles through

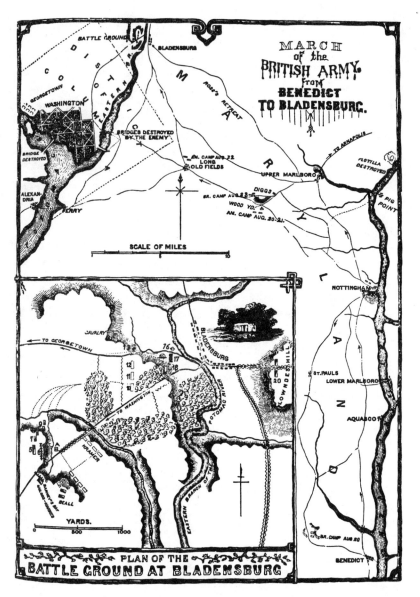

From Benson J. Lossing, *The Pictorial Field-Book of the War of 1812* (New York, 1869; New York: Benchmark Publishing Corp., 1970), p. 929.

Maryland without meeting a single American soldier. He camped at Upper Marlboro that day, barely more than a dozen miles from Washington. He did not move out his troops toward Washington the next day until two o'clock in the afternoon. Winder was confused by the tardy movement of the British. He conceived a variety of movements that they could make, and this indecision delayed any positive steps to retard their advance. Upper Marlboro, he explained to the Committee, was "at the point from whence he could take the road to Bladensburg, to the Eastern Branch bridge, or Fort Washington, indifferently, or it might be to cover his march upon Annapolis."[22]

Ross's movements continued to confuse Winder. Instead of taking the road which led north to Bladensburg, he marched by the road toward the Eastern Branch bridge, and he camped about nine miles from Washington on the evening of August 23. Winder now believed that Fort Washington might be the objective, particularly in view of new information that the enemy fleet was coming up the Potomac River. Uncertain of the enemy objective, Winder withdrew across the Eastern Branch bridge into Washington. From there, he explained, he could harass the enemy if they moved toward Fort Washington, or follow him if he reversed his march and moved toward Annapolis, or he could rush to Bladensburg if that became the enemy objective.[23] Winder now had approximately 2500 men at the Eastern Branch bridge and five miles to the north another army of about the same number. More soldiers arrived in Washington that evening.

On the morning of August 24 Winder wrote Armstrong that he had established his headquarters near the Eastern Branch bridge, and he asked for "the assistance of council from yourself and the government." For some unexplained reason, the letter was delivered to Madison, who recorded: "Not doubting the urgency of the occasion, I opened and read it, and it went on immediately by the Express to Genl. Armstrong." Armstrong was angered that the President had opened a letter addressed to him. This incident, and Madison's other activities during the preceding week, was apparently taken by Armstrong as signifying a lack of confidence. The lack of deference given to his opinions by Winder, the aggressive attitude of Madison, and the bustling activity of Monroe added to his feeling of insecurity, and he wore his wounded pride openly. He tarried an hour before going to Winder's headquarters. Madison reported that Armstrong had been "impatiently expected, and surprize at his delay [was] manifested."[24]

Armstrong's wounded pride was evident when he recorded the events of the morning of August 24 for the House Committee. Referring to Winder's request for counsel he wrote, "This letter was late in reaching

me. It had been opened, and passed through other hands." When he arrived at the headquarters, he noted, "General Winder was on the point of
joining the troops, at Bladensburg, whither, it was now understood, the
enemy was also marching. I took for granted that he had received the
counsel he required; for, to me, he neither stated doubt nor difficulty, nor
plan of attack or of defence." Madison noted that Armstrong "was asked
whether he had any arrangement or advice to offer in the emergency. He
said he had not; adding that as the battle would be between Militia and
regular troops, the former would be beaten." Truthful as this might have
been, it was injudicious, and reports of his statements and attitude on the
eve of the battle were later twisted, embellished, and used against him.[25]

Secretary of the Treasury George W. Campbell, who lived in the
same rooming house as Armstrong, noticed the secretary's sullen attitude.
He related to the House committee that he approached Armstrong and
asked whether the movement of the troops were made on his advice and
whether he would give any suggestions for their movements. "He gave me
to understand," Campbell wrote, "that the movements which had taken
place were not in pursuance of any plan or advice given by him; that General Winder, having been appointed to the command of the district, including the city, and the means assigned for its defense placed at his disposal, he was considered as having the direction of their application." He
also informed Campbell that he would not interfere unless the president
approved. This prompted Campbell to approach Madison to recommend
that Armstrong be given authority to assist Winder. "I told him," Madison
recorded, "I could scarcely conceive it possible that Genl. Armstrong
could have so misconstrued his functions and duty as secretary of war."
Madison nevertheless talked to Armstrong and expressed surprise at his
reserve and his scruples in offering advice. He stated that he hoped Armstrong had not construed the reprimand of August 13 as restraining him in
the exercise of the functions of his office. He suggested that Armstrong
proceed to Bladensburg and aid Winder. Any problem of authority
would be settled instantly by Madison who would be on hand. Armstrong replied that he had not put such a construction on the August 13
letter, and that he would go to aid Winder.[26]

Armstrong perhaps inferred more from this conversation than
Madison intended. His statement to the House Committee was vague. He
noted that his understanding was that he should go to Bladensburg and
"give such directions as were required by the urgency of the case." He continued, "I lost not a moment in fulfilling this intention, and had barely
time to reconnoitre the march of the enemy, and to inform myself of our
own arrangements, when I again met the president, who told me that he

had come to a new determination, and that the military functionaries should be left to the discharge of their own duties, on their own responsibilities." He added with a trace of bitterness, "I now became, of course, a mere spectator of the combat."[27] The implication was that Madison had committed the direction of military operations to Armstrong and then at a critical moment intervened and withdrew his sanction. Armstrong may also have been hinting that the events of the day would have had a different result had he been allowed to remain on the field. Madison later denied that he had given Armstrong authority to command or that he could have legally done so.

Winder's force, along with most of the Cabinet, arrived at Bladensburg just as the British army came into view. The Americans now totaled approximately 6000, while the British force amounted to not more than 3500. There was, however, a vast difference in the quality of the two armies, and the numerical advantage of the Americans was negated by improper battlefield alignment. Winder had little time to inspect the line of battle, indeed he was apparently ready to concede the victory, for in the brief time he was on the field he instructed the troops to be sure that when they retreated they do so by the Georgetown road. Moreover, he placed his force too far behind the Maryland militia, commanded by Brigadier General Tobias Stansbury, to sustain them in the initial shock of the British assault. Perhaps the crucial factor in determining the outcome of the battle, however, was the interference of secretary of state Monroe with the arrangement of the troops made by General Stansbury. Without Stansbury's knowledge and without authority, Monroe rearranged the troops in such a manner that it exposed them to a devastating fire from the enemy. Their flight precipitated the rout of the American force. Armstrong later characterized Monroe as a "busy and blundering tactician," and he hinted that Monroe's actions may have been deliberate. Monroe was no doubt well-intentioned. He probably thought he was helping the American commanders. Nevertheless, his formation of the troops without authority had disastrous consequences.[28]

Whether Armstrong recognized the weakness of the deployment of the troops is questionable. Madison reported that he asked Armstrong if he had suggested any improvement in the arrangements to Winder. "He said that he had not, that from his view of them they appeared to be as good as circumstances admitted." Armstrong informed Spencer that he had been about to give "an entirely different order of battle" when Madison withdrew his authority. This was happy for him, he asserted, "for as the event showed, there was not time for doing it." The disciplined British regulars easily turned the American flanks, and the raw militia broke even before General Ross committed his main force. The battle quickly turned into a rout, and the American troops fled back toward Washington. The only stiff resistance met by the British was from Commodore Barney's sailors, who had followed the army from Washington. The retreat stopped at the Capitol, where Winder consulted with Armstrong and Monroe. He recommended that a stand not be made at Capitol Hill. The disorganized state of his troops, he argued, made it necessary to retire to the heights above Georgetown where he could collect his troops. Both ministers agreed. The responsibility for this order was soon attributed to Armstrong by the inhabitants of Washington, who now began to focus all of their anger upon him.[29]

General Walter Smith, who commanded the city militia, did not even mention Monroe's presence at the Capitol in his report to the House Committee. According to Smith, he and his troops halted at the Capitol and asked for orders from Winder, who "conferred for a few moments with General Armstrong." The order was then given to retreat through Washington and Georgetown. "It is impossible to do justice to the anguish evinced by the troops of Washington and Georgetown on the receiving of this order," Smith related, "The idea of leaving their families, their houses, and their homes, at the mercy of an enraged enemy, was insupportable. To preserve that order which was maintained during the retreat, was now no longer practicable."[30]

Considering the circumstances, the decision was probably correct. Nevertheless, the humiliation of defeat and the failure to fight again were difficult for the troops to accept. It was widely believed that Washington could have been successfully defended. One officer remarked, "I have not met a man who was not of the same opinion with me on that score." Armstrong characterized the charge that he had prevented Winder from defending the Capitol as "a total perversion of the truth." In later years he even claimed that he had recommended making a stand but was outvoted by Winder and Monroe.[31]

The British entered Washington early in the evening of August 24 and burned the public buildings, including the Capitol and the President's Mansion. Most of the public records had been removed to safety, and Dolley Madison had hastily removed many valuable articles from the President's House. The Cabinet scattered. According to prearrangement, Armstrong and Campbell went to Frederick, Maryland. However, in a last-minute change of plan, Madison and the remainder of the Cabinet went into Virginia. In the next few days there was considerable confusion. The British evacuated Washington on the evening of August 25. On August 27, Fort Washington was abandoned upon the approach of a British naval squadron. The next day Alexandria capitulated.[32]

Madison and Monroe returned to Washington on August 27 after the British had retired from the city. There was, according to Monroe, "an universal wish that the active direction of military affairs should be committed to me." Certainly Monroe's activity had attracted favorable notice. He alone of all the major government figures escaped censure for the burning of Washington. Winder was at Baltimore and Armstrong at Frederick, and in the confused state of affairs Madison acceded to the demand and appointed Monroe military commander and secretary of war *ad interim*. This decision, whether Madison intended it or not, was sufficient to show the citizens of Washington that both Winder and Armstrong were no longer in favor. Monroe took what measures of defense he could and managed to quiet the alarm of the city and restore a semblance of order.[33]

Armstrong returned to Washington on August 29. Public hostility against him was running high. One participant in these events recalled a "bitter and general feeling of resentment" against Armstrong and that "he was openly and extensively denounced as a traitor." His "effigy was drawn on the walls of the Capitol after its conflagration, [and] suspended from a gallows with the superscription of 'Armstrong the Traitor.'" A heartless remark was also widely ascribed to him. Informed at Frederick of the burning of the public buildings at Washington, Armstrong was quoted as saying "that the City would make as good a sheep walk as before, and was never fit for anything else."[34] His seeming indifference to the fate of the District in the past was now used against him, and his views were so twisted that the people now believed that he had wished this calamity upon them. Everything that had happened, in this view, could be traced to Armstrong. Also, several wealthy men of the city feared that the burning of the public buildings would be seized as a pretext for the removal of the government to another place. Armstrong, as one contemporary noted, "had no sympathies in common with the people of the District and he would have been glad to see the seat of government removed." This sentiment, "he was not at all solicitous to conceal."[35]

The evening before Armstrong's arrival, the city militia held a mutinous meeting. They adopted a resolution denouncing Armstrong as the willing cause of the destruction of Washington, and they further pledged they would no longer serve under his orders. Shortly after arriving in Washington Armstrong visited the militia in their camp. One eye-witness claimed that his first notice of Armstrong's presence "was from the loud voice of Mr. Charles Carroll . . . refusing his proffered hand, and denouncing his conduct."[36] Armstrong left. Shortly afterward, a delegation was sent to the president to inform him, as Madison recorded, "that every officer would tear off his epaulettes if General Armstrong was to have

anything to do with them," but they also informed him that "Mr. Monroe
. . . was very acceptable to them." Madison replied to the delegation that
Armstrong would give no further orders.[37]

Madison visited Armstrong that evening to discuss the "violent
prejudices" against the Administration, particularly against the secretary
of war. He related the message of the militia. Armstrong replied that the
excitement was "altogether artificial, and that he knew the sources of it,
and the intrigues by which it had been effected." He claimed that the excitement was founded on falsehoods, but he also noted that it was evident
that he could not stay in the city. He offered to resign or, alternatively, retire from the scene for a while and visit his family in New York. Strangely,
Madison refused to accept his resignation, but he agreed that a temporary
retirement by Armstrong might be desirable. Armstrong denied any deficiency on his part in the defense of the city, but Madison replied that he
could not truthfully agree that Armstrong had done "all that ought to
have been done, and in proper time." When Armstrong insisted that he
had omitted no steps for the defense of the city, Madison again disagreed
and stated that "it was the duty of the Secretary of War not only to execute plans or orders committed to him, but to devise and propose such as
would, in his opinion, be necessary and proper." Armstrong had never
been scrupulous or backward in these matters before, but with regard to
the city of Washington, "he had never himself proposed or suggested a
single precaution or arrangement for its safety, everything done on that
subject having been brought forward myself."[38] Although Madison probably did not understand it, that had been part of the problem.

Armstrong left Washington the next day for Baltimore. While there
he wrote a letter to the editors of the Baltimore *Patriot*, which was published on September 3. He denied the many accusations against him: that
he had ordered the retreat at Bladensburg; prevented Winder from defending the Capitol; ordered the withdrawal from Fort Washington; or
ordered the Navy Yard burned. He also denied that he had failed to collect
a sufficient force; noting that a militia force of fifteen thousand was
authorized, to which were added more than a thousand regulars. The reasons the militia were not collected, he asserted, were "altogether extrane-
ous from the government, and entirely beyond its control." He also noted
sarcastically that from what was known of the enemy force, "if all the
troops assembled at Bladensburg, had been faithful to themselves and to
their country, the enemy would have been beaten and the Capitol saved."
The next day, September 4, he submitted his resignation to Madison.[39]

Armstrong's letter to the Baltimore *Patriot* was basically the position he always took with regard to the Washington affair: that no action

was lacking on his part, that errors attributed to him belonged to others, and that in any event the failure occurred on the battlefield where the Americans had displayed a singular want of nerve. There was some truth in what he wrote, just as there was in what Madison had stated earlier. In the final analysis, the judgment as to Armstrong's culpability for the burning of Washington rests on whether he as the secretary of war was ultimately responsible for the defense of Washington. Most historians have asserted that he was, and they have dealt with him harshly, while at the same time ridiculing the fumbling efforts of those around him. Madison's biographer, Irving Brant, while acknowledging that Madison had general responsibility, assigned the blame to Armstrong, asserting that his "neglect and resistance could hardly have been greater if the motive had been sabotage." Henry Adams, on the other hand, asserted that "Armstrong was the only man connected with the defense of Washington whom no one charged with being ridiculous." In truth, if Armstrong was responsible, then he was not only ill-served by those under and above him, he was also victimized by an uncanny set of circumstances and a bizarre series of events that strains our credulity even today. Armstrong did permit himself to write wistfully to Daniel Parker early in 1815, "I regret that Gen. Jackson was not at Washington during the disgraceful occur[r]ences there."[40]

The circumstances of Armstrong's removal have received almost no attention. In fact, his forced resignation has been taken by historians as inferential evidence that he was responsible for the burning of Washington. The reasons why he was singled out as the scapegoat by the citizens of Washington have already been explained. In his letter to the Baltimore *Patriot*, Armstrong noted that his removal was attributable to the "humors of a village mob, stimulated by faction and led by folly." In his letter to Spencer on September 3 he noted, "If these show that we have no govt., it is not my fault. The same troops, a miserable village militia, who, at the instigation of Alex. C. Hanson, dictated terms with regard to me, dictated also the appointment of Monroe, as Major Gen. of the District & in this capacity, he commands in chief." He added pointedly, "It is a well-known fact that to this man's interference in the arrangements on the 24th Ult. much of our misfortune on that day was owing." He concluded disgustedly, "With men of such imbecility I cannot longer connect myself. I have therefore renewed my resignation by letter to the Presid[en]t & am therefore on my way home."[41]

Armstrong's reference to Alexander C. Hanson, editor of the extremely partisan Federalist paper of Georgetown, the *Federal Republican*, sparked a lively controversy many years later. In effect, Armstrong charged Madison with bad faith by bowing to the demands of a group of Federalists for his dismissal. Such a deputation apparently did visit Madison, but to warn him of threats against his life and not for the ostensible reasons suggested by Armstrong. In 1845, two years after Armstrong's death, Thomas L. McKenney, one of the messengers sent by General Smith to Madison demanding Armstrong's dismissal, published an account of the Washington affair which disparaged Armstrong's assertions that Monroe had been responsible for his dismissal from office. Armstrong's son, Kosciuszko, responded in a harsh "Review," in language worthy of his father, which in turn provoked a "Reply" by McKenney to this assault. Kosciuszko returned to the fray once again to give an "Examination" of McKenney's testimony. Then the controversy was dropped. Much of the contention was over the credibility of the Hanson visit and whether McKenney was a member of that delegation. McKenney denied that he was, and he presented testimony that denied the existence of that group. Kosciuszko, on the other hand, presented testimony from several sources attesting to the existence of the cabal. Little light was shed by this dispute, except to reveal that the allegations that Monroe had been responsible for Armstrong's removal from office, as McKenney phrased it, "remained a source of deep disquiet to harass Mr. Monroe to the hour of his death." Kosciuszko's defense revealed that his father always believed there was a conspiracy to effect his removal.[42]

What is striking about Armstrong's dismissal is that he had no defenders. He had very few friends in Washington, and apparently none who were willing to step forward to defend him from attack. His superior, Madison, felt no compelling reason to defend him and willingly complied with the militia's demand for his removal. In truth, Madison was under heavy attack for his own failures at Washington and, consciously or unconsciously, he was perhaps relieved that the anger of the city had focused on Armstrong and not on him. In the Cabinet, only Secretary of the Treasury Campbell was willing to defend Armstrong, but he had little influence and was soon to resign. Secretary of the Navy Jones detested Armstrong, and he would not modify his view even when his wife informed him that Armstrong had the kindness to call upon her on his way through Philadelphia to assure her of her husband's well-being. She noted that Armstrong had spoken very kindly of him. Jones replied, "Would to God! I could return the compliment. I receive it as the more estimable as coming from one whose nature and habits forbid him to speak well of any man." He labeled Armstrong's letter to the Baltimore *Patriot* "a poor subterfuge," and he speculated that Armstrong would "attack all hands. He is full of venom but without a sting. Though I abhor the means employed to coerce the President to dismiss him," he continued, "I am glad we are clear of him even for the short time I shall remain." Jones himself was harshly criticized for ordering the Navy Yard burned, and four days after this letter, on September 11, he resigned.[43]

James Monroe, of course, gained the most from Armstrong's departure. He had been extremely active during the Washington debacle, in marked contrast to Armstrong. Shortly after the event, Monroe wrote to his son-in-law, George W. Hay, detailing and explaining his conduct. Curiously, he seemed unaware of his self-serving attitude: "I had a horror, at remaining here, to be involved indiscriminately in the censure, which would attach to others, and which so eminently belonged to the Secry. of War," he wrote, ". . . I hoped to place myself most distinctly on my own ground, not only, as to the part I had acted, in regard to the defence of this city, but certain traits of character, on which I set some value, and which it required some exertion on my part to bring it into view."[44]

Monroe's actions did attract favorable notice, but they were hardly beneficial to the American cause. From beginning to end, from the scouting activities to his placement of troops on the battlefield at Bladensburg, to his assumption of the War Department and the military command of the District, his actions do him little credit and may be aptly termed illadvised meddling. Armstrong later asserted that there was a malevolent intent behind Monroe's activities, namely to destroy the secretary of war's usefulness. "Cunning and deception were the principal agents," he asserted, "but to these were given an extension, activity, and flagitiousness, which altered their character, if not their names, and sublimated them into crimes against the state." Monroe, he charged, "became in a great degree, the executor of his own project." During the Washington affair, he asserted, "the dispassionate inquirer cannot overlook the fact, that every interposition involved an error — and that every error directly contributed to the disgrace of our arms and the destruction of the Capitol."[45]

The position that Monroe always took in relation to Armstrong's occupancy of the War Department was that his failures and subsequent dismissal were the result of his incompetence and misconduct. He had always considered Armstrong unworthy of the position. He was certain that there was nothing improper in his opposition to Armstrong's measures or in his assumption of Armstrong's post after the burning of Washington. It was the judgment of Henry Adams, however, that "Monroe's act, whether such was his intention or not, was a *coup d'etat* . . . Monroe, instead of giving Armstrong in his absence such support as might have sustained him, took a position and exercised an authority that led necessarily to his overthrow."[46] Monroe was aware that Armstrong's removal might be imputed to him, but he seemed incapable of recognizing that his actions in any way influenced the decision to remove his rival. Typical of this attitude was his application to Madison to assume the War Department permanently. Madison had made no move to fill the post, and Monroe after waiting a decent period to be asked, finally ventured to recommend on September 25 that he be appointed. Characteristically, he based his claim on his need to preserve his reputation:

> By taking charge of the Dept. twice, and withdrawing from it a second time, it may be inferred that I shrink from the responsibility, from a fear of injuring my reputation; and this may countenance the idea, that the removal of the other was an affair of intrigue, in which I partook, especially in the latter instance, from selfish and improper motives; and did not proceed from his incompetency or misconduct. It seems due therefore to my own reputation, to go thro' with the undertaking, by accepting permanently a trust, which I have not sought, never wished, and is attended with great responsibility and hazard. By taking the place all clamour will be silenced. It is known here at least that I was put into it, when the other could no longer hold it.[47]

Monroe was appointed. Despite his disclaimers, he had been conspicuously available for the public to turn to when they soured on Armstrong. As Adams noted, Monroe's actions seriously undermined Armstrong's tenuous hold on his office: "Between conscious intrigue and unconscious instinct no clear line of division was ever drawn. Monroe, by one method or the other, gained his point and drove Armstrong from the Cabinet."[48]

It was widely believed that Armstrong would lash out in all directions after his humiliation at Washington, but he was content for a time to allow matters to take their own course. He believed, rather naively, that the congressional committee investigating the burning of Washington would somehow exonerate him. He wrote to Spencer on September 29, "An investigation, honestly & carefully conducted, will do much good." He noted that Richard M. Johnson, who headed the committee, was his friend. The committee, however, after drawing statements from virtually all of the participants, merely rendered a report recapitulating the event and made no effort to assign blame.

Armstrong was disappointed, and he complained to Spencer that Attorney General Richard Rush had "mistaken or misrepresented" Armstrong's conversation with President Madison prior to the battle of Bladensburg. He also disputed John Van Ness's statement which depicted Armstrong as indifferent to the defense of the District. "That I was so to his many importunities & impertinences, is true," he wrote, "but the secret of his ill-humor & injustice comes out — he wanted to command! A fellow who has not military knowledge enough to mount a Corporal's guard; wanted to command an army & against a regular and scientific British general! I put an end to this consumate impudence & folly & of course offended this mighty Kinderhook Hero." He concluded with what may be considered at once his analysis of his problems as secretary of war and a fair statement of his philosophy of life: "In the discharge of my duty, I have never hesitated to cease pursuing its most obvious dictates, and giving offence to bad or incompetent men, hence it is, that all my signal enemies are of one or the other of these two descriptions."[49]

Armstrong recognized, of course, that he had made many enemies. He indicated to his friends that this was the real reason for his resignation. "It was only when I saw that my usefulness to the public, was gone, that I quitted the ship," he informed Spencer. "The cause of my retiring from the War Dept. is before the public," he noted to New York Congressman John W. Taylor early in November 1814, "To me it appeared to be sufficient. Conscious of no crime & seeing the worst imputed to me without a shadow of proof — and perceiving no disposition in any member of the administration excepting the late Secy. of the Treasury, to put down these calumnies, & a positive intention on the part of the President to give them effect & extension . . . I could not take a course, different from that I pursued. It was the safest for myself, and I did & do solemnly believe it was the best for the public." He elaborated: "From the moment I went into the Dept. untill I left it, there was a strong undercurrent incessantly laboring to undermine me, even at the expence of public safety and honor." Now that he was gone this problem was removed. He said much the same to his former chief clerk, Daniel Parker. "I am much more at ease, than while in the red leather chair," he wrote, "I am far from intrigues & intriguers & do not wish to be nearer them."[50]

Armstrong believed he saw evidence of the continuing enmity of the Virginians even after he was out of office. When General Wilkinson's oft-delayed court-martial was convened in January 1815, Madison and Monroe deliberately contrived the case, he believed, to assure Wilkinson's acquittal and further blacken Armstrong's reputation. He predicted to both Spencer and Parker before the trial that from the composition of the court-martial board as well as the failure to call certain key witnesses, that the obvious purpose was Wilkinson's acquittal. "What can we think of a Gov't," he wrote Spencer on January 25, "that . . . withholds from this court, the testimony necessary to convict him?" The motive for all this was obvious. "It is to give W. a triumph over *me* in public opinion!

Unable to reach me by fair means, they resort to foul—they bribe a prisoner & a culprit with hopes of impunity, to make his own defence a dia-
tribe upon me. This will be circulated in every paper, & the facts really belonging to & governing the case, will be unknown."[51]

The conduct of the trial lends credence to Armstrong's charges.
General Scott was not called to testify until midway through the trial, and
it was then discovered that the government had named him president of
another court-martial in progress. His testimony would certainly have
been adverse to Wilkinson. Other key witnesses, such as Generals Brown
and Gaines, or Colonel Joseph Swift, were not even called. Moreover,
and perhaps most shocking by today's standards, of the thirteen members
of the court-martial board, nine, including the president of the board,
Major General Dearborn, testified on behalf of the defendant Wilkinson.
Not surprisingly, the board acquitted Wilkinson of all charges in their decision on March 21, 1815. Armstrong merely pointed out to Spencer that
he had predicted the result. "Ours is a curious state of morals," he wrote,
and he lamented that there were so many "parisites . . . willing to do the
dirty work of a master, who can either reward or punish them." Although
he could not prove the source was Monroe, he asserted, "the bottom of
the mischief is there & I know it."[52]

Surprisingly, despite expectations to the contrary, Armstrong did
not take up his pen against his enemies until 1816. Ironically, he has been
credited with a pamphlet that he did not write signed "Spectator," while a
more important pamphlet that he did write has been overlooked. He was
widely identified by his contemporaries as "Spectator," perhaps because
he referred to himself as such in his report to the House Committee. Appearing early in 1816, "Spectator" exculpated Armstrong's conduct,
sneered at the interference of Madison and Monroe, and placed the blame
on General Winder. The pamphlet provoked a rejoinder by a nephew of
Winder, who not only defended Winder from the assaults of "Spectator"
and pointed out that his conduct had been commended by a court of enquiry, he also savagely attacked Armstrong, who he believed to be the author of "Spectator." General George Izard, who was criticized in an aside
by "Spectator," also believed Armstrong was the author. Armstrong denied authorship, however, and Izard published this denial in his pamphlet
defending his conduct in the campaign of 1814.[53]

Armstrong's denial is not perhaps conclusive, but if he were the author of "Spectator," it would have been more characteristic to have defi-
antly confirmed his authorship, or to have contemptuously refused to answer. The evidence indicates that the author of "Spectator" was William
Elliot, the chief clerk in the Patent Office at Washington. The pamphlet
was published in February 1816, and a month later, on March 12, 1816,

Armstrong wrote Spencer that "Old Elliot says his pamphlet has worked wonders at Washington." He also indicated that he was still working on his pamphlet. Further, Elliot included "Spectator" in a work he published in 1822, noting that "it bears evident marks of having been written by someone well acquainted with the subject."[54]

Armstrong's pamphlet was disguised as an "Exposition of the motives which induced the representatives of the people, in the late caucus at Washington, to oppose the nomination of Mr. Monroe." Spencer suggested the mode of attacking the congressional caucus, which nominated the candidate for the presidency, as being undemocratic. After finishing the pamphlet, however, Armstrong was unable to publish it in the Albany *Argus* as he had expected. The editor, Jesse Buel, although friendly to Spencer and Armstrong, could not open the columns of the *Argus* to any attack upon Monroe without sacrificing himself. "The caucus has ruined everything," Spencer lamented.[55] Armstrong's pamphlet was eventually published in Washington, perhaps through the auspices of William Elliot. This fact also had the advantage of virtually assuring Armstrong's anonymity.

In his pamphlet Armstrong charged that "the whole weight of the republican party, for fifteen years past, [has] been artfully wielded [by the Virginians] to cut off from popular respect and estimation the most distinguished characters in other parts of the United States." Prominent in that list was Armstrong himself, who "experienced perpetual embarrassment" in the War Department due to the "unusual interference of a great civil officer of state," namely James Monroe. After the capture of Washington, "the particular and personal friends of Col. Monroe, uniting with the Federalists, insulted him on the streets of Washington, and Madison discarding him from office, gave the fatal blow to his reputation." For his purposes, Armstrong was also quite generous to De Witt Clinton. Clinton had erred by his apostasy in 1812, but Monroe had done worse in his defection in 1808, yet Monroe had been forgiven but not Clinton. More to the point, fifty-four representatives had opposed Monroe in the caucus, representing over two million people. Only the eleven votes cast by the Virginia delegation had won the nomination for Monroe (65-54). Armstrong asserted that they would not go into the caucus until certain of success, and they were known to be pledged to support Monroe even if the caucus nominated someone else. As for Monroe's qualifications, Armstrong surveyed his diplomatic and political career skeptically. "His best friends allow him to be but of moderate capacity, and slow of comprehension . . . But thus ordinarily gifted, Col. Monroe has furnished unequivocal evidence that his lust for power is insatiable."[56]

Armstrong had struck telling blows against the caucus, which was being attacked in many quarters as undemocratic. This caused a response by Charles Pinckney, under the pseudonym of "A South Carolinian." Pinckney speculated that the pamphlet was probably not the work of any of the dissenting members of the caucus. He noted that it had been ascribed to De Witt Clinton or his friends, but others suspected that William H. Crawford's friends were involved. Armstrong's name was not mentioned, perhaps because he was not considered a contender for the presidency. Despite Armstrong's vigorous, recognizable style, his authorship of this pamphlet was not discovered by his contemporaries and has remained undiscovered until now. In any event, it enjoyed wide circulation. Pinckney alleged that 10,000 copies of the "Exposition" were being circulated by Monroe's enemies. He defended Monroe's qualifications admirably, but it was clear that he held the caucus in no such high esteem. He merely commended it as the "most practicable" system of nomination.[57] Armstrong's and Pinckney's pamphlets foreshadowed the debate over the caucus a few years later. The election of 1816 was, in fact, the last effective use of the caucus as a device for naming candidates for the Presidency. The Republicans soothed the wounds caused by their caucus fight of 1816, and Monroe easily defeated Rufus King, the last Federalist candidate for the presidency.

After the election of 1816 Armstrong turned to more congenial pursuits, such as agriculture, writing, studying, and occasional forays into polemics. Spencer urged him to return to politics, but Armstrong, realistically assessing his shattered reputation, refused. Spencer persisted, but even with his massive influence in New York he was unable to procure Armstrong's election to the Senate. The friends of Governor Tompkins and Martin Van Buren, anxious to show their support for the Administration, combined to block Armstrong's election. As late as 1819 Spencer was still trying, but Armstrong gave him no encouragement. He was happily engaged in agricultural pursuits and occupied on two writing projects, one on agriculture and another on military history. "You see how completely I am detached, as well by business as by taste, from everything political," he declared to Spencer on December 22, 1819. The only thing that could bring him back to labors of that kind, he asserted, would be to further the career of Spencer, or "any association of enlightened and honest men, who would declare an open war on the present weak & corrupt administration of our national affairs."[58] No such coalition loomed on the horizon, and Armstrong settled into an extended, fruitful, comfortable retirement.

12

LAST YEARS

JOHN ARMSTRONG SPENT MOST OF THE LAST YEARS of his life on his estate in New York's Dutchess County. The village of Lower Red Hook was about three miles from the Hudson River, and Armstrong's residence was along the east bank just south of Lower Red Hook Landing (present-day Barrytown), several miles upstream from Kingston. The Catskill Mountains loomed beyond the west bank of the river. Rents from possessions on both sides of the river provided him with a steady income throughout his life. His estate, "La Bergerie," contained 728 acres, a portion of which continued under leasehold to others to provide an additional source of income. This particular region along the east side of the Hudson River was the domain of the Livingston-Beekman clan. Their homes, many still standing today, dot the landscape for some twenty or thirty miles along the river and comprise a unique legacy of a once-powerful and important family.

Armstrong's mansion was not completed by 1815, but they were forced to occupy the house prematurely when a fire destroyed their temporary residence on February 12, 1815. Armstrong also constructed fine wooden barns and a frame farmhouse, which are still in use, at about this same time, and he is thought to have had a small landing stage on the river and a modest mill on the Mudder Kill, a small stream that ran through his property down to the river. It is not known today how long his French Merino sheep continued to flourish at La Bergerie, but a family tradition recalls the sale of a prize ram for an astounding $1500.[1]

In time the whimsical name of La Bergerie was dropped and the name by which the estate is known today, Rokeby, was adopted. Armstrong's daughter, Margaret, is credited with this name. She saw similarities between the English ravines described in Sir Walter Scott's epic poem, "Rokeby," published in 1813, and "Devil's Gorge," a ravine cut by the Mudder Kill. The Armstrongs briefly shared their house with another family, for Horatio married Mary Hughes of Baltimore on December 27, 1814. The Armstrongs first grandson was born at Rokeby on September 28, 1815. He was named John after his grandfather Armstrong. The next to marry was Margaret. She occasionally visited the Spencers in Albany to enjoy the social life of the town, and she happened to meet William B. Astor, the son of John Jacob Astor, at a party given by the De Witt Clintons. A romance developed and they were married on May 20, 1818, at Rokeby. It was a good match. Astor married his son into a landed, aristocratic family with useful political connections, and Armstrong married his daughter to the son and principal heir of the richest man in America. The first Astor child, Emily, was born at Rokeby in 1819. Neither John, Robert, nor Kosciuszko ever married. Henry married Mary Drayton Simons of South Carolina, described as "a fervent convert to Methodism," on May 1, 1823. They eventually had six children, five of whom lived beyond infancy, but because none of these children ever married, John and Alida had living descendants only through Horatio and Margaret.[2]

Alida did not live to see Henry married. She died in the home parlor at Rokeby on Christmas Day 1822 from the long debilitating effects of rheumatism. She was a proud woman and despite her mild disposition, she had a strong character. She shared with her husband an aristocratic sense of duty, place, and honor. One individual who knew her well asserted that she "could not be charged with having ever made an imprudent or an unkind speech."[3] She was well-educated and cultivated — an excellent wife for a husband who was a scholar, politician, and statesman. Yet, if she had a failing, it was that she did not curb the mean spirit and the political and polemical excesses of her husband. There is sufficient evidence from her letters to show that she faithfully supported and sustained her husband through all of his political battles and commiserated with him in his defeats.

John and Alida Armstrong had provided their children with the best education possible to prepare them for a role of leadership. In their children's careers, however, they were undoubtedly disappointed. Horatio and Henry showed an inclination for farming, and they assumed the task of managing the estate, collecting rents, and overseeing tenants on the lands in the Catskills. In March 1822 they began a tanning establishment, but it was not a success. Robert remained in the army. John and Kosciuszko read law in the office of John C. Spencer, son of Ambrose Spencer, but only John became a lawyer. He established an office at nearby

A very early photograph showing the south front of Rokeby, more or less as General Armstrong built it. Photo prior to 1858. Armstrong's daughter, Mrs. Astor, is probably the lady in black. *Rokeby Collection, courtesy of Mrs. Richard Aldrich and sons, Barrytown, New York*

Rhinebeck and, except for a period in Maryland, continued in this practice the remainder of his life. John flirted briefly with politics by serving as a delegate to the People's Party Convention at Utica in 1824; as a member of the State Assembly in 1825; and as Rhinebeck Town Supervisor in 1840. Kosciuszko never did find his niche in life. He was an amateur painter and litterateur who was popular with the children of the Astor family as a kindly, if somewhat eccentric, bachelor uncle. He spent most of his life in the household of the Astors.

Armstrong exerted himself during these years of retirement to harass his two old enemies, James Wilkinson and James Monroe. Ambrose Spencer had urged Armstrong to "dispel the vile slanders of ignorance & villainy" of Wilkinson's *Memoirs of My Own Times* when it was published in 1816. Armstrong had difficulty in finding a suitable place to publish his review of Wilkinson's *Memoirs*, but he did eventually in a magazine founded by Colonel Charles K. Gardner, a former aide-de-camp of Armstrong's during the War of 1812. The first article in the first issue of *The Literary and Scientific Repository and Critical Review* of June 1820 began Armstrong's lengthy review. Two further articles followed, bringing the total length of his critique of Wilkinson to eighty-five pages. The articles were anonymous, but Armstrong's style and his caustic wit were easily recognizable. Armstrong also assaulted Monroe in the same magazine, both in his critique of Wilkinson and in a short biographical sketch of his brother-in-law, Chancellor Livingston, who had died in 1813. Although Monroe suffered under the stings of Armstrong's attacks, he saw the wisdom of remaining silent. "I do not think that the writer of these caluminous essays, can injure me," he wrote his son-in-law, Samuel L. Gouverneur, "let him say what he will . . . I am certain that he has no claim with the public, of a nature to enable him to injure any one."[4]

Armstrong believed, however, that his essays were having an effect upon the public. He wrote Gardner in March 1822, "A few more attacks on M[onroe] will send him out of office in a very bad odor." Spencer, of course, applauded Armstrong's efforts to bring Monroe's Administration down in the public estimation. He accused Monroe of "undermining the Constitution," and he declared that he was a "piece of clay in the hands of potters." He exhorted Armstrong to greater efforts "to expose one of the meanest & most corrupt administrations, with which we have ever been cursed — in doing this you will deserve well of the Country, & at the same time will pay up old scores & expose a man who has hunted you down."[5] In truth, the more Armstrong wrote the less effective he became. He appeared to be a carping critic, dispensing calumny and abuse, and it destroyed his credibility.

Armstrong carried on his vendetta against Monroe even after Monroe's death on July 4, 1831. John Quincy Adams wrote a eulogy praising Monroe's deeds, and in doing so, perhaps inadvertently, by implication he insulted Armstrong. Consequently, Armstrong deemed a response to these "misrepresentations" to be "unavoidable." He explained to one of his confidants, Henry Lee, the son of "Light Horse Harry" Lee, that "the ex-President not only committed the blunder of mistaking a lucky intriguer, for a sage and hero, but was silly and wicked enough to mask, under his praises of Monroe, an attack upon me." He noted that he had confined his reply to the affair at Washington and to Monroe's "diplomatic *services* — if the word can, in any sense, be adapted to what in that walk, he ever said or did."[6]

Armstrong's pamphlet, tasteless as it was and demeaning to its author, arose out of frustration and a profound disgust that his version of the events had once again been distorted and perverted to serve other ends. Spencer congratulated Armstrong and noted that Adams "deserved it at yours hands, & the stripes have been well laid on." Armstrong replied that Adams's pamphlet "was one of malignant character & intended to perpetuate falsehoods, got up in 1814 by Monroe and his partisans, with the view of breaking me down in public opinion & in effect which, by the by, it was too successful." He added, "I have by no means exhausted my quiver." Adams would find that "he would have better shewn his friendship for his friend and Patron, had he been more discreet and better instructed with regard to the actual conduct and real character of that imposter."[7]

Armstrong's attacks upon Wilkinson and Monroe were efforts to place his version of these events on the record to counter the supposed distortions by his enemies. The Washington affair and his conduct as secretary of war occupied most of his attention, but he also dealt with the Newburgh Addresses, which had certainly been prejudicial to his career. He ruefully admitted to General Joseph Swift in 1813 that "had he been one year older, he would not have written them; that they had been a millstone hung about his neck through his life."[8] It should be remembered that Armstrong knew very little of the activities of the nationalists in Philadelphia and that his role in the Newburgh Affair had been confined essentially to that of a letter writer.

In January 1820 he wrote Timothy Pickering, long involved in public life and a knowledgable observer of the events at Newburgh in March 1783. Disguising himself with the anagram name of "John Montgars," Armstrong stated that he was writing a history of the Revolutionary War and asked for Pickering's interpretation of the events at Newburgh. He was seeking confirmation of his belief that Washington's strong reaction arose not from the content of the Addresses, but from a letter from John Harvie of Virginia warning of a dangerous conspiracy, which Washington produced and read at the meeting of March 15. Pickering was suspicious that "Montgars" was Armstrong, and he replied evasively. Perhaps because Armstrong had mistakenly identified the author of the letter to Washington as Harvie and not Joseph Jones, Pickering had no recollection that Washington had read a letter at the meeting. Even in 1825 when Pickering revealed to Armstrong that he knew Montgars was Armstrong,

Pickering still asserted that no letter was read at the meeting. Yet had he merely checked his own file of letters, he would have discovered from his own testimony that Washington had indeed read such a letter.[9]

Armstrong had already given his interpretation of the event in a review of Judge William Johnson's biography of General Nathanael Greene in 1823 in the *United States Magazine*, as Gardner's magazine was now called. Johnson asserted that Gouverneur Morris and not Armstrong was the real author of the Addresses. Armstrong demolished this theory and admitted publicly for the first time that he was the author. This admission obviously reflected a certain pride of authorship, although he still felt compelled to defend his action. He reproduced Washington's letter to him of 1797 as evidence of Washington's understanding of the affair.[10]

During this period Armstrong also wrote a series of articles for the editor of the Albany *Argus*, Jesse Buel, on the state of agriculture in the United States, which was published in book form entitled *A Treatise on Agriculture* and signed "A Practical Farmer." The work was heavily documented and offered the latest scientific advice on farming, and it was well-received. Buel, the publisher, was destined to have an extensive influence on the study of agriculture in the United States through the pages of his very successful and influential magazine, *The Cultivator*, which had a circulation of over twenty thousand. The two men corresponded frequently on agricultural matters. Armstrong encouraged Buel's project for the founding of a state agricultural school, and Buel in turn encouraged Armstrong to add additional chapters to the *Treatise* on the kitchen garden and fruit garden. An expanded version of the *Treatise* (which ran to 282 pages) was published in 1839. Attesting to the utility and readership of this expanded work is the fact that Harper and Brothers republished it in 1864.[11]

As the years passed, Armstrong was counted as one of the survivors of the thinning ranks of Revolutionary War veterans. He sat, for example, for the painter John Trumbull for the great tableau, "The Surrender of Burgoyne at Saratoga," which is now prominently displayed in the Great Rotunda of the United States Capitol. He also participated in the orgy of patriotism when General Lafayette visited the United States in 1824. When Lafayette toured the Hudson River Valley in September 1824, Armstrong participated in the ceremonies honoring Lafayette, and he traveled with his old friend on part of the tour.[12]

Lafayette's visit and the deaths of former Presidents Thomas Jefferson and John Adams on July 4, 1826, the fiftieth anniversary of the Declaration of Independence, profoundly affected many Americans and stimulated a great interest in the Revolutionary generation. Armstrong became

a beneficiary of this sentiment. Under the Act of May 15, 1828 the government finally fulfilled the promise made shortly after the Newburgh incident. He was paid $3000, or five years full pay, and as a Revolutionary
veteran he was placed on an annual pension of $600, which he received
until his death in 1843.[13]

The interest in the Revolutionary generation also stimulated efforts
to collect and preserve manuscript materials of the Revolution. One of
the best known collectors of Americana was Jared Sparks, a former editor
of the *North American Review*, who edited the George Washington papers, a task he completed in 1837. He also collected and published the diplomatic correspondence of the Revolution, edited the correspondence of
Benjamin Franklin, and wrote a three-volume biography of Gouverneur
Morris.[14] In due course Sparks sought an interview with Armstrong, and
he met with him in August 1831. Armstrong, of course, possessed much
first-hand information and anecdotes about Horatio Gates, George
Washington, Charles Lee, Alexander Hamilton, James Wilkinson, Baron
von Steuben, and other Revolutionary figures. Sparks was delighted with
the information, but his *Journal* reveals that he was somewhat repelled by
Armstrong's aggressive personality. "His conversation is interesting, and
his mind full upon matters of the Revolution, and the last war," Sparks
wrote, but he added, "His opinions are decided, & he expresses them ardently and strongly. His temperament is warm, and I think his imagina-
tion, & the bias of his feelings, give a turn to his opinions not exactly in
accordance with a rigid memory or a cool judgment." Sparks quite possibly said worse, but the next four and a half lines were marked out and are
illegible. Armstrong, on the other hand, was more favorably impressed.
He reported to Spencer that he had been pleased to discover in Sparks "that
entire and decided impartiality, which is indispensable to the historian."[15]

This was the beginning of a very fruitful relationship between the
two men. Sparks repeatedly queried Armstrong about historical facts,
which invariably elicited long, informative replies, especially those relating to the character of General Gates and Kosciuszko. The exchange was
mutually beneficial. Not only did Armstrong persuade Sparks of the validity of Washington's letter to Armstrong in 1797, Sparks also enlisted
Armstrong to write two biographies for inclusion in his *Library of American Biography* series, which ran to ten volumes. Armstrong contributed a
biography of one of the Livingston brother-in-laws, General Richard
Montgomery, which appeared in volume one, and a biography of an old
family friend, General Anthony Wayne, which was published in volume
four. Both biographies suffered from a paucity of material, and neither
pleased their author.

The writing of the latter biography was interrupted by a personal tragedy, "the death of a favorite son," Robert, his fourth son born in 1797, who died in Philadelphia on October 10, 1834. Robert had made the army his career, but promotions came slowly and in 1834 after twenty years of service he held only the rank of captain. From the few letters that survive, it appears that Robert's health was very poor, although the nature of his problems are not disclosed. One of his letters to his father reveals an almost morbid preoccupation with his "negligences." A family tradition relates that he fell desperately in love with his cousin, Cora Livingston, Edward's daughter. They were forbidden to marry due to their relationship, and Robert consequently drank heavily and eventually committed suicide.[16]

Writing the biographies for Sparks also interrupted Armstrong's project to finish his *Notices of the War of 1812,* the first volume of which was published in 1836. The idea of writing a history of the War of 1812 extended back at least to the mid-1820's when he began gathering data from the War Department. He dubbed his first volume "a pigmy in every respect," but he was obviously pleased with it, for when he sent a copy to Ambrose Spencer, he noted that it had been well-received by both the *North American Review* and the Albany *Evening Journal.* It had also "brought out wasps upon me from both nests — old federalism and young Whiggism." The latter illusion was to the belief that the *Notices* were "intended to break down Gen. Harrison in the opinion of the Public." Armstrong noted to Sparks, however, that he "had begun the work long before any portion of the people of the U.S. had been mad enough to mention W. H. Harrison as a candidate for the Presidency." Actually, he continued, the book had two objects: "to give a full & faithful narrative of facts; and to apply these, whether favorable or unfavorable to individuals, the received maxims of war." The purpose was therefore "as much didactic as historical." He concluded, referring once again to Harrison, "If the prevailing monomania has dressed up one of my blunderers, and exhibited him in a suit of old tattered Regimentals, as a fit successor for George Washington — is it my fault?"[17]

Armstrong did not begin the second volume until after the election of 1836 to avoid the imputation that it was involved in the political intrigues of the day. He was nevertheless determined to continue the second in the manner of the first, as he informed Sparks, "that is, freely and truly, without regard to individuals, dead or alive, or to governments which never die." Ill health, many interruptions, and even the state of the economy delayed the publication of the second volume. Armstrong was obliged to find a new printer when the first could not pay his journeymen or even buy paper. Eventually, the effects of the Panic of 1837 moderated and the second volume appeared in 1840.[18]

Armstrong's *Notices* have been frequently cited but little understood by historians of the War of 1812. The two volumes have been dismissed as thin in substance and frequently marred by his biases. The *Notices* are not particularly useful today as a resource work. The narrative portion of the two volumes, for example, amounts to less than 370 pages. While the chief value of the work lies in the perspective it gives of the man who served as the secretary of war during the War of 1812, the didactic purpose of the *Notices* has been all but ignored. A unique feature of each chapter is the "Remarks" section where Armstrong assumed the role of a military critic applying the maxims of war to the narrative noting where they had been properly or improperly applied. Thus in the first volume Harrison's activities were found to be particularly wanting in military acumen.

Although many perceived this volume as simply a vehicle to attack Harrison, Armstrong asserted to Spencer in 1840 that he "never had any personal ill-will to Harrison nor ever intended to him an injury. What I said of his professional conduct was merely a discharge of historical duty, which could not be dispensed with." Armstrong even confessed to his son Henry in 1840 that "on the maxim that the smaller evil is to be preferred to the greater," Harrison would have his vote for the presidency. That he had arrived at this amazing concession through extensive rationalization was evident when he added, "Even his unfitness for the office gives me one security — that arising from a competent cabinet."[19]

Wilkinson and Monroe did not escape censure in the *Notices*, but Armstrong's passages dealing with them were noticably more restrained than his previous attacks upon them. James Madison lived long enough to read the first volume. While he conceded that Armstrong's style was good, he thought it too epigrammatic. He also supposed that he would be subjected to attack in the second volume. When this conversation was reported in the newspapers shortly after Madison's death in 1836, Armstrong expressed to Spencer his regret at "the old gentleman's going out of the world under this belief — for it is unfounded. His sin," Armstrong continued, "grew out of his terrors, & however an infirmity like this, might have lessened my reverence for the man, it had no tendency to destroy my belief in the general purity of his official conduct."[20]

An intended work on the Revolutionary War was never completed. He had contemplated such a work perhaps extending back to the 1780s. He assiduously collected throughout his life a vast amount of documents, anecdotes, and other memorabilia relating to the Revolution. He evidently worked diligently on his project after completing the *Notices*, for he reported to Spencer on January 6, 1842, "my health is tolerably good, enabling me to work about four hours a day; a power which if prolonged for another year will carry me through the war of the revolution." In April he noted optimistically that his work was progressing and that he hoped to finish that year. However, for reasons that are not clear, the manuscript was never published. Possibly, as one source indicates, the manuscript might have been destroyed by a fire, but there are no other contemporary sources to confirm that as fact.[21]

Undoubtedly, one of the most remarkable aspects of Armstrong's long years in retirement was his enduring friendship with Ambrose Spencer. Spencer had been one of his major sponsors, and Armstrong owed his advancement in politics to a great extent to the sturdy support of Spencer, who by virtue of his position as Chief Justice of the New York Supreme Court remained a powerful figure into the 1820s. Under the New York Constitution of 1777, the judges of the Supreme Court sat with the governor as the Council of Revision and exercised the veto over legislative bills. This mired the judges deeply in politics, and they were subject to bitter attacks from many quarters. The accumulation of assaults upon the defects of the Constitution coincided with the rising tide of democratic sentiment and led to the calling of a Constitutional Convention at Albany in August 1821. One result of the Convention was a provision in the Constitution that all of the present political offices, including the judiciary, were to become vacant on December 31, 1822, and Spencer lost his position.[22]

The New York Constitutional Convention of 1821 was only one example of the change that was taking place in American politics. The liberalization of the franchise, one of the foremost changes, led to the democratization and at the same time a vulgarization of politics that was very displeasing to Armstrong. A constant lament in his letters was about the decline of political morality. In December 1826, for example, he wrote Spencer, "Votes are notoriously bought and sold at our elections (of all kinds) as in the rotten boroughs of Great Britian, and, unless a remedy be found, indicate an unavoidable subversion of the present form of gov't." He wrote in the same vein in January 1827 to his old chief clerk of the War Department, Daniel Parker. "The mischief of the times," he began, "is that the generation who used to call a spade a spade, has gone by, & that hocus pocus is everywhere substituted for fair dealing."[23] Despite his lament about politicians, Armstrong was a very knowledgeable and astute observer of national politics.

When Spencer was elected as a member of the Twenty-First Congress from the Albany district in 1828, he and Armstrong disagreed on the

John Armstrong, Jr., attributed to John Wesley Jarvis. *Courtesy of the National Portrait Gallery, Washington, D.C.*

Ambrose Spencer by John Wesley Jarvis. *Courtesy of the New-York Historical Society, New York City*

merits of Andrew Jackson. Spencer took a strong anti-Jackson position in
Congress. Armstrong, on the other hand, favored most of Jackson's policies, including Indian removal, the low tariff policy, and the Maysville
road veto. Yet he tempered his admiration of Jackson's policies with occasional reproach for particular acts, such as Jackson's involvement in the
so-called Eaton affair. Spencer's opinion of Jackson grew to a passionate
dislike for the man and his principles. "Genl. Jackson," he wrote in August
1832, "is not only an ignorant, but a very lawless & wicked man . . . I
now detest & loath him as a perfect Barbarian." He was particularly upset
by Jackson's veto of the Bank of the United States recharter bill, and he
added to his friend, "I shall be disappointed & mortified if after all his
folly & tyranny, you are yet his adherent."[24]

Armstrong nevertheless continued an adherent of Jackson, partly
because the Jacksonians flattered him by consulting his views and seeking
his advice on such local appointments as postmasters. His brother-in-law
Edward Livingston was also appointed secretary of state by Jackson in
1831. He did please Spencer by criticizing Jackson's conduct in the Bank
War, but as late as 1836 Spencer professed to be filled with wonder that
Armstrong, "a Philosopher and Patriot could entertain the least regard or
respect for an Administration so contemptible as this is, to find you pre-
ferring such an ignorant & inconsistent dolt as Genl. Jackson, to a man of
the transcendent powers of Clay."[25]

Such differences on political matters, however, did not diminish the
close friendship between the two men. Both realized their friendship tran-
scended mundane political issues. In truth, most of their comments on the
passing political scene were detached and quite often amounted to nostalgic reveries. They agreed more often than they disagreed. Both lamented
the lowered tone of politics and the decline of the caliber of men in government, and in the nature of the older generation passing judgment on
the younger, they agreed, as Spencer phrased it, "we are rapidly going
down hill." Epitomizing this view was Spencer's ejaculation to Armstrong
upon the election of Van Buren in 1836: "Martin Van Buren is to be our
next President!!! Who would, a priori, having a personal acquaintance
with him, have believed it possible?" He added, "I do not deny to him
acuteness of mind, & taste, but his education was extremely defective, &
his acquired knowledge very circumscribed." Spencer was consoled, however, "by the reflection that the change about to take place must be for the
better."[26]

On June 25, 1836, to please his daughter Margaret and arrange a
patrimony for his sons, Armstrong sold Rokeby to his son-in-law, William B. Astor, for $50,000. He informed Spencer that the sale price was

$20,000 less than he could have gotten on the open market. He also sold his mills on the Sawkill (with about forty acres of land) for $30,000, and two other small farms for $11,000. "I am still the owner of forty three tracts, small & great, in this town," he continued, "and have begun to build a cottage on one of them, situated in the village of Red Hook, which I shall keep as a summer residence."[27]

These transactions were necessary because Armstrong had sacrificed his own patrimony. In April 1814 his brother James had written from Carlisle, "What little estate I now possess consists chiefly of my farm near this town," and he added that his fortunes had sunk almost every year. He had accumulated a debt of "four or five thousand Dollars exclusive of the debt I owe you." If he could sell his farm at a high price, he wrote, he would be able to pay off his debts and leave a sufficient sum to each of his surviving children (who numbered five, two having died in infancy). James noted that it was "very consoling" to receive assurances from his brother "that whatever may be my Fate, my Family may expect to find in you a Friend & Protector."

His brother's estate continued to dwindle, and in July 1821 James asked for a conveyance of the remainder of the Kittanning Tract, "the only means that I can possibly devise by which I may be enabled to relieve myself from my present embarrassment." James acknowledged that this was an "extraordinary request after all the sacrifices you have so generously made in this way already," but he assured his brother that he would "pay . . . to the last farthing what is due you." This was, of course, a face-saving statement. Armstrong was touched by his brother's plight, and he signed over the remainder of the Kittanning Tract, from which he had never realized any profit. According to a family tradition, Alida drew her husband aside and asked him to consider his own children, and he in response gestured towards the Catskills and said, "My dear, do you not own these mountains? Can you not endow your children with their slopes?" She agreed and Armstrong gave away his patrimony. Years later, the discovery of vast coal deposits on these western Pennsylvania lands may have caused him some pangs of regret. James died in May 1828.[28]

Armstrong's hero-worship, as evidenced by the naming of his sons for persons he admired, provided unexpected benefits in the form of legacies for his sons. Horatio Gates's will provided $2500 for his namesake.[29] Thaddeus Kosciuszko, in June 1806, in Paris, executed a codicil to his original will of 1798 providing Kosciuszko Armstrong a sum of $3704. When Kosciuszko died on October 15, 1817, Armstrong laid claim to the inheritance on behalf of his son, who was still a minor, but the matter became involved in legal entanglements that eventually resulted in four separate United States Supreme Court decisions. Kosciuszko Armstrong never did receive the bequest.[30]

Armstrong provided very well for his children. In his will he distributed more than 4000 acres of land apiece to Horatio, Henry, and Kosciuszko. John received 340 acres and a farm of unspecified acreage but equivalent to $20,000. Margaret, who already had Rokeby, received houses and lots in Poughkeepsie. In addition, Armstrong distributed $56,000 in cash among his five surviving children. It was obvious that he sought to provide equally for his children.[31]

Late in 1836 Armstrong purchased a 247 acre farm in Maryland near Brookland Ville, which is today only a few miles from the city limits of Baltimore. Horatio had purchased a farm located nearby at Govanstown in what is now the northwest portion of the city of Baltimore. Armstrong intended to maintain a summer home in Red Hook, to which the name "Way Side" was later given, reflecting its location on the New York to Albany Post Road. It was finished in the early summer of 1837 on a lot of eight and a half acres. Later a large stable, a summer kitchen, a workhouse, and a grape house were added.[32]

Armstrong had an extremely active life, considering his age, but his letters in the late 1830s gave evidence of his recognition of his mortality. The state of his health became a preoccupation in his letters, accompanied by a growing nostalgia. It was for sentimental reasons, no doubt, that he journeyed southward to Baltimore in the fall of 1837 through central Pennsylvania and Carlisle, past the scenes he had known as a youth. His health complaints were common enough for his age. He had frequent headaches, his old lament of pain and inflammation of the eyes continued to plague him, and there were his usual rheumatic cramps and pains of the joints. An attack of dyspepsia early in 1837 yielded, as he informed Spencer, "to a compound of rhubarb & soap (two pills taken after each meal) and abstemious living."[33]

Armstrong also complained that long winters and the cold weather were more and more difficult to bear. Despite his intentions to spend the winter of 1838–1839 in the South, he remained in Red Hook, and he gave over his farm in the South to his son Henry. No doubt the frequent travel bothered him, and he was apparently happier living in Red Hook. However, Henry was unhappy with his situation (according to family tradition his wife and Horatio's wife did not like each other), and in the spring of 1839 Armstrong returned to Maryland and gave possession of his Red Hook home to Henry. John and Kosciuszko went with their father to assist in running the farm. Armstrong was visited on his farm in Decem-

The Armstrong residence in Red Hook, New York, where Armstrong died in 1843. Built in 1837 by Armstrong, it became the home of his son Colonel Henry B. Armstrong and his sons. The house burned ca. 1923. The mansard roof was added in mid-century after Armstrong's death. *Courtesy of the late Maynard Ham*

ber 1839 by a descendant of his old Revolutionary commander, General Hugh Mercer, who noted that although Armstrong was then eighty years old, "he is in good health, & his mind still active & vigorous."[34]

Armstrong returned to Red Hook in the summer of 1840 to assist Henry in making some alterations on the house. He never returned to Maryland. His decision probably arose simply from a desire to remain in Red Hook and a longing to lead a more orderly life. The farm near Baltimore was sold, and John and Kosciuszko returned to Red Hook. Horatio remained on his farm in Maryland, where he died in 1859. John died in Rhinebeck in 1852. Kosciuszko died in 1868, and Henry died in 1884 at the age of ninety-two. Margaret died in 1872.

Late in December 1841 Spencer wrote a long, warm, and reflective letter to his old friend Armstrong. "We have been acquainted with each other forty-five years," he wrote, "& I take pleasure in saying, for the greatest portion of that time our relations have been most friendly & intimate. This to me has been a source of high gratification." He reminded Armstrong that both were advanced in years. "When shall we meet again?" he asked. "This thought often occurs to me & I hope that we may live to meet once more." Armstrong replied warmly, and he offered to write Spencer's biography if Spencer would write his, "so that our friendship may live after one dies."[35] There is no record indicating whether the two men ever effected a last meeting. Spencer died in 1848 at the age of eighty-three.

In March 1843 Armstrong was stricken by another illness. Unlike so many times before, his body did not respond, and the debilitating effects took their toll. On March 28 the Reverend Kearny, Rector of St. Paul's Episcopal Church in what is now Tivoli, New York, wrote to Spencer that his friend was not expected to survive much longer. Armstrong, he reported with a certain lack of clarity, was confined to bed with the "combined effects of loss of appetite and that debility which is attendant on extreme old age." He did not appear to suffer, nor had he during any period of his confinement. "His mind, which notwithstanding his advanced years, was yet, clear, composed, and self-possessed." He had just administered Holy Communion to Armstrong at his request. Armstrong, he noted, had done much reading of the Bible in the last year, apparently influenced, the Reverend Kearney implied, by Spencer's conversion.[36] Although Armstrong's father had been almost fanatically devout, or perhaps because of that, Armstrong belonged to no established church throughout his life. References to religion in his letters do not exist. Perhaps he was an agnostic or possibly an eighteenth-century Rationalist. It is probable that the persuasions of his daughter Margaret, who was a devout Episcopalian, and Henry's wife, who was a fervent Methodist, had more influence upon his Bible reading than the report of Spencer's conversion. Perhaps also, Armstrong was unconsciously preparing himself for death, which he realized was imminent.

Death came to John Armstrong a few minutes before 1 P.M. on Saturday, April 1. Henry related to Spencer the last minutes of his father's life. He suffered little pain, and he retained consciousness to the last. Toward the end he declared that he saw his way clear and asked Henry's wife "to make a short prayer." These were his last words. Mrs. Armstrong prayed and asked to sing a hymn. She had sung the first verse, but the room was small and Armstrong asked by a gesture for her to stop. He then took on a peaceful composure and died.[37] He was buried on April 4 at 11 A.M. in a family burial vault in the Rhinebeck Cemetery. Spencer noted on the letter from Henry that he and Armstrong had enjoyed "a warm unbroken friendship" since 1797. "I admired, loved & venerated him more than any other man." He concluded, and it is a fitting epitaph: "No man was so much misunderstood or so much misrepresented."

EPILOGUE

IN MANY WAYS ARMSTRONG REMAINS AN ENIGMA. Perhaps Martin Van Buren came the closest to capturing the essence of Armstrong's personality when he characterized it as "eminently pugnacious." Armstrong was indeed aggressive, not in the physical sense, but in the disputatious sense. Whether he delighted in his controversies or not is conjectural (more probably he did), but it can be said that he never side-stepped or avoided a dispute. He was also cynical and sarcastic and his demeanor was haughty and contemptuous — not endearing qualities. His mind was first rate, but his perception of his intellectual superiority was perhaps greater than its actual merit. He was ambitious, but he masked it with a casual indifference. He nevertheless expected that the public would recognize and claim his talents. It does appear, however, that he really did not care for, nor did he ever seek, public adulation.

In retrospect, Armstrong himself must bear most of the blame for the failures of his public career. The Newburgh Addresses may have been intemperate, but they may be ascribed to the quixotic passions of youth, as he admitted himself later in life. Through the whole affair, Armstrong may be easily imagined as one of the most offended officers by the supposed wrongs of Congress to the Revolutionary Army. He may have been guided by an exaggerated sense of morality, but he paid a price in his career and in his reputation. On the other hand, his actions in the Pennamite War seem to have been directed more by a sense of loyalty to his state than any question of right or wrong. His commitment to repression of the Connecticut settlers undoubtedly worked against a resolution of the business.

Loyalty was not a ruling passion, however, when he switched his allegiance from the Federalist party to the Republican party. Opportunism seems to have been a motivating factor here, and his timing was right for advancement in the party that took power in 1801. Nevertheless, there is no reason to doubt his commitment to his newly adopted party.

These factors of morality, loyalty, and opportunism are not, of course, mutually exclusive, and they appear to have been blended together in his actions as minister to France. The Virginians Jefferson and Madison, duly valuing intellectual attainments as well as family ties to the powerful Livingston clan, advanced Armstrong's career by selecting him for this position. He was ill-suited to be a diplomat because of his personality. He was neither gregarious nor ingratiating. Instead, he was petulant and morose as the French quickly learned. Under normal circumstances he would have been a failure, but events transpired that uniquely fitted his disposition as well as his talents. The contemptuous and rapacious policies of the French toward American commerce deeply offended his sense of morality, and his loyal commitment to his country's honor engaged his talents for polemics. It is doubtful that France could have paid more dearly in terms of its national honor under any other minister. Armstrong stripped away all the superficialities and pretenses of respectability of French policies and exposed their essentially criminal character mercilessly to the French leaders and, of course, to his own superiors and the American people. His departure was opportunely timed to appear to be on a note of triumph. The fact is, however, that Armstrong's ability to change French policies was virtually nil and at no time during his ministry was he able to stave off the ever-increasing level of violence toward American commerce.

While Armstrong's failures as minister were masked by "success," his successes as secretary of war have been obscured by his "failure," the burning of Washington. There are indeed reasons for considering Armstrong a failure as secretary of war. His vacillating instructions to his commanders, as well as his inconsistency in adhering steadfastly to a fixed objective, were undoubtedly factors in the failures of the American armies. His interference with his commanders and the experiment of the secretary of war actually proceeding to the front, while marking a more aggressive direction from the War Department, proved to be more detrimental than effective. Armstrong was also an indifferent administrator, but surprisingly this is the area where he made the greatest contribution. Under him the Rules and Regulations for the Army were developed, there was the beginning of the General Staff, he carefully marshalled and on the whole sensibly allocated the meager funds at his disposal, he improved the accountability of the supply system, and most significantly, he advanced to the top commands many young military leaders who were destined to direct the American army up to the Civil War.

Armstrong's most grievous failing, in retrospect, was that his nature forbade him to placate potential enemies. He never hesitated to utter the unvarnished truth, at least as he saw it, regardless of the consequences. He was seemingly incapable of accepting the possibility that other men were entitled to their perception of truth. He cared little whether he gave offense by his opinions, or to whom he gave offense. As a result many men never forgave his slights and schemed against him, which cost him dearly and frustrated his political advancement.

It was perhaps a sign of the times that a man with such an abrasive personality, who alienated virtually everyone he came in contact with, could have advanced in politics as far as he did. It was characteristic of the political system of that day to recognize talent and family connections more than political appeal. This should remind us that a pleasing personality is not the only sign of talent nor success the only measure of achievement. Undoubtedly, had Armstrong been more likable he would have achieved more, but his faults should not blind us to his merit or to his genuine contributions to his country.

NOTES

ABBREVIATIONS

AHR	*American Historical Review*
ASP	*American State Papers*, Foreign, Military, and Indian Affairs
DAB	*Dictionary of American Biography*, edited by Dumas Malone, et al.
HLHU	Houghton Library, Harvard University
HSP	Historical Society of Pennsylvania, Philadelphia, Pennsylvania
LC	Manuscript Division, Library of Congress, Washington, D.C.
MdHS	Maryland Historical Society, Baltimore, Maryland
MHS	Massachusetts Historical Society, Boston, Massachusetts
MVHR	*Mississippi Valley Historical Review*
NYHS	New-York Historical Society, New York, New York
NYPL	New York Public Library, New York, New York
NYSL	New York State Library, Albany, New York
PMHB	*Pennsylvania Magazine of History and Biography*
SCP	*Susquehannah Company Papers*, ed., Robert Taylor
WD/LR	War Department, Letters Received, Registered Series, National Archives
WD/LS	War Department, Letters Sent, National Archives
WMQ	*William and Mary Quarterly*, Third Series

1 – REVOLUTIONARY SOLDIER

1. The Armstrong family background is drawn from many varied and frequently contradictory accounts. See William M. Darlington, "Major General John Armstrong," *PMHB* (1877), 1:183–87; E.H. Emmons, "John Armstrong and his Descendants," *Kittochtinny Historical Society Papers* (1923), 9:299–332; James Evelyn Pilcher, "John Armstrong

of Kittanning and his Sons," *The Old Northwest Genealogical Quarterly* (July 1908), 11: 159-180; Milton E. Flower, *John Armstrong, First Citizen of Carlisle* (Carlisle, 1971); Robert G. Crist, *The Land in Cumberland called Lowther* (Lemoyne, Pa., 1957).

2. The best account of the Kittanning expedition is William A. Hunter, "Victory at Kittanning," *Pennsylvania History* (July 1956), 22:3-34. Other accounts are John S. Fisher, "Colonel John Armstrong's Expedition against Kittanning," *PMHB* (1927), 51:1-14; "Armstrong's Bicentennial Celebration," *The Picket Post* (July 1956), 33:39-40. Armstrong's account is in *Colonial Records of Pennsylvania* (Harrisburg, 1851), 7:257-263, and *Pennsylvania Archives*, 1st Ser. (Philadelphia, 1853), 2:767-775.

3. Autobiographical fragment, ca. 1826, Rokeby Collection. Apparently written by Armstrong to provide his son Kosciuszko with information for a proposed biography, this biographical fragment unfortunately goes only as far as the first year of the Revolutionary War.

4. Ibid.; Armstrong to Sparks, Aug. 8, 1834, Sparks Papers, HLHU.

5. Kosciuszko Armstrong, draft biography, Rokeby Collection. The draft biography covers information only through the Revolutionary War.

6. Armstrong to William B. Reed, Sept. 13, 1839, Joseph Reed Papers, NYHS. Armstrong's account of the battle of Princeton is in Armstrong to Hugh Mercer, Oct. 6, 1839, ibid. See also, Christopher Ward, *War of the Revolution* (2 vols., New York, 1952), 1: 306-18; Alfred Hoyt Bill, *New Jersey and the Revolutionary War* (Princeton, N.J., 1964), 37-41.

7. Bruce Lancaster, *From Lexington to Liberty: The Story of the American Revolution* (Garden City, N.Y., 1955), 131. The standard biography was Samuel W. Patterson, *Horatio Gates* (New York, 1941), but it has been replaced by a new biography by Paul David Nelson, *Horatio Gates* (Baton Rouge, 1976).

8. A recent study concluded that Arnold was primarily responsible for the quarrel. See Paul David Nelson, "The Gates-Arnold Quarrel, September, 1777," *New-York Historical Society Quarterly*, no. 3 (July 1971), 55:235-252. See also Armstrong to Sparks, Mar. 28, 1834, Sparks Papers, HLHU. Armstrong's role in this affair is mentioned by many historians, for example, W. M. Wallace, *Appeal to Arms* (New York, 1951), 166-167.

9. Accounts of the Conway Cabal may be found in Edmund C. Burnett, *The Continental Congress* (New York, 1941), 281-297; and Bernard Knollenberg, *Washington and the Revolution, a Reappraisal: Gates, Conway and the Continental Congress* (New York, 1940), 37-77. This account refutes the arguments that any cabal existed.

10. Colonel William Malcolm to Armstrong, Jan. 9, 1779, Armstrong Papers, Force Transcripts, L.C.; Kosciuszko to Armstrong, Mar. 3, 1779; Kosciuszko Papers, Polish Museum of America, Chicago.

11. Armstrong to Gates, Aug. 10, 11, 12, 19, 22, 1779, Gates Papers, NYHS.

12. Armstrong to ?, n.d. [fall of 1779], William Armstrong Papers, Force Transcripts, LC.

13. Gates to Samuel Huntington, Oct. 27, 1779, National Archives, RG 360, Papers of the Continental Congress, Letters of Maj. Gen. Horatio Gates, 1775-1782.

14. Ward, *Revolution*, 2:717-734; Armstrong to Gates, Aug. 2, 1780, George Measam to Armstrong, Sept. 11, 1780, Armstrong to Gates, Sept. 20, 1780, Gates Papers, NYHS.

15. Armstrong to Gates, Jan. 14, 1781, ibid.

16. Burnett, *Continental Congress*, 512, 530, 532.

17. Louis Clinton Hatch, *The Administration of the American Revolutionary Army* (New York, 1904), 144-152; Richard H. Kohn, "The Inside History of the Newburgh Conspiracy: America and the Coup d'Etat," *WMQ*, 3rd Ser. (Apr. 1970), 27:190-195. The

petition may be found in Worthington C. Ford, et al., eds., *Journals of the Continental Congress, 1774–1789* (34 vols., Washington, D.C., 1904–1937), 24:291–293.

18. Hamilton to Washington, Feb. 13, 1783, Harold C. Syrett and Jacob E. Cooke, eds., *The Papers of Alexander Hamilton* (26 vols., New York, 1961–1979), 3:253–255. Merrill Jensen, *The New Nation* (New York, 1950), viewed this letter as an invitation to join the plot. Kohn, "Newburgh Conspiracy," 203n, interpreted it as a tip-off to the threat posed by the Gates group. Hamilton said privately that he wrote Washington because he "wished him to be the conductor of the army in their plans for redress, in order that they might be moderated and directed to proper objects." "Notes," Feb. 20, 1783, in William T. Hutchinson, William M.E. Rachal, Robert A. Rutland, et al., eds., *The Papers of James Madison* (12 vols. to date, Chicago, 1962–), 6:266.

19. Washington to Hamilton, Mar. 4, 1783, Syrett and Cooke, eds., *Hamilton Papers*, 3:277–279.

20. Jones to Washington, Feb. 27, 1783, Washington Papers, LC.

21. Washington to Jones, Mar. 12, 1783, Ford, ed., *Washington Writings*, 10:174–175.

22. Kosciuszko Armstrong, draft biography, Rokeby Collection.

23. Gates to Armstrong, June 23, 1783, quoted in George Bancroft, *History of the Formation of the Constitution of the United States of America* (2 vols., New York, 1882), 1:318; Armstrong to Gates, Apr. 29, 1783, Gates Papers, NYHS.

24. Ibid.; Charles R. King, ed., *The Life and Correspondence of Rufus King . . .* (6 vols., New York, 1894–1900), 1:621–622.

25. Ford, *et al.*, eds., *Journals*, 24:297.

26. Pickering to Samuel Hogdon, Mar. 16, 1783, Timothy Pickering Papers, MHS, 34:147–148; Washington's speech of Mar. 15 is in Ford, *et al.*, eds., *Journals*, 24:306–311; John Fiske, *The Critical Period of American History, 1783–1789* (Boston, 1888), 110; Kosciuszko Armstrong, draft biography, Rokeby Collection.

27. Ford, ed., *Washington Writings*, 10:174–177.

28. Cobb to Pickering, Nov. 9, 1825, Pickering Papers, MHS, 32:183–184; Washington to Hamilton, Mar. 12, Apr. 16, 1783, Syrett and Cooke, eds., *Hamilton Papers*, 3:286–288.

29. Washington to Hamilton, Mar. 12, 1783, ibid., 286–287; General Orders, Mar. 11, 1783, Ford, *et al.*, eds., *Journals*, 24:297–298; Pickering, "Notebooks," Pickering Papers, MHS, 46:329.

30. Josiah Quincy, *The Journals of Major Samuel Shaw . . .* (Boston, 1847), 104.

31. Pickering to Samuel Hogdon, Mar. 16, 1783, Pickering Papers, MHS, 34:145–149; Ford, *et al.*, eds., *Journals*, 24:310–311.

32. Hatch, *Revolutionary Army*, 177–178. This act still did not provide for the settlement of accounts, which touched all ranks.

33. Washington to Hamilton, Apr. 4, 1783, and Hamilton to Washington, Apr. 8, 1783, Syrett and Cooke, eds., *Hamilton Papers*, 3:315–321.

34. Washington to Hamilton, Apr. 16, 1783, ibid., 3:329–331.

35. Armstrong to Gates, May 9, 1783, Gates Papers, NYHS.

36. Armstrong to Gates, June 26, 1783, Emmet Collection, NYPL; Hatch, *Revolutionary Army*, 181–187.

37. Armstrong to Gates, Apr. 29, 1783, Gates Papers, NYHS.

38. Washington to Armstrong, Feb. 23, 1797, in John C. Fitzpatrick, ed., *The Writings of George Washington . . .* (39 vols., Washington, D.C., 1931–1944), 35:397; Cobb to Pickering, Nov. 9, 1825, Pickering Papers, MHS, 5:183–184.

39. See Kohn's reply to my article, C. Edward Skeen, "The Newburgh Addresses Reconsidered," *WMQ* (Apr. 1974), 31:272–290; Kohn, "Rebuttal," ibid., 31:290–298.

2 – POLITICIAN AND PATRICIAN

1. "Extract from the Diary of William Rawle," *PMHB*, no. 2 (July 1898), 22:253. Armstrong was always equivocal in his views of Washington. General Joseph G. Swift reported in 1813 that Armstrong "spoke of General Washington in highest terms of respect for his integrity and patriotism, but not respectfully of his genius." Harrison Ellery, ed., *The Memoirs of General Joseph Gardner Swift* (Worcester, Mass., 1890), 124.

2. Armstrong to Gates, Apr. 29, 1783, Gates Papers, NYHS. He applied for the position in October. See Armstrong to James Potter, Oct. 15, 1782, Gratz Collection, HSP; *Pennsylvania Archives*, Ser. 1, 9:650.

3. Armstrong to John Armstrong, Sr., Feb. 26, 1783, Armstrong Misc., NYHS.

4. Armstrong to Gates, Apr. 29, 1783, Gates Papers, NYHS.

5. J.S. Biddle, ed., *Autobiography of Charles Biddle* (Philadelphia, 1883), 208–209.

6. Robert L. Brunhouse, *The Counter-Revolution in Pennsylvania, 1776–1790* (Harrisburg, 1942), 9–10. In the fall of 1782 Dickinson was the object of a bitter attack by "Valerius." Deborah Logan, a cousin of Dickinson, recorded in her diary on August 31, 1814, on the "best authority" her knowledge of Armstrong's authorship. See Charles J. Stille, *The Life and Times of John Dickinson, 1732–1808* (1891, Reprint, New York, 1969), 423. The Logan account, however, is full of errors, and beyond the fact that she heard this information, her account is useless.

7. Resolution of the General Assembly, *Pennsylvania Archives*, 1st Ser., 9:762, 10:199, 365–366, 11:150–154.

8. Armstrong to William Maclay, May 2, 1783, Armstrong to Gen. James Potter, May 2, 1783, ibid., 10:46–47. See also Armstrong to Robert Morris, June 7, 1783, Armstrong to Sheriffs, July 30, 1783, Sheriff of Bucks County to Armstrong, July 3, 1783, ibid., 10:63, 67.

9. The proceedings of the Trenton trial are in Robert J. Taylor, ed., *The Susquehannah Company Papers* (11 vols., Ithaca, N.Y., 1969), 7:144–246.

10. The literature on the Wyoming controversy is scant and highly charged emotionally. Both William L. Stone, *The Poetry and History of Wyoming* (New York, 1841), and Charles Miner, *History of Wyoming* (Philadelphia, 1845), are extremely biased in favor of the Connecticut settlers. The most valuable source is the *Susquehannah Company Papers*, edited by Robert J. Taylor, not only for the documents (which extend far beyond mere company papers), but also for the stimulating and illuminating introductions to each volume. Unfortunately, Armstrong left no record that might illuminate his actions during this period.

11. Minutes of the Pennsylvania Council, July 29, 1784, *Pennsylvania Archives*, 1st Ser., 10:591.

12. Jackson to Gates, Aug. 6, 1784, Emmet Collection, NYPL; Armstrong, Sr., to Armstrong, Jr., Aug. 10, 1784, Rokeby Collection.

13. Sydney George Fisher, *The Making of Pennsylvania* (1896, Reprint, Port Washington, N.Y., 1969), 304, repeats the charges without reservation. Boyd and Armstrong to Dickinson, Aug. 2, 7, 1784, Taylor, *SCP*, 8:17, 20–22.

14. The incident is reported in two not impartial accounts. See John Franklin to William Samuel Johnson Eliphalet Dyer, and Jesse Root, Oct. 11, 1784, ibid., 8:104–120, and

Robert Martin to James Potter and William Montgomery, Aug. 14, 1784, ibid., 8:31-33.

15. Nicholas Kern to Armstrong, Aug. 22, 1784, ibid., 8:37; Armstrong to Dickinson, Aug. 24, 1784, ibid., 8:31-33.

16. Dickinson to Armstrong, Aug. 24, 30, 1784, ibid., 8:38-40; Armstrong to Franklin, Sept. 3, 1784, Armstrong to Dickinson, Sept. 14, 1784, 8:47, 70-71.

17. Commissioners to Dickinson, Oct. 1, 1784, ibid., 8:86-88.

18. *Colonial Records of Pennsylvania*, 14:216-219. Armstrong replaced General James Wilkinson who had left the state. Minutes of the Pennsylvania Council, Oct. 5, 1784, Taylor, *SCP*, 8:92-94.

19. Armstrong to Dickinson, Oct. 25, 1784, ibid., 8:133-135.

20. Armstrong to Wyoming Inhabitants, Oct. 20, 1784, ibid., 8:127-128; Armstrong to Dickinson, Nov. 15, 1784, ibid., 8:154-155.

21. Ethan Allen to William Samuel Johnson, Aug. 15, 1785, ibid., 8:255-256; William Hooker Smith, Samuel Hoover, and Abraham Westbrook to William Montgomery, May 14, 1786, ibid., 8:326-327.

22. Act of the Pennsylvania General Assembly, Dec. 24, 1785, ibid., 8:282-284; Extract of Proceedings of General Assembly, Sept. 23, 1786, ibid., 8:406.

23. Clajon to Gates, May 14, 1783, Gates Papers, NYHS. Clajon, a Frenchman who had lived in America for a long time, died on July 30, 1784, at about age sixty.

24. Armstrong, Sr., to Armstrong, Jr., May 20, 1783, Rokeby Collection.

25. Edmund C. Burnett, ed., *Letters of Members of the Continental Congress* (7 vols., Washington, D.C., 1936), 3:570.

26. Armstrong to William Irvine, June 20, 1787, Irvine Papers, HSP.

27. Jensen, *New Nation*, 356; Archer B. Hulbert, "The Methods and Operations of the Scioto Group of Speculators," *MVHR*, no. 4 (Mar. 1915), 2:56-73.

28. Ibid.; John McAuley Palmer, *General Von Steuben* (New Haven, 1937), 369.

29. Hulbert, "Scioto Group," *MVHR*, 2:56-73; Ford, et al., eds., *Journals*, 33:686; Burnett, *Letters of MOC*, 3:659n.

30. Armstrong to Gates, May 30, 1788, Gates Papers, NYHS.

31. Steuben to William North, Sept. 18, 1788, quoted in Palmer, *Steuben*, 363.

32. George Dangerfield, *Chancellor Robert R. Livingston of New York, 1746-1813* (New York, 1960), 27-29.

33. Armstrong to Gates, May 30, 1788, Gates Papers, NYHS.

34. Armstrong to Gates, Apr. 7, 1789, ibid.

35. Dangerfield, *Livingston*, 245-246.

36. Armstrong to Gates, Apr. 7, 1789, Gates Papers, NYHS. David Humphreys was a warm friend and a former aide to General Washington.

37. Armstrong to Gates, July 10, 1789, ibid.

38. Armstrong to Alida Armstrong, Dec. 24, 1789, Rokeby Collection.

39. Typescripts of deeds dated Feb. 1, 2, June 3, 4, 14, 15, 1790, ibid. The deeds of June 4 and 15 were recorded in 1844 in the Ulster County records, DB 62-281, DB 62-284. For legal reasons, the transfer was first made by John and Alida to Catherine, Alida's sister, who then deeded the lands to John.

40. Armstrong to Gates, July 30, 1790, Gates Papers, NYHS.

41. Armstrong to Gates, Oct. 14, 1791, Oct. 1792, Nov. 21, 1792, ibid.

42. Armstrong to Gates, Oct. 8, 1792, ibid.

43. Armstrong to Benjamin Walker, Feb. 28, 1799, John Armstrong Papers, Misc., NYHS.

44. Armstrong to Gates, Apr. 13, 1793, Gates Papers, NYHS.

45. Armstrong to Gates, June 23, 1794, ibid. Armstrong noted the birth occurred "on Sunday Week," which would fix the date as June 15. The family Bible lists the birthdate as June 16.

46. Armstrong to Edward Livingston, Dec. 24, 1794, Livingston Papers, John Ross Delafield estate; Armstrong to Gates, Jan. 16, 1795, Gates Papers, NYHS.

47. John Armstrong, Sr.'s will is in the Cumberland County (Pa.) Courthouse in Carlisle, Will Book F, 1795–1803. See also James Armstrong to Armstrong, Mar. 14, 1795, Rokeby Collection.

48. Armstrong to Gates, Aug. 5, 1795, Gates Papers, NYHS; Armstrong to Edward Livingston, June 5, July 5, 20, 1795, Delafield photostats, NYHS.

49. Family Bible, Rokeby Collection.

50. Armstrong to Gates, Nov. 13, 1797, Gates Papers, NYHS.

51. James Armstrong to Armstrong, Dec. 4, [1797] Rokeby Collection.

52. Armstrong to Gates, Nov. 13, 1797, Gates Papers, NYHS; William Henry Egle, *Some Pennsylvania Women During the War of the Revolution* (Harrisburg, 1898), 11–12.

53. Armstrong to Rufus King's Agent, Oct. 4, 1798, Rufus King Papers, NYHS.

54. Metchie J.E. Budka, trans. and ed., *Under Their Vine and Fig Tree*, by Julian Ursyn Niemcewicz (Elizabeth, N.J., 1965), 195–200.

55. Armstrong to Gates, May 30, 1788, Gates Papers, NYHS.

56. Armstrong to Gates, Mar. 14, 1793, ibid.

57. Armstrong to Gates, Jan. 12, 1793, ibid.

58. Dangerfield, *Livingston*, 257–259, 261.

59. Alfred F. Young, *The Democratic Republicans of New York: The Origins, 1763–1797* (Chapel Hill, 1967), 292n, citing Dangerfield, agrees. Armstrong to Ambrose Spencer, Dec. 11, 1833, Rokeby Collection.

60. Friedrich Kapp, *The Life of Frederick William Von Steuben* (New York, 1859), 584–585.

61. Hamilton to Armstrong, Apr. 1, 1793, Rokeby Collection.

62. Armstrong to Gates, Apr. 13, May 19, 1793, Gates Papers, NYHS.

63. Armstrong to Gates, Feb. 19, 1794, Aug. 5, 1795, ibid. James Armstrong to Armstrong, Apr. 18, 1794, Rokeby Collection.

64. See Edward P. Alexander, "Jefferson and Kosciuszko: Friends of Liberty and of Man," *PMHB* (Jan. 1968), 92:87–103; Armstrong to Edward Livingston, Dec. 28, 1797, Delafield photostats, NYHS.

65. Armstrong to Gates, Feb. 4, 1796, Armstrong Misc. Papers, NYPL; Armstrong to Gates, Aug. 26, 1797, Feb. 18, 1798, Gates Papers, NYHS.

3 – SENATOR

1. Stephen G. Kurtz, *The Presidency of John Adams: The Collapse of Federalism, 1795–1800* (New York, 1957), 305; Noble E. Cunningham, Jr., *The Jeffersonian Republicans: The Formation of Party Organization, 1789–1801* (Chapel Hill, 1957), 126; John C. Miller, *The Federalist Era, 1789–1801* (New York, 1960), chapter 13.

2. Jabez D. Hammond, *The History of Political Parties in the State of New York . . .*, 3rd ed. (2 vols., Cooperstown, 1844), 131.

3. [John Armstrong,] "To the Senate and Representatives of the United States, in Congress assembled" (Poughkeepsie, 1798), 2 fol. pages, NYPL.

4. Hammond, *History of N.Y.*, 1:132.

5. A good summary of Spencer's career is Julian P. Boyd, "Ambrose Spencer, " in Johnson and Malone, eds., *DAB*, 17:443–445. See also Daniel D. Bernard, *A Discourse on the Life, Character, and Public Services of Ambrose Spencer* (Albany, 1849). The quotation is from Henry Adams, *History of the United States of America during the Administrations of Jefferson and Madison* (9 vols., New York, 1890), 1:229.

6. Hammond, *History of N.Y.*, 1:154. The source of the vote is Spencer to Armstrong, Mar. 9, 1839, Rokeby Collection.

7. Armstrong to Thomas Tillotson, Jan. 13, 1801, Armstrong Misc., NYPL.

8. Ibid.

9. Gates to Jefferson, Feb. 10, 1801, Jefferson Papers, L.C.; Edward Livingston to R. R. Livingston, Jan. 29, 1801, R. R. Livingston Collection, NYHS; Armstrong to Tillotson, Feb. 23, 1801, Armstrong Misc., NYPL.

10. Armstrong to Tillotson, Jan. 13, 30, 1801, ibid.; Armstrong to Peters, Feb. 16, 1801, Richard Peters Papers, HSP.

11. *Annals*, 6th Cong., 2nd Sess., 758; Armstrong to Tillotson, Feb. 23, 1801, Armstrong Misc., NYPL; Adams, *History*, 1:30–31.

12. Gallatin to Jefferson, Sept. 14, 1801, in Henry Adams, ed., *The Writings of Albert Gallatin* (3 vols., Philadelphia, 1879), 1:52.

13. Armstrong to Edward Livingston, Nov. 22, 1801, Delafield photostats, NYHS; Armstrong to Gates, Nov. 22, 1801, Gates Papers, NYHS.

14. Armstrong to Gates, Jan. 8, Feb. 10, 1802, ibid.; Hammond, *History of N.Y.*, 1: 183–184; Madison to Gates, Mar. 10, 1802, Emmet Collection, NYPL.

15. Alida Armstrong to R. R. Livingston, Oct. 4, 1802, Gratz Collection, HSP. The birthdates of the children are found in the Armstrong family Bible, Rokeby Collection. It records Edward's death as July 30.

16. Gardenier was later a congressman. Edward L. Merrit, "Barent Gardenier," *A Paper Read before the Ulster County Historical Society* (Kingston, N.Y., 1931); [John Armstrong,] *Letters Addressed to the Army of the United States in the Year 1783: With a Brief Exposition, etc.* (Kingston, N.Y., 1803). Armstrong sent Jared Sparks (Oct. 28, 1836, Sparks Papers, HLHU), a statement by Jesse Buel, dated Dec. 18, 1830, and a statement by Lafayette, dated July 6, 1808, which certified the authenticity of Washington's letter. Armstrong loaned the original (apparently never returned) to the Italian historian, Carlo Botta, who published a history of the American Revolution in 1809. On the whole, Botta was harshly critical of the Newburgh Addresses. See George Alexander Otis, trans., *History of the War of the Independence of the United States of America*, by Charles Botta (2 vols., Reprint, New York, 1970), 2:452–459.

17. Armstrong to Clinton, June 26, 1802, quoted in Noble E. Cunningham, Jr., *The Jeffersonian Republicans in Power: Party Operations, 1801–1809* (Chapel Hill, 1963), 206.

18. R. R. Livingston to Alida Armstrong, Sept. 5, 1803, Rokeby Collection.

19. James Armstrong to Armstrong, Sept. 29, 1803, May 12, 1804, ibid.

20. Clinton to Armstrong, Nov. 10, 1803 (covering a commission of the same date), ibid.; Memorandum dated Mar. 17, 1806, in Everett Somerville Brown, ed., *William Plumer's Memorandum of Proceedings in the United States Senate, 1803–1807* (New York, 1923), 52.

21. Armstrong to R. R. Livingston, Feb. 4, 1804, R. R. Livingston Collection, NYHS.

22. Armstrong to Gates, Dec. 30, 1803, Gates Papers, NYPL. A good discussion of the Jeffersonian social order and the Merry incident is Joel Larus, "Pell Mell Along the Potomac," *WMQ*, 3rd Ser. (July 1960), 17:349–357.

23. Armstrong to Spencer, Dec. 18, 1803, Rokeby Collection; *Annals,* 7th Cong., 1st Sess., 213–215; Charles F. Adams, ed., *Memoirs of John Quincy Adams* (12 vols., Philadelphia, 1875), 1:309. Armstrong's lack of loyalty made no difference. Pickering was convicted and removed.

24. Armstrong to Spencer, Feb. 28, 1804, Rokeby Collection; Adams, *Memoirs of J. Q. Adams,* 1:313. On the election, see Dixon Ryan Fox, *The Decline of Aristocracy in the Politics of New York, 1801–1840* (New York, 1919), ed. by Robert V. Remini (Harper Torchbook edition, 1965), 62–63.

25. Armstrong to Spencer, June 4, 1804, Rokeby Collection.

26. Jefferson to Armstrong, May 26, 1804, Jefferson Papers, LC.

27. Armstrong to Jefferson, June 2, 1804, ibid.

28. Armstrong to Edward Livingston, July 18, 1804, Delafield photostats, NYHS.

29. Armstrong to Spencer, June 4, 1804, Rokeby Collection; Armstrong to Gates, June 2, 1804, Gates Papers, NYPL.

30. Jefferson to Armstrong, July 11, 1804, Jefferson to Skipwith, July 11, 1804, Jefferson Papers, LC.

31. Armstrong to Madison, July 15, 1804, Madison Papers, LC.

32. Alida Armstrong to Edward Livingston, Aug. 30, 1804, Delafield photostats, NYHS; Armstrong to Madison, Aug. 6, 1804, National Archives, RG59, State Department, Diplomatic Despatches, France, vol. 10; Madison to Armstrong, Aug. 21, 1804, National Archives, RG59, State Department, Diplomatic Instructions, All Countries, 6:252–253.

33. Armstrong to Warden, Aug. 24, 1804, Warden Papers, MdHS.

34. Armstrong to Madison, Oct. 20, 1804, State Dept., Dipl. Des., Fr., vol. 10.

35. Alida Armstrong to Edward Livingston, Dec. 26, 1804, Delafield photostats, NYHS.

36. Armstrong probably delivered this address in English. He could translate written and comprehend spoken French, but his secretaries served as his translators. His knowledge of French improved with time. The ceremonial, Jefferson's letter, and Armstrong's address, may be found in a letterbook entitled "Papers and Documents of the American Legation at Paris," Rokeby Collection (copy in NYHS).

37. Armstrong to Madison, Dec. 24, 1804, State Dept., Dipl. Des., Fr., vol. 10.

4 – MINISTER TO FRANCE

1. Alida Armstrong to R. R. Livingston, Sept. 2, [1807,] R. R. Livingston Collection, NYHS.

2. Frederick Hall, "Letters from France: Modern Paris," *The Literary and Philosophical Repertory* (1812–1816), Letters 1–17, vol. 1; Letters 18–28, vol. 2; Letter 12 (Mar. 1814), 1:401–411.

3. Alida Armstrong to Edward Livingston, Jan. 10, 1806, to [Janet Montgomery,] Feb. 5, 1806, J. R. Delafield Estate Papers; Armstrong to Charles Willson Peale, May 31, 1809, Peale-Sellers Papers, American Philosophical Society, Philadelphia.

4. Irving Brant, *James Madison, The President, 1809–1812* (Indianapolis, 1956), 151.

5. Alida Armstrong to Horatio Armstrong, 29 Germinal (Apr. 18), 1805, Rokeby Collection.

6. Alida Armstrong to Edward Livingston, Aug. 10, Dec. 26, 1805, Jan. 10, 1806, Mar. 11, 1807, J. R. Delafield Estate Papers; Armstrong to Warden, Sept. 14, 1808, Warden Papers, MdHS.

7. Alida Armstrong to Edward Livingston, Apr. 11, 1807, Rokeby Collection.

8. Alida Armstrong to Edward Livingston, Jan. 19, 1806, J. R. Delafield Estate Papers.

9. Alida Armstrong to R. R. Livingston, July 22, 1807, R. R. Livingston Collection, NYHS.

10. Hall, "Modern Paris," Letter 21 (Sept. 1814), 2:98–103; Alida Armstrong to Gertrude Lewis, June 27, 1807, Rokeby Collection.

11. This portrait is now in the Independence Hall Museum, Philadelphia.

12. John Bassett Moore, ed., *History and Digest of the International Arbitrations to which the United States had been a Party* . . . (6 vols., Washington, D.C., 1898), 5:4434, 4440.

13. The commissioners examined and verified all the accounts approved by the French bureaus. If the board disagreed, they submitted their opinion to Livingston, and he in turn gave his opinion to the minister of the treasury, whose decision was final. Ibid., 5: 4435.

14. Board of Commissioners to Armstrong, Nov. 30, 1804, in William Maclure, *To the People of the U.S.* (Philadelphia, 1807), 87.

15. *ASP, For. Rel.*, 2:774–775; Armstrong to Madison, Nov. 26, 1805, State Dept., Dipl. Des., Fr., vol. 10.

16. Armstrong to [Marbois,] Dec. 5, 1804, in [John Armstrong,] "A Friend to Truth and Justice," *Examination of the Memorial of the Owners and Underwriters of the American Ship the New Jersey* . . . (Philadelphia, 1806). His letterbook copy varies in stating the annual profit at "20 per cent" (Letterbook, NYHS), but the larger figure is probably correct.

17. Armstrong to Madison, Dec. 30, 1804, State Dept., Dipl. Des., Fr., vol. 10; Madison to Armstrong, Nov. 10, 1804, State Dept. Dipl. Instrs., All Countries, 6:264.

18. J. R. Livingston to Armstrong, Jan. 2, 1805, Armstrong photostats, NYHS; Armstrong to Marbois, Jan. 5, 1805, Rokeby Collection; Armstrong, *Examination*, 27.

19. Ibid., 63; Armstrong to Madison, Nov. 26, 1805, State Dept., Dipl. Des., Fr., vol. 10.

20. Memorial of Philip Nicklin and Robert Eaglesfield Griffith of the City of Philadelphia, Merchants, to James Madison, Esq., Secretary of State, July 25, 1805, copy in Rokeby Collection.

21. Madison to Armstrong, Aug. 25, 1805, State Dept., Dipl. Instrs., All Countries, 6:308.

22. Armstrong to Madison, Nov. 16, 1805, State Dept., Dipl. Des., Fr., vol. 10; Jefferson to Armstrong, Feb. 14, 1806, Jefferson Papers, vol. 156, LC.

23. Armstrong to Madison, Mar. 9, 1806, State Dept., Dipl. Des., Fr., vol. 10.

24. *Annals*, 9th Cong., 1st Sess., 603–604.

25. Adams, *History*, 3:153; Adams, *Memoirs of J. Q. Adams*, 1:421. See also, Brown, ed., *Plumer's Memorandum of Proceedings*, 52, 456. Jefferson urged his friend Wilson Cary Nicholas to accept a position with Armstrong and Bowdoin because of the "cloud of dissatisfaction" with Armstrong, but Nicholas declined. Jefferson to Nicholas, Apr. 13, 1806, Ford, ed., *Jefferson Writings*, 8:434–435.

26. Armstrong to Madison, June 2, 1806, State Dept. Dipl. Des., Fr., vol. 10; Madison to Armstrong, Oct. 26, 1806, Madison Papers, LC. Madison included letters favorable to Armstrong in the documents submitted to the Senate. See Henry Waddell to Nicklin and Griffith, Feb. 24, 1806, Waddell to Madison, Feb. 26, 1806, in *ASP, For. Rel.*, 2:775.

27. Rush to Adams, Oct. 24, 1806, in L. H. Butterfield, ed., *Letters of Benjamin Rush* (2 vols., Princeton, 1951), 2:934.

28. Armstrong, *Examination*, 53, 78.

29. Ibid., 107–119. The file on the *New Jersey* case in the National Archives, Records of the Court of Claims, amount to approximately 1100 pages. There is no reference to an award being made to Nicklin and Griffith.

30. Armstrong to Madison, Feb. 14, 1805, State Dept., Dipl. Des., Fr., vol. 10. Armstrong blamed the delays on the negligence of the claimants or their agents, and the French doctrine of oppositions. Armstrong to Madison, Feb. 17, Apr. 28, 1806, ibid.

31. Armstrong to Madison, May 20, 1807, ibid.

32. Armstrong to Madison, June 28, 1807, ibid.

33. Henry Bartholomew Cox, *The Parisian American: Fulwar Skipwith of Virginia* (Washington, D.C., 1964), 155–156.

34. Barnet to Madison, July 24, 1806, National Archives, RG59, State Department, Consular Despatches, Paris.

35. Skipwith to Madison, Aug. 1, 1806, ibid.; [John Armstrong,] *Two Letters from F. Skipwith Esq. to General Armstrong: With the General's Answers and Sundry Documents* [Paris,] 1806 [*sic*, 1807], 125–128.

36. Skipwith to Armstrong, July 24, 1806, State Dept., Consular Des., Paris; Skipwith to Armstrong, Aug. 14, 1806, Armstrong, *Two Letters*, 35–37; ibid., 188–191.

37. Armstrong to Jefferson, Jan. 2, 1806 [*sic*, 1807], Jefferson Papers, vol. 155, LC.; Armstrong to Madison, Mar. 2, 1807, State Dept., Dipl. Des., Fr., vol. 10; Skipwith to Madison, Sept. 11, 1807, State Dept., Consular Des., Paris.

38. Copy in Armstrong, *Two Letters*, 289–291.

39. Skipwith to Minister of Exterior Relations, Feb. 23, 1808, State Dept., Consular Des., Paris; Skipwith to Jefferson, Mar. 8, 1808, ibid.

5 – MINISTERIAL POLITICS

1. Quoted in Adams, *History*, 2:72, 68.

2. Quoted in Clifford L. Egan, "The United States, France, and West Florida, 1803–1807," *Florida Historical Quarterly* (Jan. 1969), 47:235.

3. Ibid., 47:229.

4. Monroe to Madison, Dec. 16, 1804, in Hamilton, ed., *Monroe Writings*, 4:277–297. See also Isaac Joslin Cox, *The West Florida Controversy, 1798–1813* (Baltimore, 1918), 113–116; Adams, *History*, 2:310–313.

5. Armstrong to Madison, Dec. 24, 1804, State Dept. Dipl. Des., Fr., vol. 10; Irving Brant, *James Madison, Secretary of State, 1800–1809* (Indianapolis, 1953), 260–261.

6. Armstrong to Monroe, May 4, 1805, Monroe Papers, NYPL.

7. Madison to Armstrong, June 6, 1805, State Dept., Dipl. Instrs., All Countries, 6: 301–306.

8. Armstrong to Madison, Aug. 10, 1805, State Dept., Dipl. Des., Fr., vol. 10.

9. Monroe blamed Livingston, asserting that he had assured the French that the United States would eventually pay for the Floridas. He advised that Livingston not be given any honors when he returned to America. Monroe to Madison, July 6, 1805, Monroe Papers, NYPL. The Administration did receive Livingston coolly. See Dangerfield, *Livingston*, 397.

10. Adams, *History*, 3:69–78.

11. Armstrong to Madison (with enclosures), Sept. 10, 1805, State Dept., Dipl. Des., Fr., vol. 10.

12. Adams, *History*, 3:106–108.

13. Monroe to Armstrong, Sept. 2, 1805, in Hamilton, ed., *Monroe Writings*, 4: 312–313.

14. Armstrong to Monroe, Sept. 18, 1805, Monroe Papers, NYPL; Bowdoin to Erving, Nov. 3, 1805, Bowdoin-Temple Papers, Part II, *Collections* of the Massachusetts Historical Society (Boston, 1907), 7th Series, 6:254–256; Sullivan to Erving, May 5, 1806, Monroe Papers, NYPL.

15. Erving to Bowdoin, Nov. 19, 1805, Bowdoin to Erving, Nov. 28, 1805, Bowdoin-Temple Papers, 6:260, 262–265; Armstrong to Madison, Dec. 22, 1805, State Dept., Dipl. Des., Fr., vol. 10.

16. Bowdoin to Monroe, Jan. 5, 1806, Monroe Papers, NYPL; Armstrong to Monroe, Jan. 7, 1806, Monroe Papers, LC.

17. Bowdoin to Erving, Jan. 7, 15, 1806, Bowdoin-Temple Papers, 6:280–282, 283–287.

18. Bowdoin to Monroe, Feb. 5, 1806, Monroe Papers, LC.; Armstrong to Jefferson, Feb. 17, 1806, Jefferson Papers, vol. 156, LC.

19. Bowdoin to Jefferson, Mar. 1, 1806, Bowdoin to Madison, Mar. 9, 1806, Bowdoin-Temple Papers, 6:294–295, 296–297.

20. Madison to Armstrong and Bowdoin, Mar. 13, 1806, Hunt, ed., *Madison Writings*, 7:192–200; Skipwith to Monroe, May 3, 1806, Monroe Papers, NYPL.

21. Armstrong to Madison, May 4, 1806, State Dept., Dipl. Des., Fr., vol. 10.

22. Bowdoin to Armstrong, May 2, 3 (2 letters), 1806, Armstrong to Bowdoin, May 2, 3, 4, 1806, ibid.; Bowdoin to Monroe, May 30, 1806, Monroe Papers, NYPL.

23. Irving Brant could find "no tangible evidence" that Armstrng "fell in with the schemes of corruption," but he concluded nevertheless that "Armstrong's failure to tell his government about the schemes of Parker, which Bowdoin freely reported, hardly suggests a righteous revulsion against them." Brant thus gratuitously confirmed Bowdoin's suspicions and condemned Armstrong of guilt by association. Brant, *Madison, Sec. of State*, 366.

24. Bowdoin to Erving, June 30, 1806, Bowdoin-Temple Papers, 6:314. A chronology of these events is outlined in Armstrong to Madison, Oct. 10, 1806, State Dept., Dipl. Des., Fr., vol. 10; Adams, *History*, 3:386.

25. Bowdoin to Erving, Oct. 1, 1806, Bowdoin-Temple Papers, 6:338–339.

26. Armstrong to Madison, Oct. 10, 1806, State Dept., Dipl. Des., Fr., vol. 10.

27. Alida Armstrong to Edward Livingston, Dec. 8, 1806, J. R. Delafield Estate Papers.

28. Bowdoin to Erving, Oct. 28, 1806, Bowdoin-Temple Papers, 6:346.

29. Bowdoin to Jefferson, May 1, 1806, State Dept., Consular Des., Paris. The Somers document is in French.

30. Jefferson to Bowdoin, July 10, 1807, Bowdoin-Temple Papers, 6:397–398.

31. These documents are enclosed in Armstrong to Madison, Jan. 23, 1810, State Dept., Dipl. Des., Fr., vol. 11.

32. Armstrong to Madison, May 6, 1810, Madison Papers, LC; Madison to Armstrong, Oct. 29, 1810, Rokeby Collection.

33. Armstrong to Prince of Benevento, June 12, 16, 1807, enclosed in Armstrong to Madison, June 24, 1807, State Dept., Dipl. Des., Fr., vol. 10; Armstrong to Madison, Aug. 9, 11, 1807, ibid.

34. Armstrong to Madison, Aug. 15, 23, 1807, ibid.

35. Madison to Armstrong and Bowdoin, July 15, 1807, Bowdoin-Temple Papers, 6: 400–401.

36. Madison to Armstrong and Bowdoin, Aug. 2, 1807, State Dept., Dipl. Instrs., All Countries, 6:436–437.

37. Madison to Armstrong, Oct. 18, 1807, ibid., 6:433–435.

38. Bowdoin to Armstrong, Aug. 1, 1807, Armstrong to Bowdoin, Aug. 17, 1807, Bowdoin to Armstrong, Aug. 19, 1807, Bowdoin-Temple Papers, 6:402, 401, 407–409.

39. Armstrong to Bowdoin, Aug. 30, 1807, ibid., 6:416–420.

40. Bowdoin to Armstrong, Sept. 10, 14, 1807, Armstrong to Bowdoin, Sept. 11, 16, 1807, ibid., 6:421–423, 426–429, 425–426, 430.

41. Bowdoin to Erving, Sept. 20, Oct. 11, 1807, ibid., 6:430–431, 433–435.

6 – DEFENDER OF NEUTRAL RIGHTS

1. Armstrong to Monroe, Sept. 18, 1805, Monroe Papers, NYPL; Monroe to Armstrong, Nov. 14, 1805, Hamilton, ed., *Monroe Writings*, 4:370.

2. Armstrong to Madison, Mar. 9, 1806, State Dept., Dipl. Des., Fr., vol. 10.

3. Madison to Armstrong, Mar. 14, 1806, State Dept., Dipl. Instrs., All Countries, 6:322–325.

4. Armstrong to Madison, Dec. 24, 1806, Mar. 29, 1807, State Dept., Dipl. Des., Fr., vol. 10. See also, Armstrong to William Lee, Dec. 24, 1806, State Dept., Consular Des., Bordeaux; Armstrong to Monroe, July 7, 1807, Monroe Papers, LC.

5. Armstrong to Madison, Sept. 24, 1807, State Dept., Dipl. Des., Fr., vol. 10.

6. Armstrong to U.S. Consuls, Oct. 6, 1807, ibid.

7. Armstrong to Champagny, Nov. 12, 1807, ibid.; Napoleon to Champagny, Nov. 15, 1807, quoted in Adams, *History*, 4:110. On the *Horizon* case, see Edward Channing, *The Jeffersonian System* (New York, 1906), 210–211.

8. Armstrong to Madison, Nov. 15, 1807, State Dept., Dipl. Des., Fr., vol. 10.

9. Armstrong to Madison, Dec. 27, 1807, ibid.

10. Napoleon to Champagny, Jan. 12, 1808, quoted in Adams, *History*, 4:292; Champagny to Armstrong, Jan. 15, 1808, *ASP, For. Rel.*, 3:248.

11. Armstrong to Champagny, Jan. 27, Feb. 5, 1808, State Dept., Dipl. Des., Fr., vol. 11.

12. Armstrong to Champagny, Feb. 8, 1808 (2 letters), Champagny to Armstrong, Feb. 13, 1808, Marginal note on Armstrong to Decres, Feb. 13, 1808 (enclosed to Madison), ibid.

13. Armstrong to Madison, Feb. 15, 1808, ibid.; Armstrong to Madison, Feb. 22, 1808, *ASP, For. Rel.*, 3:250.

14. Madison to Armstrong, Feb. 8, 1808, State Dept., Dipl. Instrs., All Countries, 6:443–447; Armstrong to Champagny, Apr. 2, 1808, Armstrong to Madison, Apr. 5, 1808, *ASP, For. Rel.*, 3:251.

15. Armstrong to Madison, Apr. 23, 1808, State Dept., Dipl. Des., Fr., vol. 11.

16. Madison to Armstrong, May 2, 1808, State Dept., Dipl. Instrs., All Countries, 6:458–461; Armstrong to Madison, June 29, July 25, 1808, State Dept., Dipl. Des., Fr., vol. 11.

17. Jefferson to Armstrong, May 2, 1808, Jefferson Papers, LC.; Jefferson to Thomas Mann Randolph, June 28, 1808, Ford, ed., *Jefferson Writings*, 9:197–199.

18. Brant, *Madison, Sec. of State*, 445.

19. Armstrong to Madison, June 25, July 23, 1808, State Dept., Dipl. Des., Fr., vol. 11.

20. Armstrong to Jefferson, July 28, 1808, Jefferson Papers, LC.; Jefferson to Madison, Aug. 12, Sept. 13, 1808, Ford, ed., *Jefferson Writings*, 9:203–204, 208–209.

21. Armstrong to Champagny, Aug. 6, 1808, *ASP, For. Rel.*, 3:255; Frank E. Melvin, *Napoleon's Navigation System* (New York, 1919), 73–76.

22. Madison to Armstrong, July 21, 1808, *ASP, For. Rel.*, 3:254; Madison to Armstrong, July 22, 1808, Hunt, ed., *Madison Writings*, 8:36–37.

23. Armstrong to Madison, Aug. 28, 1808 (enclosing Armstrong to Talleyrand, Aug. 26, 1808), State Dept., Dipl. Des., Fr., vol. 11; Armstrong to Madison, Aug. 30, 1808, Madison Papers, LC.

24. Armstrong to Warden, Sept. 1, 2, 4, 12, 13, 14, 15, 24, 1808, Warden Papers, MdHS.

25. Armstrong to Madison, Oct. 20, 1808, State Dept., Dipl. Des., Fr., vol. 11. Armstrong approved of Haley's conduct. See Armstrong to Madison, Nov. 24, 1808, ibid. See also Armstrong to Champagny, Oct. 20, 1808, and Armstrong to Madison, Oct. 25, 1808, ibid.

26. Armstrong to Madison, Nov. 24 (with postscript, Dec. 1), Dec. 6, 12, 14, 26, 1808, Jan. 2, 1809, ibid.

27. Armstrong to Madison, Feb. 16, 1809, State Dept., Dipl. Des., Fr., vol. 11; Adams, *History*, 4:444–451. See also, Jefferson to Armstrong, Mar. 6, 1809, Jefferson Papers (Coolidge Collection), LC.

28. Armstrong to Madison, Mar. 25, 1809, State Dept., Dipl. Des., Fr., vol. 11.

29. Armstrong to Madison, Feb. 16, Mar. 25 (with enclosure), 1809, Armstrong to Champagny, Mar. 23, 1809, ibid. On the development of the French policy, see Melvin, *Napoleon's Nav. System*, Chapter 3.

30. Adams, *History*, 5:141; Armstrong to Smith, July 24, 1809, State Dept., Dipl. Des., Fr., vol. 11. See also Armstrong to Madison, June 6, 1809, Madison Papers, LC.

31. Armstrong to Madison, Sept. 18, 1809, ibid.; *Further and Still More Important Suppressed Documents* (Boston, 1808). The title implies a previous publication, but none of that description has been found.

32. Brant, *Madison, President*, 37–38.

33. Champagny to Armstrong, Aug. 28, 1809, Armstrong to Champagny, Sept. 8, 1809, Armstrong to Smith, Sept. 16, 1809, State Dept., Dipl. Des., Fr., vol. 11.

34. Armstrong to Smith, July 26, 1809, ibid.; Armstrong to Madison, Aug. 20, 1809, Madison Papers, LC. Information relating to the trip is in Alida Armstrong to R. R. Livingston, Aug. 20, 1809, R. R. Livingston Papers, NYHS; Armstrong to Sylvanus Bourne (U.S. Consul at Amsterdam), Aug. 7, 1809, Armstrong to Smith, Aug. 20, 1809, State Dept., Dipl. Des., Fr., vol. 11.

35. Champagny to Armstrong, Aug. 22, 1809, *ASP, For. Rel.*, 3:325–326.

36. Armstrong to Samuel Smith, Sept. 16, 1809, Dreer Collection, HSP; Armstrong to Jefferson, Sept. 19, 1809, Jefferson Papers, LC.

37. Armstrong to Smith, Oct. 25, 1809, State Dept., Dipl. Des., Fr., vol. 11. Melvin, *Napoleon's Nav. System*, 154–155, asserts that Armstrong orchestrated this movement, but he does not adequately document this contention.

38. Armstrong to Smith, Oct. 18, Nov. 10, 1809, State Dept., Dipl. Des., Fr., vol. 11.

39. Armstrong to Smith, Nov. 18, Dec. 10, 1809, ibid.

40. Ibid.

41. Armstrong to Smith, Jan. 28, 1810, ibid.; Napoleon to Cadore, Jan. 19, 1810, quoted in Adams, *History*, 5:228–229.

42. Armstrong to Cadore, Feb. 21, 1810 (marginal comment dated Feb. 25), State Dept., Dipl. Des., Fr., vol. 11. Madison's view of Armstrong's terms is in Smith to Armstrong, June 20, 1810, State Dept., Dipl. Instrs., All Countries, 7:101–102.

43. Armstrong to Smith, Mar. 10, 1810, State Dept., Dipl. Des., Fr., vol. 11. The figure of six million is based on calculations in Adams, *History*, 5:242–243.

44. Napoleon to Cadore, Mar. 20, 1810, quoted in Adams, *History*, 5:234–235.

45. Armstrong to Madison, May 25, 1810, Madison Papers, LC. Jarvis's reports to Armstrong are dated Mar. 9, 22, 26, 29, Apr. 2, 7, 17, 28, 1810, and his final report of May 18, 1810, State Dept., Dipl. Des., Fr., vol. 11.

46. Bourne to Smith, May 20, 1810, quoted in Melvin, *Napoleon's Nav. System*, 154.

47. Adams, *History*, 5:246–247.

48. Armstrong to Smith, July 10, 1810, State Dept., Dipl. Des., Fr., vol. 11.

49. Napoleon to Cadore, July 19, 1810, quoted in Adams, *History*, 5:252; Adams, ed., *Memoirs of J. Q. Adams*, 2:150–151, 168.

50. Cadore to Armstrong, Aug. 5, 1810, *ASP, For. Rel.*, 3:386–387.

51. Armstrong to Madison, Aug. 5, 1810, Madison Papers.

52. Quoted in Adams, *History*, 5:260.

53. Armstrong to Madison, Aug. 15, 1810, Madison Papers, LC.

54. Armstrong to Smith, Aug. 24, 1810, State Dept., Dipl. Des., Fr., vol. 11; Adams, *History*, 5:260.

55. Brant, *Madison, President*, 221. See also Armstrong to Jonathan Russell, Sept. 26, 30, 1810, Russell Papers, Brown University Library, Providence, R.I.

56. The quotation is from Armstrong to Smith, Aug. 7, 1810, State Dept., Dipl. Des., Fr., vol. 11. The proclamation was based on Armstrong's letter to Pinkney, which reached the United States in late September. See Madison to Armstrong, Oct. 29, 1810, Hunt, ed., *Madison Writings*, 8:114–117.

57. Roger H. Brown, *The Republic in Peril: 1812* (New York, 1964), 25.

58. Armstrong to Pinkney, Sept. 29, 1810, *ASP, For. Rel.*, 3:389; Armstrong to Russell, Sept. 30, 1810, Russell Papers, Brown Univ.

59. Armstrong to Smith, Sept. 10, 1810 (with postscript dated Sept. 12), State Dept., Dipl., Des., Fr., vol. 11; *ASP, For. Rel.*, 3:387.

7 – RETURN TO POLITICS

1. Biddle achieved notoriety as the president of the Second Bank of the United States and as the chief adversary of President Andrew Jackson. Charles Biddle served as the secretary of the Constitutional Convention in 1787.

2. Armstrong to Jefferson, July 28, 1808, Jefferson Papers, LC.

3. Armstrong to Madison, Nov. 19, 1807, State Dept., Dipl. Des., Fr., vol. 11; Armstrong to Smith, June 6, 1809; ibid., vol. 11; Barnet to Smith, June 24, 1809, State Dept., Consular Des., Paris. Barnet eventually sent the Registers to the State Dept. See John Graham to Madison, Aug. 24, 1810, Madison Papers, LC.

4. Newspaper extracts, Warden Papers, MdHS. See also Warden to Duane, Jan. 10, 1810, ibid., enclosing supplementary documents, and Warden to Joel Barlow, Jan. 1, 1809 [*sic*, 1810], ibid.

5. Armstrong to Madison, Mar. 18, 1810, Madison Papers, LC.

6. Armstrong to Warden, Sept. 6, 10, 1810, Warden to Armstrong, Sept. 9, 10, 1810, Madison Papers, LC.

7. Armstrong to Madison, Mar. 3, 1811, ibid.; Jefferson to Armstrong, Aug. 5, 1809, Jefferson Papers, LC.; Armstrong to Warden, Sept. 13, 1810, Warden Papers, MdHS; McRae to Warden, Sept. 24, 1810, ibid.; McRae to Smith, Nov. 9, 1810, State Dept., Consular Des., Paris.

8. Burr to Edward Grinwold, Aug. 3, 1810, in Matthew L. Davis, ed., *The Private Journal of Aaron Burr* . . . (2 vols., New York, 1838), 2:29; Armstrong to Smith, Mar. 10, 24, June 7, July 18, State Dept., Dipl. Des., Fr., vol. 11.

9. Russell to Armstrong, June 30, 1810, Robert Bailey to Armstrong, Sept. 14, 1810, Russell Papers, Brown Univ.

10. Armstrong to Russell, Nov. 19, 1810, Christopher Meyer to Russell, Jan. 3, 1811, ibid.

11. Ibid.

12. W. Lewis to Armstrong, Nov. 25, 1810, J. M. Taylor to Armstrong, Nov. 26, 1810, Society Collection (Misc.), HSP; Daniel W. Coxe to Armstrong, Nov. 28, 1810, Rokeby Collection.

13. Armstrong to R. R. Livingston, Dec. 3, 1810, R. R. Livingston Collection, NYHS; Armstrong to Short, Nov. 10 [*sic*, 30?], 1810, Dreer Collection, HSP.

14. Armstrong to Alida Armstrong, Dec. 9, 1810, Rokeby Collection; Philadelphia *Aurora*, Dec. 17, 1810.

15. Armstrong to Alida Armstrong, Dec. 20, 27, 1810, Jan. 24, 1811, Rokeby Collection. Armstrong's claims were never paid.

16. Jefferson to Madison, Dec. 8, 1810, Jefferson Papers, LC.

17. Armstrong to Madison, Mar. 3, 1811, Madison Papers, LC.

18. Wilkinson to Callender Irvine, Feb. 6, 1811, Dickinson College Library, Carlisle, Pa.; Armstrong to Russell, Mar. 5, 1811, Russell Papers, Brown Univ.

19. Madison to Jefferson, Mar. 18, Apr. 1, 1811, Madison Papers, LC; Jefferson to Madison, Apr. 7, 1811, ibid., Ser. 2; Madison to Jefferson, Apr. 19, ibid., Ser. 1.

20. Madison removed Warden in 1814. "Be assured he is not the man he passed for with all of us originally," Madison wrote Jefferson. "His apparent modesty & suavity cover ambition, vanity, avidity (from poverty at least) & intrigue." Madison to Jefferson, Oct. 23, 1814, ibid. Warden was replaced by Isaac Cox Barnet, who held this position until his death on Mar. 8, 1833. Warden remained in Paris, devoting the remainder of his life to intellectual pursuits. He published many books and articles and belonged to many learned societies. He died in 1846.

21. Armstrong to Alexander Phonin, Dec. 17, 1811, Misc. Papers, NYSL. According to family tradition, the sheep were a gift from Napoleon.

22. Armstrong to Spencer, Feb. 15, 1811, Rokeby Collection; Armstrong to Alexander Phonin, Dec. 17, 1811, Misc. Papers, NYSL.

23. Armstrong to Spencer, Mar. 11, 1811, Rokeby Collection.

24. Armstrong to Spencer, Jan. 12, 1812, Spencer to Armstrong, Apr. 9, 1812, ibid.

25. Armstrong to Spencer, Apr. 29, May 23, 1812, ibid.

26. Armstrong to Eustis, June 12, 1803 [? *sic*, 1812] Eustis Papers, MHS; Tompkins to Porter, June 20, 1812, Hugh Hastings, ed., *Public Papers of Daniel D. Tompkins* (Albany, 1902), 2:633–634; Eustis to Armstrong, July 7, 20, 1812, WD/LS, 6:12.

27. DeAlva S. Alexander, *A Political History of the State of New York* (New York, 1957), 1:204; Armstrong to Southwick, Aug. 17, 1812, John Armstrong Misc., NYHS.

28. Raymond Walters, Jr., *Albert Gallatin, Jeffersonian Financier and Diplomat* (New York, 1957), 248; Armstrong to Duane, Aug. 20, 1812, "Selections from the Duane Papers," *Historical Magazine*, 2nd ser. (Aug. 1868), 4:60–61.

29. [Ambrose Spencer,] "The Coalition," in [Anon.,] *The Pilgrims of Hope: An Oratorio* (Albany, 1820).

30. [John Armstrong,] *Hints to Young Generals by an Old Soldier* (Kingston, 1812); Armstrong to Alida Armstrong, Aug. 8, 1812, Rokeby Collection.

31. Gallatin to Monroe, Dec. 1812, Monroe Papers, LC.

32. Monroe to Jefferson, June 7, 1813, Hamilton, ed., *Monroe Writings*, 5:264; Gallatin to Madison, Jan. 4, 1813, cited in Irving Brant, *James Madison, Commander in Chief, 1812-1836* (Indianapolis, 1961), 127.

33. Gallatin to Madison, Jan. 7, 1813, ibid.; Adams, ed., *Memoirs of J. Q. Adams*, 5:434; Rush to Madison, [Jan. 1813,] in Brant, *Madison, Comm. in Chief*, 128.

34. Cong. Ed., *Madison Letters*, 3:384, in a statement by Madison in 1823, entitled: "Review of a Statement Attributed to Gen. John Armstrong," 373-385.

35. Madison to Armstrong, Jan. 14, 1813, Armstrong to Madison, Jan. 17, 1813, Madison Papers, LC; Brant, *Madison, Comm. in Chief*, 128; *Niles' Weekly Register*, Jan. 16, 1813, 3:320.

36. Armstrong to Spencer, Jan. 25, 1813, Spencer to Armstrong, Feb. 1, 1813, Rokeby Collection.

37. Jefferson to Armstrong, Feb. 8, 1813, Washington, ed., *Jefferson Writings*, 6:103.

8 – SECRETARY OF WAR

1. Adams, *History*, 6:395; Richard Peters, ed., *Public Statutes at Large of the United States of America*, II (Boston, 1848), Acts of Mar. 28, May 14, 1812 (I Stat. 696, 732); Emory Upton, *The Military Policy of the United States* (Washington, D.C., 1917), 93-94. See also Erna Risch, *Quartermaster Support of the Army: A History of the Corps, 1775-1939* (Washington, D.C. 1962), 117-133; Marguerite M. McKee, "Service of Supply in the War of 1812," *The Quartermaster Review* (Mar. 1927), 6:49; Leonard D. White, *The Jeffersonians: A Study in Administrative History, 1801-1829* (New York, 1951), 217-218. James R. Jacobs, *The Beginning of the U.S. Army, 1783-1812* (Princeton, N.J., 1947), 363, 383, called Eustis "essentially a military tinker . . . He concerned himself with details so much that he lost track of missions and principles . . . As Secretary of War, he was a piddling incompetent."

2. James D. Richardson, ed., *A Compilation of the Messages and Papers of the Presidents* (10 vols., Washington, D.C., 1900), 1:499; *Annals*, 12th Cong., 1st Sess. (House), 1355-1374. See also Daniel Parker to Armstrong, [Jan. 1813,] Parker Papers, HSP.

3. Richardson, *Messages*, 1:504; Brant, *Madison, Comm. in Chief*, 135-136; Gallatin to Monroe, Jan. 1813, Monroe Papers, LC; Peters, II Stat. 819.

4. Ibid., 816. See Armstrong's report to the Senate, Dec. 27, 1813, *ASP, Mil. Af.*, 1: 384-385.

5. Ibid., 1:425ff. L. D. Ingersoll, *A History of the War Department of the United States* (Washington, D.C., 1879), 61. See the generally favorable estimate of Risch, *Quartermaster Support*, 153.

6. Peters, II Stat. 801; Brant, *Madison, Comm. in Chief*, 167. Ogden and Davy declined.

7. *ASP, Mil. Af.*, 1:432; John Armstrong, *Notices of the War of 1812* (2 vols., New York, 1836, 1840), 1:236-237; Ross to Parish, Mar. 16, Apr. 6, 13, 1813, Edward Ross Papers, LC.

8. Ross to Parish, Apr. 16, 22, 1813, ibid.; Francis B. Heitman, comp., *Historical*

Register and Dictionary of the United States Army . . . (2 vols., Washington, D.C., 1903), 1:846.

9. J. Mackay Hitsman, *The Incredible War of 1812* (Toronto, 1965), 109.

10. McKee, "Supply," *Quartermaster Review*, 6:46–47; Jackson to Armstrong, Nov. 20, Dec. 30, 1813, John S. Bassett, ed., *Correspondence of Andrew Jackson* (Washington, D.C., 1926), 1:355–357, 423–428; Jackson to Gen. John Floyd, Dec. 27, 1813, WD/LR. Sometimes commanders did not call upon the contractors to fulfill their contracts. See the complaints of Elbert Anderson against Gen. Hampton, Sept. 8, 1813, and Orr and Greeley against Gen. Harrison, Jan. 17, 1814, WD/LR. By the war's end the officers decidedly preferred the commissariat system. See Monroe to John C. Calhoun, Dec. 23, 1814, National Archives, War Department, Secretary's Office, Confidential and Unofficial Letters Sent, p. 10.

11. *ASP, Mil. Af.*, 1:428–431; Irving to Armstrong, June 30, 1813, WD/LR; Armstrong to Irvine, July 25, Aug. 7, 1813, WD/LS, 7:22, 33. The six Issuing Commissaries were assigned (1) with Gen. Harrison; (2) with Gen. Pinckney; (3) at Niagara; (4) at Sackett's Harbor; (5) at Lake Champlain; (6) at New Orleans.

12. Gallatin to Madison, Mar. 5, 1813, Adams, ed., *Gallatin Writings*, 1:532–533; Walters, *Gallatin*, 256–258; Gallatin to Secretaries of War and Navy, Apr. 17, 1813, Madison Papers, LC; Adams, ed., *Gallatin Writings*, 1:535–538.

13. Adams, *History*, 7:384; Jones to A. J. Dallas, Sept. 25, 1814, in Brant, *Madison, Comm. in Chief*, 327.

14. Barbour to Armstrong, Feb. 7, May 29, 1813, WD/LR; Armstrong to Barbour, Mar. 22, 1813, WD/LS, 6:332–333.

15. Shelby wrote Armstrong on Aug. 13, 1814 (WD/LR), that delays in paying the troops was "damping the ardour of our Citizens for public service." See also Robert Brent (Paymaster of the U.S.) to Armstrong, Aug. 19, 1814, Madison Papers, LC.

16. Armstrong to Duane, Mar. 21, 1813, *Historical Magazine* (Aug. 1868), 4:61–62. In the fall of 1813, in preparation for the invasion of Canada, Armstrong shifted $600,000 from the Ordnance Department to clothing and $800,000 from fortifications to subsistence for the army.

17. Armstrong to Swartwout, Apr. 25, May 4, 1813, WD/LS, 6:381, 404–405.

18. Armstrong to Madison, Sept. 5, 1813, Madison to Jones, Sept. 16, 1813, Madison Papers, LC. See also Daniel Parker to Callender Irvine, Oct. 13, 1813, WD/LS, 7:57.

19. Upton, *Military Policy*, 92; Armstrong to John W. Eppes (chairman of Ways and Means Committee), Feb. 10, 1814, *Niles' Weekly Register*, Apr. 9, 1814, 6:94; Armstrong to G. M. Troup, Jan. 2, 1814, WD/Reports to Congress.

20. Alec R. Gilpin, *The War of 1812 in the Old Northwest* (East Lansing, Mich., 1958), 176–179; Brent to Armstrong, Feb. 1814, *Niles' Weekly Register*, Apr. 9, 1814, 6:95.

21. Armstrong to Madison, Dec. 5, 1813, Madison Papers, LC; Monroe to Madison, Dec. 27, 1813, ibid.

22. Armstrong to Troup, Jan. 1, 1814, WD/Reports to Congress; Peters, II Stat. 94; *Annals*, 13th Cong., 2nd Sess. (Senate), 576–83; Dr. James Mease (Philadelphia) to Armstrong, Aug. 2, 8, 1814, WD/LR; Armstrong to Mease, Aug. 6, 1814, WD/LS, 7:275; Duane to Armstrong, July 12, 1814, WD/LR; Armstrong to Duane, July 15, 1814, *Historical Magazine* (Aug. 1868), 4:63; Duane to Armstrong, Aug. 25, 1814 (enclosing a 15-page project), WD/LR.

23. *ASP, Mil. Af.*, 1:514–17. Monroe, like Armstrong, cited the Revolutionary experience. See Adams, *History*, 8:267–80.

24. Upton, *Military Policy*, 96.

25. Dearborn to Armstrong, Feb. 14, 1813, WD/LR.

26. Wilkinson to Armstrong, Aug. 6, 1813, *ASP, Mil. Af.*, 1:463; Armstrong to Wilkinson, Aug. 9, 1813, WD/LS, 7:33–34; Wilkinson to Armstrong, Dec. 26, 1813, WD/LR.

27. Flournoy to Armstrong, June 15, 1814, WD/LR.

28. Freeman Cleaves, *Old Tippecanoe* (New York, 1939), 218; Armstrong to Harrison, Mar. 3, 1814, Logan Esarey, ed., *Messages and Letters of William Henry Harrison* (2 vols., Indianapolis, 1922), 2:631.

29. Armstrong to Harrison, Apr. 25, 1814, ibid., 2:645; Armstrong to Holmes, Apr. 25, 1814, WD/LS, 7:172; Croghan to Harrison, [n.d.,] in Robert B. McAfee, *History of the Late War in the Western Country* (Bowling Green, 1919), 449–52.

30. Harrison to Armstrong, May 11, 1814, Esarey, ed., *Harrison Letters*, 2:647–648; Armstrong to Madison, June 18, 1814, Madison Papers, LC.

31. Adams, ed., *Gallatin Writings*, 1:538–539; Monroe to Madison, [Feb. 25?] 1813, Monroe Papers, LC. Irving Brant, *Madison, Comm. in Chief*, 205–206, questions the authenticity of this letter's date. Harry Ammon, *James Monroe: The Quest for National Identity* (New York, 1971), 634–35, disagrees. Nevertheless, the contents certainly reveal Monroe's feelings, and they were undoubtedly communicated to Madison verbally.

32. In a draft of a letter to Madison written on Sept. 25, 1814, Monroe wrote that Armstrong "excluded me from the command of the northern army last campaign." Hamilton, ed., *Monroe Writings*, 5:293n. Armstrong's statement is quoted in Rufus King, Memorandum, June 27, 1813, King, ed., *Correspondence*, 5:320. See also C. Edward Skeen, "Monroe and Armstrong: A Study in Political Rivalry," *The New-York Historical Society Quarterly* (Apr. 1973), 57:121–147.

33. Wilkinson to Monroe, Aug. 8, 1813, Monroe Papers, LC; Hampton to Monroe, June 13, 1813, Monroe Papers, NYPL.

34. Monroe may have been encouraged in his belief that he was charged with an oversight of the War Department by a letter sent to him (not to Parker) by the president in Sept. 1813 asking him to forward the plans for military operations in the South. Madison to Monroe, Sept. 1, 2, 1813, Madison Papers, LC.

35. Adams, ed., *Memoirs of J. Q. Adams*, 6:3–6. When Monroe took over the War Department in 1814, he forced Parker to give up his position as chief clerk. Madison then appointed Parker as the Adjutant and Inspector General with the rank of brigadier general. See Parker to Madison, Oct. 29, 1814, Monroe Papers, LC.

36. Monroe to Madison, Dec. 27, 1813, ibid.

37. John W. Taylor, Memorandum, Jan. 12, 1814, John W. Taylor Papers, NYHS.

38. Rufus King, Memorandum, Jan. 1814, King, *Correspondence*, 5:370–371; King to Morris, Jan. 17, 1814, ibid., 5:365.

39. Brant, *Madison, Comm. in Chief*, 233. The report is in *ASP, Mil. Af.*, 1:439–488.

40. *Annals*, 13th Cong., 2nd Sess., 1521.

41. There is uncertainty about the most daring and successful appointment, that of Jacob Brown to major general. Henry Adams, *History*, 7:407–409, credits Armstrong, but Irving Brant, *Madison, Comm. in Chief*, asserts that Madison was responsible. Wilkinson charged that Scott was promoted to discredit him, but Scott's promotion was well-merited. Wilkinson, *Memoirs of My Own Times* (3 vols., Philadelphia, 1816), 3:367n; Charles Winslow Elliott, *Winfield Scott: The Soldier and the Man* (New York, 1937), 135–136.

42. *Annals*, 13th Cong., 2nd Sess., 856–858; Monroe to Hay, Mar. 11, 1814, Oct. 17, 1813, Hay to Monroe, Mar. 14, 1814, Monroe Papers, NYPL. See the comments of Zebulon Shipherd (Fed., N.Y.), *Annals*, 13th Cong., 2nd Sess., 1519–1520.

43. Brant, *Madison, Comm. in Chief,* 207, quoting William Jones; Monroe to Hay, Mar. 11, 1814, Monroe Papers, NYPL.

44. Wilkinson, *Memoirs,* 1:741n, 762.

45. Madison to Armstrong, May 25, 1814, Madison Papers, LC.

46. The correspondence relating to this incident is conveniently gathered in Madison's "Review of a Statement attributed to Gen. John Armstrong," Cong. Ed., *Madison Letters,* 3:373–385.

47. Madison to Armstrong, June 15, Aug. 10, 1814, Madison Papers, LC.

48. Madison to Armstrong, July 27, 1814, Armstrong to Madison, July 27, 1814, ibid.

49. Madison to Armstrong, Aug. 4, 1814, Cong. Ed., *Madison Letters,* 3:415.

50. Madison to Armstrong, Aug. 13, 1814, ibid., 3:417–419.

9 – THE CAMPAIGN OF 1813

1. Armstrong to Eustis, Jan. 2, 1812, Armstrong, *Notices,* 1:235–237.

2. Armstrong memorandum to Cabinet, Feb. 8, 1813, *ASP, Mil. Af.,* 1:439–440.

3. Alfred Thayer Mahan, *Sea Power in its Relations to the War of 1812* (2 vols., Boston, 1905), 2:31, 33.

4. Armstrong to Dearborn, Feb. 10, 1813, *ASP, Mil. Af.,* 1:439–440; Armstrong to Dearborn, Feb. 15, 1813, WD/LS, 6:293–294; Armstrong to Porter, Feb. 12, 1813, ibid., 6:464–465; Armstrong to Lt. Christopher Vandeventer, Feb. 12, 1813, ibid., 6:465–466; General Orders, Feb. 12, 1813, National Archives, Adjutant General's Office, General Orders, 1812–1817, 3:36.

5. Armstrong to Dearborn, Feb. 15, 1813, WD/LS, 6:293–294; Armstrong to Porter, Feb. 23, 1813, ibid., 6:466; Armstrong to Dearborn, Feb. 24, 1813, *ASP, Mil. Af.,* 1:440; Armstrong to Dearborn, Mar. 4, 1813, WD/LS, 6:314–315.

6. Armstrong to Dearborn, Mar. 10, 1813, ibid.

7. Armstrong to Spencer, Feb. 28, 1813, Rokeby Collection; Armstrong to Duane, Mar. 16, 1813, *Historical Magazine* (Aug. 1868), 4:61.

8. Dearborn to Armstrong, Mar. 3, 9, 14, 16, and n.d., 1813, WD/LR. See also Dearborn to Madison, Mar. 13, 1813, Madison Papers, LC.

9. Armstrong to Dearborn, Mar. 29, Apr. 8, 1813, WD/LS, 6:338–339, 354–355.

10. Adams, *History,* 7:72–98; Alec R. Gilpin, *War in the Old Northwest,* chapter 7; Harry L. Coles, *The War of 1812* (Chicago, 1965), chapter 4; McAfee, *Late War,* chapter 3.

11. Harrison to Monroe, Dec. 12, 1812, Jan. 4, 6, 15, 1813, Monroe to Harrison, Dec. 26, 1812, Jan. 7, 21, 1813, Esarey, ed., *Harrison Letters,* 2:293–299, 299–307, 309–310, 265–269, 312–313, 325–326; Adams, *History,* 7:86–98; Harrison to Armstrong, Feb. 11, 1813, Esarey, ed., *Harrison Letters,* 2:357–358.

12. Armstrong to Harrison, Mar. 5, 7, 1813, ibid., 2:379–380, 380–381. See also Armstrong to Harrison, May 4, 1813, ibid., 2:430–431; Armstrong to Captain Thomas S. Jessup, Mar. 9, 1813, WD/LS, 6:310.

13. Harrison to Armstrong, Mar. 17, 1813, Shelby to Harrison, Mar. 20, 27, 1813, Harrison to Shelby, Mar. 1813, Esarey, ed., *Harrison Letters,* 2:387–392, 394–395, 398–399, 341–342.

14. Harrison to Armstrong, Mar. 27, 28, 1813, ibid., 2:400–404, 404–405; Richard M. Johnson to Armstrong, Mar. 31, 1813, Duncan McArthur to Armstrong, Mar. 30, 1813,

Thomas Worthington to Armstrong, Mar. 31, 1813, WD/LR; Armstrong to Huntington, Apr. 1, 1813, WD/LS, 6:343-344.

15. Harrison to Shelby, Apr. 9, 1813, Esarey, ed., *Harrison Letters*, 2:416-417; Harrison to Armstrong, Apr. 17, 1813, ibid., 2:418-419.

16. Armstrong to Harrison, Apr. 11, 18, 1813, ibid., 2:417, 421; Armstrong to Cass, Apr. 28, 1813, WD/LS, 6:390-392.

17. Gilpin, *War in the Old Northwest*, 181-190; McAfee, *Late War*, 280-295. See also Harrison to Armstrong, May 5, 9, 1813, Esarey, ed., *Harrison Letters*, 2:431-433, 438-440.

18. Armstrong to Duane, Mar. 16, 1813, *Historical Magazine* (Aug. 1868), 4:61; Harrison to Armstrong, Apr. 21, 1813, Esarey, ed., *Harrison Letters*, 2:424-425.

19. Armstrong to Duane, Apr. 29, 1813, *Historical Magazine* (Aug. 1868), 4:62.

20. Meigs to Armstrong, Apr. 11, 1813, Worthington to Armstrong, Apr. 10, 1813, McArthur and Cass to Armstrong, Mar. 31, 1813, WD/LR; Armstrong to Harrison, Apr. 11, 1813, Harrison to Armstrong, May 13, 1813, Esarey, ed., *Harrison Letters*, 2:417, 442-447.

21. Owings to Armstrong, May 2, 1813, Cass to Armstrong, Apr. 18, May 8, 1813, Harrison to Armstrong, May 26, 1813, Cass to Armstrong, June 16, 1813, McArthur to Armstrong, June 30, 1813, WD/LR.

22. Armstrong to Johnson, Feb. 26, 1813, Esarey, ed., *Harrison Letters*, 2:375; Johnson to Armstrong, Apr. 13, 1813, WD/LR. Johnson's Volunteers were authorized by the Act of Feb. 25, 1813, Peters, II Stat. 804.

23. Armstrong to Dearborn, Apr. 19, 1813, WD/LS, 6:439-441.

24. Armstrong to Dearborn, June 19, 1813, ibid., 6:459-460; Adams, *History*, 8:162; John K. Mahon, *The War of 1812* (Gainesville, Fla., 1972), 151-152.

25. Armstrong to Dearborn, July 6, 1813, *ASP, Mil Af.*, 1:449; Madison to Henry Lee, Feb. 1827, Cong. ed., *Madison Letters*, 3:562.

26. Adams, *History*, 8:163-170; Mahon, *War of 1812*, 147-149.

27. Armstrong to Dearborn, June 19, 1813, WD/LS, 6:459-460; Armstrong to Lewis, July 1, 3, 9, 1813, ibid., 7:1, 4, 9; Armstrong to Boyd, July 1813, ibid., 7:7-8.

28. Lewis to Armstrong, July 5, 23, 1813, Porter to Armstrong, July 27, 1813, WD/LR.

29. Jackson to Monroe, Jan. 7, 1813, quoted in Adams, *History*, 7:207; Monroe to Wilkinson, Jan. 30, 1813, Monroe to Pinckney, Jan. 13, 1813, WD/LS, 6:276, 268-269.

30. Armstrong to Jackson, Feb. 5, 1813, Bassett, ed., *Jackson Correspondence*, 1:275-276; Wilkinson to Monroe, Feb. 9, 1813, WD/LR; Wilkinson to Armstrong, Feb. 23, Mar. 2, 1813, ibid.

31. Wilkinson to Armstrong, Mar. 9, 1813, ibid., Wilkinson to Jackson, Mar. 8, 1813, Bassett, ed., *Jackson Correspondence*, 1:290-291; Col. Covington to Wilkinson, Mar. 15, 1813, WD/LR.

32. Jackson to Armstrong, Mar. 15, 1813, Bassett, ed., *Jackson Correspondence*, 1:291-292; Blount to Armstrong, Apr. 6, 1813, WD/LR.

33. Armstrong to Jackson, Mar. 22, 1813, Bassett, ed., *Jackson Correspondence*, 1:300; Jackson to Armstrong, Mar. 22, 1813, ibid.

34. Crawford to Madison, Mar. 3, 1813, Madison Papers, LC; Wilkinson to Monroe, Feb. 9, 1813, WD/LR.

35. Armstrong to Wilkinson, Mar. 10, 12, 1813, Wilkinson, *Memoirs*, 3:341-342; Royal Ornan Shreve, *The Finished Scoundrel* (Indianapolis, 1933), 275-276.

36. Wilkinson to Armstrong, May 23, 1813, WD/LR. Gen. Winfield Scott declared later, possibly on inside information, "The selection of this unprincipled imbecile was not

the blunder of Secretary Armstrong." Winfield Scott, *Memoirs of Lieutenant General Scott* (New York, 1864), 1:94.

37. Armstrong to Madison, July 25, 1813, Madison Papers, LC.

38. Wilkinson's career is surveyed by Isaac Joslin Cox in Malone, ed., *DAB*, sv "Wilkinson, James (1757 – Dec. 28, 1825)."

39. Wilkinson to Armstrong, Aug. 6, 1813, *ASP, Mil. Af.*, 1:463–464; Armstrong to Wilkinson, Aug. 8, 1813, WD/LS, 7:60; Wilkinson, *Memoirs*, 3:88n.

40. Armstrong, *Notices*, 2:23–24; Wilkinson, *Memoirs*, 3:347–349; Hampton to Armstrong, May 19, July 13, 1813, WD/LR; Hampton to Armstrong, Aug. 22, 1813, Madison Papers, LC.

41. Hampton to Armstrong, Aug. 22, 1813, ibid.; Wilkinson to Armstrong, Aug. 26, 1813, *ASP, Mil. Af.*, 1:465.

42. Armstrong to Hampton, Aug. 25, 1813, Madison Papers, LC; Hampton to Armstrong, Aug. 31, 1813, WD/LR.

43. Wilkinson to Armstrong, Aug. 21, 1813, *ASP, Mil. Af.*, 1:465; Armstrong to Madison, Aug. 28, 1813, Madison Papers, LC; Armstrong to Duane, Sept. 18, 1813, *Historical Magazine* (Aug. 1868), 4:63.

44. Adams, *History*, 7:115–127; Perry to Harrison, Sept. 10, 1813, Esarey, ed., *Harrison Letters*, 2:539.

45. Harrison to Armstrong, Sept. 27, 30, Oct. 9, 1813, ibid., 2:551, 556, 558–565.

46. Harrison to Armstrong, Sept. 15, 1813, ibid., 2:541; Armstrong to Harrison, Sept. 22, 1813, ibid., 2:544–545; Harrison to Armstrong, Oct. 22, 24, 1813, ibid., 2:589, 589–590.

47. Armstrong to Harrison, Nov. 3, 1813, ibid., 2:595–596; Harrison to Armstrong, Nov. 8, 11, 1813, ibid., 2:596–598, 600–601; Cleaves, *Old Tippecanoe*, 211; *Niles Register*, Dec. 18, 1813, 5:263–264.

48. Wilkinson to Armstrong, Sept. 18, 1813, Armstrong to Wilkinson, Sept. 18, 22, 1813, *ASP, Mil. Af.*, 1:467, 468, 469; Wilkinson to Armstrong, Sept. 20, 1813, WD/LR.

49. Armstrong to Madison, Sept. 21, 26, Oct. 4, 1813, Madison Papers, LC; Armstrong to Hampton, Sept. 25, 28, 1813, *ASP, Mil. Af.*, 1:459, 460. For an account of Chauncey's activities, see Mahan, *Sea Power*, 2:51–61.

50. Armstrong to Madison, Oct. 8, 19, 1813, Madison Papers, LC.

51. Armstrong to Wilkinson, Oct. 19, 1813, *ASP, Mil. Af.*, 1:471–472; Wilkinson to Armstrong, Oct. 19, 1813, WD/LR.

52. Armstrong to Wilkinson, Oct. 20, 1813, *ASP, Mil. Af.*, 1:473; Armstrong to Madison, Oct. 20, 1813, Madison Papers, LC. See also Ellery, ed., *Swift Memoirs*, 112, 115; Jacobs, *Tarnished Warrior*, 288–291; Thomas Robinson Hay, "Some Reflections on the Career of General James Wilkinson," *MVHR* (Mar. 1935), 21:471–494.

53. Hampton to Armstrong, Sept. 22, 25, Oct. 4, 1813, *ASP, Mil. Af.*, 1:459, 460; Hampton to Armstrong, Nov. 1, 1813, WD/LR.

54. Armstrong to Swartwout, Oct. 18, 1813, WD/LS, 7:94; Wilkinson, *Memoirs*, 3: 71n; Armstrong to Madison, Nov. 11, 1813, Madison Papers, LC.

55. Wilkinson to Armstrong, Oct. 28, 1813, Armstrong to Wilkinson, Oct. 30, 1813, *ASP, Mil. Af.*, 1:473, 474; Wilkinson to Armstrong, Nov. 3, 1813, WD/LR.

56. Wilkinson to Hampton, Nov. 6, 1813, ibid.; Hampton to Wilkinson, Nov. 8, 1813, *ASP, Mil. Af.*, 1:462; Hampton to Armstrong, Nov. 12, 1813, ibid., 1:462–463; Hampton to Armstrong, Nov. 13, 1813, WD/LR.

57. Wilkinson to Hampton, Nov. 12, 1813, General Order, Nov. 13, 1813, *ASP, Mil. Af.*, 1:463, 479.

58. Armstrong to Madison, Nov. 8, 9, 11, 14, 19, 1813, Madison Papers, LC.

59. Wilkinson to Armstrong, Nov. 15, 17, 24, 1813; Wilkinson to Hampton, Nov. 26, 1813, WD/LR; Armstrong, *Notices*, 2:24–44.

60. Madison to Wirt, Sept. 30, 1813, Hunt, ed., *Madison Writings*, 8:262–265; Madison to Armstrong, Oct. 30, 1813, Madison Papers, LC.

61. Armstrong to Madison, Nov. 25, 1813, ibid.

62. Adams, *History*, 8:201–295; Cass to Armstrong, Jan. 12, 1814, *ASP, Mil. Af.*, 1: 487–488.

63. Harrison to Armstrong, Nov. 11, 1813, Esarey, ed., *Harrison Letters*, 2:600–602; Armstrong to McClure, Nov. 25, 1813, *ASP, Mil. Af.*, 1:485.

64. Scott to Armstrong, Dec. 31, 1813, ibid., 1:483; McClure to Armstrong, Dec. 25, 1813, WD/LR.

65. McClure to Armstrong, Dec. 10, 1813, ibid.; Madison to Armstrong, Dec. 29, 1813, Cong. Ed., *Madison Letters*, 3:395.

10 – THE CAMPAIGN OF 1814

1. Mrs. Richard Aldrich (Margaret Livingston Chanler), "Memoirs of Rokeby," typed manuscript, ca. 1900, Rokeby Collection. The style is not typical of the American Federal style of houses built in the Hudson Valley, 1790–1830. The design is fairly complex and imaginative, indicating that Armstrong either brought the plans with him from France or engaged an architect.

2. Approximately 16,000 hard bricks and 1000 soft bricks arrived between August and early October 1812, Farm Account Book, 1812–1813, Rokeby Collection. The exterior (bearing) walls were fieldstone, 30 inches thick, and stuccoed on the outside. The original house was nearly square (61 feet x 63 feet), with two and a half stories, and with dormered attic rooms. The roof was hipped and a skylight at the peak lit the central hall on the second floor, around which four of the six bedrooms, each with a dressing room, were arranged. The basic first-floor plan was symmetrical, with a central hall as the axis and three rooms on each side, with a curved staircase at the back of the hall. Two service wings, two stories high, each 12 feet wide and 17½ feet deep, and each extending 7½ feet beyond the easterly and westerly flanks of the main portion of the house were either added then or shortly thereafter. The configuration was in the shape of a "T," with the two service wings creating an open court on the north side. With the wings, the house contained about thirty rooms. In its time it was the largest house in the region.

3. Aldrich, "Memoirs of Rokeby," Rokeby Collection.

4. Flournoy to Armstrong, May 29, 1813, WD/LR; Armstrong to Flournoy, June 24, July 4, 1813, WD/LS, 6:479, 7:5–7.

5. Wilkinson to Armstrong, July 6, 1813, WD/LR.

6. Armstrong to Commander, 3rd Regt., U.S. Infantry, July 3, 1813, Armstrong to Governors Willie Blount (Tenn.) and David Mitchell (Ga.), July 13, 1813, Armstrong to Pinckney, July 26, 1813, WD/LS, 7:11–12, 14, 21.

7. Hawkins to Armstrong, July 20, 1813, *ASP, Ind., Af.*, 1:849; Hawkins to Governor David Mitchell, July 27, 1813, WD/LR; Adams, *History*, 7:216–234.

8. Mitchell to Armstrong, July 29, Aug. 9, 24, 31, Sept. 14, 1813, Blount to Armstrong, July 30, Aug. 1, 1813, WD/LR; Parker to Mitchell, Sept. 5, 1813, Parker to Ward & Taylor (contractors), Sept. 3, 1813, WD/LS, 7:40–41, 56.

9. Blount to Armstrong, Sept. 8, 1813, WD/LR.

10. Blount to Armstrong, Sept. 28, 1813, ibid.; Madison to Armstrong, Oct. 11, 30, 1813, Armstrong to Madison, Oct. 20, 1813, Madison Papers, LC.

11. Armstrong to Madison, Sept. 26, 1813, Madison to Armstrong, Oct. 8, 1813, ibid.; Adams, *History*, 7:235-245.

12. Madison to Armstrong, Oct. 11, 1813, Madison Papers, LC. The appointment, however, was not made until Nov. 7, after Mitchell declined reelection as governor. Parker to Pinckney, Oct. 18, Nov. 7, 1813, WD/LS, 7:58-59, 65-66; Pinckney to Armstrong, Nov. 23, 30, Dec. 2, 4, 1813, WD/LR.

13. Armstrong to Madison, Nov. 24, 25, 1813, Madison Papers, LC.

14. Armstrong to Harrison, Dec. 29, 1813, Esarey, ed., *Harrison Letters*, 2:613-615; McArthur to Armstrong, Oct. 6, 1813, Cass to Armstrong, Dec. 17, 1813, Tompkins to Armstrong, Dec. 24, 1813, WD/LR; Armstrong to Harrison, Jan. 1, 1814, Esarey, ed., *Harrison Letters*, 2:615-616.

15. Wilkinson to Armstrong, Dec. 24, 1813, WD/LR; Armstrong to Wilkinson, Jan. 1, 1814, WD/LS, 7:91-92; Tompkins to Armstrong, Jan. 7, 9, 1814, WD/LR.

16. Wilkinson to Armstrong, Jan. 7, 16, 18, 1814, ibid.

17. Tompkins to Madison, Jan. 3, 1814, Hastings, ed., *Tompkins Papers*, 3:411-413; Madison to Tompkins, Jan. 25, 1814, Cong. Ed., *Madison Letters*, 2:580.

18. Armstrong to Wilkinson, Jan. 30, 1814 (2 letters), WD/LS, 7:116-117; Wilkinson, *Memoirs*, 3:367n, 1:617; Elliot, *Winfield Scott*, 139-141.

19. Wilkinson, *Memoirs*, 3:365n; Elliot, *Winfield Scott*, 139-141.

20. Flournoy to Armstrong, Jan. 24, 1814, WD/LR; Armstrong to Flournoy, Feb. 8, 1814, WD/LS, 7:122.

21. John H. Eaton, *The Life of Andrew Jackson* (Philadelphia, 1824), 157-163; Pinckney to Armstrong, Apr. 22, 1814, WD/LR.

22. Flournoy to Armstrong, June 15, 1814, ibid.; Armstrong to Flournoy, July 25, 1814, WD/LS, 7:263-264.

23. Armstrong to Wilkinson, Mar. 24, 1814, Armstrong to Izard, Mar. 24, 1814, Armstrong to Hampton, Mar. 16, 1814, WD/LS, 7:147, 145, 141; Adams, *History*, 8:25-26; Hitsman, *Incredible War*, 181-182.

24. Armstrong to Brown, Feb. 28, 1814, Armstrong, *Notices*, 2:213-214.

25. Ibid.

26. Brown to Armstrong, Mar. 21, (two letters), 24, 1814, WD/LR; Tompkins to Armstrong, Mar. 30, 1814, ibid.

27. Armstrong to Brown, Mar. 20, 1814, WD/LS, 7:146.

28. Brown to Armstrong, Apr. 8, 29, 1814, WD/LR; Armstrong to Gen. Edmund P. Gaines, Apr. 26, 1814, WD/LS, 7:173; Armstrong to Izard, Apr. 28, May 6, 1814, ibid., 7:176-177, 186.

29. Armstrong, *Notices*, 2:64.

30. Armstrong to Madison, Apr. 30, 1814, WD/Letters Sent to the President; Armstrong to Brown, June 2, 1814, WD/LS, 7:215.

31. Madison to Armstrong, May 4, 1814, Madison Papers, LC; Armstrong to Madison, Apr. 30, 1814, WD/Letters Sent to the President; Armstrong to Brown, May 7, 1814, WD/LS, 7:186-187.

32. Armstrong to Brown, May 25, 1814, Armstrong to Scott, May 25, 1814, ibid., 7:204, 209; Brown to Armstrong, June 3, 1814, cited in Brant, *Madison, Comm.-in-Chief*, 257.

33. Madison to Armstrong, June 3, 1814, Cabinet memorandum, June 7, 1814, Madison Papers, LC.

34. Armstrong to Brown, June 10, 1814, WD/LS, 7:257–259; Brown to Armstrong, June 17, July 6, 16, 22, 1814, WD/LR; Adams, *History*, 8:34–90.

35. Ibid., 8:32; McArthur to Armstrong, June 15, July 16, 1814, WD/LR; Armstrong to McArthur, July 27, 1814, WD/LS, 7:268.

36. McArthur to Armstrong, July 31, Aug. 8, 1814, WD/LR; Armstrong to McArthur, Aug. 8, 1814, WD/LS, 7:276–277.

37. Jackson to Armstrong, June 13, 1814, WD/LR; Armstrong to Jackson, June 25, 1814, WD/LS, 7:233–234.

38. Jackson to Armstrong, June 27, 1814, Cong. Ed., *Madison Letters*, 3:408; Armstrong to Jackson, July 18, 1814, WD/LS, 7:255.

39. Jackson to Armstrong, July 24, 1814, Jackson to Pinckney, July 27, 1814, WD/LR. The treaty is in *ASP, Ind. Af.*, 1:826–827.

40. Pinckney to Armstrong, Aug. 11, 1814, WD/LR (with annotations by Armstrong and forwarded to Madison); Armstrong to Jackson, Aug. 20, 1814, WD/LS, 7:297; Jackson to Armstrong, Aug. 25, 1814, WD/LR.

41. Armstrong to Izard, May 18, 1814, WD/LS, 7:197.

42. Izard to Armstrong, May 24, June 10, 1814, WD/LR; Armstrong to Izard, May 25, 1814, WD/LS, 7:205–207.

43. Armstrong to Izard, June 10, 30, 1814, ibid., 7:269–270, 289; Izard to Armstrong, June 3, 1814, Izard to Monroe, June 4, 1814, Monroe Papers, NYPL.

44. Izard to Armstrong, July 19, Aug. 7, 1814, WD/LR; William Jones to Chauncey, Aug. 13, 1814, Madison Papers, LC.

45. Izard to Armstrong, Aug. 11, 1814, WD/LR.

46. Armstrong to Brown, May 7, 1814, Armstrong to McArthur, Aug. 6, 1814, WD/LS, 7:186–187, 276; Adams, *History*, 8:99–102.

47. Izard to Armstrong, Aug. 20, 23, 1814, WD/LR; Adams, *History*, 8:100–101.

48. Armstrong to Izard, Aug. 12, 1814, quoted in Adams, *History*, 8:100. Armstrong's successor, Monroe, proposed to return the focus to the St. Lawrence by severing this line of communication, but he unrealistically planned to use a 40,000 man force. C. P. Stacey, "An American Plan for a Canadian Campaign, Secretary James Monroe to Major General Brown, February, 1815," *AHR* (Jan. 1941), 46:348–358.

11 – THE WASHINGTON AFFAIR

1. Armstrong to Duane, Mar. 16, 1813, *Historical Magazine* (Aug. 1868), 4:61; Report of the House Committee, July 31, 1813, "Spirit and Manner in which the War is waged by the Enemy," *ASP, Mil. Af.*, 1:339–382; Adams, *History*, 7:271–275.

2. Report to the Senate, June 10, 1813, *ASP, Mil. Af.*, 1:383; Armstrong to Dearborn, Apr. 15, 1814, WD/LS, 7:162.

3. Report of the House Committee on the "Capture of Washington," *Annals*, 13th Cong., 3rd Sess., 1518–1738, Van Ness Statement, 1685; Statement of the Citizens of Alexandria, ibid., 1722; Wadsworth to Armstrong, May 28, 1813, WD/LR.

4. Armstrong statement, *Annals*, 13th Cong., 3rd Sess., 1565. A fortification below Philadelphia was being financed with a loan from that city at the interest rate of 6 percent annually. See Armstrong to Thomas Leiper, July 1, 1814, WD/LS, 7:240.

5. Van Ness statement, *Annals*, 13th Cong., 3rd Sess., 1688.

6. Tatham to Armstrong, July 10, 1814, WD/LR.

7. Memorandum of the Cabinet meeting of July 1, 1814, Madison Papers, LC; Armstrong, *Notices*, 2:128.

8. Armstrong, *Notices*, 2:140, 127.

9. Winder to Armstrong, June 30, 1814, WD/LR; Winder statement, *Annals*, 13th Cong., 3rd Sess., 1601; Van Ness statement, ibid., 1686–1687.

10. Winder statement, ibid., 1577–1578.

11. Armstrong to Winder, July 12, 1814, quoted in Edward D. Ingraham, *A Sketch of the Events which preceded the Capture of Washington by the British on the twenty-fourth of August, 1814* (Philadelphia, 1849), 12; Van Ness statement, *Annals*, 13th Cong., 3rd Sess., 1685; Armstrong to Col. Wadsworth, June 28, 1814, WD/LS, 7:237; Madison to Barbour, June 16, 1814, Madison Papers, LC.

12. Winder statement, *Annals*, 13th Cong., 3rd Sess., 1602; Winder to Armstrong, July 23, 1814, ibid., 1582.

13. See Tatham's reports dated June 25, July 2, 4, 10, 13, 1814, WD/LR; Winder to Armstrong, July 7, 1814, ibid.

14. Winder to Armstrong, July 23, 1814, Winder statement, *Annals*, 13th Cong., 3rd Sess., 1581, 1603.

15. Ibid., 1607.

16. Ibid., 1603–1604.

17. Winder to Armstrong, Aug. 13, 1814, ibid., 1586, 1597.

18. Ibid., 1605–1606; Adams, *History*, 8:128–129; Walter Lord, *The Dawn's Early Light* (New York, 1972), 97–99.

19. Winder to Armstrong, Aug. 19, 1814, *Annals*, 13th Cong., 3rd Sess., 1588; Monroe to Armstrong, Aug. 18, 1814, WD/LR; Armstrong to Monroe, Aug. 18, 1814, Monroe Papers, LC; Winder statement, *Annals*, 13th Cong., 3rd Sess., 1608; Monroe to Madison, Aug. 20, 1814, WD/LR.

20. Madison to Monroe, Aug. 21, 22, 1814, Monroe Papers, LC; Armstrong to Winder, Aug. 19, 22, 1814, *Annals*, 13th Cong., 3rd Sess., 1592, 1587.

21. Armstrong, *Notices*, Appendix 29, 2:232–236.

22. Adams, *History*, 8:128–131; Winder statement, *Annals*, 13th Cong., 3rd Sess., 1609–1610, 1614.

23. Winder statement, *Annals*, 13th Cong., 3rd Sess., 1614–1615.

24. Winder to Armstrong, Aug. 24, 1814, WD/LR; Madison Memorandum, Aug. 24, 1814, Hunt, ed., *Madison Writings*, 8:295.

25. Armstrong statement, *Annals*, 13th Cong., 3rd Sess., 1566–1567; Madison Memorandum, Aug. 24, 1814, Hunt, ed., *Madison Writings*, 8:295.

26. Campbell statement, *Annals*, 13th Cong., 3rd Sess., 1735–1736; Madison Memorandum, Aug. 24, 1814, Hunt, ed., *Madison Writings*, 8:295.

27. Armstrong statement, *Annals*, 13th Cong., 3rd Sess., 1567.

28. Adams, *History*, 8:153. Monroe wrote proudly to his son-in-law, George Hay, that he had "formed the line, and made the disposition of our troops." Monroe to Hay, Sept. 7, 1814, Monroe Papers, NYPL. See also, Brant, *Madison, Comm.-in-Chief*, 301. Armstrong's statement is in Armstrong, *Notices*, 2:148.

29. Madison Memorandum, Aug. 24, 1814, Hunt, ed., *Madison Writings*, 8:297; Armstrong to Spencer, Sept. 29, 1814, Rokeby Collection; Winder statement, *Annals*, 13th Cong., 3rd Sess., 1621; Monroe statement, ibid., 1560.

30. General Walter Smith statement, ibid., 1642.

31. Lt. Col. Lavall statement, ibid., 1657; *Niles' Weekly Register*, Sept. 10, 1814, 7:6; Armstrong, *Notices*, 2:231–232. An eye-witness account refutes Armstrong's assertion. See John S. Williams, *History of the Invasion and Capture of Washington* (New York, 1857), 365.

32. Adams, *History*, 8:156–157.

33. Monroe to Hay, Sept. 7, 1814, Monroe Papers, NYPL; Monroe Memorandum, n.d., Hamilton, ed., *Monroe Writings*, 5:373–375. See also Monroe to Jefferson, Dec. 21, 1814, ibid., 5:303–304.

34. William Stewart to Thomas L. McKenney, Jan. 15, 1847, quoted in Thomas L. McKenney, *Reply to Kosciuszko Armstrong's Assault . . .* (New York, 1847), 28.

35. Williams, *Invasion of Washington*, 105. There was a brief, unsuccessful effort in Congress to remove the capital.

36. Quoted in Brant, *Madison, Comm.-in-Chief*, 313.

37. Williams, *Invasion of Washington*, 105. Williams was one of the messengers to Madison. General Walter Smith, who signed the message, was Madison's "devoted friend." Brant, *Madison, Comm.-in-Chief*, 312. See also Madison Memorandum, Aug. 29, 1814, Cong. Ed., *Madison Letters*, 3:424–426.

38. Ibid.

39. Baltimore *Patriot & Evening Advertiser*, quoted in *Niles' Weekly Register*, Sept. 10, 1814, 7:6–7; Armstrong to Madison, Sept. 4, 1814, Madison Papers, LC.

40. Brant, *Madison, Comm.-in-Chief*, 316–318; Adams, *History*, 8:155; Armstrong to Parker, Mar. 4, 1815, Parker Papers, HSP.

41. Armstrong to Spencer, Sept. 3, 1814, Rokeby Collection.

42. Thomas L. McKenney, *Memoirs, Official and Personal* (2 vols., New York, 1845); Kosciuszko Armstrong, *Review of T. L. McKenney's Narrative of the Causes which, in 1814, led to General Armstrong's Resignation of the War Office* (New York, 1846); Thomas L. McKenney, *Reply to Kosciuszko Armstrong's Assault upon Col. McKenney's Narrative . . .* (New York, 1847); Kosciuszko Armstrong, *Examination of Thomas L. McKenney's Reply to the Review of his Narrative, &c.* (New York, 1847).

43. Jones to Eleanor Jones, Sept. 7, 1814, Jones Papers, HSP; Jones to Madison, Sept. 11, 1814, ibid.

44. Monroe to Hay, Sept. 7, 1814, Monroe Papers, NYPL.

45. [Armstrong,] "Answer to the Queries of D. F., in our Third Number, Addressed to the reviewer of Wilkinson's Memoirs," *Literary and Scientific Repository and Critical Review* (July 1821), 3:127, 136.

46. Adams, *History*, 8:159.

47. Monroe to Madison, Sept. 25, 1814, Hamilton, ed., *Monroe Writings*, 5:294–295. There is an addendum to this letter (not sent) that may have been added at a later date rationalizing at length the contents of this letter.

48. Adams, *History*, 8:161.

49. Armstrong to Spencer, Dec. 22, 1814, Rokeby Collection. Rush had some doubts about his testimony. He wrote George W. Campbell on Nov. 2 that he could not say for certain whether Armstrong's statement to the committee was true or not. Rush to Campbell, Nov. 2, 1814, George W. Campbell Papers, LC.

50. Armstrong to Spencer, Nov. 4, 1814, Rokeby Collection; Armstrong to Taylor, Nov. 8, 1814, John W. Taylor Papers, NYHS; Armstrong to Parker, Mar. 4, 1815, Parker Papers, HSP.

51. Armstrong to Spencer, Nov. 25, Dec. 22, 1814, Jan. 25, 1815, Rokeby Collection; Armstrong to Parker, Dec. 19, 1814, Parker Papers, HSP.

52. The transcript of the trial is conveniently published, along with Wilkinson's notations, in the third volume of Wilkinson's, *Memoirs*. Armstrong to Spencer, Apr. 13, 1815, Rokeby Collection.

53. Rider H. Winder, *Remarks on a Pamphlet entitled "An Enquiry respecting the Capture of Washington by the British, on the 24th of August, 1814 . . ." By Spectator* (Balti-

more, 1816); George Izard, *Official Correspondence with the Department of War relative to the Military Operations of the American Army under the Command of Major General Izard* . . . (Philadelphia, 1816); Armstrong to Izard, Apr. 25, 1816, ibid., v.

54. Armstrong to Spencer, Mar. 12, 1816, Rokeby Collection; William Elliot, *The Washington Guide* (Washington, D.C. 1822), 26–51. Recent historians who have attributed "Spectator" to Armstrong include Brant, *Madison, Comm.-in-Chief*, 317–318, and Glenn Tucker, *Poltroons and Patriots* (2 vols., Indianapolis, 1954), 2:622. See [William Elliot,] *An Enquiry respecting the Capture of Washington by the British, on the 24th of August 1814 . . . By Spectator* (Washington, D.C., February 1816).

55. Spencer to Armstrong, Jan. 26, Feb. 10, Apr. 2, 1816, Rokeby Collection.

56. [John Armstrong,] *Exposition of the Motives for Opposing the Nomination of Mr. Monroe for the Office of President of the United States* (Washington, D.C., 1816). Armstrong's informant was congressman, later governor of Kentucky, Joseph Desha. See Armstrong to Spencer, Mar. 12, 1816, Spencer to Armstrong, Apr. 2, 1816, Rokeby Collection.

57. "A South Carolinian," [Charles Pinckney,] *Observation to shew the Propriety of the Nomination of Colonel James Monroe, to the Presidency of the United States by the Caucus at Washington. In which a Full Answer is given to the Pamphlet entitled "Exposition of the Motives for Opposing the Nomination of Mr. Monroe as President of the United States"* (Charleston, S.C., 1816).

58. Spencer to Armstrong, Feb. 14, 1819, Armstrong to Spencer, Dec. 22, 1819, Rokeby Collection.

12 – LAST YEARS

1. Armstrong to Spencer, Mar. 18, 1815, Rokeby Collection; Aldrich, "Memoirs of Rokeby," Rokeby Collection.

2. Aldrich, "Memoirs of Rokeby," Rokeby Collection; Family Bible, Rokeby Collection. Eight Astor children were born; six survived infancy.

3. Julia Delafield, *Biographies of Francis Lewis and Morgan Lewis* (New York, 1877), 202.

4. [Armstrong,] "Review of Memoirs of My Own Times by Maj. Gen. James Wilkinson," *Literary and Scientific Repository and Critical Review* (June and Oct. 1820), 1:1–24, 441–471, and (July 1821), 3:106–137; [Armstrong,] "Biographical Sketch of the late Robert R. Livingston," ibid. (July 1821), 3:69–74; Monroe to Gouverneur, Oct. 14, 1821, Monroe Papers, NYPL. A second article by Armstrong on the same subject was titled "Negotiation for Louisiana," *Literary and Scientific Repository and Critical Review* (Oct. 1821), 3:491–503.

5. Armstrong to Gardner, Mar. 31, 1822, Gardner Papers, NYSL; Spencer to Armstrong, Mar. 31, 1820, Jan. 24, 1821, Rokeby Collection.

6. Armstrong to Henry Lee, Jan. 1, 1833, Armstrong Misc., NYHS; Armstrong to Lee, Feb. 15, 1833, Armstrong Misc., LC; [Armstrong,] *Notice of Mr. Adams' Eulogium on the Life and Character of James Monroe* (Washington, D.C., 1832). Adams noted in his diary that Armstrong had heaped the "bitterest abuse upon Mr. Monroe and me. There is nothing in it that I think needs reply." Adams, ed., *Memoirs of J. Q. Adams*, 8:522.

7. Armstrong to Spencer, July 14, 1833, Rokeby Collection; Spencer to Armstrong, July 5, 1833, ibid.

8. Ellery, ed., *Swift Memoirs*, 124.

9. "John Montgars," [Armstrong] to Pickering, Jan. 20, 1820, Pickering Papers,

MHS, 31:295; Pickering to "Montgars," Jan. 29, 1820, ibid., 15:206. See Pickering to Armstrong, July 15, 1825, ibid., 16:46; Armstrong to Pickering, Oct. 6, 1825, ibid., 32:171; Pickering to Armstrong, Sept. 15, 1827, ibid., 16:25. Pickering's account of the meeting is in Pickering to Samuel Hogdon, Mar. 16, 1783, ibid., 34:145.

10. [Armstrong,] "Review of William Johnson's Sketches of the Life and Correspondence of Nathanael Greene . . . (Charleston, 1822)," *United States Magazine* (Jan. 1823), 1:1–44. In addition to the reviews previously noted, it appears that between June 1820 and Jan. 1823 Armstrong wrote a total of nine review articles amounting to 219 pages. Other reviews that can be attributed to him include "Letters to James Monroe . . . from William King . . .;" Gleig's, "A Narrative of the Campaigns of the British Army at Washington, Baltimore, and New Orleans . . .;" and Carlo Botta's, "Storia della guerra dell' Independence degli Stati Uniti D'America . . .," *Literary and Scientific Repository and Critical Review* (Jan. and Oct. 1821), 2:37–50, 3:358–381, 255–292.

11. Harry J. Carman, *Jesse Buel: Agricultural Reformer* (New York, 1947). Armstrong to Buel, Dec. 5, 1822, Nat. Sci. MSS (Buel), Sterling Memorial Library, Yale University; Paul W. Gates, *The Farmer's Age: Agriculture, 1815–1860* (New York, 1960), 359; [Armstrong,] *A Treatise on Agriculture . . . To which is added, a Dissertation on the Kitchen and Fruit Garden* (Albany, 1839, reprinted New York, 1864).

12. Amy Ver Nooy, "Lafayette's Visit, September 16, 1824," Dutchess County Historical Society *Yearbook* (1954), 39:38–55.

13. National Archives, Revolutionary War Pension Files, 1800–1900 (RG 15), Armstrong, John (Cont., Pa), S17, 823.

14. See Samuel E. Morison's brief sketch in the *DAB*, sv "Sparks, Jared (May 10, 1789–Mar. 14, 1866)." A biography is H. B. Adams, *Life and Writings of Jared Sparks* (2 vols., Boston, 1893).

15. Sparks, *Journal*, Aug. 22, 1831, Sparks Papers, HLHU, 18–27; Armstrong to Spencer, Sept. 5, 1831, Rokeby Collection.

16. Armstrong to Sparks, Dec. 9, 1834, Sparks Papers, HLHU; Robert L. Armstrong to Armstrong, Feb. 17, 1833, Armstrong to Robert L. Armstrong, May 27, 1833, Aldrich, "Memoirs of Rokeby," Rokeby Collection.

17. Armstrong to Spencer, Mar. 15, 1836, Rokeby Collection; Armstrong to Sparks, Mar. 6, 1836, Sparks Papers, HLHU.

18. Armstrong to Sparks, Sept. 21, Oct. 28, 1836, ibid.; Armstrong to Henry Armstrong, Mar. 1840, Rokeby Collection. Volume one was published by George Dearborn and volume two by Wiley & Putnam.

19. Armstrong to Spencer, June 18, 1840, ibid.; Armstrong to Henry Armstrong, Mar. 1840, ibid.

20. Armstrong to Spencer, Jan. 1, 1837, Gratz Collection, HSP.

21. Armstrong to Spencer, Jan. 6, Apr. 20, 1842, Rokeby Collection; L. D. Ingersoll, *A History of the War Department of the United States* (Washington, D.C., 1879), 443–444.

22. An abridgement of the New York Convention debates is in Merrill D. Peterson, ed., *Democracy, Liberty, and Property: The State Constitutional Conventions of the 1820's* (Indianapolis, 1966), 125–270. See also Dixon Ryan Fox, *The Decline of Aristocracy in the Politics of New York, 1801–1840*, 229–267. Armstrong's and Spencer's correspondence relating to this convention is in C. Edward Skeen, ed., "'A Political Bear Garden . . .:' Four Letters on the New York Constitutional Convention of 1821," *New York History* (July 1978), no. 3, 59:326–342.

23. Armstrong to Spencer, Dec. 4, 1826, Rokeby Collection; Armstrong to Parker, Jan. 22, 1827, Parker Papers, HSP.

24. Spencer to Armstrong, June 28, 1831, Aug. 23, 1832, Rokeby Collection.

25. Spencer to Armstrong, June 23, 1834, Oct. 19, 1836, ibid.

26. Spencer to Armstrong, Dec. 16, 1836, ibid.; Armstrong to Spencer, Jan. 1, 1837, Gratz Collection, HSP; Armstrong to Spencer, Feb. 27, 1837, Armstrong Misc., NYHS.

27. Copies of this deed, recorded on July 12, 1836, and the deed for the sale of the mills to John C. Cruger, dated July 26, 1836, are in the Rokeby Collection. Armstrong to Spencer, July 28, 1836, Rokeby Collection.

28. James Armstrong to Armstrong, Apr. 7, 1814, July 10, 1821, Rokeby Collection; Aldrich, "Memoirs of Rokeby," Rokeby Collection.

29. Isaac J. Greenwood, "Major General Horatio Gates," *The New England Historical and Genealogical Register* (July 1867), 21:252–256.

30. Kosciuszko was represented at various times by his uncle Edward Livingston, Henry Wheaton, and Francis Scott Key. William Wirt, the Attorney General, represented the other side. Justice Joseph Story delivered the opinions of the Court. *Armstrong v. Lear*, 12 Wheaton 169 (1827); *Armstrong v. Lear*, 8 Peters 52 (1834); *Estho v. Lear*, 7 Peters 130 (1833). Thaddeus Kosciuszko's estate was finally settled in 1852. The Supreme Court ruled that the will left in Jefferson's hands was overruled by a later one of 1816. *Ennis v. Smith*, 14 Howard 400; Edward P. Alexander, "Jefferson and Kosciuszko: Friends of Liberty and of Man," *PMHB* (Jan. 1968), 92:101–102.

31. A copy of the will is in the Rokeby Collection.

32. Armstrong to Spencer, Jan. 1, 1837, Gratz Collection, HSP; Armstrong to Spencer, June 22, 1837, Henry E. Huntington Library, San Marino, Calif.

33. Armstrong to Spencer, Feb. 27, 1837, Armstrong Misc., NYHS.

34. Armstrong to Henry Armstrong, Mar. 5, 1839, Henry Armstrong to Armstrong, June 28, 1839, Rokeby Collection. See also Aldrich, "Memoirs of Rokeby," and Armstrong to Spencer, Apr. 30, 1839, ibid.; Armstrong to William B. Reed, July 8, 1839, Joseph Reed Papers, NYHS; Note, dated Dec. 1839, on a letter, Armstrong to Hugh Mercer, Oct. 6, 1839, ibid.

35. Spencer to Armstrong, Dec. 28, 1841, Misc. Papers, NYSL. Spencer expressed the same sentiments in a letter on May 25, 1842, Rokeby Collection. See also Armstrong to Spencer, Apr. 20, 1842, ibid.

36. The Rev. Kearny to Spencer, Mar. 28, 1843, ibid.; Daniel D. Bernard, *A Discourse on the Life, Character, and Public Services of Ambrose Spencer* (Albany, 1849), 102–103.

37. Henry Armstrong to Spencer, Apr. 3, 1843, Rokeby Collection.

BIBLIOGRAPHICAL ESSAY

I HAVE RELIED VERY HEAVILY upon primary sources in this biography, as the footnotes will attest. (For a complete listing of all the sources used, the footnotes should also be consulted.) Secondary sources were little used, for they were often found to be untrustworthy and too scant to be of much value. There is no significant collection of Armstrong letters to be found in any depository, but there are Armstrong documents located in well over a hundred collections scattered across the United States. Many of these letters, however, are routine correspondence and shed little light on his personal life. The paucity of materials accounts to a large extent, I am sure, for the lack of historical interest in Armstrong. I have reconstructed his career based primarily upon official documents and records, but fortunately, in the collections of other individuals, I have found many Armstrong materials that filled in many gaps and gave a personal dimension to the colder, more formal official letters.

MANUSCRIPT MATERIALS

By far the most valuable collection of Armstrong materials available to the public is the William Astor Chanler Collection of Armstrong photostats in the New-York Historical Society. This collection contains the bulk of what I have referred to as the Rokeby Collection. I have had the privilege of working with the original letters, due to the generosity of Mrs. Richard Aldrich and her two sons, Richard and John Winthrop. Rokeby, an estate along the Hudson River near Barrytown, New York, was built by Armstrong and enlarged by William B. Astor, and it still reflects the grandeur of the past. Many of the buildings on the estate date from the Armstrong period. The visits I made there added greatly to my understanding of the setting and the style of life of the Armstrongs.

The Rokeby Collection is particularly valuable because it contains an extensive correspondence between Armstrong and Ambrose Spencer. The bulk of these letters, however, date from 1812. A few letters from Armstrong's father, his brother, and letters to his future wife, Alida Livingston, are in the collection, as are a few letters to and from his children. A large number of letters dating from the Ministry in France are also in the collection, but they are duplicates of those to be found in the official correspondence. Approximately four chapters of a draft biography of Armstrong written by Kosciuszko Armstrong is in the collection. It does not go beyond the 1780s. His early chapters roughly parallel an autobiographical fragment, circa 1826, also in the Rokeby Collection.

The estate also has Armstrong's personal library, many of the books with his annotations. The Family Bible is also there, which was useful for family genealogy. There are a few miscellaneous items, including copies of many deeds involving Armstrong's land transactions, a farm account book (1812-1813), commissions, and a few letters from other correspondents, but not nearly the number that might be expected. Armstrong apparently kept no letterbook or retained copies of what he wrote to others. There is a remote possibility that Armstrong's collection of letters were retained by his son Henry and that they were destroyed in a fire in the 1920s. A trove of Armstrong letters may yet appear.

The New-York Historical Society also holds the Horatio Gates Papers, which were indispensable in delineating Armstrong's early life. Other collections in the New-York Historical Society that were valuable include the Robert R. Livingston Papers, John W. Taylor Papers, Rufus King Papers, Albert Gallatin Papers, Baron von Steuben Papers, Armstrong Miscellaneous Papers, the Edward Livingston photostats in the J. R. Delafield Collection, and the Joseph Reed Papers. The New York Public Library also has a collection of Horatio Gates Papers and a valuable collection of the James Monroe Papers, which shed much light on Armstrong's career in France as well as in the War Department and additionally on Monroe's and Armstrong's varied disputes. The Emmet Collection was of some value too. The library also has an extensive collection of rare books and pamphlets. Interestingly, some of those used had once been Armstrong's personal copies and included his annotations. These were no doubt given to the library by the Astor family.

The New York State Library has the Charles K. Gardner papers, which were useful for Armstrong's years in retirement. The Jonathan Russell Papers in the Brown University Library filled a gap in the years 1810-1812. The Jared Sparks Papers in the Houghton Library of Harvard University contain an extensive correspondence between Armstrong and Sparks primarily relating to Revolutionary matters and of little value for biography, but it is extremely interesting and rich in anecdotes. In the Massachusetts Historical Society, the following collections were very useful: the Timothy Pickering Papers and the James Bowdoin Papers in the Bowdoin-Temple Collection. Also consulted were the William Eustis Papers, the Henry Dearborn Papers, and the Jacob Brown Papers.

The Historical Society of Pennsylvania had several collections of value, including the Simon Gratz Collection and the Frank M. Etting Collection of miscellaneous correspondence. The Daniel Parker Papers had an extensive letterpress duplication of Armstrong's War Department correspondence, but there was little personal correspondence. The William Irvine Papers and the William Jones Papers were also helpful. In the Maryland Historical Society the David Bailie Warden Papers contain some personal insights into the French interlude.

The Manuscript Division of the Library of Congress has several valuable collections that illuminate certain aspects of Armstrong's career. The papers of Thomas Jefferson, James Madison, James Monroe, and Andrew Jackson were all very helpful, particularly the Madison Papers. Also in the Library of Congress, the Edward Ross Papers shed some light on Armstrong's private life while secretary of war. The Armstrong Miscellaneous Papers, the George Washington Campbell Papers, the George Washington Papers, and the William C. Rives Papers (containing many Madison letters), were also consulted.

For Armstrong's public career, the collection of official documents in the National Archives is indispensable. Many record groups were consulted and used. The two most valuable were the records of the State Department and the War Department. In the Department of State (Record Group 59), the most useful were: Diplomatic Instructions, Letterbook; Despatches from United States Ministers to France; and Despatches from United States Consuls in Paris and Bordeaux. In the Department of War Papers (Record Group 107), the most useful were: Letters Received by the Secretary of War, Registered Series and Irregular Series; Letters Sent by the Secretary of War Relating to Military Affairs; Letters Sent to the President by the Secretary of War; and Reports to Congress from the Secretary of War.

EDITED PUBLICATIONS

Armstrong's duties as Secretary of the Supreme Executive Council of Pennsylvania may be traced in the Pennsylvania *Archives*, Series One. This series also contains much about Armstrong's role in the Wyoming affair, but Robert J. Taylor, ed., *The Susquehannah Company Papers* (11 vols., Ithaca, N.Y., 1935–1969), is indispensable for an understanding of this controversy. Worthington C. Ford, et al., eds., *Journals of the Continental Congress, 1774–1789* (34 vols., Washington, D.C., 1904–1937), and Edmund C. Burnett, ed., *Letters of Members of the Continental Congress* (8 vols., Washington, D.C., 1921–1936), cover Armstrong's role in the Congress under the Articles of Confederation. For Armstrong's career in the Senate of the United States, the *Annals of Congress* is the basic source. The *American State Papers, Foreign Affairs*, was useful in covering Armstrong's activities in France, and the *Military Affairs* and *Indian Affairs* were likewise valuable in studying Armstrong's role as secretary of war. The *Public Statutes at Large* served as the source of laws passed during the War of 1812. Charles F. Adams, ed., *Memoirs of John Quincy Adams* (12 vols., Philadelphia, 1874–1877), were helpful at several points, as was Charles R. King, ed., *The Life and Correspondence of Rufus King* (6 vols., New York, 1894–1900). The Bowdoin-Armstrong correspondence in the Massachusetts Historical Society, *Collections*, part II, Seventh Series, was very useful in illuminating their controversy. Also valuable for national politics were: Stanislaus Murray Hamilton, ed., *The Writings of James Monroe* (7 vols., New York, 1898–1903); Henry Adams, ed., *The Writings of Albert Gallatin* (3 vols., Philadelphia, 1879); John Spencer Bassett, ed., *Correspondence of Andrew Jackson* (6 vols., Washington, D.C., 1926–1933); Gaillard Hunt, ed., *The Writings of James Madison* (9 vols., New York, 1900–1910), and the Congressional Edition, *Letters and Other Writings of James Madison* (4 vols., Philadelphia, 1865). Others consulted and used were John C. Fitzpatrick, ed., *The Writings of George Washington* (39 vols., Washington, D.C., 1931–1940); Paul L. Ford, ed., *The Writings of Thomas Jefferson* (10 vols., New York, 1892–1899); Andrew A. Lipscomb and Albert E. Bergh, eds., *The Writings of Thomas Jefferson* (20 vols., Washington, D.C., 1903–1905); H. A. Washington, ed., *The Writings of Thomas Jefferson* (9 vols., Washington, D.C., 1853–1854); Logan Esarey, ed., *Messages and Letters of William Henry Harrison* (2 vols., Indianapolis, 1922); Hugh Hastings, ed., *Public and Military Papers of Daniel D. Tompkins, 1807–1817* (3 vols., Albany, 1898–1902); and James D. Richardson, ed., *A Compilation of the Messages and Papers of the Presidents, 1798–1897* (10 vols., Washington, D.C., 1897–1900).

NEWSPAPERS

Newspapers were not used extensively as they added little information about Armstrong's career. The most useful were the *Niles' Weekly Register*, actually almost a news magazine; the Washington *National Intelligencer*, essentially an administration newspaper; the *Albany Argus*, edited initially by Armstrong's friend, Jesse Buel; and the Philadelphia *Aurora*, which was the newspaper edited by William Duane.

BIOGRAPHIES, MEMOIRS, AND SECONDARY SOURCES

There are only two historical works that deal at any length with Armstrong's career. One is Henry Adams, *History of the United States During the Administrations of Thomas Jefferson and James Madison* (9 vols., New York, 1889–1891), which is generally favorable in his treatment of Armstrong. Despite his detractors, the Adams volumes are still the most valuable work on this period. The other work is Irving Brant, *James Madison* (6 vols., Indianapolis, 1948–1961), which is very unfavorable to Armstrong. The two thus have an adversary relationship. Adams apparently did not have access to the Madison Papers presently in the Library of Congress, which were available to Brant, but despite Brant's claims to the contrary, this writer believes that Adams's grasp of the facts and his interpretations are more accurate. Beyond the Adams and Brant volumes, most secondary works add very little to an understanding of Armstrong, and these works have, in fact, contributed most of the misinformation about Armstrong. There is no biography of Armstrong's closest friend, Ambrose Spencer, and one is badly needed. Information about his life may be found in Daniel D. Bernard, *A Discourse on the Life, Character and Public Services of Ambrose Spencer* . . . (Albany, 1849), and William B. Sprague, *A Discourse Commemorative of the Late Hon. Ambrose Spencer* . . . (Albany, 1849), in Joel Munsell, comp., *Memorial of Ambrose Spencer, Former Chief Justice of the Supreme Court of the State of New York* . . . (Albany, 1849). The first really adequate biography of General Horatio Gates is the recently published *General Horatio Gates: A Biography* (Baton Rouge, 1976), by Paul David Nelson, but the coverage of the postwar years when the Armstrong-Gates friendship flourished is very thin. Formerly the standard biography of Gates was Samuel White Patterson, *Horatio Gates: Defender of American Liberties* (New York, 1941), which adds some information about Armstrong's and Gates's relationship. George Dangerfield, *Chancellor Robert R. Livingston of New York, 1746-1813* (New York, 1960), is an excellent biography, but it contains little about Armstrong. As for Armstrong's protagonists, a recent and satisfactory biography of James Monroe is Harry Ammon, *James Monroe, The Quest for National Identity* (New York, 1971), but he almost studiously ignores the differences between Armstrong and Monroe. To understand James Wilkinson, one must consult his *Memoirs of My Own Times* (3 vols., Philadelphia, 1816), but it is not good history. Two biographies will balance out Wilkinsons's views: James Ripley Jacobs, *Tarnished Warrior: Major-General James Wilkinson* (New York, 1938), and Royal Ornan Shreve, *The Finished Scoundrel* (Indianapolis, 1933). Other works of value are: Winfield Scott, *Memoirs of Lieutenant General Winfield Scott* (2 vols., New York, 1864); and Harrison Ellery, ed., *The Memoirs of General Joseph Gardner Swift* (Worcester, Mass., 1890). Useful biographies include Freeman Cleaves, *Old Tippecanoe: William Henry Harrison and His Times* (New York, 1939); Marquis James, *Andrew Jackson: The Border Captain* (Indianapolis, 1933); Raymond Walters, Jr., *Albert Gallatin: Jeffersonian Financier and Diplomat* (New York, 1957); and Henry Bartholomew Cox, *The Parisian American: Fulwar Skipwith of Virginia* (Washington, D.C., 1964).

Armstrong's early career in Pennsylvania and in Congress are touched upon in Robert L. Brunhouse, *The Counter-Revolution in Pennsylvania, 1776-1790* (Philadelphia, 1942), and Edmund Cody Burnett, *The Continental Congress* (New York, 1941). Armstrong's activities in New York politics is adequately covered in Jabez D. Hammond, *The History of Political Parties in the State of New York* (2 vols., Buffalo, 1850), and touched upon in De Alva Stanwood Alexander, *A Political History of the State of New York* (4 vols., New York, 1906-1909), and Dixon Ryan Fox, *The Decline of Aristocracy in the Politics of New York, 1801-1840* (New York, 1919). There is scant information in the secondary sources about Armstrong's activities in France, except in the aforementioned volumes of Adams and Brant. However, Isaac Joslin Cox, *The West Florida Controversy, 1798-1813* (Baltimore, 1918); Frank E. Melvin, *Napoleon's Navigation System* (New York, 1919); and Bradford Perkins, *Prologue to War: England and the United States, 1805-1812* (Berkeley, 1961), touch on various aspects of Armstrong's career.

Armstrong's role as secretary of war is rarely and only briefly mentioned in most of the standard accounts of the War of 1812. General histories that are useful include Harry L. Coles, *The War of 1812* (Chicago, 1965); J. Mackay Hitsman, *The Incredible War of 1812* (Toronto, 1965); Alfred Thayer Mahan, *Sea Power in its Relations to the War of 1812* (2 vols., Boston, 1905); and John K. Mahon, *The War of 1812* (Gainesville, Fla., 1972). Armstrong's own work, *Notices of the War of 1812* (2 vols., New York, 1836–1840), is useful only for giving Armstrong's opinions on the war. Benson J. Lossing, *The Pictoral Field-Book of the War of 1812* (New York, 1868), has some valuable maps. Of Armstrong's administration of the War Department, there is no adequate account. Portions of his activities may be found in Emory Upton, *The Military Policy of the United States* (Washington, D.C., 1917); L. D. Ingersoll, *A History of the War Department of the United States* (Washington, D.C., 1879); and Leonard D. White, *The Jeffersonians: A Study in Administrative History* (New York, 1951). The Washington incident has received better coverage and greater study than perhaps any other aspect of the War of 1812. Unfortunately, much of it has been so-called "popular history," and many errors and distortions have been the result. Depending upon the predisposition of the author, it appears, this incident may be seen in many different ways. An older, detailed, but somewhat biased account, is John S. Williams, *History of the Invasion and Capture of Washington* (New York, 1857). Much like it, although briefer, is Edward Duncan Ingraham, *A Sketch of the Events which Preceded the Capture of Washington by the British* . . . (Philadelphia, 1849). A recent, more balanced account, is Walter Lord, *The Dawn's Early Light* (New York, 1971).

INDEX

JOHN ARMSTRONG, Jr.

was composed in 10-point Compugraphic Palatino and leaded two points,
with display type also in Compugraphic Palatino,
by Metricomp Studios;
printed by sheet-fed offset on Glatfelter 50-pound acid-free Antique Cream,
Smythe-sewn and bound over boards in Joanna Arrestox C,
by Maple-Vail Book Manufacturing Group, Inc.;
and published by

SYRACUSE UNIVERSITY PRESS
SYRACUSE, NEW YORK 13210